THE
AMERICAN ALPINE
JOURNAL

1990

THE AMERICAN ALPINE CLUB
NEW YORK

ISSN 0065-6925
ISBN 0-930410-43-2

Manufactured in the United States of America

*Articles and notes submitted for publication
and other communications relating to*

THE AMERICAN ALPINE JOURNAL

should be sent to

THE AMERICAN ALPINE CLUB
113 EAST 90th STREET
NEW YORK, NEW YORK 10128-1589 USA
(212) 722-1628

THE AMERICAN ALPINE CLUB

OFFICIALS FOR THE YEAR 1990

THE AMERICAN ALPINE JOURNAL

VOLUME 32 • ISSUE 64 • 1990

CONTENTS

COLD SWEAT ON MAKALU .... *Pierre Beghin* 1

KUMBHAKARNA—MY WAY .... *Tomo Česen* 7

THE NORTHEAST RIB OF KWANGDE CENTRAL .. *Alan Kearney* 14

MOUNT RUSSELL'S EAST FACE .... *Charles Townsend* 21

FORAKER'S INFINITE SPUR .... *Mark Bebie* 28

HUNTER'S NORTHWEST FACE .... *Conrad Anker* 37

EROICA, MOUNT HUNTER .... *Roy Ruddle* 39

MOOSE'S TOOTH AND HUNTINGTON .... *James Quirk* 43

DENALI'S WEST RIB SOLO IN WINTER .... *David Staeheli* 50

ONE HUNDRED YEARS OF CROSSINGS OF
    GREENLAND'S INLAND ICE .... *Gunnar Jensen* 54

THE FIRST TWENTY-SEVEN YEARS .... *Benjamin G. Ferris* 66

SIR GEORGE EVEREST'S 200TH BIRTHDAY ...... *Audrey Salkeld* 71

HENRY S. HALL JR. MEMORIAL EVEREST
    RELIEF MODEL .... *Bradford Washburn* 75

CLIMBING ETHICS .... *AAC and Mountain Tools* 76

GLACIERS OF ALASKA AND ADJACENT YUKON
    TERRITORY AND BRITISH COLUMBIA .. *William Osgood Field* 79

CLIMBS AND EXPEDITIONS 151

BOOK REVIEWS .... *Edited by John Thackray* 315

IN MEMORIAM 337

CLUB ACTIVITIES .... *Edited by Frederick O. Johnson* 357

AAC BOOKS 369

    VIGNETTES .... *Mignon Linck*

COVER: Part of the National Geographic/Boston Museum of Science
    Map of Mount Everest, 1:50,000, 1988. It is used with
    permission of the National Geographic Society and the Boston
    Museum of Science.

FRIENDS OF
THE AMERICAN ALPINE JOURNAL

THE FOLLOWING PERSONS HAVE MADE CONTRIBUTIONS
IN SUPPORT OF THE CONTINUED PUBLICATION OF
THE AMERICAN ALPINE JOURNAL

Cold Sweat on Makalu

PIERRE BEGHIN, *Groupe de Haute Montagne*

F OR HALF AN HOUR our group had been clustered about the radio at our 4900-meter Base Camp at the foot of Makalu. Guy Chaumerueil, leaning over the radio-telephone, was about to explain to Parisian motorists stuck in rush-hour traffic, among others, how our adventure was progressing. Electronic magic!

"Good! You are ready in the studio. I'll put on the tape."

Tumlingtar, a miniscule airstrip surrounded by rice paddies drowned under the monsoon. It was there that four members of the French national expedition had been landed by a small Nepalese Twin-Otter plane to start the long approach march. Fifty mostly bare-footed porters. Water and mud everywhere . . . . and the famous leeches. On the tenth day, the formidable south face of Makalu is just around the corner.

And Guy could tell it all in two minutes!

This approach march under the monsoon! I had the impression of penetrating an interminable curtain of fog and rain to emerge somehow some day on the other side: at the end of the earth. An expanse of sand strewn with huge boulders, a little bit of grass and before us a 2500-meter-high wall, Makalu's south face.

After Gérard Vionnet gave up during the approach, we were only three climbers, and although Alain Ghersen and Michel Cadot are very strong technically, tough and enthusiastic, they had never had high-altitude experience. Three climbers to pioneer a direct route on Makalu's south face is little enough. In 1975, fifteen Yugoslavs—among them the best climbers of that day—were needed to climb the only other route on the face. Six high camps, much fixed rope and a huge degree of obstinacy. No one has succeeded since.

The rock wall which makes up the bottom half of the face is cut from right to left by a very steep ramp that ends near the Yugoslav route at 7300 meters: 1100 meters of gullies, rock walls, ice bombardments, snow funnels and precipitous ridges. It is there that we climb. Everywhere, enormous stalactites detach themselves under the effect of the sun and scatter all over the wall in a fracas of broken glass. This is wide-spread by nine in the morning. By noon, it is a debacle.

On September 21 and 22, we climb a good part of the ramp. Toward 6800 meters, I work my way up a slanting gully bordered by threatening stalactites. The ice is fragile, a veneer over rock. Twelve meters above my last protection,

I find myself on a snow-covered slab with a vague nick for my left hand. I jam the point of my ice axe into a miniscule crack, catch my balance and bang in a piton. Above rises a vertical wall. After a few meters of traction, the angle slackens a little. Another almost vertical gully subject to short bombardments has good ice. I set foot on a snow slope that collects the debris of all kinds that the mountain wants to rid itself of. Alain and Michel follow. We fix some rope. Towards 7000 meters, after they decide to descend, I attack a long, very steep ridge and continue on alone. The ridge ends in a toboggan of ice festooned with stalactites. At 7100 meters, I too descend.

At the end of September, our first summit try is stopped by one of those storms for which only the Himalaya has the secret: 48 hours without the slightest lull.

Everywhere expeditions give up, fall back on their respective Base Camps. The snow cover soon mounts up to a meter. Glacial dampness seizes the region. In turn, each of us grasps a shovel to dig out the sagging tent, to get warm and to pass the time.

On October 2, we make the grand departure. At 5800 meters, we find the tent at Camp I crushed under the weight of the snow. Inside, it is a swimming pool. The sleeping bags, the down clothing, the gloves and socks are learning how to swim. To continue looks bad, but by good luck the sun beats down and at the end of the afternoon, everything has dried.

After some hours of dozing, a midnight departure lacks charm. The bowl of tea and the little crackers sit heavily on the stomach, the packs are too heavy, the night too dark, Makalu too tall.

Near the bergschrund, we lose our way. Above, the south face is only a black mass in an inky night. Except for the North Star, we have no landmarks. We climb too far to the right. We lose hours crossing avalanche gullies, climbing snowy humps. Finally we're back on the route.

Soon the sun emerges from behind the south ridge. An instant later, it is already too hot. The light is blinding. At the end of the morning, at 7100 meters, I decide to halt. Alain and Michel have fallen far behind. I am almost ready to descend to look for them when a head emerges. Only at mid afternoon have they turned up, worn out by the heat and the 1300 meters of difficult climbing.

The bivouac is frightful. With three of us in a badly pitched two-man tent, sleeping is a real achievement. One stirs and the other two groan. At dawn, my two companions decide to quit.

There I am alone. Above, there are 1400 meters to the summit, of which 1000 are very difficult. I have kept a dozen pitons, two deadmen, two 40-meter ropes and minimal bivouac gear. I have practically no food.

At 7300 meters, in order to escape from the ramp, there is only a 25-meter-high rock step covered with unconsolidated snow. I surmount a vague spur or rather a pile of unstable blocks. A good piton! I take off my rucksack and one of my ropes and self-belay myself on the other. It takes me three hours to overcome the last overhanging zone; expanding flakelets, portable handholds, choked cracks rise above an impressive void. The pitons go in only a few

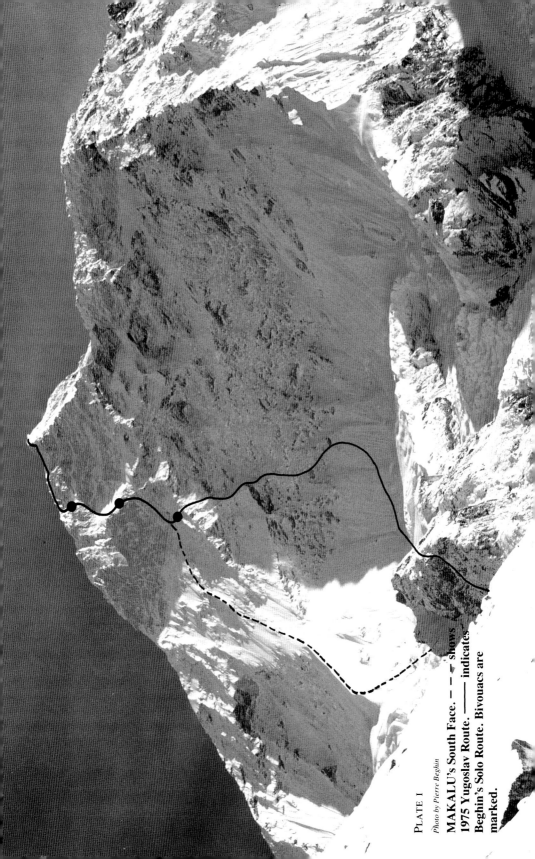

PLATE 1

Photo by Pierre Beghin

MAKALU's South Face. – – – shows 1975 Yugoslav Route. ———— indicates Beghin's Solo Route. Bivouacs are marked.

centimeters. Then, I can remove them with my fingers. Certainly, this is one of the most exposed passages I have ever climbed in the mountains.

At midday I join the Yugoslav route. I continue up delicate terrain: slabs covered by a thin layer of snow that barely supports my weight. My crampons scratch on the rock beneath. Then follows a long traverse rising to the right. Finally at 7600 meters, some thin bands of ice lead me to the left. I contact Guy on the radio and tell him that I can get out only by climbing up. To descend what I have climbed would make no sense.

By mid afternoon, I decide to halt for an early bivouac. In the night, the wind chases the snow over my tent. The platform is etched away little by little.

The next morning, October 5, I am madly anxious to get going ahead of the sun. Gradually I get my second wind. Snow slopes seem to lead to the west buttress, far to my left. This is an illusion. I know, having studied the face, that they do not meet.

I approach 8000 meters. The slope steepens considerably. Higher is a succession of verglaced walls: an impassable chute dominated by a vertical cliff where the rare cracks dribble ice. Where to go?

Curiously, I scarcely feel the precariousness of my situation. I know I have to do what I have to do. Each difficulty demands so much concentration that, in my mind, the previous one disappears instantly. I find again, here, confusedly, sensations I felt long ago on solo ascents in the Alps.

Suddenly my rope is caught fast. I can't go down to free it. A knife slash and I am free. Little bothered, I keep on unanguished. A horizontal traverse takes me to the west ridge. It is too late to get to the summit before nightfall and the last passages have exhausted me nervously and physically. I bivouac at 8100 meters, higher than I ever have before. It is an icy, fantastic night. Violent electrical storms strike distant Nepalese hills. I look down on them. In a totally unreal silence, lightning flashes off the clouds.

When the next morning I continue up the west ridge, I am greeted by a piercing wind. Swirls of snow rise from the slopes. The sky is cloudy, which accentuates the cold. I fear for my hands and feet.

From false summit to false summit, the ridge never ends. The snow is heaped up on the north slope and dangerous cornices hang far out over the south. All alone, I exhaust myself breaking trail. Once or twice, I straddle the ridge with my left leg in the shade, the right one in the sun.

At nearly 8400 meters, a 20-meter-high vertical rock wall bars the whole ridge. With crampons on my feet and my hands encased in mittens, I climb clumsily up this last obstacle. With each gust I cling to the slope. A hump, then another beyond it still higher. The afternoon has started. At 2:45 P.M. the three ridges converge under me. Nothing is higher.

New space unfolds: the desert mountains of Tibet to the north, Everest and Lhotse closer, far to the east Kangchenjunga. All are surrounded by a myriad of peaks I do not know.

Without a moment's delay, I plunge into the descent of the normal route. Way down, toward Makalu Col, I spy four tiny points: Spanish tents. All goes

PLATE 2

Photo by Alain Ghersen

Ice Gully at 6700 meters on MAKALU.

well. I lose altitude fast. Soon I am on slopes overloaded with snow. Not a track. None of the other expeditions have made the summit. It is sundown. Through the swirling snow, I see the tents of Camp III of the Spaniards nearby.

Suddenly, the whole slope is in motion: a huge windslab avalanche, 300 meters across. I am hurled head first. I try to swim, but efforts are in vain against many tons of snow. Two hundred meters lower, I emerge, unhurt. I have lost one of my ice axes and my walkie-talkie.

Minutes later, I am at the tents. I call out. A tent opens. I plunge in onto the reclining figures in their sleeping bags.

"Pierre! You're coming from the summit?" It's my Catalan friend, Carlos Valles. He is stupified to see me. I'm offered tea. Gradually, I warm up, getting back feeling in my hands and feet. Outside the cold is terrible. Carlos tells me that his thermometer reads $-30°$ C.

On October 7, I continue my descent. At Makalu Col, blinded by drifting snow, I cannot find the Spanish fixed ropes. I start down a long 45° couloir. The vast, easy Chago Glacier lies 1000 meters lower. Halfway down, the snow suddenly changes with crust over loose snow. Before I can really take stock, the whole slope has let go. It is the same scenario as the night before. I glide head first at crazy speed, I am submerged, then flung about. I am hurled over two ice walls. The snow cushions my fall. Interminable seconds! Hideous fear! Four hundred meters lower, the avalanche comes to rest. I am tossed free. With my heart racing, I sit there, totally stupified. I have lost much: my second ice axe, my mittens, the camera, the stove . . . . and a lot of adrenalin!

Nervously exhausted, I stagger to Camp I on the normal route. Now I am out of danger. Despite fatigue, I savor the moment. There is no doubt that I have lived through the most difficult and most uncertain of my mountain adventures. I will set out again, but nothing I undertake will really ever be as it was before.

Summary of Statistics:

AREA: Mahalangur Himalaya, Nepal.

NEW ROUTE: Makalu, 8463 meters, 27,766 feet, Direct South Face, Summit reached on October 6, 1989 (Beghin).

CLIMBING PERSONNEL: Pierre Beghin, leader, Michel Cadot, Alain Ghersen.

Kumbhakarna—My Way

Tomo Česen, *Planinska Zveza Slovenije, Yugoslavia*

FOR A YEAR, I debated with myself whether to try to climb Kumbhakarna solo. At one time, I spent an entire fortnight thinking of nothing else. After all, its direct north face was considered one of the most difficult in the world. Today, of course, I am delighted that I eventually went and I do not regret my decision to climb the face alone.

The north face of Kumbhakarna was first reconnoitered by New Zealanders in 1975. (At that time, the peak was known by climbers as *Jannu*, although it appears that the name has no local usage. The present official name is used throughout this article.) In 1982, a strong French team headed by Pierre Beghin spent two months on the face, eventually changing to the northeast ridge, but not climbing to the summit. In his account in the *American Alpine Journal, 1983* on page 219, he states, "It was the most moving experience I had ever had in the Himalaya because of the harshness of the wall. None of us had ever seen such a cold, steep face. The last 3000 feet were like the Cima Ovest's north face in the Dolomites with much overhanging in the last 1500 feet. When we discovered how smooth this part of the face was, we headed for the northeast ridge." The latter route was eventually climbed by Japanese in 1986. This Japanese route was ascended again in October, 1987, first by Netherlanders, two of whom were killed on the descent, and then by Frenchmen Beghin and Erik Decamp.

The season last winter was for me perfect preparation of such difficult Himalayan climbing, not so much physically as psychologically, a very important aspect. Taxing solo winter ascents, such as the *Pilier Rouge* on Mont Blanc, the north faces of the Eiger, the Matterhorn and the Grandes Jorasses and the south face of the Marmolada, convinced me that I was psychologically strong enough for a solo ascent amongst the Himalayan giants. With some success, I tried to keep from thinking about Kumbakharna, but as I packed my equipment two days before my departure, from then on, like it or not, my thoughts always dwelt on the climb.

Dr. Jani Kokalj, who accompanied me to the mountain almost by chance, was a good companion. Along with the liaison officer and Chindi, the cook, who also served as sirdar, we made a great team. We established Base Camp on April 22 at 4600 meters at the edge of the Kumbhakarna Glacier. The following day and for several days after, Jani and I went to the foot of the face and other good viewpoints. This was also essential for acclimatization. The upper part of the north face was clearly visible from Base Camp, but the lower part presented a puzzle which I wanted to solve as soon as possible. The beginning of the route did not look encouraging. The face started with an icefall, which from our side of the glacier looked like heaped-up ice cubes, threatening to tumble down at any moment. But I was even more interested in the upper part of Kumbhakarna's upper face: ice gullies, a smooth overhanging granite wall, interspersed with giant roofs. A fantastic sight! I could see that I needed a different strategy from my original one on the upper face. Before leaving home, I knew I could not plan an exact route. Although the threat of huge avalanches and falling séracs was not unacceptably great, whistling blocks of ice and rocks were proof that the face was extremely dangerous. Most of this falling ammunition ended in the funnel at the bottom of the middle of the face. That was why I knew that it was essential to make that part of the climb during the night when much was frozen in place.

Dawn on April 27 was cloudy. During lunch, the sun's rays eventually pierced the clouds. How quickly one's mood can change! Chindi was a master of his craft. I decided to take along some of his cheese custards as well as crackers, tins of fish and drinks. Around early afternoon, I left with Jani, who accompanied me to the start of the glacier. My fantastic mood matched the weather.

Alone on the glacier, I felt exhilarated, a good sign, and I was already in complete control of my feelings. I hung pitons and a spare ice-axe blade on my harness, put crampons on my feet and an ice axe in each hand. I had a rope and, of course, a helmet. My rucksack contained only spare clothing, gloves, glasses, food, drink, a sleeping bag and a bivouac sack. Truly, not much gear. To climb the 9250-foot-high north face of Kumbhakarna thus, was, apart from everything else, a great challenge.

After 200 meters of steep, initial warming up, I came to the first 10-meter-high vertical ice. Four hours later, at dusk, the lower part of the face was behind me and I rested for ten minutes. The valley below was already dark, but up here I could see satisfactorily despite the late hour. I kept on climbing in the night. I was thankful that the falling rock and ice were easing off. Climbing this section in the day would have been suicide, but the night represented safety. There were 200 meters, perhaps a little more of cramponing 70° to 80° ice up a steep couloir as well as some difficult rock.

The new day broke when I reached the top of the icefield. I had to make a right turn to the next icefield, which was separated from the last one by the first really problematic part of the route. Very steep ice and granite slabs alternated. I oriented myself on the séracs at the beginning of the middle icefield. There was no possibility for protection in the crackless rock. I was glad to reach the top of the steep ice gully that led to the less steep icefield below some huge séracs. I rested.

A short rock step separated me from the final part of the face. Ice, rock, more ice, always followed by granite slabs. The exit from this section was something special. A gently sloping slab blocked the way to the last icefield before the vertical exit from the face. Without crampons and gloves and some 6000 meters lower, this might have been easy, but here it was quite a different matter. I couldn't remove my crampons and plastic double boots are hardly suitable for

COLOR PLATE 2

Photo by Tomo Česen

North Face of KUMBHAKARNA.

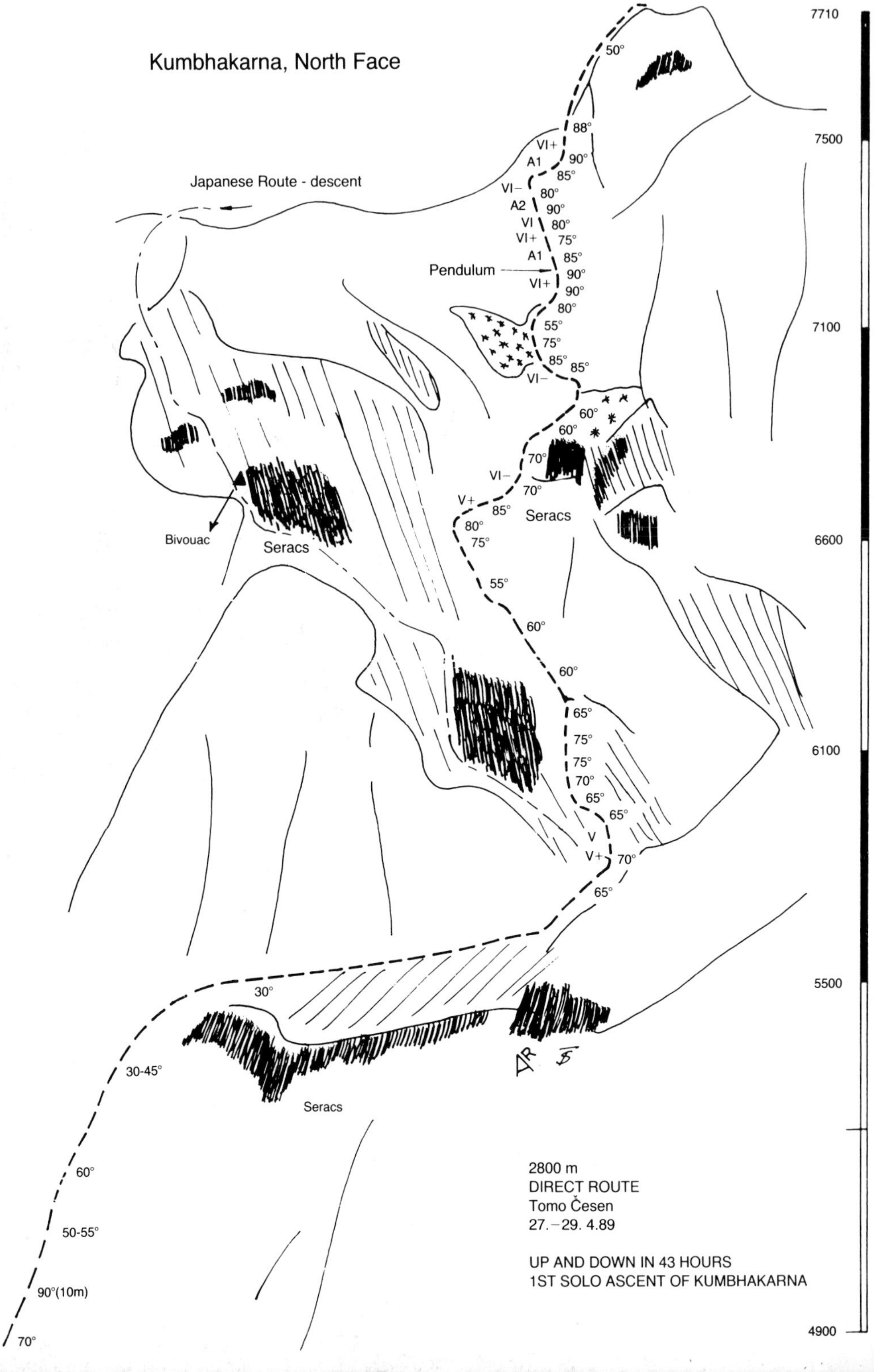

Kumbhakarna, North Face

7710

50°

7500

Japanese Route - descent

88°
VI+
A1   90°
         85°
VI−   80°
A2   90°
VI   80°
VI+   75°
         A1   85°
Pendulum ──── 90°
VI+   90°
         80°
         55°
         75°
         85° 85°
         VI−

7100

60°
60°

VI−   70°
V+   70°
         85°
80°   Seracs
75°

Bivouac

Seracs   Seracs

6600

55°

60°

60°

65°
75°
75°
70°
65°

65°

V
V+   70°

65°

6100

5500

30°

30-45°

Seracs

60°

50-55°

2800 m
DIRECT ROUTE
Tomo Česen
27.−29. 4.89

90°(10m)

UP AND DOWN IN 43 HOURS
1ST SOLO ASCENT OF KUMBHAKARNA

70°

4900

PLATE 3

Photo by Tomo Česen

**KUMBHAKARNA's North Face.
Ascent was by solid line on right.
Descent was by 1986 Japanese Route
on left.**

delicate friction climbing. I leaned unhappily with my hands on the slab and my crampons in the thin ice below. I clawed with an ice axe at some small ice crystals. Eventually I felt enormous relief when my axe at last hit solid ice. This section was definitely not for the faint-hearted!

What was ahead, though, deserves a particular description. The face above 7000 meters called for all my technique, but even more for psychological strength. I stared upward at an unbelievable scene. Only there, at 7000 meters, did I realize what lay in store. But there was no way back. A vertical gully was filled with thin ice, sometimes interrupted by a few meters of rock. The rock appeared good, although it was clear that rock climbing with crampons would be very difficult. The feeling of uncertainty, which gives climbing a peculiar attraction and which I need from time to time, suddenly vanished. In these moments of utmost concentration, the world around you no longer exists. You have to use to the limit all your capabilities, strength and a good sense of balance.

The nearly vertical slabs were covered with ice, no more than ten centimeters (four inches) thick. The consistently 80° to 90° slabs were on an average 30 to 40 meters high. My suffering was both psychological and physical. Due to the thin air, I couldn't climb these without resting, but resting, hanging on a perilously inserted ice axe, was anything but pleasant. There were at least ten such slabs. There were some easier options, but they were not visible from below. I could only guess at the best route upward. I needed to use aid pitons on four occasions as the rock was too difficult to climb free with my crampons on. There was no place to remove them or it would have been too dangerous. Fortunately, some cracks were wide enough for me to jam in my foot, relax the tension on my arms and get a short rest.

At the end of the rock, there was always ice again, hard, black, green, sometimes rotten, but almost always steep. On one occasion, I had to perform a pendulum; a narrow ice gully lost itself in granite above, up which there was no way. Vertical rock rose above, left and right. I noticed a tiny crack above me; I climbed slowly almost to the top of the ice tongue with great care because it could easily have broken off. I hammered in a piton, threaded the rope, descended a little and swung to the side. Thus, I reached the continuation of the ice gully to the left.

I was slowly approaching the ridge, although there were extremely difficult sections right up to the crest. Suddenly I almost stumbled into the soft snow on the ridge. The summit of Kumbhakarna was very close, and the ridge leading to it presented no technical difficulties. I felt drained; I'd had enough of this kind of torture. I reached the summit just after 3:30 P.M. in deteriorating weather. To the south was a sea of gray clouds.

The usual afternoon worsening of weather would prevail that day too. For that reason, I wanted to descend the Japanese route as far as was possible. I had to rappel to reach the upper icefield of the Japanese route. Because the weather began to resemble a proper storm, there was no point in sitting it out in the middle of a 55° to 60° icefield. Heavy snowfall and strong, cold winds forced me into temporary shelter in a crevasse among the séracs.

The seemingly endless bivouac was marked by chattering teeth, quivering muscles, looking at my watch and hoping the last few days' weather pattern would prevail. With howling winds sweeping snowflakes in every direction, fog and darkness, I felt it lasted far too long. In the middle of the night, the storm finally abated. I continued down immediately. From the crevasse I descended among the séracs for 100 meters. It was not the right way and led to a 15-meter-high vertical ice cliff. Not feeling like retracing my steps, I decided to rappel. At the edge of the sérac I chiseled an ice mushroom with my ice axe and fixed the rope with a sling. Although this maneuver appears close to madness to the uninitiated, such an ice mushroom holds weight without danger.

The ice slopes leading to the lower séracs sometimes surprised me with black ice. During the day, I could have sought a better route, but in the darkness I descended the most direct line. Among the lower séracs I zigzagged left and right to stay among them for as long as possible and on the final section to the plateau I rappelled a few more times. The icefall in the jumbled mess of the Kumbhakarna Glacier was a mere formality. I chose a much easier route than for my ascent, albeit a more dangerous one. I told myself that if the séracs hadn't collapsed for a whole week, they'd last another hour or two.

And finally it was all over. When there is no more danger and the way ahead is easier, concentration falls. My walk across the glacier resembled the staggering of a drunk returning from a night out. Halfway to Base Camp, Jani came toward me with a broad smile on his face. It was wonderful to see another human, especially one who had kept his fingers crossed through my climb. It took me five hours to reach Base Camp from the foot of the face, although it normally would have taken two. I was exhausted. After great effort on three days and with very little food, my stomach was not prepared for a feast. Only liquids went down easily. That afternoon we drank a lot.

Some people thought that the north face of Kumbhakarna could not be climbed in the way I had chosen. I did not agree and felt that I would succeed. For me personally it is important that matters in which I believe so much I must resolve in my own way. And Kumbhakarna is only a part of what I believe in.

Summary of Statistics:

AREA: Kangchenjunga Himal, Nepal.

NEW ROUTE: Kumbhakarna (Jannu), 7710 meters, 25,294 feet, via the direct North Face, April 27 to 29, 1989 (Tomo Česen, solo); the ascent took 23½ hours; the descent took 18 hours.

The Northeast Rib of Kwangde Central

ALAN KEARNEY

I THOUGHT THAT LIVING IN Kathmandu would offer greater climbing opportunities than my home in Bellingham, Washington. When Bellinghamsters aren't watching the slug races, they manage to pull off an occasional alpine climb. You can see the mountains from Kathmandu, but getting to them is another matter. I realized that when my wife took a job with CIWEC Clinic and we moved to Nepal for two years.

Back in Bellingham, our friends wrote about the exceptionally cold winter we were missing. I went insane imagining all the ice climbs that had never formed during my eight years living there. In January it was hot and dusty in Nepal. I continued to mountain-bike the dirt roads in the Kathmandu valley and fend off screaming kids that frequently threw rocks at me and latched onto the rear of my bike on steep hills. I was plenty sick (on the average once a month) and was tired of being hounded for money by the locals. Other climbers breezed through town, picked up permits and went climbing. I did not have a job and was beginning to get depressed.

I lived for March 2 when Carlos Buhler and Martín Zabaleta would arrive and I could join them on Cho Oyu. At this point, you may be wondering how many years I spent in Kathmandu before Carlos and Martín showed up to bear me away to the mountains. Only three months!

When at last they flew in, I became very nervous and excited at the same time. I was enthusiastic about leaving Kathmandu and apprehensive about climbing to 8000 meters. On previous trips, I had been slow to acclimatize, had never been above 20,500 feet and at least once had altitude sickness. My past record showed that I possessed an aptitude for climbing small beautiful mountains and not big ugly ones. I often wondered about climbers' motives and my own. What was the fascination with trying to ascend the really high peaks? Many of them are not attractive and even less so with so much garbage accumulating at the Base Camps. At least, Carlos and Martín were keen on keeping the trip small and thus impacting the mountain less. This was an approach I always favored.

After hiking for nine days from Jiri to Namche Bazar, Carlos pointed out to me that he thought Ama Dablam one of the five most beautiful mountains of the

Plate 4

Photo by Alan Kearney

KWANGDE CENTRAL.

world. What were the other four? He listed Gasherbrum IV, Nameless Tower, Machapuchare and Cerro Torre. He was diplomatic to include Cerro Torre and it did make me feel better. Since Sue had joined us at Lukla, I had been hit with an intestinal bug but was finally starting to recover at Namche.

We veered away from the Everest path westward toward Dramo and Thame Og. To the southwest rose several trekking peaks that sported steep technical faces and summits of reasonable height, a modest 20,000 feet or so. The scenery improved and I stated that Thame looked like a combination of Alaska and Patagonia, plus the culture of course.

The truly beautiful Thame valley wound northward toward the Nangpa La. I began to think I would have a good trip after all, and Sue was happy to be away from work and out of the city. Having tea served in bed by the cook boy on frosty mornings was luxurious. The pace had been steady and each day we gained less than 1000 feet until Chocsumba. Lhakpa Dorje, our sirdar, stated that there were no campsites until we gained Lunag at 16,300 feet, a rise of 1800 feet in one shot. There was no problem for anyone else, including Carlos' 63-year-old mother, but I got pulmonary edema. Sue stayed with me while the expedition went to Base Camp at 17,200 feet.

The following day, Sue and I descended to Chocsumba and the day after to Thame Og at 12,500 feet. The slightest rise in the trail made me gasp and Sue finally took my ten-pound pack. I sat on a boulder and wept. Fear and a sense of uselessness and failure gripped me. My lungs were trapped in a vise and I spent twenty minutes climbing a 150-foot slope. On the other side, when we began the gradual drop to Chocsumba, I could breathe a tiny bit better. But my brain was hammered with pain and my heart was crushed. Why did I travel to the other side of the world just to live in a city ten times the size of my home town, hike for two weeks and then get altitude sickness? Even Sue, with her expert medical training, didn't realize what was happening inside me or how fast pulmonary edema kills. I *did* know; I had lost a friend on Aconcagua in 1985 when he and his wife were guiding a group of clients.

The next sixteen days consisted of descent to Namche, rest, a very gradual reascent to Base Camp, seeing Carlos and Martín briefly, waving goodbye to Sue, carrying a load to 18,000 feet and getting pulmonary edema a second time. I left Base Camp immediately with the cook and reached Marulung in one day, a drop of 4000 feet. Cho Oyu was out of the picture!

I hiked slowly on down to Thame alone, and although despondent, I was glad to be alive. Thame was so picturesque I lingered there for several days, reading and hiking, and eventually ambled down the trail toward Namche. The surrounding peaks teased me, but my spirit was gone as were any climbing partners. Between Dramo and Namche, I encountered Rob Newsom. I was happy to see anyone I knew. He had not come to climb Nuptse as originally planned but had a permit for Kwangde, a peak directly to the south. But the face he and Gordy Kito intended to climb was devoid of ice and anticipating a long rock climb, he went in search of used pitons in Namche. The scalp hunters in Namche wanted $8.00 per pin and so he came back with none. I wasn't anxious to return to Kathmandu and volunteered my hardware if we could get porters to bring it down from the Cho Oyu Base Camp.

Rob said that I ought at least to come to their Base Camp for a day or two and, if I wanted, to join their small expedition for the climb. Imagine an unused power eggbeater that has sat on the shelf for years and has just been plugged in. Every part functions smoothly as though it had never been discarded. I literally hummed with excitement.

I sensed something wrong when Rob said in his Louisiana drawl, "We came to do an ice climb and there's no ice. I'm not too psyched." I was grateful for a chance to do any climbing and logged his remark away without further thought. The day was hot and we took our time in reaching Base Camp in the village of Hungo. Gordy and Rob parked a huge North Star tent on the grass in a stone corral. The elevation was 11,800 feet and the air warm, an ideal place to finish my recovery. Rob was in the grips of an intestinal disorder and I sent a note to the Cho Oyu Base Camp to try to get my gear brought down to Hungo. Seven days passed during which my gear arrived. I made a carry to the north face of Kwangde's north peak. Rob was still pretty sick.

On April 15, Gordy and I moved to a high camp in two stages, having changed our objective to the northeast rib of Kwangde's lower summit. Rob came up on the night of April 17 and the three of us fixed ropes across steep snow and up two pitches of rock on the 18th. I was feeling good, having finally lost any trace of a cough, Rob had kicked his diarrhea and Gordy seemed in good spirits. Beneath the surface, I still sensed a lack of interest in the climb on the others' part. It was not in the condition they had hoped and there was a question of rockfall on the face we intended to try. I didn't think it was that bad, but Rob felt the danger excessive. During the past week, I had become remotivated, the route looked reasonable and the weather was perfect. It is possible that my perception of the hazards were smothered by my desire to climb something.

The next morning, the three of us climbed easy snow to 16,500 feet, just below a snow-and-ice gully leading to the fixed ropes. As we neared the couloir, it ejected a large rock that slid 100 yards down the snow slope and stopped. Rob announced that he would not be doing the climb and when I asked Gordy about the route, he felt the same. My position was tenuous, being a guest on their expedition. Although I had had my share of bad times since arriving in Nepal, here was a chance to wipe out those feelings of failure and depression. I had no intention of offending anyone. I felt I could solo the route, doing it for purely personal reasons. I told Rob that I would leave the first fixed rope in place so that he could retrieve his camera, Gore-Tex coat, Jümars and North Wall hammer that he had left hanging from a piton the day before.

Rob replied, "No, you don't understand. I'm never going up that mountain again. My life's worth more than that gear. If you can bring some of it down, that's OK, but I'm not going back up." I said that if that were true, I would pull the first rope on the traverse and use it higher. Doing so would cut me off from his gear as my intended rappel would not descend past that spot. Naturally I

didn't expect them to wait at Base Camp with nothing to do while I was climbing, but I guess I hoped they would.

I was plenty nervous that first morning as I climbed hard snow and ice back up to the start of the ropes. I was determined to right the wrongs and leave Nepal having climbed a summit or at least having made a good effort. This situation could turn things around. The trick was staying alive.

As I began the first self-belayed pitch above the high point of the fixed ropes, a baseball-sized rock tore through the air and vaporized on the slabs nearby. Perhaps Rob was right about the danger and I was being a fool. It appeared that after a couple of pitches I would be on a rib between two concave faces and thus safe from rockfall. Completing those three pitches and reaching safer climbing took the remaining afternoon and part of the next morning. Consequently, my first bivouac was filled with apprehension, as I was in the danger zone.

I chose to rope solo the lower two-thirds of the route and carry a stove, bivy sack, thin Polarguard bag and four days of food. By moving slowly, I would lessen the chances of getting altitude sick a third time. This style may seem archaic in the present world of extreme fifth-class free soloing, but it was appropriate for me. Attempting a new route alone brought to mind the thoughts expressed by the late Renato Casarotto, "The factors which motivate me to climb are the need for action, a desire for the unknown and a longing for mental and physical commitment—which may be total!"

Commitment was the key word. I kept telling myself that I could rappel at any time if the difficulties looked bad. The second day was more cheerful than the first. I was climbing on the crest of the rib and away from the intermittent rockfall on either side. The climbing was enjoyable when leading and a real grunt when reascending the rope with the pack and hardware. Far below, I could see the yellow dot of Rob and Gordy's tent in the corral.

In Hungo, they were probably drinking a hot mug of coffee and watching me through binoculars. I was munching on a granola bar and speculating on how to scale a 70-foot featureless wall. When it came to rope soloing, I had been a dunce and now this simple unclimbed route was asking me to produce direct-aid techniques. With my maximum ability at A2+, I lurched upward, making mistakes straightaway, running into dead ends, standing on pins that shifted and tiny slings looped over small flakes. It was a pleasure to resume free climbing and in one more short pitch to reach a suitable bivouac ledge.

A nearby snow patch provided water for dinner and from the warmth of the sack I watched the moon rise over Kusum Kanguru. I felt there was a possibility of succeeding as I had climbed ten pitches in two days and another five or six would put me on ground that I could climb unroped. There was one more obstacle on the agenda for Day Three: a smooth black granite slab some two pitches in length. If I could solve the slab puzzle and altitude sickness did not return, the route would go.

Three pitches of moderate and enjoyable climbing led to the slab on my third day on the mountain. Previous to this climb, the longest time I had spent alone on a route was measured in hours and not days. Down in Hungo, the tent was barely visible and above, the black slab had fallen into the evening shadows. Cracks seemed to lead halfway up the slab, but beyond I could only see some seams and then nothing. It would have been reassuring to have had a bolt kit.

For a hundred feet I laybacked, stemmed, traversed left on thin holds and then jammed up a hand-crack. I continually placed stoppers and Friends and paid out the single 8.5mm rope through prusiks attached to my harness. I stuck a N° 4 Friend behind a block on a ledge and continued climbing up and left 40 feet higher. It was increasingly difficult the farther I climbed from the last piece. Close to large face holds to the left, I carefully smeared with my right foot, edged with the left and pulled up on a couple of rounded crystals to reach easier climbing.

The elevation was roughly 18,700 feet and although the slab was now below me, there still remained 1000 feet to the top. I rearranged rocks at the bottom of a snowbank and settled in for supper. During the night, I developed a cough and thought it might be the beginning of pulmonary edema again. But Day Four was clear and warm and the cough did not worsen. In two-and-a-half hours I climbed unroped up third-class with a couple of spots of 5.7. I reached the top at 10:30 A.M. on April 22, my 38th birthday.

Before tackling the descent, I reflected on the last five months of my life. From an incredibly low state of enthusiasm and health, I felt I had come a long way in a short span. Although Kwangde was not a striking peak and low by Himalayan standards, I had finished the climb in good style. The ascent was by a new route, though it will never stir the imagination or become a classic. For me, it was the perfect means to rebuild my cheerful attitude, eradicate my recent doubts and give me new strength to deal with living in a foreign country. If Sue ever took another job outside the United States, I wouldn't whine constantly, so long as there were slug races to watch.

Summary of Statistics:

AREA: Rolwaling Himalaya, Nepal.

NEW ROUTE: Kwangde Central, 5957 meters, 19,544, feet, Northeast Rib, Summit reached April 22, 1989 (Kearney).

PERSONNEL: Alan Kearney, Gordon Kito, Robert Newsom.

Mount Russell's East Face

CHARLES TOWNSEND

WE HAD SEEN THE PEAK both from Hunter and Foraker—it stood out like a shark's fin on the horizon—and the Washburn photos in the rangers' notebooks got us even more fired up. Mount Russell had been climbed three times, and by two different routes, but Dave Auble and I were attracted by a potential line that split the dramatic east face. It boasted five thousand feet of unexplored terrain and shot up in a straight line from the glacier to the summit.

Unfortunately neither of the established routes offered a viable descent for us. They both simply point the wrong way and would leave us far from Base Camp. In both 1987 and 1988, we had been daunted by the prospect of becoming committed to the increasingly steep and poorly-protected face, knowing that the only logical descent involved down-climbing the entire route. Nevertheless, we went back to the east face this spring, armed with some hardware, bivouac gear and information gleaned from two previous forays on the lower part of the route. We found that if we trimmed down the food and fuel and left the tent behind, a small paraglider would just fit into each pack. The paragliders opened up new options, but we still told our pilot to look for us at the foot of the northeast ridge, in case we couldn't—or wouldn't—jump. It is flat enough to land a Cessna there and so we figured he could bump us down to Base Camp, and we'd pay him more or something.

The first day saw us gain the Douglas Boulder—an obvious snowy shoulder that defines the base of the route—and work up endless slopes to Camp I at 8000 feet. We were still on familiar terrain on the second day, but this time we blew past our previous Camp II and found a more sheltered spot. We were already even with our former high point and into the sculpted rime that characterizes the entire upper route. Nowhere, save the Wishbone Arête, had we encountered such volumes of the stuff. It built up in frothy, feathery layers that exaggerated the size of whatever it clung to, resulting in grotesque, overhanging, unconsolidated heaps of crud. It was sort of pretty to look at, though.

Time did not pass quickly that second night. The relentless winds kept the bivy bags flapping with a steady noise all night, and we had to keep vigil for spindrift leaks. Dave had been coughing and hacking during the whole climb and he was getting pretty hoarse by now. The consolation was that he couldn't sing. That man can retain the same annoying tune in his head for weeks at a stretch.

PLATE 6

Photo by Bradford Washburn

**MOUNT RUSSELL's East Face.
Arrow shows take-off point for the
Paragliders.**

A whole day of unusual mixed climbing followed: snaking up gullies of green, cement-like water ice, looping horns to protect tenuous rock pitches, flicking the rope behind odd projections of rime. Dave's offer to lead the worst run-out, spark-inducing mixed pitches met with little argument. After several hours, we reached the imposing *Tower of Rubble.* What a grand feature: a spire of loose rock stacked up at a ridiculous angle with scattered icy bits that somehow held it together. A slender ridge, *The Tightrope,* linked the tower to the main face and so we shinnied across it, straddling the knife edge as we went. The dizzying drop helped keep us alert. Just above, at about 10,500 feet, a notch carved from the ridge gave us a decent, if exposed, place to spend a beautiful night.

In the morning, Dave and I were reminded how tedious it can be to break camp when each piece of gear is just *asking* to be dropped. Clip this in; unclip that. The problem with steep faces is that you never can relax and toss your hat over there in the snow. It leads to a prolonged anxiety that's not so evident anywhere else.

We had hoped to summit the next day, but our pace slowed as the climbing became more intricate with each pitch. There is a huge, exposed amphitheater up there that funnels down to the *Luge Run*, an uninterrupted gully to the right of our route that would dump you out on the glacier nearly five thousand feet below. We had watched debris, including one of our flukes, exit the face via that route. Just looking down there made us feel nauseous. It also encouraged us to hug the rime towers to the left. Like Hobbit Couloir back home in New Hampshire, we were just able to squeeze through a tiny slot in the rock, half stemming and half chimneying. Thankfully, it popped us back onto the ridge proper, and we reckoned it was in the bag.

No such luck! In fact, the final ridge proved the most memorable of all. Faced with an endless series of rime-encrusted gargoyles, we began to chip away at them, protected by little more than the classic Alaskan belay: "If you fall down that side, I'll jump down this side." The vertical crud resisted orthodox technique, and by pawing at it again and again, we just made it steeper. Nor would our tools stick in the marbles overhead. Additional insult was added by the constant shower of junk that we raked down on ourselves; it filled the space behind our glasses and poured down our collars.

The worst of these gargoyles required a sort of overhanging girdle traverse. Dave pointed out that he'd be left dangling if he fell while seconding that bit and so I slid the prusiks I'd borrowed from him back along the rope before I got too far along. From his belay straddling the ridge, he could only watch me flailing and wonder which of us would have a tool shear out and be launched backward off the overhang. What a grunt! It slowed us so much that we had to bivouac in deteriorating weather about five hundred feet short of the top. Lots of snow fell that night which produced serious shivering, but the summit day dawned clear. Dave still couldn't shake his cough; he said he felt like a refugee from a TB ward.

A solid, green-ice gully led up from our last bivouac on the face; it ended at a tiny saddle between two tottering gargoyles. Dave belayed there, digging

Dave Auble on the "Tower of Rubble" on RUSSELL's East Face.

himself in and driving his tools horizontally into the crud. The cleft over his head was tight enough to stem, and that got us atop the last tower guarding the upper slopes. One more snowy bridge was taken *à cheval*, and everything seemed to merge together. We knew we were close. Dave led through and arrived on the summit where we actually felt comfortable enough to unrope for the first time in five days. We lounged in the sun and shot photos of our new view to the west, lingering on top for more time than we usually allow ourselves.

While it might have been possible to launch from the summit itself, swirling clouds indicated that conditions were not appropriate for flying. We started down on foot. Dave was out in front when suddenly the rope went tight. I looked up, but he was gone. It was the first time that either of us had ever gone into a crevasse past the armpits. I could feel him squirming around like a fish on a line, and so I figured he was all right and just needed time to work things out. He eventually emerged, spluttering, snow-covered and furious. I was elected Crevasse Dowser for the rest of the day and led off down the ridge in failing light.

After a single rappel off an ice cliff, we found a level bivy spot on a tiny promontory overlooking the head of the glacier. It was about a thousand feet down from the summit, and it looked as if a long day would get us down to the base of the northeast ridge where we could wait for a plane. The view was spectacular, since our prow dropped away on three sides. It was a beautiful night, and our spirits were high.

We awoke to a storm that lasted five days, during which it increased to a fury that we hadn't believed possible. We never moved from our perch in the bivouac bags. For at least one entire day, the wind rose to such a force that we could not even communicate, though we sat shoulder to shoulder. We had only a few hard candies left and grew weaker and more dehydrated as the storm wore on. The feeling of being completely disoriented began to overwhelm us both. Our sense of time became distorted and the whiteout erased any visual reference point. The whole situation was surreal. Even our fear, being so prolonged, was more like numbness.

With all that time to sit and think, we speculated that Mount Russell's position at the extreme southwest corner of the Alaska Range might account for its unusual weather and that odd rime formation. Neither of us knew much about such things, but we found it interesting to hear Adams Carter later describe similar weather that his party encountered on the northeast ridge of the peak in 1966 when they were "driven off by a horrendous storm." In all his climbing, it was the only time he can remember ever saying to himself, "This is survival." Twenty-three years later, we felt the same way.

We were several days overdue by the time the storm abated, but having been spotted from the air, we were reassured that local pilots and the Denali Park Rangers were aware of our situation. One rappel off a bollard started us heading down to the notch, where we began several hours of slogging along the level portion of the ridge. Fatigue barely let me lift my feet. Dave was burdened with the dual task of plowing a waist-deep trench and then all but dragging me

Plate 8

Photo by Bradford Washburn

The East Face of MOUNT RUSSELL.

through it. We continued until near the 10,000-foot level, where we found a launch site and probed it out. Dave unrolled his paraglider, waited for the right wind and launched, carefully avoiding a narrow crevasse near the lip.

When it was clear that he had landed, I pulled up my chute, took a few steps and went off the edge. There was a sudden drop, followed by a reassuring lift of the wing, and I was airborne. Sailing directly in front of the face, I was too distracted by the lure of Base Camp to enjoy the incredible view of the route. Before long, I landed in a heap near Dave a few hundred yards from the tent.

Ten days on the hill; eight minutes in the air. Sitting at Base Camp and enjoying our bottomless cache of food and beer, we stared back up at the face. The frothy rime was in shadow now, and we tried to pick out the features of the route. Two pounds of fig newtons disappeared in minutes. Still looking up, Dave seemed puzzled by something. Finally he asked, "Can you still call it alpine-style if it takes three years?"

Summary of Statistics:

AREA: Alaska Range.

NEW ROUTE: Mount Russell, 3557 meters, 11,670 feet, East Face, Summit reached May 11, 1989 (David Auble, Charles Townsend). Descent from 10,000 feet by paraglider.

Foraker's Infinite Spur

MARK BEBIE

WEATHER FOCUSES YOUR CHOICES in the mountains. Jim Nelson and I read many books during the three weeks we spend at the 14,000-foot camp on Denali. That, and a lot of skiing—the storms are dropping much dry powder. We are on Denali trying to acclimatize and become comfortable with the range before we try Foraker. Some people create fantastic snow shelters, and I also notice that the trail between camps and the leftover-food dump is well packed. During a break in the storm cycle, a volleyball game even breaks out. A packed stuff sack is the ball, and a rope is strung between skis for the net. With some twenty countries represented, this international social event is no wilderness experience. It almost seems urban. One Korean calls it "McKinley City." Small groups materialize from time to time to discuss how they all can deal with the lousy weather, but no amount of talk can change matters—mountains aren't moved by democratic vote.

Our time is running, so if we are going to climb Foraker, we had better get going. We blunder our way down toward the landing strip in a storm, until we lose the wands. We spare ourselves the frustration of trying to rediscover the trail, and we camp where we are.

The next day is the start of a long period of good weather. It takes us two days to recognize this, as we lazily prepare for Foraker, sharpening tools, organizing food and helping to smooth out the rutted landing strip. Noticing that the weather pattern has indeed changed, we make plans to leave.

Just after midnight on June 14, we begin the ten-mile approach to the Infinite Spur. Alpenglow distracts the flight of butterflies in my stomach. This is the biggest, most remote climb I have ever attempted. Without a decent photograph, the description of the first ascent is little more than a collection of words. A lot of unknowns. And who are we? Just a couple of guys from the Cascades. The only thing that is certain is that the route has been climbed once before.

We ski independently on the hard snow to the first pass, where we rope up and travel on foot the rest of the way. Even at this early hour, the warmth of the day has changed the last bit of the couloir over the second pass into waist-deep sugar. That minor aggravation is soon taken care of. One rappel leads to a camp on the flat glacier as a light drizzle starts. The rain lasts only through the night, and in the morning we turn the shoulder for our first view of the Spur. It is immense. As we walk up to its base, we mentally break the climb into pieces. This huge puzzle begins to fit together. There is surprisingly little snow on the lower rock, even after Anchorage's wettest May in 55 years.

PLATE 9

Photo by Bradford Washburn

The South Face of MOUNT FORAKER. The Infinite Spur is marked.

Jim Nelson on Pitch 46, the first of
three crux pitches on FORAKER.

PLATE 11

Photo by Mark Bebie

Nelson on Pitch 60 on FORAKER. He was placing his third ice screw just before his fall.

We decide to start on a rock buttress left of center. Abandoning sleds and ski poles, we begin punching up the avalanche debris. Approaching the rock, I see rappel slings from a previous attempt. Since the initial rock is steep and our packs are heavy, we haul the leader's pack while the second jümars the pitch. By eight P.M., we have climbed five pitches. We stamp out a platform at a snowy spot on the rock spur and begin the two-hour evening routine—water, nuts, ramen, tea. For the first time in a month, we are really climbing and glad to have this project under way.

The next day is varied: easy rock, hard rock, pack hauling, unconsolidated snow over rock, and a snow slope with mixed bands leading to our next bivouac at midnight. The tent doesn't fit so very well here. In this land of 24-hour daylight, our schedule is not subject to that of the sun. We sleep and eat when we need to, and climb when we can. We leave our site at noon. As we climb, the weather deteriorates. After six pitches, we are at the ice arête, and it is pointless to continue in a snowstorm. After we have hacked the ice for two hours, the platform looks big enough, but the tent hangs over the edge.

By noon, we are moving again. A gorgeous day. The arête begins easily, step-kicking with ice-screw belays. At almost every belay, we take off our packs. They are just too heavy to wear all the time. There are no bivouac sites on this arête. We don't want to cut another ice platform and so at midnight we start into the crux pitches.

At our bivouac later that morning, we reflect on the seriousness of those three poorly protected pitches. There we were, some 45 pitches up the route with no possibility of retreat, traversing a tremendously exposed loose wall, dulling our ice tools in a gully of garbage rock and thin ice. I remember the last pitch very well. Jim led it and dumped the most relentless barrage of ice, snow and stones that has ever fallen on me. We were even—I did just the same thing to him on the previous pitch. After two hours in that belay, I cursed anything and everything. Rarely had I been so cold. After two additional pitches of steep ice, the ridge leveled out and we stamped a platform on the only snow around, a pillow perched atop the ridge. Our anchors for the night were five ice screws about thirty feet away, and below us! Both of us had opened our water bottles during the night climbing by beating the frozen lids on our axes, but we find that both lids are cracked. Mine I repair with duct tape, but Jim's is ruined. He tosses it. After 23 pitches in 20 hours, we are ready for a brew and sleep.

We climb the next ten pitches of the Spur on the left side. The Spur gains little elevation here but is steep sided with a sharp crest. The ice is excellent, we are well rested, the sun is out and we are in a spectacular spot. But our ice tools are dull. Shouldn't we have brought along a file? Looking back at our previous bivouac, we shudder to see that we were soundly sleeping atop a cornice.

Our 60th pitch leads onto the hanging glacier. Jim knows that I have no belay in the unconsolidated snow and so he looks as if he is being his usual safe self by putting in three screws in the sérac. But the sérac is giving him trouble. The ice is brittle. He is in an off-balance move to get around a bulge when he starts fishing with his tools in the powder snow. With only six feet to go before we are on easy terrain, he plunges off. I have always wondered about those Soviet titanium screws, but the top one stops him, full pack and all, after fifteen feet. Thoughts of broken ankles, pulled shoulders and other horrors flash through my mind. Fortunately Jim is only breathing hard. He says he spied good ice just before he peeled off. He is up on the second try, and I find it awkward even with his coaching. Knee-deep snow leads to a sérac where we have room to unrope for the first time since leaving the glacier below. The tent is soon up. We dive in as the weather deteriorates.

Our first avalanche arrives at about three A.M. It drops a foot of snow on the tent. We move the tent up closer under the sérac. The second avalanche comes in the early morning, but this time it goes over us. Countless avalanches pour over us during the four-day storm. Avalanches and wind-driven snow around the tent require constant attention to keep from getting crushed. We wait for lulls to make our exits and entrances in order to minimize the snow that blows in the tent door. Twice, we push with our backs against the walls to hold back the driven snow. The wind howls so loudly that we can't hear each other speak. We read our books—both of them twice. After three days, conversation drifts around to how long we have each gone without food. We still have plenty, but how long is this storm going to last? From two A.M. until ten A.M. on the fourth day, the wind roars.

Then, suddenly, it stops. What has happened to four days of snowfall and avalanches? Scoured away by the wind! Even the knee-deep snow of four days ago has gone. A surreal staircase of footprints leads up to us from the last belay. Our original tent platform looks as if we had just packed up the tent. It is one of the most amazing mountain phenomena I have ever seen. There is no trace of fresh snow! It is as if the storm had never occurred.

The sun is out and the heat is unbearable as we plod out of camp. Higher, on the ice, the breeze picks up, and climbing is fun again. Pilot Doug Geeting flies by below us since we were expected out the day before, but he doesn't see us. The summit at midnight. We brew up as we watch a beautiful sunset over the northern horizon.

By three A.M. we are down to 14,000 feet on the southeast ridge. Since we have cold conditions on the lower part of the ridge which will keep the snow hard, we continue our descent that evening. After the double-corniced ridge, we are forced to bivouac because of the clouds. We don't sleep; we just eat the rest of our food. Geeting is buzzing around again, but he misses us once more.

When the clouds drop around midnight, we continue. The southeast ridge is not a trivial route. Belayed down-climbing leads to four rappels off rock. Shortly we are punching in to our knees in the slide debris. Soon, we are on the moraine and level ground where Geeting finally finds us. In the late June sun, we struggle with the soft, wet mushy snow, trying to get to our cache of skis, sleds and cans of fruit cocktail. Five miles later, we are at the landing strip. Beer rarely tastes so good. We toast to our safe return as we relate the tales of our 13-day adventure.

We are glad we went heavy: 11 days of food and, as it turned out, 15+ days of fuel. This enabled us to keep our strength up and to climb at a safe pace. A

couple of days of "extra" food does not weigh that much on a climb this long. Instead of being tempted to go for it during a lull in the storm, we could afford to be patient. I have read many accounts of people heading for the summit with something like a single chocolate bar and no water—basically running on fumes, and a lot of hope. Here, the margin of safety is already thinned enough by the cold, and the conditions which can change. No amount of wishful thinking will ever tame Alaska.

Summary of Statistics:

AREA: Alaska Range.

SECOND ASCENT: Mount Foraker, 5303 meters, 17,400 feet, via the Infinite Spur, a 13-day Climb, Summit reached on June 24, 1989 (Mark Bebie, James Nelson).

Hunter's Northwest Face

CONRAD ANKER

Get worse, stay the same or get better—Foolproof Denali Weather Forecast

OPERATING THE KAHILTNA BASE Camp for the month of May provided an ideal job between climbs. People from around the world embarked on pilgrimages to the snowy summits of the Alaska Range. Some returned with a better grasp on their abilities, while others returned frustrated, demanding instant taxi service. Each morning as I gathered weather data, the crowned heads of the Alaska Range played with the sky. Every now and then, the sky would clear: Denali dominating the north, the subtle and elusive Foraker to the west, and the north face of Hunter to the east. Of this spectacular horizon, the northwest edge of Mount Hunter drew my attention most. A new line to climb existed, but how safe was it? I added another column to the weather log, noting avalanches and the position of the sun on the diamond-shaped northwest face.

In the third week of June, having observed the face for seven weeks, I felt a reasonably safe route could be climbed in a two-day push to the summit plateau. To share an adventure with a friend is the essence of a fun climb. My partner, Seth Thomas Shaw, is very much a "top-hand" and is always keyed for excitement. We adjusted our sleeping habits in preparation for continuous 24-hour climbing. By the time we were ready to set off, a four-day storm rolled in. Our imaginations had plenty to ponder. It was time to be patient, as impatience brings worse weather.

Jim Nelson and Mark Bebie skied into camp after climbing the Infinite Spur on Foraker, ready to celebrate and reminisce on their experience. The energy of a successful climb creates a contagious exuberance, which coupled with a few glasses of home brew can motivate even the laziest of climbers. Suddenly, the route seemed to be in shape and the weather stabilizing.

By packing light, we hoped to travel more quickly. With food for five days, we had the idea of scaling the face in a 48-hour dash. In the event of inclement weather, we would have to choose between retreat and several low-calorie bivouacs. As the route appeared to be steep, we planned on mixing wall and water-ice techniques for rapid progress. The leader would lead on a single 100-meter 9mm rope with a day pack; the second would follow on ascenders with the heavier pack. The rack was pared to a minimum: 8 screws, 2 pickets, 5 pins, 7 nuts and 20 carabiners. With the light rack we found reliance in each other and our skills; not in a sack of hardware.

The first 1500 feet were (and always will be) susceptible to sérac-triggered avalanches. One must spend little time in the gambling den or great losses can be incurred. A three-tiered bergschrund separated the ice from the snow slope. ST is a magnet on 5.11, yet the loose, overhanging snow had him wriggling like a husky in a snow drift. Several rope-lengths later, we met the first rock band, the designated tea spot. While we brewed, the weather began to deteriorate. The snow cascaded down and doused the tea. A sign to get moving.

Two pitches later, the spindrifts had not abated. In fact, they were becoming large enough to spoil the fun. We found a granite ledge on which to set up the tent. Wet as mops, we flopped into the tent and began rationalizing about the situation. It was best to make no decisions until the storm was over; going down was as senseless as going up. Fortunately, twenty hours later the sky cleared, exposing Denali and Foraker. The sun sneaked around the ridge and began drying us out. Our spirits rose as the crisp blue sky enticed us to further adventure.

The main rock band provided the setting for inspirational climbing in the eight-P.M. sunlight. Three pitches of interesting climbing gave way to the final icefields. Seven 100-meter rope-lengths beyond the bivouac, we stopped for tea. As we savored it, Jim Okonek flew a pattern above the southeast fork of the Kahiltna. Seeing a plane was a welcome sight. Our spirits were boosted. A few more pitches of steep ice and we stood below the cornice. One last unknown before the sanctity of the summit plateau. ST, in a happy manner, tunneled through the big lip.

We set up our tent and promptly were lulled into a deep sleep. Our second bivouac in three days lasted 26 hours as a snowstorm had pinned us. At nine P.M. on July 3, we left the high camp for the final 1300 feet to the summit. The climbing was easy and we enjoyed our position in the Alaska Range. The weather was clear and still. Hunter cast a long shadow to the southeast. On the eve of the Fourth of July, we took a moment on the summit to ponder the Valdez oil spill. The disaster has raised the awareness of oil consumption in our nation, and new guidelines have been established to protect marine environments. Yet, as a nation, our ravenous appetite for oil is slowly but surely taking its toll on the atmosphere. Will the Alaska Range always be blessed with clean air?

The west ridge of Hunter, our descent route, is not a casual snow plod. Tricky crevasses and cornices reminded us that concentration was required as we went downwards. A slip could speed up the rate of descent past the point of enjoyment. Twenty hours after standing on the summit, we bivouacked for the last time, as the glacier was too warm for safe travel. A clear night froze the surface and we marched back to the landing strip. We stood in awe of the mountain, happy to have shared a secret with it.

Summary of Statistics:

NEW ROUTE: Mount Hunter, 4442 meters, 14,573 feet, via a new route on the Northwest Face, Summit reached on July 3, 1989 (Conrad Anker, Seth Thomas Shaw).

Eroica, Mount Hunter

ROY RUDDLE, *Alpine Climbing Group*

WHEN JONATHAN PRESTON AND I met for the first time at an Alpine Club symposium in North Wales in November 1988, we were both very keen to visit Alaska. Our friendship and mutual trust were cemented during the first half hour when we found out that we had both attempted a particular new route in Peru on a little known peak called Trapecio, Jonathan in 1988 and I in 1985.

I had been inspired by Mount Foraker's unrepeated French Ridge in Donald Goodman's history *(AAJ, 1987)* and after I had shown Jonathan one picture, that became our objective.

We flew to Base Camp on the Kahiltna Glacier's west fork at midday on May 17 thanks to Doug Geeting, John Rowland and Tom Waite, just 36 hours after leaving London; we set about settling into a routine and developing a good feel for our huge objective. To warm up, we chose to attempt Mount Hunter's west ridge but had to turn back early on the third day when we were confronted by a slope in prime avalanche condition. It groaned and cracked as we stepped on it.

After a day's rest, we still felt in need of a true shake-down route and therefore skied, under very low cloud cover, into the valley below Hunter's south face. We remained in our tent by the base of the southwest ridge until seven P.M. on May 24 when suddenly the clouds lifted and exposed Mount Hunter's 5000-foot south face. On the left side of the face, a slender, narrow line stood out, being both elegant and safe. A series of ice slopes and gullies led to a 1200-foot rock buttress which joined the summit plateau at 12,000 feet at the same point as the southwest ridge. There was no need to confer about the objective as the line appeared out of the cloud. All that remained was to pack our gear and decide when to commence climbing.

The following day the weather was ominously unsettled with alternate patches of blue sky and heavy cloud. Our plan was to leave late in the afternoon and climb as much of the face as possible in the night—"less daylight" would be more accurate—when objective danger would theoretically be at a minimum with the snow and ice harder. At five P.M. we ate a huge meal, packed and waited in a state of readiness in our tent, pondering whether we should go or stay put, bearing the weather in mind. At 9:30 P.M. optimism and "nothing ventured, nothing gained" philosophy won.

We skied up the valley for an hour to a point where we could cut switchbacks up onto an elevated tributary glacier leading to the avalanche runnel at 7500 feet

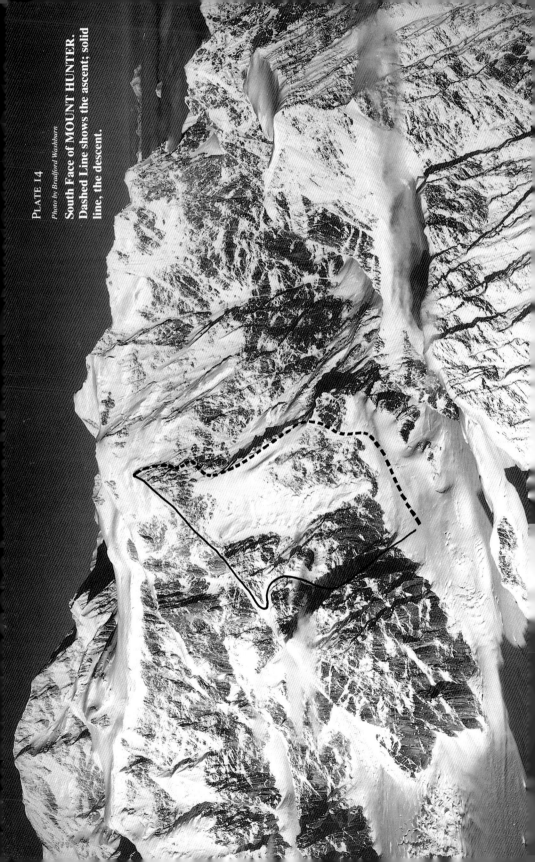

from which we intended to start. Leaving our skis parked upright, I forced the trail up the runnel, starting in knee-deep 30° snow and ending, an hour later, with a struggle through 50° chest-deep powder to a thin ridge crest, which provided instant exposure. Jonathan pushed through and we were soon moving together up perfect névé slopes, crossing to a slender gully between baby séracs on one side and granite outcrops on the other. Together we raced up the gully, pausing briefly at the top to arrange our first belay before negotiating a powdery bulge at 9500 feet. Above, we squirmed our way around crevasses and between séracs to a 40° ice slope leading to the base of the rock buttress. At 5:30 A.M. we were at 10,800 feet.

From our camp on the glacier we had both examined the final rock buttress carefully through my 200mm camera lens. It appeared that we should be able to tackle the buttress directly up reasonably angled snow gullies. Now that we had reached the buttress, we found that the snow in these gullies was a few inches of fine powder, sitting on smooth granite. Accordingly, we traversed right, looking for an alternative. After 150 meters, Jonathan belayed me below a feasible-looking upward line. I tried it and admitted defeat after 30 runnerless feet when the snow disappeared and the rock assumed a rock-climbing-shoe friction structure.

I resumed our crablike movement, willing to traverse all the way to the central sérac band and to tackle that directly, but still hoping for an easy line up. Jonathan found it, and after 150 meters he led up a steep gully to a small col. He sat down on a wide snow ledge on the col. He was about to remove his sack to put a brew on when the ledge fell off and left him dangling on the rope, inspecting what was left of the cornice. Once he was safely connected to rock, I followed. Giving the cornice a wide berth, I led up sustained mixed ground. A combination of solid placements and tiptoeing across slabs brought me to a balancy traverse to the right across a wall, with my front points resting in a horizontal crack and nothing for my hands. Above, I squirmed into a bottomless leaning chimney and nudged my body up, jamming knees and sack in opposition while I sought placements for my axes. There was no room for feet or crampons here! At the top of the chimney, I ran out of rope and adopted a bridged-cum-bi-chacal-pick-belay posture while Jonathan climbed halfway to give me 75 feet more slack. This enabled me to reach a proper belay, bridged across the next groove. Above, Jonathan bouldered over two short overhanging walls before dropping into an icy gully. There he gobbled a full pack of chocolate Hob Nobs in record time to re-energize his exhausted body.

I led the gully, sprinting a few steps at a time and front-pointing on adrenalin to combat my exhaustion, until I ran out of rope. Jonathan continued, past my axe-pick belay, to a small rock outcrop from which I pushed on to the complex forked bergschrund. Unable to exit right, I attempted to pad across the snow bridge covering the left exit. Just as I thought I was on solid ground, a huge hole opened under me—but nothing that a quick foot cum belly flop wouldn't fix. At 2:30 P.M. I suddenly found myself at 12,000 feet on the summit plateau, a few yards from two domed tents!

As I belayed Jonathan from a snow stake, Dave Karl, a member of a four-man American team repeating the southwest ridge, emerged from a tent and stared at me.

"Where the devil did you come from?" Satisfied that I was not an aparition, he wandered over to share the brew he had just made, most welcome after seventeen hours of continuous climbing.

While Jonathan and I dug our tent in, Dave's partners returned from a successful bid for the south summit. We retired to our tent to eat and brew endless cups of tea while a snowstorm raged outside. At 6:30 A.M. on May 28, we emerged. The weather was very unsettled and a summit attempt seemed extremely foolhardy. We elected to descend the southwest ridge with the Americans.

A 150-meter traverse brought us to the start of ten abseils. Unfortunately, Cory Brettman was the first man down, which meant that our ropes stretched six feet short of his second and third anchors. (Cory was much heavier than either of us.) Jonathan had the worst job, down-climbing to each anchor, holding onto our rope, while I remained clipped into an ice screw, ready to catch him if he should slip! By the fourth anchor point, we managed to get Cory to reduce his abseil lengths to normal proportions.

After ten hours, the descent was complete. We retrieved our skis and prepared to return to Base Camp. The following evening it began to snow, continuing almost without a pause for eight days. When the weather did clear, the slopes giving access to Foraker's French Ridge were laden. With each ray of sunshine, avalanches rumbled and we knew that for 1989 at least our chances of repeating that ridge were gone.

At the end of June we returned to England, feeling overjoyed at our ascent of Eroica and planning to return in 1990 to what is, in my opinion at least, the finest place on earth. We were both sad that we were unable to reach Mount Hunter's true summit, but having joined the southwest-ridge route on the summit plateau, above all of both routes' technical difficulties, we stand by our claim to have made the first ascent of the south face.

Summary of Statistics:

AREA: Alaska Range.

NEW ROUTE: Mount Hunter, 4441 meters, 14,570 feet, First Ascent of *Eroica* on the South Face; Ascent ended at the Junction of the Eroica and Southwest-Ridge Routes at c. 12,000 feet, May 25 to 28, 1989 (Jonathan Preston, Roy Ruddle).

Moose's Tooth and Huntington

JAMES QUIRK, *Unaffiliated*

D AVE NETTLE AND I hadn't been in Talkeetna for more than ten minutes when we descended on the bar at the Fairview Inn. One of the folks present was Doug Geeting, our pilot. We mentioned to him that we were going to climb Mount Huntington and that he would be flying us to the Upper Tokositna Glacier. His eyes narrowed and he launched into a rubber-faced account of a flight to the Tokositna in winter. The story ended with Doug looking me straight in the eye and saying, "I thought I was going to die." With Doug's last words ringing in our ears, all the planning, scheming and dreaming ended, and our Alaskan adventure began. Our plan had been to climb Mount Huntington's west face via the Harvard route, made famous by Dave Roberts' book, *Mountain of My Fears*, and the tragic death of Ed Bernd on the first ascent.

While we still remembered what the sun looked like, we were waiting, like everyone else, to be flown into Denali National Park. The droning of planes awakened us from a peaceful slumber on Day Two in Talkeetna. Getting a flight to the Tokositna Glacier requires perfect weather, and Doug assured us that this was not going to happen soon. We decided to settle on flying into the Sheldon Amphitheater below the Moose's Tooth and give that peak's west ridge a shot rather than hanging off bar stools in Talkeetna for another night.

Immediately after landing, Dave and I began to fidget, unable to sit out the day on the glacier. Promising ourselves to take it easy, we started climbing. Since the Moose's Tooth was not our main objective, we hadn't studied the route description. Traveling past the original start, we opted for a couloir that rises on the south side of the west ridge. From there we would follow the entire ridge. Ten hours later, after quivering up some 5.7 snow- covered slag, we decided to sleep.

Day Two on the west ridge found us tired and unmotivated after the long sprint from Talkeetna. Having joined the German route at 7600 feet, we meandered up the ridge, shooting for a 9000-foot col which looked within easy striking distance and a likely bivouac spot. In the col, we found 50° to 65° alpine ice and not a flat spot in sight. We ended up climbing simultaneously for two hours before we found rocks to bivouac under. We had hoped for an easy day and discovered that Alaskan "easy" is still damned hard.

PLATE 15

Photo by Bradford Washburn

MOOSE'S TOOTH rises from Ruth Glacier. The new variation started at the foot of the buttress in the center.

The next morning was perfectly clear. After about 350 feet of moderate climbing, we were on the west summit of the Moose's Tooth. We knew from the route description in *The Fifty Classic Climbs* that the Germans who made the first ascent had left ropes at a couple of key spots where they had rappelled to make climbing back a possibility. Slowly, we began to realize that this maneuver requires at least two ropes. We had only one!

As we dropped into Englishman's Col, our sense of commitment increased exponentially with each step. Dave climbed down into the col to search for a way around rappelling into it. I watched his form disapppear over a small rise, hoping beyond hope that one of us would have the guts to call this climb folly. I heard a shout for me to follow. Four years of college and all I could think was, "Oh hell!"

After Dave had put his foot through a cornice and almost fallen 3000 feet onto the Buckskin Glacier, we started to climb out of the col. Now I don't mean to complain, but my ice-climbing experience was limited to screwing around on ice "boogers" in the Tahoe region. Peering at Dave's butt disappearing over a small rise on 80° ice, I realized that I'd traveled a long way to learn how to ice climb, a real initiation under fire.

After surmounting the ice bulge, we emerged on the ridge and from here moved together towards the true summit. Climbing this ridge will go down as one of the most incredible experiences of my entire life. It was like standing on the biggest wave in the world, suspended by clouds and fear, listening to Hendrix's version of *Kiss the Sky*, naked. And people wonder why we climb!

Upon reaching the true summit along with the afternoon clouds, we looked back and could reminisce about the climbing of the day. We sat smugly on the summit, visually panning the mile-long ridge and noting all the high points of the day, or the places we almost turned back; take your pick. Our ascent appears to be the third of the whole west ridge to the main peak. Actually the direct start had been done before, but we were the first to climb this variation and go on to the main summit.

Suddenly, like a slap across the face, it dawned on me that we had to go back over the same ridge. Arghh! However, the ground we had to return on was now familiar and, for the first time all day, we were heading toward food and sleep, which made a big difference in motivation and velocity.

Returning to Base Camp on the Ruth Glacier under perfect skies we heard a rumor that two other climbers had been flown to the Tokositna Glacier the day before. Armed with this knowledge, we successfully "sand-bagged" Doug Geeting into giving the thumbs up for flying us to the upper Tokositna. The flight went without a hitch, but there is something incredibly disconcerting about your pilot jumping up and down in the snow, much happier than you are about having made a safe landing.

Once in the Tokositna basin, our thoughts immediately strayed from the Harvard route and to a magnificent ramp system to the left of the Harvard route and to the right of the Coulton-Leach route. It looked as if this ramp linked with the Harvard route but, as usual, we didn't have a clue. After a short discussion, Dave said, "Jim, I think we should go there." "Oh . . . OK," I replied.

PLATE 16

Photo by Bradford Washburn

**MOUNT HUNTINGTON, showing
the Nettle-Quirk Route.**

At 8:30 on the bitterly cold morning of May 23, we started up the initial snow slopes with four days of food and bivouac gear. The first part of the route above the schrund, which looked easy from below, turned into steep ice climbing. We wondered what the ramp would be like.

The weather had been perfect: clear and cold. However, small clouds began moving in and a light snow started to fall. I looked back at Denali and whistled to myself at the top two-thirds which were covered with huge lenticular clouds. Alaskan weather anxiety began to set in and eat away at my fortitude.

After climbing the lower snowfield, we traversed left for 200 feet. We then ascended the snowfield, which was at least 50°, and ended at the base of the prominent ramp system that angles up and right to join the Harvard route. The first four rope-lengths of the ramp were actually steep steps with sections of vertical and 75° water ice.

A short section of vertical and then 50° ice led to a narrow gully with 55° black ice that was on the outside half of the ramp. Dave led off. Sixty feet into his lead, the tinkling of icy snow could be heard far above us. I looked up to see a white wave of snow engulf Dave and thought, "This is what it feels like just before you die . . ." The snow hissed all around us and the pressure built up on the anchors and on Dave, hanging precariously from his tools, twenty feet above his last screw. Dave claims to this day he couldn't tell what was tighter, the grip on his tools or his sphincter. Three big spindrift avalanches swept over us before we could climb out of this chute. As I pulled up to the belay, all I could think about was going down. I looked at Dave and with a demonic gleam in his eye he said, "Well, it looks as if we're in for all fifteen rounds now."

The next seven pitches climbed the left side of the ramp gradually steepening and hugging a rock wall. From there we could see the spindrift avalanches like clockwork shoot down the gully to where we had been. Emotionally and physically drained, we reached the top of the ramp and angled up and right to a rocky section where we found an old bolt anchor and other signs of the Harvard route. Searching in vain for a place to lie down that wasn't being bombarded by spindrift, we decided to move in the only direction that made any sense: up.

Continuing right at the top of the ramp and then climbing straight up through a rock band brought us to the base of the summit icefield. We moved together to the only rocks we could see on the face, hoping we would be able to bivouac there. It was our last option aside from the summit. Finding a ledge on these rocks, we began to chop away at the ice as another spindrift avalanche swept over us. We reached this spot at 6:30 A.M. on May 24 in a full-blown storm. At this bivy, I fell asleep and dreamed that people had rented my sleeping bag. They were really happy; they had gotten a room with a view.

We rested and brewed for seven hours and then decided to go for the summit. On top, two hours later, instead of exultation, all I felt was relief and dread. Brutally tired and looking forward to a long, intricate descent, the specter of Ed Bernd played across my mind. Below us, an avalanche swept down the face.

Many hours later, we made the last rappel down our ascent route. Our tracks on the glacier had been covered by numerous avalanches. We wallowed through waist-deep snow and collapsed. That night the weather socked in and it was ten days before we even made radio contact with anyone. It was another four before a plane could fly in and pick us up.

Dave and I played a lot of cribbage in those two weeks. I ended up losing the thirty-second game of our tournament and had to buy the beer when we were flown out. The route on Huntington had taken us 36 hours to complete and we waited 336 hours on the glacier to be flown out. The wait was worth it, but it would have been better if I had brought marked cards.

Summary of Statistics:

AREA: Alaska Range.

ASCENTS: Moose's Tooth, 3150 meters, 10,335 feet, via Entire West Ridge, Third Ascent of the Main Summit, May 14 to 16, 1989.

      Mount Huntington, 3731 meters, 12,240 feet, via a new route between the Harvard and the Colton-Leach routes, May 23 and 24, 1989.

PERSONNEL: David Nettle, James Quirk.

Denali's West Rib Solo in Winter

David Staeheli

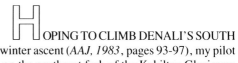OPING TO CLIMB DENALI'S SOUTH
Face solo in the style of its first winter ascent (*AAJ, 1983*, pages 93-97), my pilot
friend Paul Claus set me down on the southeast fork of the Kahiltna Glacier on
February 25. I had finally found time between guiding jobs to make the attempt,
which I had been planning for two years. Originally, I intended to try the Cassin
Ridge; so, armed with route description on a sheet from a yellow legal pad and
several years of hearsay, I was ready to give it a go.

A very intense cold spell had gripped Alaska during the early part of the
month, but this finally gave way to a warm spell with powerful winds out of the
north. On our approach to the mountain, the wing tips of the Piper Supercub
made huge figure-eights as Claus battled the turbulence. I was glad to be put
down on the relative safety of the glacier. On landing, the plane had skidded
across the tops of colossal sastrugi before flopping belly-deep in a snow drift. We
dumped out a mountain of gear and unstrapped my 14-foot ladder, which had
been lashed Alaska-style to the plane's belly. It took time to dig the plane out
before Paul gunned the plane and left me in a cloud of spindrift.

To my surprise, I was not alone. It seems that climbing Denali in winter is
getting popular. At Kahiltna Base, there were four climbers: three Austrians who
had just completed an ascent of the West Buttress and a solitary Japanese, who
was waiting there for his three companions. They were already six days overdue.
With consistent high north winds, it was looking grim. Two weeks later, they
were spotted below Denali Pass, frozen, having succumbed to cold and fero-
cious gales. Denali in winter, or in any season, can be very unfriendly. With that
thought in mind, I began my odyssey up the mountain the next day.

My traveling rig was unusual: two sleds hooked in tandem towed by a
14-foot aluminum ladder suspended from my pack. This was my insurance
against a crevasse fall. At first, it took me five minutes to climb in. After lining
everything up, I would step in between the middle rungs of the ladder and strap
on my skis. Then I would hoist the pack up, leaving the ladder suspended around
my waist. Hooking my sit harness into the ladder was the final step before I
lurched off along the glacier. The whole carnival train, all 21 feet of it, would
have been an amusing sight if anyone had been around to see it.

PLATE 17

Photo by Bradford Washburn

**MOUNT McKINLEY's South Face.
The Western Rib is in the left center;
the Cassin Ridge in the right center.**

To approach the south face of Denali, either the Cassin Ridge or the West Rib, one first must ascend the main Kahiltna Glacier from Kahiltna Base to the northeast fork and climb this so-called "Valley of Death" to the upper basin, hoping not to be swept away by an avalanche. My first day was pretty much what I expected, hard but not impossible. I placed Camp I just short of the northeast fork. The next two days proved hellish as the weather turned sour with heavy ground blizzards. Wearing a 14-foot ladder while threading through crevasses and trying to maintain balance against 30-knot gusts of wind is not fun. Progress was limited to a mile a day for the next two.

Camp IV was at the base of the big icefall, my next obstacle. It took two days to force my way through as I had to resort to load carries. The ladder became a nuisance and it was impossible to wear here. As with all icefalls, it was an enigmatic maze until every last secret passage had been found. I was grateful to establish Camp V at 11,200 feet at the base of the West Rib couloir.

Until then, I had intended to climb the Cassin Ridge. I had several equipment problems, the most pressing being my boots. I had bought a new model and found them not as warm as they had been made out to be. Every day, it was a struggle to keep my feet from freezing. Looking up at the sunless ice chute leading to the Cassin Ridge, I realized that if I continued, I would suffer severe frostbite. A much wiser and more profitable idea was to climb the West Rib instead. Not having researched this route meant that I had to rack my brain to remember everything I had ever heard about it. I made a short reconnaissance up the couloir and decided on it.

The next day, I carried a load up the couloir, often using a 300-foot piece of 7mm rope. After establishing a cache just short of the "snow domes," I returned to camp.

On day eight, I broke camp and moved up the couloir. In the gully the climbing varied from step-kicking to front-pointing on nearly impenetrable boiler-plate ice. Since previous winter attempts had found the gully to be mostly all ice, I considered myself lucky. Crossing the snow domes was the trickiest part of the whole climb. I was forced to use double tools and front-points on wide-open exposed slopes. A very happy camper dug his tent into a bergschrund that night. The next few days saw me carrying loads and moving to Camp VI at 15,000 feet and Camp VII (Balcony Camp) at 16,300 feet.

Through this time, the weather was mostly windy with a fair amount of sunshine. What really surprised me was that the average daily temperatures continued to rise as I gained altitude. The coldest I had recorded was $-28°$ F down on the northeast fork. On the summit day, I arose to a very comfortable 5° F. A veritable heat wave. In researching other winter ascents, I found such a temperature inversion is not uncommon.

Although I was on the steepest terrain yet, the summit day, March 11, was uneventful. I concentrated particularly hard while climbing the "Orient Express," scene of many a fateful accident. I was amazed when I came to the "Football Field" at 19,500 feet to find that the winds of the past month had carved the most spectacular sastrugi I had ever seen. They were up to four feet high with underhangs of five or six feet.

The weather on the summit was the clearest in all my years of standing there. I had no feeling of exhilaration, though, as I was now facing the most dangerous part of any climb, the descent. Climbing carefully down, I reached Balcony Camp seven hours after leaving it.

The next morning, I left Balcony Camp via the West Buttress to descend to my next camp at 7800 feet at Ski Hill. Carelessness on the descent is not unusual. I managed to contract a case of what I call "mechanically induced frostbite" on several toes. That night at Ski Hill, I was treated to one of the best northern lights shows in years in probably the best location to see them. The next day, at Kahiltna Base I was able to flag down bush pilot Doug Geeting. By early afternoon, my fiancée and several excellent friends plied me with 'burgers and champagne at Talkeetna.

This was the first solo winter ascent of Denali by a technical route. Winter mountaineering in the Alaska Range is serious business, but not without rewards. Fourteen people have stood on McKinley's summit in winter but six of them have died. I believe that all the winter accidents can be traced to poor judgment, carelessness or inexperience with local conditions. Alaskan climbs can be safer in winter, especially if the main objective hazards are icefalls or avalanches at altitude. I believe my success was good luck, but luck is made as well as found.

Summary of Statistics:

AREA: Alaska Range.

SOLO WINTER ASCENT: Denali (Mount McKinley), 6193 meters, 20,320 feet, via West Rib of the South Face, Summit reached on March 11, 1989 (David Staeheli).

One Hundred Years of Crossings of Greenland's Inland Ice*

GUNNAR JENSEN, *Arctic Expeditions Adviser, Denmark*

M ORE THAN ONE HUNDRED YEARS ago, in the autumn of 1888, the ice-covered interior highlands of Greenland were explored by the Norwegian polar explorer, Fridtjof Nansen, during his scientific expedition across the Inland Ice from Umivik at Gyldenløves Fjord to Nuuk/Godthåb. This historic centenary brought about increased interest. A record of nine expeditions completed crossings in memory of Nansen in 1988. Naturally, the question arises, "How many expeditions have crossed Greenland's Inland Ice?"

One normally thinks of crossings from East to West Greenland or vice versa. The route used by most is from Angmagssalik to Søndre Strømfjord. One solo Japanese crossed the Inland Ice from north to south in 1978 and another expedition from south to north in 1988.

The following list does not include expeditions that had to be rescued after calling by emergency radio, those that were evacuated by the authorities against their wishes and those that had to give up the crossing and requested evacuation. Expeditions rescued after completing the crossing are included but this is recorded in the remarks. The list gives the following: The year; the members with the leader's name first; the route; the dates of the expedition (often with the number of days on the ice); remarks.

1. 1888; Norwegians Fridtjof Nansen, Otto Neumann Sverdrup, Kristian Kristiansen Trana, Oluf Christian Dietrichson, Samuel Johannesen Balto, Ole Nielsen Ravna; Umivik, Austmannadalen, Nuuk; August 15 to October 3 (40 days); ski, sleds, sail.

2. 1892; American Robert Edwin Peary, Norwegian Eyvind Astrup; McCormick Fjord, Navy Cliff, McCormick Fjord; May 14 to August 5 (97 days); ski, snowshoes, 2 sleds, 14 dogs. Support team of Langdon Gibson and Dr. Frederick A. Cook followed the expedition for 13 days and 200 kms with two sleds.

---

*Drawings are from Fridtjof Nansen's *First Crossing of Greenland*, courtesy of Rare Books Collection, Wellesley College.

IN ONE CASE WE HAD TO PASS THROUGH A NARROW CLEFT'
(By E. Nielsen, from a photograph)

3. 1895; Americans Robert Edwin Peary, Hugh J. Lee, Matthew A. Henson; Bowdoin Fjord, Navy Cliff, Bowdoin Fjord; spring until June 25; 3 sleds, 42 dogs. Support team of 6 eskimos, 3 sleds, 18 dogs.

4. 1910; Danes Ejnar Mikkelsen, Iver P. Iversen; Shannon Ø, Danmark Fjord; March 24 to May 18 (51 days); ski, sleds, dogs. Support team of Hans P. Olsen, Georg Poulsen and Wilhelm Laub with 3 sleds followed until April 10.

5. 1912; Danes Knud Rasmussen, Peter Freuchen, Greenlanders Uvdloriaq, Inukitsoq; Clements Markham Gletscher, Danmark Fjord, Cairn built by Peary, Thule/Dundas; April 14 to September 15; ski, sleds, dogs. Accompanied by eskimos with 8 dog teams on the first 173 kms from Neqe.

6. 1912; Swiss Alfred de Quervain, Paul-Louis Mercanton, Roderick Fick, W. Jost, H. Hoessly, K. Gaule, A. Stolberg; Eqip, Angmagssalik; June 20 to July 21; ski, 3 sleds, 25 dogs. De Quervain, Mercanton and two more made the crossing while the three others carried out scientific research in the marginal area.

7. 1912-3; Danes Jens Peter Koch, Lars Larsen, German Alfred Wegener, Icelander Vigfus Sigurdsson; Danmarks Havn, Storstrømmen; July 24, 1912 to July 17, 1913; ski, sleds, sails, 16 horses, 1 dog. First wintering on the ice. Descent from the ice on July 4, 1913 east of Prøven.

8. 1917; Danes Knud Rasmussen, Lauge Koch, Greenlanders Hendrik Olsen,

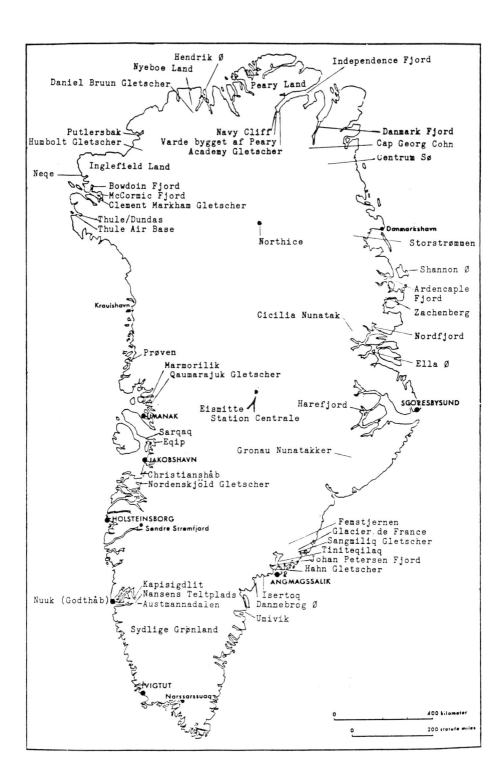

Hendrik Ø
Nyeboe Land
Independence Fjord
Daniel Bruun Gletscher
Peary Land
Navy Cliff
Danmark Fjord
Putlersbak
Varde bygget af Peary
Cap Georg Cohn
Humbolt Gletscher
Academy Gletscher
Centrum Sø
Inglefield Land
Neqe
Bowdoin Fjord
McCormic Fjord
Clement Markham Gletscher
Thule/Dundas
Thule Air Base
Danmarkshavn
Northice
Storstrømmen
Shannon Ø
Ardencaple
Fjord
Krauishavn
Zachenberg
Cicilia Nunatak
Nordfjord
Prøven
Ella Ø
Marmorilik
Qaumarajuk Gletscher
Eismitte
Harefjord
SGORESBYSUND
Station Centrale
UMANAK
Sarqaq
Eqip
Gronau Nunatakker
JAKOBSHAVN
Christianshåb
Nordenskjöld Gletscher
HOLSTEINSBORG
Femstjernen
Søndre Strømfjord
Glacier de France
Sangmiliq Gletscher
Tiniteqilaq
Johan Petersen Fjord
Hahn Gletscher
ANGMAGSSALIK
Kapisigdlit
Nansens Teltplads
Isertoq
Nuuk (Godthåb)
Austmannadalen
Dannebrog Ø
Umivik
Sydlige Grønland

IVIGTUT
Narssarssuaq

0   400 kilometer

0   200 statute miles

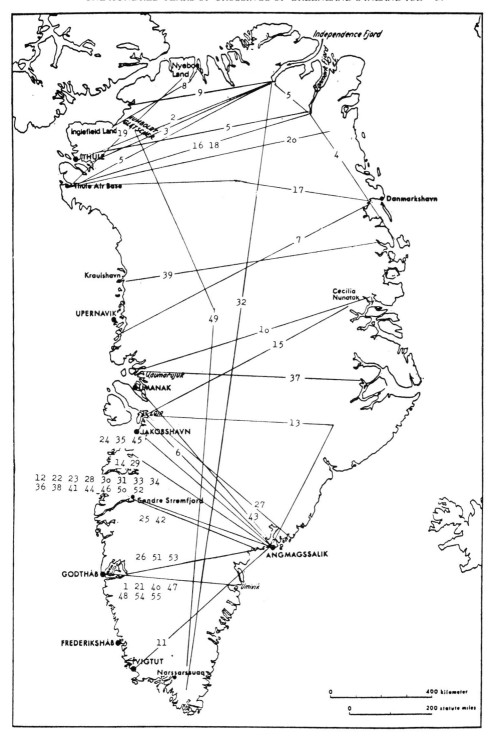

THE CARAVAN ON THE MARCH   (*By A. Bloch, from a photograph*)

Ajako, Nasaitordluarsuk, Inukitsoq, Swede Thorild Wulff; Daniel Bruun Gletscher, Inglefield Land, Thule/Dundas; August 4 to October 22; ski, sleds, dogs. Olsen disappeared at Hendrik Island. Wulff died after descent from the ice.

9. 1921; Dane Lauge Koch, Greenlanders Inuiterk, Etukussuak, Nugapiin guak; Independence Fjord, Putlersbak; June 26 to August 12; ski, 3 sleds, 32 dogs.

10. 1931; Norwegains Arne Høygaard, Martin Mehren; Qaumarajuk Gletscher, Nordfjord; July 10 to August 18 (39 days); ski, 2 sleds, 16 dogs, sails. Distance: 1000 kms.

11. 1931; British J.M. Scott, A. Stephenson, Martin Lindsay; Angmagssalik, Ivigtut; July 1 to 29; ski, sleds, 27 dogs, sails.

12. 1931; British J. Rymill, W.E. Hampton; Angmagssalik, Søndre Strømfjord, Holsteinsborg; August 13 to October 19; ski, sleds, dogs, 2 kayaks.

13. 1934; British Martin Lindsay, Andrew Croft, Daniel Godfrey; Eqip, Gronau Nunatakker, Angmagssalik; June 3 to September 5 (95 days); ski, sleds, dogs. Longest journey without laying out depots: 1695 kms in 95 days!

14. 1936; French Paul-Emile Victor, Robert Gessain, Swiss Michel Perez, Dane Eigil Knuth; Nordenskjöld Gletscher, Angmagssalik; left on May 23 (48 days); ski, 3 sleds, 32 dogs, sails, collapsible boat.

15. 1949-50; French Paul-Emile Victor and 35 participants; A start was made on

THE START IN THE MORNING (*From a photograph*)

July 9, 1948 to bring support over the marginal zone from Eqip; three convoys set out from Eqip on July 1, 30 and August 7, 1949 for the "Station Centrale;" 8 men wintered over; from Station Centrale to Cicilia Nunatak with 5 weasels, 8 sleds, 2 trailers. Some participants of this scientific expedition went on from Cicilia Nunatak to Ella Ø.

16. 1952; Frenchman Paul-Emile Victor with American support; Thule Air-Base, Cap Georg Cohn; weasels.

17. 1952-4; British Michael Banks, C.B.B. Bull, S. Paterson and J.W. Oakley; Zachenberg, Northice, Thule Air Base; weasels, air support. 3 men wintered at Northice in 1952-3 and others 1953-4.

18. 1955; Americans and Frenchman Paul-Emile Victor; Thule Air Base, Cap Georg Cohn; tractors.

19. 1959; 40 Americans and Frenchman Paul-Emile Victor; Thule Air Base, Nyeboe Land/Peary Land, Thule Air Base; 6 D-8 tractors, 4 weasels, 1 polecat, 4 overland-train, 14 heavy sleds, and 2 aircraft and 1 helicopter.

20. 1960; Americans and Frenchman Paul-Emile Victor; Thule Air Base, Centrum Sø.

21. 1962; Norwegians Bjørn Staib, Bjørn Reese; Angmagssalik, Umivik, Nansens Teltplads; July 16 to August 22 (29 days); ski, 2 sleds, 16 dogs.

22. 1965; Scots Hugh and Myrtle Simpson, Roger Tuft, William Wallace; Johan

FIRST ATTEMPTS AT SAILING

(*By A. Bloch*)

Petersen Fjord, Søndre Strømfjord; June 20 to July 25 (36 days); ski, sleds, sails. First woman to cross the Inland Ice.

23. 1966; Finns Erik Pihkala, Eero Varonen, Viljo Haapala, Christer and Peter Boucht; Angmagssalik, Søndre Strømfjord; May 6 to June 20 (38 days); ski, 3 sleds, 30 dogs, sails.

24. 1968; Japanese Kaneshige Ikeda, Tsuguo Saotome, Katuhiko Miyoshi, Hiroshi Sagano, Tadashi Towada; Angmagssalik, Jakobshavn; July to September.

25. 1968; Norwegians Svein R. Søftestad, Øyvind Bay Gundersen, JohanGarrard; Isertoq, Søndre Strømfjord; July 10 to August 4 (24 days); ski, 1 sled, 1 pulk, 16 dogs. Accompanied to a height of 630 meters by Eilif Solberg and Henning Ingnasiussen from Isertoq.

26. 1970; West Germans Peter Lechhart, Günther Bock, Michael Dacher, Franz Martin; Nansens Teltplads, Isertoq; May 26 to July 8 (42 days); ski, 2 sleds, sails.

27. 1971; Danes John Andersen, Erik Hjemlar, Sven Poulsson, Englishman Derek Fordham; Angmagssalik, Glacier de France, Sarqaq; April 22 to June 23 (62 days); ski, sleds, sails.

28. 1973 Norwegians Ralph Høybakk, Herman Mehren; Angmagssalik, Hann Gletscher, Søndre Strømfjord; May 25 to June 25 (23 days); ski, 1 sled, 12 dogs. Helicopter from Angmagssalik to Hann Gletscher.

SAILING IN MOONLIGHT. ' WHEN THE SNOW LOOKED TREACHEROUS I HAD TO GO CAUTIOUSLY AND USE MY STAFF '

(*By A. Bloch, from a sketch by the Author*)

29. 1973; American Dennis C. McAllister and 3 others; Angmagssalik, Christianshåb; May (46 days).

30. 1974; British Joint Services Expedition; Flight Lieutenant Daniel Gleed; Shaun Marshall, Dan Drew, Tom Addison, Mike Cran, Mike Hill, Steve Bodycote, John Pollard; Søndre Strømfjord to Angmagssalik; May 4 to June 9 (37 days.)

31. 1975; Japanese Massa Masuda, Swedes Monica Masuda, Björn Albino; Angmagssalik, Søndre Strømfjord; April 7 to May 29 (50 days); ski, sled, sail; helicopter from Angmagssalik to 65° 57' N, 38° 40' W.

32. 1978; Japanese Naomi Uemura; Academy Gletscher, southern Greenland; May 21 to August 21 (93 days); ski, sled, dogs, air support. Radio contact.First solo crossing. First north-south crossing.

33. 1980; Americans Paul Erickson and 7 others; Angmagssalik, Johan Petersen Fjord, Søndre Strømfjord; June 15 to August 4; boat from Angmagssalik to Johan Petersen Fjord, ski, pulks.

34. 1981; Finns Pentti Kronqvist, Seppo Salomaki, Norwegians Arild and Kjell Bronken; Angmagssalik, Søndre Strømfjord; April 20 to May 18 (26 days); ski, sleds, sails. 3 sleds with dogs accompanied them up the Hann Gletscher to a height of 1050 meters.

35. 1982; Norwegians Morten Berle, Jan Enget, Ståle Blærsterdalen, Ola Dølven, Kjell Brennodden; Angmagssalik, Christianhåb; May 19, to June 15 (27 days); ski, pulks.

36. 1982; British W.S.L. Wooley, Iain Campbell, Ted Courtnay, Roger Daynes, David Matthews, John Beatty; Angmagssalik, Søndre Strømfjord; July 15 to August 28.

37. 1983; West Germans Arved Fuchs, Rainer Neuber; Marmorilik, Station Centrale, Harefjord; May 8 to July 16 (70 days); ski, 2 sleds, dogs.

38. 1983; Norwegian Carl Emil Petersen solo; Angmagssalik, Søndre Strømfjord; April 20 to May 17 (26 days); ski, sled, parachute. Accompanied by 2 sleds from Angmagssalik to a height of 900 meters. Petersen was 58 years old.

39. 1983; Italians Robert Peroni, Josef Schrott, Wolfgang Thomaseth; Ardencaple Fjord, Kraulshavn; June 15 to September 10 (82 days); ski, 3 sleds, sails. Distance 1050 kms.

40. 1984; Norwegians Kjell Einar Andersen, Guttom Christensen, Kåre Kullerud, Håkon Nordseth; Umivik, Nuuk; April 18 to May 26; ski, pulks. Christensen, hurt by a fall beyond Austmannadalen, was transported by helicopter to hospital.

41. 1984; Czechs Jaroslav Pavlicek, Vladimir Weigner, Miroslav Jakes; Angmagssalik, Søndre Strømfjord; September 17 to October 26 (40 days); ski, sleds.

42. 1985; French Allain Misner, Paul Valentini, Didier Drouet; Isertoq, Søndre Strømfjord; July 12 to August 3 (23 days); ski, 3 pulks. They descended near Godthåb Fjord and were rescued on August 6 by helicopter after a radio emergency call. They were three days without food.

43. 1986; Norwegians Jan Morten Ertsaas, Børge Ousland, Agnar Thoralf Berg; Angmagssalik, Umanaq; March 26 to May 1 (37 days); ski, 3 pulks, parachutes. Helicoptered to 1000 meters in Johan Petersen Fjord. Distance 800 kms.

44. 1986; Spaniards Ramón Hernando de Larramendi, José Bellido Trullenque, Pedro Guevara Martínez, Gabriel and Gonzalo Gardenas Sarralde; Angmagssalik, Jakobshavn (Søndre Strømfjord); May 6 to July 1 (42 days); ski, pulks. They departed from Tiniteqilaq on May 13. Bad weather for 20 days. Destination was changed to Søndre Strømfjord.

45. 1986; Norwegians Sjur Mørdre, Vidar Sie, Kai Knudsen, Simen Mørdre; Angmagssalik, Jakobshavn; June 16 to July 9 (23 days); ski, 4 pulks, sails. Helicopter from Angmagssalik to Femstjernen.

46. 1987; British James N. Lowther, Nicholas Hulton; Angmagssalik, Søndre Strømfjord (helicopter from Angmagssalik to Sangmiliq Gletscher); March 31 to April 29 (30 days); ski, 2 pulks, parachutes. They covered 130 kms in one day with parachutes.

47. 1988; Norwegians Asle T. Johansen, Jan Morten Ertsaas, Agnar Thoralf Berg, Roar Nese; Angmagssalik to Umivik (by helicopter), Kapisigdlit, Nuuk; March 19 to April 28 (40 days); ski, sleds, sails. All equipment was exact copies of that used by Nansen in 1888.

48. 1988; Danes Michael Haslund-Christensen, Morten Søborg, Anders Berggren, Norwegians Ole Hoff, Tor-Jostein Hunstad; this expedition followed the same route and the same time schedule as the previous expedition (47 days) and filmed it. A helicopter was used to film the ascent up and descent off the ice. Snowmobiles were flown in and used outside the marginal zone.

49. 1988; American Will Steger, French Jean-Louis Etienne, Bernard Prud'homme, Englishman Geoff Somers, Soviet Viktor Boyarski, Japanese Keizo Funatzu; east of Narssaarssuaq, Humbolt Gletscher; April 19 to June 16; ski, sled, 30 dogs, air support. First south-north crossing of the Inland Ice.

50. 1988; Spaniards Josu Iztueta Azkue, Nekane Urkia Arana, Dina Bilbao Barruetabena, Angel Ortiz Zabala, Miguel Angel Plaza Tadeo; Angmagssalik, (helicopter to 700 meters above Johan Petersen Fjord), Søndre Strømfjord; April 29 to May 24 (26 days); ski, 5 sleds.

51. 1988; West Germans Michael Krug, Martin Boick, Günther Kerber, Udo Krieger, Frank Wagner; Angmagssalik, (helicopter to Hann Gletscher in Johan Petersen Fjord), Kapisigdlit; April 28 to June 4 (36 days); ski, pulks, parachutes.

52. 1988; Swedes Lars Wallgren, Dag Aronsson, Jan O. Johansson; Angmagssalik, (helicopter to Johan Petersen Fjord), Søndre Strømfjord; June 7 to July 14 (41 days); ski pulks.

53. 1988; Italians Giuseppe Cazzaniga, Gianfranco Fasciolo, Maurizio Della Libera, Anna Bianca, Giulio Beggio, Giovanni Spinelli; Angmagssalik, 10 kms NE of Dannebrog Ø, Austmannadalen, Nuuk; June 27 to July 25 (29 days); ski, 3 sleds, sails. Helicopter from Angmagssalik to 500 meters on the ice. Helicopter from end of the ice to Nuuk.

54. 1988; West Germans Michael Vogeley, Gerhard Miosga, Walter Obster, Werner Schiller; Angmagssalik (helicopter to Umivik), Austmannadalen, Nansens Teltplads, Kapisigdlit; July 21 to August 24 (32 days); ski, 4 sleds, sails.

55. 1988; Norwegians Stein P. Aasheim, Nils U. Hagen, Odd Eliasen, Jo Toftdahl; Angmagssalik, Umivik, Austmannadalen, Nuuk. August 12 to September 9 (27 days); ski, 4 sleds, sails. All equipment was exact copies of that used by Nansen in 1888. Boat from Angmagssalik to Umivik. They departed from Umivik just 100 years after Nansen did on August 15, 1888. The sails were not used.

Coordinates for locations mentioned

Academy Gletscher	81° 40′ N, 34° 00′ W
Angmagssalik	64° 20′ N, 40° 40′ W
Ardencaple Fjord	75° 40′ N, 22° 20′ W
Austmannadalen	64° 10′ N, 50° 10′ W
Bowdoin Fjord	77° 40′ N, 68° 30′ W
Cairn built by Peary	81° 40′ N, 34° 10′ W
Cap Georg Cohn	88° 10′ N, 27° 00′ W
Centrum Sø	79° 40′ N, 25° 30′ W
Christianshåb	68° 50′ N, 51° 10′ W
Cicilia Nunatak	72° 30′ N, 28° 00′ W
Clements Markham Gletscher	77° 55′ N, 72° 00′ W
Dannebrog Ø	65° 20′ N, 39° 40′ W
Daniel Bruun Gletscher	81° 40′ N, 53° 30′ W
Danmark Fjord	81° 00′ N, 27° 00′ W
Danmarks Havn	76° 45′ N, 18° 40′ W
Eismitte	71° 25′ N, 44° 15′ W
Ella Ø	72° 50′ N, 25° 00′ W
Eqip	69° 35′ N, 50° 20′ W
Femstjernen	66° 35′ N, 36° 45′ W
Glacier de France	66° 25′ N, 35° 55′ W
Godthåb	64° 10′ N, 51° 40′ W
Gronau Nunatakker	69° 30′ N, 30° 05′ W
Hann Gletscher	65° 50′ N, 38° 20′ W
Harefjord	70° 55′ N, 28° 20′ W
Hendrik Ø	82° 10′ N, 53° 00′ W
Holsteinsborg	66° 55′ N, 53° 40′ W
Humbolt Gletscher	79° 30′ N, 63° 00′ W
Independence Fjord	79° 10′ N, 66° 00′ W
Isertoq	65° 30′ N, 39° 00′ W
Ivigtut	61° 10′ N, 48° 10′ W
Jakobshavn	69° 15′ N, 51° 05′ W
Johan Petersen Fjord	66° 00′ N, 38° 25′ W
Kapisigdlit	64° 15′ N, 50° 15′ W
Kraulshavn	74° 10′ N, 57° 00′ W
Marmorilik	71° 10′ N, 51° 15′ W
McCormick Fjord	77° 40′ N, 70° 00′ W
Nansens Teltplads	64° 15′ N, 50° 05′ W
Narssarssuaq	61° 10′ N, 45° 25′ W
Navy Cliff	81° 40′ N, 35° 00′ W
Neqe	77° 50′ N, 71° 35′ W

Nordenskjöld Gletscher	68° 30' N, 50° 30' W
Nordfjord	73° 40' N, 24° 30' W
Northice	78° 00' N, 39° 00' W
Nuuk (Godthåb)	64° 10' N, 51° 40' W
Nyboe Land	81° 10' N, 55° 00' W
Peary Land	82° 00' N, 39° 00' W
Prøven	72° 20' N, 55° 35' W
Putlersbak	80° 00' N, 65° 00' W
Qaumarajuk Gletscher	71° 10' N, 51° 10' W
Sangmiliq Gletscher	66° 15' N, 35° 50' W
Sarqaq	70° 00' N, 52° 00' W
Søndre Strømfjord	67° 00' N, 50° 40' W
Shannon Ø	75° 10' N, 18° 00' W
Station Centrale	71° 25' N, 40° 15' W
Storstrømmen	76° 50' N, 22° 30' W
South Greenland	62° 00' N, 44° 00' W
Thule Air Base	76° 30' N, 68° 50' W
Thule/Dundas	76° 30' N, 68° 50' W
Tiniteqilaq	65° 55' N, 37° 45' W
Umanaq	70° 40' N, 52° 10' W
Umivik	64° 20' N, 40° 40' W
Zachenberg	74° 30' N, 20° 30' W

HELLAND'S AND RINK'S 'NUNATAKS' (AUGUST 22) (*By the Author*)

The First Twenty-Seven Years

The Safety Report of the American Alpine Club

Benjamin G. Ferris, Jr., M.D.

$\mathbb{S}$HORTLY AFTER WORLD WAR II, in 1947, a large number, more than 300 climbing fatalities or accidents, were reported in Europe—mainly in Switzerland. Walter Wood, then president of the American Alpine Club, noted this and anticipated a similar situation in the United States. He commented:

> "No mountaineer, looking back on the 1947 climbing season, can fail to be impressed and saddened by the shocking number of fatal or near-fatal accidents that have cast a shadow on the ever-broadening enthusiasm of our sport. Nor can he content himself—if he be a true mountaineer—to sit back and assuage his conscience with the vague hope that something will be done to foster a balanced understanding of mountaineering principles. Yet, with reason, he can ask, 'What can the individual do?'
>
> "To stimulate the thinking of all mountaineers and lovers of mountainous regions, the Safety Committee of the American Alpine Club has prepared a survey of accidents which occurred in the summer of 1947, broadly analyzing the factors which caused or contributed to the tragedy. To this survey the Committee has appended recommendations, implementations of which, it believes, will succeed in fostering national respect for the high places, wider understanding of established techniques, and a saner philosophical approach to the benefits which accrue to those who would know the mountains.
>
> "I commend to you this survey, not as a finished product, but as food for thought; not as a localized effort but as a challenge to national action. Only through the cooperation of all those who love the mountains can ignorance be replaced by experience, sound discretion and mature judgment. Safe climbing means more enjoyment."[1]

These words are as timely now as they were then. *Plus ça change, plus c'est la même chose.*

The first Safety Committee was formed in 1947 by the action of Walter Wood and was chaired by William P. House. The other members were M. Beckett Howorth, Maynard M. Miller and David A. Robertson, Jr. Their report was presented as a separate booklet[2] that was later to be the format followed by similar separate reports.

Miller was the chairman of the second Safety Committee. Also serving were Ome Daiber, Howorth, Richard Leonard and I. The report for 1949, or the second report, was compiled and written by Miller and published in the *American Alpine Journal*.[3] This was the only one so published. All subsequent reports have been separate entities like the first one. Miller also wrote the third report. John Fralick and Dr. Hans Kraus were added to the committee in 1950 and Hassler Whitney took Howorth's place the next year. Fralick wrote the fourth report. He initiated the tabulation of accidents and their statistical information for the previous four years. I did the fifth report in 1952. Standardization of reports followed and it was quickly realized that critical demographic data and other specifics were not recorded. This was accomplished by a simple question-naire, completed by those individuals in the accident or rescue operations. Some accidents were reported by others from newspaper reports or personal knowl-edge of the incident. I expanded the statistical categorization of accidents. Since Miller's geological and glaciological responsibilities were making demands on his time, he resigned and I became the Chairman of the Safety Committee in 1952.

The accident report form was made more detailed and informative by Dr. Thomas O. Nevison as a part of his work as a student at the Harvard School of Public Health in 1958-59 when he was a candidate for a Master's degree in the Aerospace Program directed by Dr. Ross McFarland.

From the material collected through the reports and standardized question-naires, we were able to develop risk estimates based on estimated man-mountain days in 1954 through 1956. These man-mountain days were developed from data provided by the larger mountaineering clubs over a two-year period. We obtained estimates of man-mountain days from the National Parks, against which we could compare the accident rates and separate data for rock climbing (Yosemite) and snow climbing (McKinley) from additional information from the parks. These were rough comparisons, but they were the best we could do. We always worry about the adequacy of our information. In general our data are under-reported due either to not enough information or to persons not reporting the event. We encouraged many reports even if they resulted in duplications. We have had rare instances in which the individual(s) involved refused to report their accidents. Sometimes we have obtained the information and included the data in the statistical tables and not reported the information in the written text.

Comparisons were made with data from other sports. The mountaineering accident rates were comparable to those in other sports when "standardized" for periods of risk or exposure, but the mortalities were higher. In 1959, more detailed analyses were possible and the results were presented in graphic form. The data collected were used as a basis for two articles in the *New England*

Journal of Medicine.[4,5] in 1963. Further discussions of various aspects of mountaineering safety were presented in the *Encyclopedia of Sport Sciences and Medicine*[6] in 1971.

The Safety Report went through a series of changes in its title. The first report in 1948 was called *Mountaineering Safety: Report of the Safety Committee.* The second report in 1949 was entitled *Safety in the Mountains;* in 1950, *Safety and the Climber;* in 1951, *Alpine Accidents;* and in 1952, *Accidents in American Mountaineering,* which was used thereafter until 1962 (14th report) when it was called *Accidents in North American Mountaineering.* The last title resulted because the Alpine Club of Canada joined in collecting data for the report in 1960 and has continued to do so. Also, initially some accidents from South and Central America had been included. These were soon dropped because there were no persons available to monitor the situations and submit reports. Thus, the eventual title *Accidents in North American Mountaineering* seemed to be a more accurate description of the geographic area which was being reported on.

The accident report stimulated the development of the Mountain Rescue Association. This group was particularly active in the Western states. The following is a brief account of the Mountain Rescue Association prepared with the help of George Sainsbury.

The Mountain Rescue Association (MRA) was formed in 1959 following a decade of inter-unit summer training conferences and two years of organizational meetings. Peter K. Schoening, Western Vice-President of the American Alpine Club and a past president of the Mountain Rescue Council, was keenly aware of this development, and in anticipation of it Schoening and Sainsbury explained a proposed project to coordinate mountain-safety education and rescue at the 1958 Annual Meeting of the American Alpine Club in Philadelphia. The most visible outcome of this was the inclusion of a listing of the existing mountain rescue groups in the 1959 *Safety Report*, a practice that continues to this day.

The proposed safety-education program was presented to the MRA board by the AAC Safety Committee member John Humphreys and MRA Vice-President Darrell Looff in October, 1960 in Yakama, Washington. Samples of proposed flyers were distributed. Nine of these were eventually developed by the MRA and published by the AAC to provide basic information to climbers throughout North America interested in organizing mountain-rescue teams.

George Sainsbury was asked to direct this program at the February MRA Board Meeting in l961. Later in the year he reported on the program to the AAC Board of Councilors and the first article, "National Search and Rescue Plan," was nationally distributed with the *AAC News.* The 1961 *Safety Report* included an article about the MRA and a general endorsement of the new association by the Board of Councilors of the AAC.

A joint AAC-MRA committee composed of Sainsbury, Ezra A. Campbell and Richard Pooley was formed to develop a supplemental report on rescues and the first of these reports appeared in the 1963 *Safety Report*. At this time a rescue report form was added to the accident-report form. Results from these question-naires were used to determine how rescue operations could be improved. Three rather extensive annual rescue reports were prepared together with statistical tables, but the later reports were more sporadic. Eventually, this material was absorbed directly into the accident reports, if included at all.

Our format for the annual report was copied by some of the European climbing clubs and our questionnaire, properly modified, was used by spelunk-ers or cavers for their accident reports. I believe that our reports have been effective in educating persons to the hazards of mountain climbing and how to climb safely. Data to support this is almost impossible to come by. The best I can say is that the reports have been used repeatedly by various climbing organiza-tions in their training programs.

Our philosophy from the start of the Safety Committee was to be as objective as possible and not to point a finger directly at any person or persons. Usually the reports themselves did an adequate job of describing the problems or errors. If analyses were presented, especially by the person(s) involved, they were pub-lished. The fundamental effort was to try to let the material speak for itself and to make it useful as teaching material in learning how to enjoy mountaineering safely, which is really what Walter Wood stated in his introduction to the first report in 1947.

Very rarely has a report produced any negative reaction. Responses gener-ally have been positive. I do recall one case in which there was a question of equipment failure or misplacement by the victim. In this instance a series of letters back and forth resulted without any real animosity. In another instance, I published two accounts, one by the victim and one by the reporters or rescuers. I was concerned that neither was entirely objective and so I left it up to the reader to decide what the facts were.

I was fortunate in not becoming involved in litigations, which now seem to be increasing. I hope this unfortunate development does not get out of hand. At the start of the reports, in the late 1940s to the early 1950s, no litigation had occurred. Later, primarily as a result of an accident on Mount Temple near Lake Louise, more concern arose. I personally was not involved in that incident.

I did most of the collating, tabulating and preparation of the reports and other material that the committee members supplied from 1952 to 1973 because it seemed more efficient. The committee members and others are to be com-mended for their cooperation and the effort they contributed. They are the unsung heroes of our safety effort.

I continued as Chairman until 1974. Jed Williamson took over in 1975 and has done an excellent job since then. I have been a member of the Safety Committee from 1948 until the present.

Bibliography

[1] House, W., *Mountaineering Safety, Report of the Safety Committee of the American Alpine Club*, 1948, American Alpine Club, New York, p. 1.

[2] House, W., *Ibid*, pp. 2-24.

[3] Miller, M.M., Daiber, O., Ferris, B.G. Jr., Howorth, M.B.,and Leonard, R.M., "Safety in the Mountains, Report of the Safety Committee of the American Alpine Club," *American Alpine Journal*, September, 1949, pp. 285-304.

[4] Ferris, B.G. Jr., "Mountain Climbing Accidents in the United States," *New England Journal of Medicine, 1963, 268*: pp. 430-431.

[5] Ferris, B.G. Jr., "Mountain Climbing Safety," Ibid, pp. 662-664.

[6] Ferris, B.G. Jr., "Applied Physiology: Mountaineering," pp. 374-376; "Clinical Examination: Mountaineering," p. 462; "Acute and Subacute Injury: Mountaineering," pp. 554-556; "Chronic Injury: Mountaineering," pp. 623-624, *Encyclopedia of Sport Sciences and Medicine*, L.P. Larsons, Editor, The Macmillan Co. New York, 1971.

Sir George Everest's 200th Birthday

AUDREY SALKELD, *The Alpine Club*

$\mathcal{S}$IR GEORGE EVEREST was born two hundred years ago. It is well known that in 1849 reports reached Everest's successor as Superintendent of the Great Trigonometrical Survey of India, Andrew Waugh, of a peak in the Himalaya that appeared to be the highest in the world. Waugh suggested that the mountain should be named for his predecessor as an acknowledgement of his tremendous achievements in the survey. Although the Nepalese now call the peak Sagarmatha and the Chinese Qomolangma, much of the world recognizes primarily the name of Mount Everest.

Born in London on July 4, 1790, one of five sons of a solicitor, George Everest entered the Royal Military Academy at Woolwich at the age of 14. In 1806, he went to Java and was commissioned a lieutenant in the Bengal Artillery, an East India Company regiment. He was active in reconnaissance there, working on military surveys. In 1817, he came to India. The following year, he became an assistant to Colonel Henry Lambton, the third Surveyor General of India, who in 1800 had started a network of triangulation that was to cover the whole subcontinent, starting with Cape Comorin, the southernmost tip. Lambton lived and died by the code that the Map must go forward—no matter what—and it was a principle that Everest adopted quite naturally. In 1823, 70-year-old Lambton died in the field, and Everest succeeded him as Superintendent of the Great Trigonometrical Survey. His first act was to demand more funds and men for the work.

By 1825, Everest had extended the great arc to Kalianpur in central India, but not without its taking a great toll on his health. He returned to Britain on extended sick leave, where he remained for five years. However, he was not idle back home. He used the time thoroughly to review the latest European surveys aimed at calculating the figure of the earth and the most modern equipment. He also supervised the construction of two 36-inch theodolites, the most accurate ever made. Each weighed more than 1100 pounds and needed twelve men to carry it, three at either end of two poles. Massive stone towers were built from which observations were made; a number of these still exist. He also perfected an ingenious series of dials and differential wheels called a "perambulator." This was basically a revolution counter mounted on a wheel which could give a quick

measurement of distance if the diameter of the wheel was known. Previous ones had measured in yards and rods, necessitating complicated conversions to tenths of a mile. Everest remarked, "Since a mile is 5280 feet, I propose that the long hand shall revolve once when the wheel has been trundled over 528 feet of ground." He personally badgered his directors in London for the funds and equipment he needed until they gave in. On the strength of his persistence and personality, he was appointed by them Surveyor General of India on his return, as well as Superintendent of the Great Trigonometrical Survey.

During Everest's term of office, Lambton's network of triangulations was abandoned in favour of running a series of triangles along the meridians of longitude, connected by cross links along parallels of latitude, the "gridiron system." It remains in use today, and it afforded Everest the chance of pushing forward with the measurement of the Great Arc of the Meridian. He extended his work northward to the foot of the Himalaya at Dehra Dun, where he measured a baseline 7.5 miles long in 1834-5. Another baseline was measured at Kalianpur, near Sironj, south of Agra.

Upon retirement from the Survey in 1843, his health broken, he returned to England and married. He was knighted in 1861 and died in Paddington in 1866.

Throughout his career, Everest was a stickler for accuracy. He would not suffer fools gladly and had a fiery temper. He was as blisteringly forthright to his superiors in London as to those who worked under him in India. He never spared himself, and when his legs became paralyzed as a result of his illnesses, he would still be lifted onto a stool to perform his observations personally. He was always ready to fight for better conditions for his staff.

PLATES 19 AND 20

Photos by David Breashears

On the left is Everest's 36-inch Theodolite made by Troughton and Sims. On the right is the 24-inch Theodolite with which the height of Mount Everest was determined.

Henry S. Hall, Jr. Memorial Everest Relief Model

BRADFORD WASHBURN

IN MEMORY OF HENRY S. HALL, Jr., a new and unique exhibit is being made at the studio of Vigo Rauda in Seattle. It will be completed in mid summer of 1990 and will be first shown to the public in a place of honor at London's Royal Geographical Society during the celebration of the birth of Sir George Everest, who was born on July 4, 1790.

Henry S. Hall, Jr. served as a director or officer of the American Alpine Club from 1923 until his death in 1987. He was president from 1950 to 1952 and Honorary President from 1974 until his death. He was a trustee of the Museum of Science for many years. He left a bequest to the Museum, a tenth of which is devoted to the preparation of the large-scale map and the relief model.

This model is based on a new ultra-large-scale map of Mount Everest being made for Boston's Museum of Science under my direction by Swissair Photo+Surveys Ltd. of Zürich, Switzerland. The new Everest map is a sort of first cousin of the Everest map published by the National Geographic Society at a scale of 1:50,000 in November 1988. It covers only Everest itself, not its approaches. There are twelve sheets on a scale of 1:2500 (approximately 2 feet to the mile) with five-meter contours.

The model will measure 11 by 15 feet. It is being made of an extremely hard plastic material known as polyurethane foam. The photographs of a portion reproduced here show parts of the snowy eastern or Kangshung Face so that the pure white model, with only 2mm steps for each contour, looks very much like the real thing.

Climbing Ethics

*This was written by the American Alpine Club and Mountain Tools, Inc.
under the leadership of Sam Davidson. Many climbers contributed to its
production.*

CLIMBING IN THE UNITED STATES
is now a popular recreational activity. There are perhaps 250,000 climbers
nationwide, with visits from foreign climbers increasing. Until recently, no one
looked closely at the impact of climbing on the natural environment. Now, we
see that our increasing numbers may have an adverse impact on the lands we use,
on other users and ultimately on climbers if we fail to be responsible in our
behavior.

While many climbers are committed to "minimum impact," our growing
numbers, combined with the evolving styles and objectives of modern climbing,
are having a noticeable effect on some areas. Soil erosion, trail degradation,
defoliation of trees and bushes, litter, human waste and conflicts with other
users—all are increasing matters for concern and can be attributed directly to
increased climber use.

We have traditionally enjoyed freedom of access to climbing areas and
become accustomed to a lack of restrictions on our activities. To preserve these
freedoms, it is imperative that, as climbers, we dedicate ourselves to a code of
behavior based on self-restraint, activity demonstrating care for the environment
and concern for other visitors to mountain areas.

The following *Ten Commandments of Sustainable Climbing* are intended to
assist all climbers, both American and foreign guests, to act conscientiously
toward the environment and to promote good relations with other users, land
owners and land-management officials.

Ten Commandments of Sustainable Climbing

1. Never disturb historically, archeologically or environmentally sensitive
   areas.
2. Don't scar, chisel, glue holds onto, or otherwise deface the rock.
3. Don't place bolts near cracks or other natural protection.
4. Avoid using colored bolt hangers that contrast brightly with the rock.
5. Don't add fixed protection on established routes except to beef up questionable belay or rappel anchors.

6. Don't establish routes in heavy traffic areas such as campgrounds or directly above public trails or roads.
7. If you must leave slings at rappel stations or "back off" gear, use colors which blend in with the surrounding rock.
8. Don't throw anything—rotten slings, trash or even human waste—off climbs; it's simple: everything you start up with comes off the climb with you, not before.
9. Accept responsibility even for the impact of other climbers on the mountain environment by removing rotten slings and garbage from climbs, bivouac areas and descent routes.
10. Know and follow local regulations on climbing and restrictions on bolting, motorized bolting and chalk. Then work to change unfair restrictions through the American Alpine Club Access Committee or local climber organizations.

Dispose of human waste legally and cleanly. Human-waste disposal is a real and growing problem which no one should ignore. Follow these guidelines for disposal of human waste:

When toilets are available, use them.

Do not dispose of human waste within 50 yards of any water source or at the base of a cliff. Bury your feces at least 6 inches below the soil's surface and pack out toilet paper.

When on a route where human waste cannot be buried, dispose of it and your toilet paper in sturdy plastic bags (zip-lock or freezer bags). Seal them after use and stow them in a non-breakable, non-leak container to be carried out in your pack or haul bag. Do not leave these bags on the climb or throw them away. It is illegal to throw anything off rock walls in National Parks and a hazard in most climbing areas. When off the climb, dispose of bags in appropriate waste facilities.

Renew your commitment to "leaving no trace" of your passage during the approach, climb and descent. Clean up after yourself and others. Take along a plastic bag or hard plastic container for packing out trash. It takes little effort to stuff rotten slings, cigarette butts, food wrappers, etc. into these bags or even your pockets. If you accidentally drop gear or trash on a climb, return to the base of the route and recover it, plus any other garbage you may find in the area. Politely remind other climbers of the need for this commitment.

Always use existing means of access. Walk on trails whenever possible and avoid creating new descent routes or approaches if such routes already exist. Never make shortcuts across switchbacks.

Assume complete responsibility for yourself and your party's actions while climbing. Be sure someone (friend or family) has detailed knowledge of your plans and timetable. Do not rely on a rescue team to come to your aid. If you get into a problem, get yourself out of it. Know and practice what to do in various types of emergencies, including injury to a party member, darkness or a rapid change in the weather.

Maintain a low profile. Other users of the land have the same right to undisturbed enjoyment of the area as you do. Remember that climbers often have a highly visible and audible "presence." Whether on the cliff or in the parking lot, try to minimize this "presence." Respect hikers, bird-watchers and other visitors.

Do not break the law or trespass in order to climb. In most places, climbing is a legal and legitimate activity. Should you encounter restrictions, call the American Alpine Club Access Committee to seek an effective and permanent response.

Respect other climbers in the area. Remember safety and courtesy while climbing. Falling rock or gear is a serious hazard, so be careful when climbing above another party. Do not create a dangerous situation by passing another party on a route without their consent. If you can't pass safely and easily, don't do it.

Support projects that make us all more aware of, and responsive to, climber-impact issues. Climbers depend on natural areas for climbing. If we care for the environment and back the agencies that manage it, we help preserve the right to and enjoyment of climbing. Get involved in or start clean-up projects, organizations that protect access and the mountains and back with whatever money you can afford the acquisition and protection of climbing areas.

Spread the word! Climbers should be leaders in attention to environmental concerns and responsible behavior for other land users to follow.

Glaciers of Alaska and Adjacent Yukon Territory and British Columbia

WILLIAM OSGOOD FIELD

T HE LARGEST GLACIERS outside the Polar Regions are found in the mountain ranges which extend in a great arc north of the Gulf of Alaska from Skeena River in western British Columbia to Cook Inlet. All the highest mountains in Canada and the United States are in this area, which measures some 2200 km long and 150 to 300 km in width. These ranges culminate in Mount McKinley (Denali) (6195 m) in Alaska, and Mount Logan (5951 m) in Yukon Territory, the two highest elevations on the North American Continent, followed by Orizaba (5699 m) in Mexico, and Mount St. Elias (5490 m) on the boundary between Alaska and the Yukon.*

The glaciers of Alaska were seen but not studied by the early British, French, Russian, and Spanish navigators along the shores of North America in the 18th century. According to Davidson (1904), only the Frenchman, LaPérouse, used the word *glacier* in his account and, in his chart of Lituya Bay in 1786, may have been the first to show the positions of glacier fronts, and to have also comprehended their nature. His expedition included scientists who were probably familiar with the glaciers in the Alps. The other navigators reported in such terms as "great level tracts of snow which come to the water's edge," "solid body of ice or frozen snow," "one compact sheet of ice as far as the eye could distinguish"; and at the entrance of the present Glacier Bay, Whidby described: "two large open bays, which were terminated by compact solid mountains of ice, rising perpendicularly from the water's edge" (Davidson, 1904). The calving of

---

* At the outset we must settle on how to state distances and altitudes; whether to use metric, feet and miles, or a combination of both. Existing maps of both the U.S. and Canada use both for distance scales. However, the problem gets more complicated in dealing with heights and contour intervals. U.S. maps show altitudes in feet as is also the case in older Canadian maps, but the metric system is used exclusively in the newer Canadian maps. Rather than attempt to blend both systems, it would seem preferable in this article to favor the metric system, which although not widely used in the U.S. is becoming accepted in Canada and is the standard in most parts of the world. Accordingly, we shall favor the metric for distances and in some cases use both for altitudes, depending on the original sources. For those unfamiliar with either of these systems, it is relatively easy to convert to the metric system by using 3.28 ft. per meter, 1 mile as the equivalent of 1.61 km, or conversely, 1 foot equals 0.305 meters and 1 kilometer equals 0.62 miles.

tidal glaciers was described in such vague terms as to give the impression that most of these seafaring people did not really comprehend what they were seeing.

During the first three-quarters of the 19th century, the locations of some of the glaciers along the coast began to be shown on maps. However, detailed observations were lacking. William H. Dall's book, *Alaska and Its Resources*, (1870), had little to say about glaciers and only mentioned a few of the more prominent ones along the coast that had been seen from passing vessels. It was not until the last two decades of the century that maps and charts began to show them in detail as a result of (1) special efforts to study certain particular glaciers, (2) charts prepared by the Coast and Geodetic Survey for navigation purposes, and (3) the preliminary surveys to delineate the International Boundary between Alaska and northwestern Canada.

In the last quarter of the 19th century, more information was becoming available about the glaciers in the interior from the reports of U.S. Army and Geological Survey parties which had begun a series of reconnaissance surveys in the 1880s. Alfred H. Brook's reports of 1906 and 1911 summarized what was known of the geology and geography of Alaska and the results of his 1902 expedition from Cook Inlet to the northern side of the Alaska Range and the Mount McKinley area (Brooks, 1906 and 1911). In them he outlined and indicated on his maps what was known at the time of the glaciers in the interior.

It appears that the first effort to study the physical characteristics of glaciers in this region was made in 1863 by a party under the leadership of William P. Blake of New Haven who visited what is now Great Glacier in the Lower Stikine River Valley, British Columbia, as a guest on a Russian Naval Squadron (Blake, 1867). There followed more efforts by U.S. observers after the purchase of Alaska in 1867. In the next decade John Muir began his visits in 1879 and 1880, which led to the first observations of the glaciers in the inlets in the Coast Mountains of southeastern Alaska and in the Glacier Bay area in the southern part of the St. Elias Mountains. The reports of his work first appeared in San Francisco newspapers and later as articles in magazines and in book form. These accounts opened the way for a series of scientific studies beginning with those of George F. Wright at Muir Glacier in 1886, Harry F. Reid in Glacier Bay in 1890 and 1892, I.C. Russell in the Yakutat Bay area in 1890 and 1891, and the Harriman Alaska Expedition of 1899, which visited the glaciers along the coast, including those of Glacier Bay and Yakutat Bay and was the first scientific party to report on the glaciers of Prince William Sound. (Harriman Alaska Expedition, vols. 1 and 2 by various authors, 1901; and on Glaciology by Gilbert, vol. 3, 1903). Thus by 1900 all the principal glaciers along the southern coast had been located, their lower ends were marked on existing topographic maps and navigational charts, and many were already named.

As far as we know the first effort to attempt a treatise on the glaciers in the northwestern part of this continent was by Israel C. Russell, Professor of Geology at the University of Michigan, in his book *Glaciers of North America*, published in 1897. By then the glaciers of the Rockies and Sierra Nevada were pretty well known and some of the glaciers in the coastal mountain ranges up to

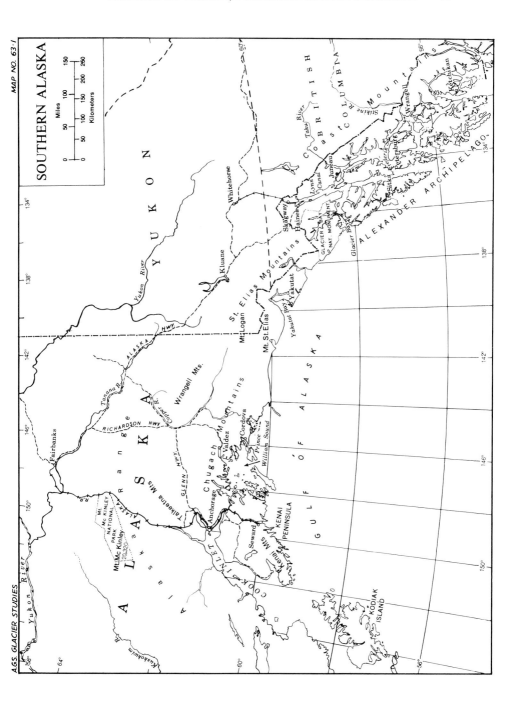

Malaspina Glacier had been visited. Russell, himself, had made two trips to Yakutat Bay in 1890 and 1891, during attempts to climb Mount St. Elias and had crossed the Malaspina and Seward glaciers on expeditions sponsored by the National Geographic Society. However, he appears to have known little of the early reports of high-mountain ranges to the north and west of Mount St. Elias, such as Vancouver's mention of "stupendous high mountains" which he had seen from Cook Inlet in 1794. As an example of how little information was then available, Russell wrote: "In the interior of Alaska and of the adjacent portion of Canada, there are many mountains that reach elevations of at least four or five thousand feet above the sea, but are bare of snow during the summer, and no glaciers are known to exist upon them." (p.197) However, uninformed as he was of the mountains of interior Alaska, he did appreciate the glacial scenery. In opening remarks, he wrote: "Until within the past few years, nearly all current knowledge of glaciers was based on the study of those in the Alps. . . . As geological and geographical explorations have been extended, it has been found that North America is not only a favorable field for the growth of these twin sciences, but in many ways furnishes the best example of continental development that has as yet been studied." He continued: "The magnificence of the field for glacial study in North America has only been appreciated within recent years, and is still unrecognized outside of a limited circle of special students." (pp.III and IV) . . . "In purchasing Alaska, the United States not only acquired a vast territory rich in natural resources, but added new wonders to her already varied scenery. . . . When we include Alaska and the adjacent portion of Canada, the field for glacial study becomes almost unlimited." (p.74).

Meanwhile, great impetus in learning the physical geography, topographic details, and the mountains and glaciers of large areas was provided by the preliminary surveys to establish the International Boundary between Alaska and British Columbia and Yukon Territory. These were carried out from 1893 to 1896 by the Canadian Boundary Survey, using photo-topographical techniques, which were relatively new at the time. These exploring and mountaineering parties delineated in considerable detail the topography of the Coast Mountains as a basis for the final determination of the boundary between southeastern Alaska and British Columbia and Yukon Territory from Portland Canal to Mount St. Elias. This series of maps marked a great advance over previous efforts.

This earliest mapping for the International Boundary was the basis for its final delineation in 1903, after which much of the area was resurveyed by both Canadian and United States parties from 1904 to 1913 and the resulting maps were published in the 1920s. These maps were superb representations for their day. They were issued over the next two decades on a scale of 1:250,000 with contour intervals on land and ice of 250 ft. These maps showed the glaciers in some detail in the areas covered, which, however, were limited to the general vicinity of the International Boundary from Portland Canal in the south, north-westward along the coastal ranges to the 141st meridian, and then northward to the northern limits of the St. Elias Mountains.

This series of maps showed many of the glaciers in considerable detail. Other areas not situated along the International Boundary were subsequently mapped in topographical surveys by the U.S. Geological Survey in Alaska and the corresponding agencies in Canada. These showed the lower ends of many glaciers in a general way and in the case of long glaciers, where their upper parts could not be easily seen, source areas were shown very sketchily or left as blank.

The accuracy of topographic mapping, especially in the rugged mountain regions changed abruptly with the advent of aerial surveys. Until then, glaciologists and others could only conjecture what were the conditions at the heads of the longer glaciers which had not yet been visited by mountaineering parties. This new mapping was carried out with both vertical and oblique aerial photography, beginning in a few localities in southeastern Alaska in 1929 by the U.S. Navy, and then extended over wide areas for aerial navigation purposes by the U.S. Army Air Corps in the series of flights for Trimetrogon photography in 1941-42. These were followed by further mapping by U.S. and Canadian Air Forces from 1948 to the 1950s, and the U.S. Coast and Geodetic Survey in other areas near the coast. These became invaluable tools for the topographer, geologist, geographer, and glaciologist, as well as for other civilian and commercial purposes. These were the basis for most of the current topographic maps of the whole area on a scale of 1:250,000 with contour intervals of 200 ft (61 m) and the larger scale series with contour intervals of 100 ft (30.5 m) in Alaska and 1:50,000 with 40 m (131 ft) contours in British Columbia and the Yukon.

The problem now is that many of the maps show the glaciers as they were twenty to forty years ago. While some sheets have been revised to show later changes in the lower end of the glaciers, in many cases where they have advanced or receded dramatically, these changes have not been recorded on more recent editions.

With this use of surveying which was developed by government and military agencies came the increasing adaptation of aerial observations and photography by scientists concerned with glaciological matters. H.F. Reid and C.W. Wright, who had done pioneering work in the 1890s and the first decade of this century, were among the first to take to the air over Glacier Bay and parts of the Coast Mountains in 1931, as part of their field work supported by The Geological Survey. However, the first serious efforts at aerial photography for glaciological purposes was probably Bradford Washburn, who, with the support of the Harvard University Institute of Geographical Exploration and the National Geographic Society, began his long series of high quality aerial photography of the glaciers in 1933 and 1934.

The use of aircraft not only for observation purposes, but also increasingly as integral parts of glaciological projects, were begun in the 1930s and came into general use in the late 1940s (Wood, 1936). Aircraft equipped with ski-wheel landing gear became used increasingly for the transport of supplies and equipment to the high-level névés. This made possible the more extensive use of heavy equipment which is now part of the required instrumentation for geophysical and glaciological investigations. As time went on, helicopters were also introduced and in recent decades have been used increasingly for glaciological research.

The systematic aerial photography of glaciers has been continued in recent decades. Austin Post of the Geological Survey began his long and distinguished efforts in the late 1950s and has continued to this day, and others in the Survey have joined in this effort in recent years, notably Larry Mayo in 1971 and more recently Bob Krimmel. While such aerial work does not take the place of detailed ground studies, it can cover more glaciers in a short period, especially those in remote areas, and provide evidence of major changes and an indication of regional trends.

In the meantime, to step ahead to the last two decades, a new technique has been developed, making use of satellite imagery, which can now record changes in the position of the termini, the surface elevations of the glaciers, and such features as the annual lower limit of the snowline on the glaciers, which is a good indicator of the state of health of a glacier.

Area of Glaciers

Gilbert (1903, p.9) estimated that glaciers in Alaska covered between 14,000 and 20,000 miles^2, which would be around 36,000 to 52,000 km^2. More recent studies based primarily on the aerial surveys of the 1940s and 1950s provide a more accurate assessment. In a report of Austin Post and Larry Mayo of the USGS, 1971, the total area of glaciers in Alaska was given as 73,000 km^2 (28,100 miles^2) which is about 5% of the area of Alaska. Subsequently, Post refined this figure to 73,360 km^2 (28,320 miles^2) and further estimated the figure for the adjacent parts of British Columbia and Yukon Territory as 28,980 km^2 (11,180 miles^2) (personal communication). This brings the estimated total of the extent of glacier ice in the Pacific Mountain system, north of the southern boundary between Alaska and British Columbia to around 102,340 km^2 (39,500 miles^2). This represents around 18% of the presently glacierized area outside the Arctic in the Northern Hemisphere.

Because of the vast amount of information now available, it becomes a formidable task to even attempt to describe the glaciers of Alaska, and the adjacent parts of British Columbia and the Yukon. Compared to even half a century ago an enormous amount has been accomplished in mapping and recording their physical aspects. The last hundred years have seen many efforts devoted to these intriguing ice masses which represent all known types of glaciers except for ice sheets which in the present world are now confined to Greenland and Antarctica. One could spend many pages in just discussing the scientific studies that have been made in the physics of ice or the observations of glacier fluctuations by terrestrial and aerial means and in recent years by satellite imagery, but this cannot be our primary purpose in this article.

In the last few years, for instance, tens of thousands of passengers on commercial and chartered aircraft, large and small ships, and busses and cars on

PLATE 22

Top photo, taken by Austin Post on August 29, 1967, shows Taku Glacier advancing toward Taku Point. In bottom left, Taku Glacier invades forest. Photo by W.O. Field, September 7, 1950. South Crillon Glacier front seen in bottom right, July 1934. Photo by Bradford Washburn.

highways have viewed many of the well-known as well as remote glaciers throughout the region. In a comparatively short article it becomes almost impossible to attempt anything but a very generalized discussion, mentioning only the highlights which have come to the attention of the writer. There are a number of points of view from which to consider such a diversity of glacial features, among which are, (1) their dimensions, distribution, and general characteristics, (2) their fluctuations and observed changes in their regimes, (3) their hydrological aspects, (4) their complicated interrelationships with climate, (5) their effects on the local and regional economy, (6) their role in the ecological studies of the succession of plant and animal life in the areas left bare by the retreating ice cover, and (7) other specific scientific studies and measurements that have been carried out on the physics and flow characteristics of glaciers widely scattered throughout the area under discussion.

It is inevitable that some most interesting observations and studies will be left out of this account. The available reports and articles are legion. We must also approach our subject without direct access to many highly significant sources of information which have appeared in recent years. Those omitted, alas, may be quite as significant and interesting as those which are mentioned.

To those of us who have spent most of a lifetime looking at glaciers, we tend to see something of special interest peculiar to each glacier. Over a period of time and a number of visits, we begin to view each of them as personalities, each with its special characteristics, behavior patterns, and features which command our attention and interest. We tend to have favorites and to dwell on them unduly. However, in the long run, it is one of our primary tasks to try to find the answers as to their state of health and the reasons why most of them, at the present time, are shrinking, while a few are advancing, to determine the general trends under way which could affect those environments in the future, and to determine the combination of climatic factors which are at work to cause these changes. Unlike the situation in many parts of the world we are privileged to see glaciers advancing over terrain not covered by ice in a century or more, as shown by trees of ancient vintage being destroyed by the ice, much as our forefathers witnessed in the Alps and elsewhere during the Little Ice Age of the 18th and 19th centuries.

Why do we find such satisfaction in studying everything we can about glaciers in general and those of Alaska and adjacent parts of Canada in particular? All of us, I think, can agree that they are beautiful and inspiring aspects of a mountain landscape, vibrant in themselves, and important in the geological processes. One obvious reason to study them is, as George Mallory commented, "because they are there." More specifically however, it is obvious that glaciers are products of a certain combination of climatic factors which indicate enough snow accumulation to more than offset the average annual rate of loss by melting. As glaciers advance or retreat they tell us that the balance between accumulation and ablation is changing or had changed during a recent period in the glacier's history. We must also take into account how such changes in their regimes can be affected by other than climatic factors, as, for instance, (1) landslides which may cover parts of a glacier in sufficient thickness to reduce surface ablation and conserve that ice for years or decades, which otherwise would normally have melted; or (2) changes in the rate of calving at tidal termini caused by changes in the depth of water.

Although most people tend to pay special attention to the large glaciers, which are more spectacular and dominate the mountain scenery, the small glaciers are also of great interest, particularly where they are found in remote mountain groups, which may mark the fringes of the glacial environment and the current glaciation level (Ostrem et al 1981). Therefore, from a glaciological point of view, because of their shorter response time than the large glaciers, the small glaciers are the more useful as recorders of climatic change for a determination of both short and long term trends in the local climate.

Where there are inhabitants living in the valleys close to glaciers, as in the Alps, the economics of the region are greatly influenced by their advance or recession. The melt from the glaciers has often been a valuable source of water, or has also caused disastrous floods through the sudden breakout of ice-dammed lakes. Advancing glaciers have destroyed farm lands, and even villages and routes of travel. Because of this, the history of these changes has been recorded in village and church records since the Middle Ages in the many Alpine valleys where glaciers are vital sources of water, for domestic and commercial use, power, and irrigation. Changes in the size of such glaciers are as important as changes in the levels of our lakes and reservoirs. Tourism, a source of important economic significance in many mountain areas, has been affected as glaciers have receded or advanced, disrupted lines of communication, or otherwise interfered with normal activities.

The situation in Alaska, British Columbia and the Yukon is somewhat less intimately related to the lives of the local people than in the Alps, yet there are many instances of the close relationship with the economy. In many places, glaciers are important sources of water. Such cities as Anchorage, with a population of over 200,000, and Juneau, the capital of the state, depend on reservoirs which are largely derived from glacial sources. Routes of travel have also been threatened by floods caused by the outbreak of ice-dammed lakes and other changes in the drainage. Tourism has also been affected by the advance or recession of glaciers.

Distribution and Size of Glaciers

Glaciers of various sizes are distributed over a large part of Alaska and the adjacent parts of British Columbia and the Yukon. Although those which terminate in tidewater are the most spectacular and tend to get the most publicity, they represent only a small percentage of the glaciers even along the southern coast of Alaska. There they tend to be concentrated in groups where the coastal mountain ranges are sufficiently lofty to attract heavy annual snow accumulation and at the same time rise so precipitously from the sea that the glaciers can easily reach tidewater and discharge icebergs. In the 1980s, there have been about 42 glaciers reaching tidewater in Alaska, of which about half actively discharge icebergs. Another seven or so terminate near tide level or vary from decade to decade between being tidal or non-tidal. All these occur in the Coast, St. Elias, Chugach, and Kenai Mountains.

Many other glaciers, whether they reach tidewater or not, also attract attention because of the scenery or special conditions at their termini. These are mostly in southern and central Alaska.

The Longest Glaciers

The longest glaciers, which are 20 km (12.5 miles) or more in length, are distributed over six of the principal mountain ranges. Table I shows the breakdown according to length based on the presently existing maps of Alaska, British Columbia, and Yukon Territory. While most of the data reflect the aerial surveys of the late 1940s to the 1960s, the figures have been changed in a few instances, where glaciers are known to have recently advanced or receded by a kilometer or more. Since there are comparatively few fluctuations greater than this, these figures, although compiled around 1970 (*Mountain Glaciers of the Northern Hemisphere*, 1975), are considered to be reasonably close to reflecting conditions in the 1980s.

The length of some of the glaciers can be given only approximately because on available maps the topography indicated by the contours on the upper névés are not sufficiently detailed to be able to determine the exact limits of the glacier basins and the divides between them. The lengths given of such glaciers can therefore be considered only as reasonable estimates, but, we believe, of the right order of magnitude.

Table 1

Mountain Ranges	20-29 km	30-39 km	40-49 km	50-59 km	60-79 km	80-89 km	Over 90 km	Totals
Coast	19	7	3	1	0	0	0	30
St. Elias	21	13	5	3	4	2	2	50
Chugach	15	10	5	1	3	0	1	35
Kenai	5	2	0	0	0	0	0	7
Wrangell	8	2	1	1	0	1	0	13
Alaska	19	7	8	1	3	0	0	38
Total	87	41	22	7	10	3	3	173

Of the thirty glaciers listed above in the Coast Mountains, twelve are entirely in British Columbia, four entirely in Alaska, and the remaining fourteen are partly in both. In the St. Elias Mountains, 27 of the 50 glaciers are in Alaska, 9 in the Yukon, and 5 are partly in Alaska and in British Columbia, 5 in Alaska and

PLATE 23

Top photo, taken on Mount Wright by H. J. Brabazon of Canadian Boundary Survey, shows Muir Glacier in 1894. Bottom photo, taken by Austin Post of U.S. Geological Survey on August 29, 1984, depicts the 40-kilometer recession.

the Yukon, 3 partly in the Yukon and British Columbia, and 1 entirely in British Columbia. In the Chugach Mountains, only one glacier flows across the International Boundary from the Yukon into Alaska. All the rest of the glaciers in the Chugach and Wrangell Mountains and in the Alaska Range are entirely in Alaska.

The other mountain groups in Alaska that do not have any glaciers longer than 20 km are on the islands of the Alexander Archipelago in southeastern Alaska; the islands of Prince William Sound and the Talkeetna Mountains in south central Alaska; the Aleutian Range on the Alaska Peninsula and its extension along the Aleutian Islands; the Brooks Range of northern or Arctic Alaska; and two small mountain groups in western Alaska north of Bristol Bay and on Seward Peninsula. In British Columbia, there are also some isolated glaciers east of the northern part of the Coast Mountains and a few on isolated mountains in the Yukon east of the St. Elias. These are of glaciological interest, but are outside our area of concern in this article.

At this juncture it may be useful to discuss the glaciers of the principal mountain ranges. We can begin at the southeastern tip of Alaska, proceeding northwesterly along the Coast Mountains of the Alaska panhandle, then along the St. Elias Mountains of Alaska, British Columbia, and Yukon Territory to the 141st meridian at Mount St. Elias. There the boundary turns north to the Arctic Coast. West of the boundary in Alaska the ranges split, with the coastal mountains extending westward as the Chugach and Kenai Mountains, ending at Cook Inlet, and the other system of ranges farther inland, extending northward to the Wrangell Mountains, then merging with the Alaska Range. The latter continues in a great arc westward, then southwestward, around the basins draining into Copper River and Cook Inlet, to where this interior mountain system reaches the coast on the west side of the mouth of Cook Inlet. These are the ranges of southeastern, south central, central or interior, and parts of southwestern Alaska, which have the largest concentration of glaciers, and all those over 20 km in length. The other mountain groups in northern, western and southwestern Alaska have smaller glaciers, many of which are more remote and seldom visited but nevertheless are also of glaciological interest.

It may seem strange that the largest glaciers are all concentrated in the southern part of the area under discussion, where conditions are generally warmer than in the areas north of Yukon River. In the colder regions of northern or Arctic Alaska, the largest glaciers are all less than nine kilometers in length, not only because the mountains do not exceed 10,000 ft (3050 m) in height, but also because the region is virtually arid. This aridity is also found in other parts of the Polar regions, which are remote from areas of open sea water which forms the main source of moisture for precipitation as snow on adjacent land areas. There, despite the fact that there is little annual melting, there is also very little precipitation, although a relatively larger part of it falls in the form of snow.

The glaciers of the Coast, St. Elias, Chugach, and Kenai Mountains are of special interest because of their size, their proximity to frequented routes of travel, and the beautiful fiord scenery and their tidal glaciers. On the other hand, many of the glaciers of the Wrangells and the Alaska Range are remote from frequented routes of travel and are somewhat eclipsed as scenic features by the huge mountains which serve as their sources.

In subsequent sections we will review each of these areas and mention the features which are deemed of special interest and such glaciological studies as have come to our attention and merit special consideration.

The Coast Mountains

In this section we are concerned with the northwestern part of the Coast Mountains which extends along the boundary between Alaska and British Columbia from Portland Canal to the head of Lynn Canal, then northward into the southern part of Yukon Territory. Local usage seems to favor the name Boundary Ranges in British Columbia and the Coast Mountains in Alaska. The glacierized area is roughly 685 km long and up to 130 km wide. There are several breaks in the range due to dissecting river valleys and ice-free passes, between which are a series of extensive icefields. The glaciers drain westward into salt water or eastward into the British Columbia rivers, most of which also eventually flow westward back across the range into the waters of the Pacific. Two of the largest of these icefields which straddle the range are locally known as the Stikine Icefield, between Stikine and Whiting rivers, and the Juneau Icefield, east and northeast of Juneau. From the former rises the highest two peaks: Mount Ratz (10,290 ft, 3137 m) and Kates Needle (10,023 ft, 3056 m); from the latter, Devils Paw (8584 ft, 2611 m). Between Portland Canal and Stikine River are 11 glaciers over 20 km in length which drain into Portland Canal, the eastern tributaries of the Stikine, and Behm Canal. All but the last mentioned are in British Columbia.

Between Stikine and Whiting rivers, draining the Stikine Icefield, are eight glaciers over 20 km long of which those over 30 km long are the LeConte (37 km), Baird (c. 48 km), Dawes (c. 41 km), South Sawyer (48 km) and Sawyer (c. 35 km). Of these, one is entirely in Alaska and the other four flow westward into Alaska from their upper névés in British Columbia. The four which discharge into tidewater are the LeConte, Dawes, South Sawyer, and Sawyer. Their spectacular termini can be reached by excursion vessels and small boats from Juneau, Petersburg, and other points on the Inside Passage.

The longest glacier between Whiting and Taku river is the Wright (38 km), which drains into the latter. Its sources are in British Columbia and its terminus in Alaska. Flowing from the Juneau Icefield and its northwestward extensions are the Tulsequah (27 km), Taku (53 km), the longest in the Coast Mountains; and the Norris (27 km), into the Taku River drainage; the Gilkey (32 km) and Meade (37 km) into rivers entering Lynn Canal; and the Llewellyn, (c. 35 km), which drains into the interior basins of the Yukon River system. Of these eight outlets of the Juneau Icefields, two are in British Columbia, three in Alaska, and three in both Alaska and British Columbia. Two glaciers northwest of the head of Lynn Canal that drain into it via Chilkat and Chilkoot inlets are over 20 km in

Miller, who had helped organize it and was in charge of the field operations for the first few years, then continued the operation from Michigan State University with additional sponsorship by the Foundation for Glacier Research, and more recently from the University of Idaho where in 1989 it is still being run with support from the National Science Foundation and other institutions. Over the years, this project has pursued the original research objectives and in addition has provided valuable training and field experience for both undergraduate and graduate students in glaciology and related disciplines.

As a result of his observations, Miller has attributed at least part of the Taku advance to the fact that its source areas are higher than those of the other glaciers draining from the icefield, and that observations indicate that these higher névés have received appreciably more snow accumulation in the last two centuries than the neighboring névés at lower level (Miller 1963, pp. 181-184).

In 1953, the AGS effort was shifted to Lemon Creek Glacier, a smaller and less complex glacier of the Juneau Icefield. This continued until 1958 (Heusser and Marcus, 1960). More recent activity is the remapping of Lemon Creek Glacier in 1989 by Melvin G. Marcus' party from Arizona State University for a determination of changes in the glacier since a similar undertaking by the AGS for the International Geophysical Year Program in 1957-1958. (Nine Glacier Maps, 1960).

Another feature of the valley was the Polaris-Taku Mine which operated for many years in the upper Taku valley, 11 km below Tulsequah Glacier. There work was disrupted almost yearly by the outbreak of ice-dammed Tulsequah Lake which discharged into Tulsequah Glacier, 8 km above the terminus (Marcus, 1960).

There are two other features about the Coast Mountains that deserve mention. One is the volcanic activity that has occurred in the recent past which is a northward extension of the more spectacular events in the Cascades from Northern California to Washington and in the coastal mountains of southern British Columbia. Three features of volcanic origin have been described. There are two dormant volcanic cones in British Columbia in the Stikine River watershed. The biggest is Edziza Peak (8135 ft, 2480 m) in the upper valley east of the main range of the Coast Mountains. Studies of the extensive ice cover of this dormant volcano were begun in 1965 and have continued intermittently since then. The second is Hoodoo Mountain (6500 ft, 1982 m) which rises between two glaciers near Iskut River. It is said to be a spectacular mountain with an ice-filled crater.

The third feature is a vent which has spewed lava and ash onto small glaciers near Mount Lewis Cass (6864 ft, 2094 m) on the crest of the Coast Mountains, a short distance into British Columbia from the International Boundary. The remains of a recent lava flow was reported by Fremont Morse in 1905 while he was surveying for the International Boundary Commission, in what was called Lava Fork of Blue River, tributary of the Unuk. He wrote that the latest outburst flow had "probably occurred within less than fifty years." (Morse, 1906, p.176) At this same place another actual outpouring onto the glaciers was observed and

PLATE 24

Rendu Glacier from Reid's Plane Table Station A (now AGS Station 4). Top photo was taken by H.F. Reid on August 30, 1892. W.O. Field's photo from the same site recorded surge as it appeared September 16, 1966.

photographed by a U.S. Navy aircraft engaged on a mapping project in the summer of 1948. The writer knows of no further word on this interesting occurrence since then.

Tourism and Transport

Tourist excursions and facilities for reaching the glaciers of the Coast Mountains have existed for many years. In the old days, steamers travelling the Inside Passage from Seattle or Vancouver to Skagway often made side trips to such areas as Taku Glacier. River passenger boats have also, for a long time, plied Stikine River the 150 km from Wrangell in Alaska, through the Coast Mountains to Telegraph Creek in British Columbia which provides beautiful river scenery and superb views of mountains and glaciers.

Other glaciers have been among the easiest for tourists to reach. Local excursion vessels now provide access to the tidal glaciers of LeConte Bay and Endicott and Tracy Arms. Points in the Taku River valley can be reached by river boats and float planes providing access to the several glaciers at the upper end of the inlet and the lower reaches of the river. On the flats almost opposite the advancing Hole-in-the-Wall Glacier, a distributary tongue of the Taku, is Taku Lodge, which has operated there for most of the last few decades. Not far up river is also the scenic Twin Glacier Lake, accessible by river boats.

In Juneau a highway connects the city with Mendenhall Glacier, where a Forest Service Center provides facilities for the many sightseers who come by car and bus. From the Juneau Airport local aircraft also provide trips over the Juneau Icefield and the local glaciers. Helicopters are also available for sightseeing trips from the heliport on Gastineau Channel outside the city.

In bygone days, glaciers near Skagway were accessible to hikers. Lawrence Martin reports that in the early years of this century, Denver Glacier, 9 km up the East Fork of Skagway River from the town of Skagway, was "visited annually by hundreds of tourists." (Tarr and Martin, 1914, p. 6). In recent years it is seldom visited, partly because, as a 1958 AGS party learned, the glacier has receded far back up its valley.

In the 18th and 19th centuries ships travelling the Inside Passage along Frederick Sound and Stephens Passage between Petersburg and Juneau often encountered icebergs floating out from LeConte Glacier at the head of LeConte Bay, Dawes Glacier at the head of Endicott Arm, South Sawyer and Sawyer glaciers at the head of Tracy Arm, and Taku Glacier at the head of Taku Inlet. Since then these glaciers have either retreated substantially or have become non-tidal so that icebergs are now hardly ever seen along these shipping channels and are not considered a serious risk to navigation.

St. Elias Mountains

The St. Elias Mountains extend for some 300 km along the coast and somewhat over 400 km farther inland in Canada with a width varying from 125 to 200 km. Of the 13 peaks in Alaska and the Yukon over 4572 m (15,000 ft), nine of them are in the St. Elias Mountains. Of these, eight are in what is known as the Icefield Ranges, and one in the Fairweather Range. As Wahrhaftig points out (1965, p. 41), the "drainage is almost entirely by glaciers."

The St. Elias can be divided roughly into two parts: the southern, situated south of Alsek River, which includes the glaciers draining from the Fairweather Range and the lower mountains to the east in the Alsek and Chilkat ranges; and the northern, dominated by the Icefield Ranges and its subsidiary ranges where the most extensive névés and long valley glaciers in North America are located.

The best-known glaciers of the southern area are situated (1) in the valleys of the rivers flowing into the northwestern part of Lynn Canal, (2) on the west side of Lynn Canal, (3) in Glacier Bay, and (4) those to the west which drain southward into Taylor Bay, westward into the Gulf of Alaska, and northward into Alsek River and its principal tributary, the Tatshenshi in northern British Columbia. The longest and best-known glaciers in this area, proceeding from the northeast to the south, then to the west and north are: the Tsirku (c. 22 km) at the head of Tsirku River; Davidson (20 km) on the west side of Lynn Canal; and in Glacier Bay, proceeding counter-clockwise, the Casement (c. 30 km), McBride (c. 24 km), Riggs (27 km), Muir (c. 20 km), Carroll (c. 42 km), Grand Pacific (c. 46 km), Margerie (c. 39 km), Johns Hopkins (26 km), Lamplugh (31 km), and Reid (21 km). To the west draining southward from the Fairweathers is the Brady (48 km); to the northwest along the Coast, the La Perouse (26 km), Fairweather (33 km), and the Grand Plateau (c. 50 km); and flowing northward into Alsek River from the Fairweathers, the Alsek (31 km). The following glaciers reach tidewater in this area: the McBride, Riggs, Muir, Grand Pacific, Margerie, Toyatte, Tyeen in 1989, Johns Hopkins, Gilman, Hoonah, Kashoto, Lamplugh, and Reid in Glacier Bay; and the La Perouse, North Crillon, and Lituya along the outer coast.

Glacier Bay is one of the most interesting localities on earth for the study of glacier fluctuations, due to its many glaciers in a relatively small area, their diversity of behavior, and the long-term trends which now extend back to the end of the last Ice Age. An explanation of the causes of these changes is the ultimate goal, but is still lacking partly because of inadequate data on the interrelationships between glacier behavior and the meteorological record. U.S. Weather stations have existed at a number of places around the area, but at no locality nearer the glaciers than several tens of kilometers, and only occasionally have data been obtained on the glaciers themselves.

Some glaciers have receded dramatically in the last two centuries while others, only a few, are larger now than in the late 18th century. The wealth of historical information now available is due to studies by glacial geologists, geobotanists, and glaciologists which extend the knowledge of the fluctuation of these ice masses to a century before the first observations. Two unusual sources of information which have been of enormous help are (1) the photographic record and (2) the mapping which has been undertaken since the middle 1890s.

Systematic observations of glacier fluctuations in Glacier Bay were begun by H.F. Reid in 1890 and 1892 (Reid 1892 and 1896) and have been carried on intermittently up through 1989 by various observers representing many different organizations, both private and governmental. The list of reports issued over this 100-year period and an outline of the results obtained would fill a book, so must be greatly abbreviated in this article. The writer has been associated with this work since his first visit to the bay in 1926 (Field, 1926). In recent years further significant efforts have been made by members of the Geological Survey and the National Park Service through both aerial and terrestrial observations.

Until the late 1920s almost all the glaciers of the bay had been in recession. However, in the last sixty years, the glaciers at the heads of Tarr and Johns Hopkins inlets began to readvance and have both moved forward in the order of 2 to 2½ km. It is probably significant that they both drain from high névés in the highest parts of the Fairweather Range. Elsewhere in the northern inlets there has been little net recession, while in the southern inlets, where mountains and névés are lower, there has been continued recession which in some valleys can be described as in an advanced stage of deglaciation. Muir Glacier, which receded over some 40 km from 1890 to 1980 has since then stabilized at the head of its fiord, so the enormous retreat since the Little Ice Age maximum of the 18th century has now ended in most of the upper reaches of the bay, while still continuing in the areas of lower elevations. Needless to add, trends in the next few decades will be watched with great interest and, let us hope, will be closely monitored. On the western and northern slopes of the Fairweather Range, the fluctuations vary from advance in Lituya Bay, to relative stability at La Perouse Glacier, and recession elsewhere.

At this point it would seem appropriate to add a word about the Muir which in 1883 seems to have been the first glacier in Alaska to be visited by a passenger steamer (Scidmore 1884), as well as the first one to be studied in some detail by a scientific party headed by George F. Wright, in 1886 (Wright 1887). With its former tributaries it has remained over the years one of the most frequently visited by tourists as well as scientists. A century ago, it was some 66 km long and according to H.F. Reid in 1890 the area of ice was estimated to be about 350 miles [2] (900 km^2) (1892, p.26). Since then recession has amounted to some 46 km during which four large tributaries have become independent, so that by the 1980s its area appeared to be less than 150 km^2. At the present position of the terminus, the ice surface in Reid's time was at around 2750 ft.

However, during this time three of its former tributaries have lost less than 10% of their areas, and have receded only from one to seven kilometers since becoming independent of the Muir. The reason for the Muir's much greater retreat seems primarily due to its having terminated in deep water where calving has been very active. This recession of the Muir merits our consideration because it appears to be by far the greatest known recession of any valley glacier in North America, and very probably anywhere else in the temperate regions.

While the recession of the Muir is perhaps the most spectacular during the past century, historically, it is eclipsed by the opening up of Glacier Bay since the middle of the 18th century. The age of the trees now growing on the terminal moraine at the mouth of the bay together with other geological features show conclusively that the whole bay was filled with a huge glacier which attained its maximum length in what is generally known as the Little Ice Age in the middle of the 18th century. At that time this giant glacier occupied all of what is now Glacier Bay and was around 126 km long, which would have been surpassed at the present time only by Bering Glacier in the eastern Chugach. Apparently recession set in soon after the middle of the 18th century and amounted to a few kilometers by the time Vancouver's party charted the coast in 1794. After that, the recession continued up what is now lower Glacier Bay. Although it was seen by the local Tlingit Indians who hunted seals in the area, there were no reliable observations of the position of the terminus until Muir's visit in 1879 and 1880 (Muir, 1895 and 1915). However, the age of the trees growing along the shores of the areas vacated by the ice provide the successive positions of the terminus during at least part of the recession (Cooper, 1937; Lawrence, 1949; Heusser, 1960).

At the present time in the Fairweather Range at the northwestern end of Glacier Bay, where the great glacier of the 18th century had its principal sources, is a series of huge basins with a head wall extending from Mount Quincy Adams (13,560 ft, 4134 m) southward to Mount Crillon (12,726 ft, 3879 m). This area remains the source of the various glaciers which drain into Johns Hopkins Inlet with its two active tidal glaciers and four others that in 1989 also reached high tide. This fiord, in the opinion of many people, is one of the most spectacular in Alaska, with surrounding peaks, such as Mount Abbe (9200 ft, 2805 m) and Mount Cooper (6780 ft, 2067 m), rising directly from tidewater. Two centuries ago this fiord was filled with ice up to an elevation of 5000 to 6000 ft (1520 to 1830 m), for as recently as 1894, Boundary Survey Sheet No. 16, surveyed in 1894, showed the ice level after over a century of recession at around 2000 ft at the present position of the Johns Hopkins terminus.

It may appear that this great recession, that took place from the middle of the 18th century until the 20th century, is a continuation of the recession since the last Ice Age, which is generally thought to have ended about 10,000 to 12,000 years ago. However, this is not the case, for remnants of old trees which grew along the shores of lower Glacier Bay and had been reported as early as the 1880s, as well as geological evidence, have now provided dates of an ecosystem that existed along the shores of the lower bay from 10,000 to 7000 years ago, indicating that in that period the glaciers were greatly recessed, perhaps even farther back than they are today. The subsequent advance which culminated in the 18th century had apparently begun in the period 2800 to 2200 B.C. (Goldthwait, 1966).

One of the most interesting features of the region is the presence of the Brady Icefield which has two northern outlet glaciers, the Lamplugh and the Reid, both tidal, flowing into upper Glacier Bay; and the main southern flow terminating on a bar at the head of Taylor Bay, which is 35 km west of the mouth of Glacier Bay. This icefield complex of some 480 to 490 km² is now almost the same size as it was in the 19th century, and its surface level has apparently been lowered only a few tens of meters from high-level trimlines that date from about 1876 (Bengtson, 1962, p.84). This example of relative stability which Bengtson described as ". . . substantially in equilibrium . . . " on one ice mass and the huge shrinkage over the last two centuries of its larger neighboring ice sheet which occupied the present Glacier Bay is one of the paradoxes which remain to be adequately explained.

One aspect of glacier fluctuations which has caused considerable excitement in recent years has been what are known as surging glaciers, sometimes referred to in the press as "galloping glaciers." Such occurrences have taken place in many parts of Alaska, and have been noted since at least the first decade of this century. At least ten glaciers have been known to surge in the Glacier Bay area. Three are of special interest because the frequent observations have indicated a most interesting pattern of repetition. The three, which are all in separate widely-scattered inlets are the Carroll, a long valley glacier; the Rendu, a smaller valley glacier; and the Tyeen, a relatively small hanging glacier in Johns Hopkins Inlet. The first two have either advanced vigorously, or became heavily crevassed, indicating unusual activity in their terminal areas, whereas the Tyeen pours out of its inner valley and descends some 600 m to tidewater over a distance of 1½ to 2 km. All these surges end a year or two after the initial advance, and the terminal ice then becomes stagnant or disappears.

The amazing feature is the apparent synchroneity of the surges at these three glaciers during the last five decades. All were activated between 1943 and 1950, 1965 to 1966, and 1987 to 1989. Between each surge they all have resumed their previous condition. As far as we know there are no other instances of surges occurring elsewhere where different glaciers responded both in the same period and with such comparable results, but this aspect of glaciology is still in its infancy and many new discoveries will undoubtedly be made in the next decades.

Because the early scientists who visited Glacier Bay realized its extraordinary history of change and its other unusual features, the idea of setting it aside for scientific research and protection led to its being made a National Monument. William S. Cooper, through his connection with the Ecological Society of America, was instrumental in this process leading to the establishment of the Glacier Bay National Monument by President Coolidge on February 16, 1925. The proclamation stated: "This area presents a unique opportunity for the scientific study of glacial behavior and of resulting movements and development of flora and fauna and of certain valuable relics of ancient interglacial forests." (Cooper, 1956, p.18). Since 1925 the area has been enlarged at least twice and in 1980 gained further recognition by being designated as a National Park.

Probably no other uninhabited region of this size and complexity has received more attention over the last few decades than has been directed toward the area now included in Glacier Bay National Park and Preserve. One reason for this is the valuable cooperation of the Park Service in providing logistical support to scientific parties, primarily in the form of transportation by boat to various points of study. Perhaps the fairest, but not the most scientific, way to

PLATE 25

Photo by Austin Post

Johns Hopkins Glacier (right) and
Gilman Glacier (left) on August 16,
1961. By 1989, the Johns Hopkins
had advanced to meet the Gilman.
Mount Crillon on left and Mounts
Wilbur and Orville on right.

deal with the work accomplished is to mention primarily the long-term efforts, some of which have continued over decades. However, that is not to imply that some short-term studies are not of value, because sometimes they may disclose crucial events.

We have already discussed the simplest effort of all, the measurement of changes in the glaciers which began with the observations by John Muir in 1879 and 1880 and have continued for the ensuing 110 years. Many individuals and organizations have taken part. These observations have been greatly enhanced by National Park Service personnel, the frequent photographic flights by USGS's Austin Post and his colleagues and others and by other scientists in glacial geology, ecology, and environmental matters.

Prominent in the last few decades is the research of William S. Cooper of the University of Minnesota, from 1916 to 1935 (Cooper 1923, 1931, 1937, and 1939) and his assistant and successor Donald B. Lawrence, also of the University of Minnesota from 1941 to 1989 (Lawrence 1949). Cooper's and Lawrence's influence and encouragement of research on the environment, and marine and terrestrial ecosystems, carried out by Park Naturalists and other personnel, have also been invaluable. Lawrence was also influential in the founding of the Friends of Glacier Bay in the late 1970s to work as an independent group with the Park Service and others and in the planning of the First and Second Glacier Bay Symposia in 1983 and 1988.

Another series of glacial geology studies were initiated in Glacier Bay by Richard P. Goldthwait in 1959 as part of the program of the Institute of Polar Studies (IPS), The Ohio State University. He had already been the scientist on Bradford Washburn's Harvard-Dartmouth Expedition in 1934 (Goldthwait 1936), and had also been a member of the AGS party in Glacier Bay on the IGY Glaciology Program of 1958.

His new research consisted of directing graduate students in various aspects of glacial geology and glaciology in the Muir Inlet area, and later extended to other parts of the National Monument. They included studies of remnant and active glaciers, ecology and the environment. Several of these researchers continued the original study as faculty members at other universities. Unfortunately, space does not permit more details about these worthy efforts in this article.

Other than observations of remnant ice masses, such as Burroughs Glacier (Taylor 1962, and Michelson 1971) and McBride Remnant (Haselton 1966), regimen studies were carried out on Casement Glacier (Peterson 1970). The post-glacial history of the region by Goldthwait and his associates also determined some of the major geological and glaciological events that had taken place over the last 10,000 years (Goldthwait 1966).

Interesting work has also been done in the fiords themselves including additional soundings in Muir and Wachusett inlets by a USGS team led by Austin Post in 1972. These have special importance because of the changes that have taken place in these inlets due to the fluctuations in the glaciers and the rapid rate of sedimentation in the inlets. Other research in marine geology in these same inlets has been done by a party led by Bruce Molnia, USGS (Molnia, 1986).

Tourist travel has been attracted over the years by the glaciers, fiords, spectacular mountains, vegetation, aquatic and terrestrial animals, and the renewal of the biological environment in the vast areas which have been deglaciated over the last two centuries. The steamer "Queen" brought the first boat load of tourists in 1883 (Scidmore 1885). Such visits were continued until September 1899 when Muir Glacier, following a series of strong earthquake shocks, calved so heavily that ships could not approach close enough for satisfactory views of the ice front (Gilbert 1903, pp. 23-24). The steamer visits then came to an end. Finally, visits by tourist vessels began again in the summer months in the 1950s and have been followed more recently by large cruise ships from Seattle and Vancouver. Muir Glacier and the other tidal glaciers of Muir Inlet were the main scenic attractions until the 1970s, but as the Muir has continued to recede, making the approach longer, and the other glaciers became less spectacular, the favored route for cruise ships has shifted to the northwest arm of Glacier Bay where both Tarr and Johns Hopkins inlets are easier to reach and now offer more tidal glaciers, fiord scenery, and views of the lofty Fairweather Range.

In the 1950s, the National Park Service established an administrative headquarters at Bartlett Cove near the entrance of Glacier Bay, and subsequently built Glacier Bay Lodge. It is now run by a concessionaire who also operates excursion vessels for trips to both arms of the bay. A few kilometers away is Gustavus Airport, built as an emergency air strip during World War II, where regular commercial service is maintained and which serves as a base for charter flights over the whole area. Small cruise ships and private vessels also bring visitors into Glacier Bay during the summer months.

Beyond Brady Glacier, which has already been mentioned, is the La Perouse which drains high névés between Mounts Crillon and La Perouse and is the only glacier that discharges directly into the Gulf of Alaska. Such icebergs as are calved from its 3-km-long ice front do not last long and soon break up in the waves and swells of the open ocean. The glacier varies from at times being a relatively inactive low ice cliff on the beach at high-tide level, to a high active ice cliff, which at least twice in this century has been estimated to reach a height of over 75 m. These appear to be genuine surges.

Northward along the coast from La Perouse Glacier is Lituya Bay, one of the most spectacular and interesting localities along the whole coast of Alaska. Its modern history begins with the French navigator La Pérouse's visit in 1786. He called it Port des Français, but the name Lituya, which is based on a Tlingit Indian name, has been officially adopted. La Pérouse charted the bay in which two large glaciers are shown in what he called the Western Basin (now Gilbert Inlet) and two at the head of the Eastern Basin (now Crillon Inlet). Unlike on other early charts, these glaciers were recognized and marked as such. This is believed to be the first fairly accurate map showing the termini of Alaskan glaciers in which the details of the surrounding topography can now be recongized.

La Pérouse's chart of Lituya Bay can be readily compared with conditions as they are today. Since then a great change has occurred in the glaciers. During the late 18th century both sets of glaciers in the eastern and western arms coelesced and advanced so that the four tidal termini of 1786 had been reduced to two by the late 19th century. These advances have continued so that by now their termini are four to five kilometers farther forward than two centuries ago, and are still advancing slowly as their outflow of sediment and moraine gradually fill up the head of the inlet.

During the violent earthquake of July 9, 1958 along the Fairweather Fault, which occupies the trench forming the head of the bay, there occurred another episode which ranks among the more dramatic natural events of this century. A great landslide estimated to have a volume of 40 million m^3 fell from the oversteepened slopes above Gilbert Inlet partly onto Lituya Glacier and partly into the inlet. About 400 m of the lower part of the glacier was destroyed, and an enormous wave was generated with a splash effect which wiped out the vegetation up to a height of 530 m on the southwestern point of the inlet. At its origin, the wave was over 60 m high and became lower as it moved down the bay, stripping the trees and other vegetation along both shores about 13 km to the entrance. Three fishing boats were at anchor inside the entrance. Two were swept over the spit into the Gulf; one survived with its two passengers able to describe what they saw, while the other boat was swamped and not seen again. A third was swamped inside the bay, but the two individuals aboard escaped in a dory. Subsequently, Lituya Glacier grew out once again to its pre-1958 position and resumed its slow advance (D.J. Miller 1960 and F.E. Caldwell 1986).

Alsek River

Some 75 km along the coast northwest of Lituya Bay is Dry Bay at the mouth of Alsek River which drains extensive areas of northern British Columbia and southern Yukon Territory. It is one of the wildest rivers in North America with glaciers entering its valley and in some cases discharging into the river itself.

Only one large glacier, the Alsek (31 km) drains from the east and is entirely in Alaska with its sources in the northwestern part of the Fairweather Range. Most of the rest of the larger glaciers flow from western and northern sources in the part of the St. Elias Mountains known as the Icefield Ranges where are located the highest peaks, the largest glaciers, and the most extensive ice fields. The upper source of Alsek River is Kaskawulsh Glacier (75 km) in Yukon Territory, which drains not only into Kaskawulsh River, tributary of the Alsek, but also into the Kluane Lake drainage of the Yukon River system. Whichever is dominant varies from time to time, but here we assume the former to be the main outlet. The other glaciers of this area that are longer than 30 km and their relationship to the National and Provincial boundaries proceeding downstream are: the Dusty (54 km) and Lowell (73 km), both in the Yukon; the Fisher (45 km) and Tweedsmuir (70 km) (*ICE*, No. 43, 1973) in both the Yukon and British Columbia; and the Vern Richie (46 km) in British Columbia; entirely in Alaska is the Novatak (35 km), which drains lower level icefields between the Brabazon and Icefield Ranges.

An important feature of Alsek River are the instances when such glaciers as the Lowell, Fisher, or Tweedsmuir have advanced across the river and formed ice dams which impounded large lakes in the valley above. One such lake, referred to by geologists as Recent Lake Alsek (Kindle 1953) was caused by an advance of Lowell Glacier, probably in the early part of the 19th century. This dam is believed to have been 150 m high and caused the impounded lake to extend some 90 km up the valley, into Haines Junction on the Alaska Highway. When these lakes drained, they caused floods in the valley below and onto the delta at Dry Bay where the river empties into the Gulf of Alaska.

The surges in recent years of these glaciers have been studied: that of the Tweedsmuir in 1952 to 1954 and 1973 to 1975 (*ICE*, No. 44, 47, 50); and of Lowell Glacier in 1983 to 1984 (*ICE*, No. 59). Those of recent years were detected on satellite imagery as well as on aerial photos. Although these recent surges reached the river, they were not powerful enough to dam its flow. However, these events stimulated more careful examination of the surges and the features of the basin of Recent Lake Alsek by G. Holdsworth and M. Alford of the Geological Survey of Canada (*ICE*, No. 43) and G.K.C. Clarke and J. Schmok of the Geophysics Department, Univ. of British Columbia (*ICE*, No. 77, 85). They also found that Lowell Glacier had dammed Alsek River five to six times in the last 2800 years (*ICE*, No. 50).

In this century minor floods have been reported near the mouth of the river at Dry Bay. In August, 1909, a native village had to be abandoned as the river rose 5 to 5½ m and for two weeks icebergs and tree trunks floated down the swollen river. Another record of heavy ice in the river occurred shortly after the July 1958 earthquake when it appears that the flow of the river was temporarily blocked by ice discharged from one of the glaciers (Davis and Sanders 1960). It is quite possible that any one of these glaciers may advance again causing the formation of another ice-dammed lake and the ensuing flood when the dam collapses.

The Icefield Ranges

North and northwest of the Alsek River are the highest parts of the St. Elias Mountains, now known as the Icefield Ranges, which are mostly in Yukon Territory. This area includes the highest peaks. Those over 15,000 ft. (4572 m) are in order of height: Mounts Logan (19,525 ft, 5951 m), St. Elias (18,008 ft, 5489 m), Lucania (17,147 ft, 5226 m), King Peak (16,971 ft, 5171 m), Mounts Steele (16,664 ft, 5074 m), Bona (16,421 ft, 5005 m), Wood (15,885 ft, 4842 m), Vancouver (15,700 ft, 4785 m), Churchill (15,638 ft, 4766 m) and Hubbard

(15,015 ft, 4577 m). These peaks are surrounded by icefields from which flow some of the longest glaciers outside the Polar Regions with surface elevations ranging from roughly 2000 to 3600 m.

North of the Icefield Ranges are subsidiary ranges such as the Kluane and Donjek ranges with small glaciers fronting on the interior valleys of the Yukon River watershed. The Brabazon Range rises to the southwest, along the coast in Alaska between Alsek River and Yakutat Bay. Although less than 2000 m high, it supports a number of medium size glaciers. The longest of these, besides Novatak Glacier of the Alsek River drainage, already noted, are the Chamberlain-Rodman (22 km) and the Yakutat (c. 25 km). Neither of them reach the coast. Their sources range from 1500 to 2500 m and are lower than those in the higher parts of the Icefield Ranges to the north. This seems too low an altitude for them to maintain their present sizes under late 20th century climatic conditions and there is some evidence that they are shrinking rather rapidly.

Yakutat Bay

In the Yakutat Bay area are a series of glaciers which drain into Russell Fiord, Disenchantment Bay, Yakutat Bay itself, and the Gulf of Alaska. These are, from east to west, the East Nunatak (c. 30 km), West Nunatak (c. 20 km), Variegated (21 km), Hubbard (c. 125 km), Turner (24 km), Lucia (24 km), Hayden (26 km), and the Malaspina-Seward complex (113 km) between Yakutat Bay and Icy Bay to the westward. Of these the East Nunatak, Variegated, Turner, Lucia, and Hayden are entirely in Alaska but have all or parts of their sources in either British Columbia or the Yukon. As previously indicated, we consider the western end of the Icefield Ranges to be at Mount St. Elias, where the coastal ranges continue to the west as the Chugach Mountains.

Proceeding north from Mount St. Elias are three large glaciers draining into the westward flowing Chitina River, tributary of the Copper. The Chitina and Logan glaciers coalesce near their termini, but insofar as flow of ice is concerned, they can be considered as virtually separate ice streams. The Logan is about 87 km in length, Chitina (c. 77 km), Barnard (54 km), and Hawkins (35 km). Both the Logan and the Chitina have their sources in Yukon Territory and terminate in Alaska, while both the Barnard and Hawkins are entirely in Alaska.

East of the Chitistone and Skolai passes are the northward-flowing glaciers draining into White River, tributary of the Yukon. These are from west to east: Russell Glacier (39 km), Klutlan (c. 88 km), Steele (35 km), Spring (c. 34 km), Donjek (65 km), and Kluane (c. 36 km). Russell Glacier is entirely in Alaska, the Klutlan has some sources in Alaska but terminates in the Yukon, and the remaining four are entirely in the Yukon.

This complex of glaciers that drain from the Icefield Ranges form the largest concentration of glaciers and icefields on this continent. The northward flow is into the Yukon River system, eastward into Alsek River, southward into the Gulf

PLATE 26

Photo by Austin Post

Lowell Glacier discharging into the Alsek River. August 14, 1961.

of Alaska, and westward to Icy Bay, Bering Glacier of the Chugach Mountains, and the Copper River basin. Over half of the area of ice is in the Yukon Territory.

Scientific Observations

Since 1890 (Russell 1892 and 1893) scientific observations have been carried out in the part of the St. Elias Mountains now called Icefield Ranges.

In this article it is virtually impossible to do full justice to the research on the many glaciers which radiate from the huge reservoir of interconnected névés extending for roughly 125 km north to south and 115 km east to west. Over the last half century there have been too many participants for all to be mentioned nor can their reports be cited. The author apologizes for whatever serious omissions occur, and emphasizes that there is no intended slight to any of the scores of scientists who have made valuable contributions.

The research efforts at the principal glaciers which have emerged as especially worthy of discussion are the Seward-Malaspina complex, the Hubbard, Variegated, Donjek, Steele, and its neighboring glaciers, such as the Trapridge in the Hazard Lake area. The range of subjects investigated have included regimen, depth measurements, glacial-meteorology and climatology, hydrology, surging glaciers, and ice-dammed lakes.

Two related projects covered many glaciers and a large part of the Icefield Ranges and were the longest and most comprehensive studies in the area. These were concerned with the high mountain environment which had its inception in the several expeditions organized by Walter A. Wood under the sponsorship of the American Geographical Society (AGS) beginning in 1935 (Wood 1936). From these, Wood developed what was called Project Snow Cornice which had eight field seasons from 1948 to 1958 under the additional sponsorship of the Arctic Institute of North America (AINA), with support from the U.S. Office of Naval Research and other U.S. and Canadian government agencies as well as several universities and other organizations in both countries. It was in the first year of this project (1948) that Robert P. Sharp of California Institute of Technology developed a long-term program of glaciological research which served as an important guideline for the ensuing years (Sharp 1948).

The general objectives of Project Snow Cornice were continued in the Icefield Ranges Research Project (IRRP) from 1961 to 1968 and the High Mountain Environment Project.

The general objective as stated by Wood (IRRP Scientific Results Vol. 1, 1969, p. xi) was "This project seeks understanding of the multiple facets that comprise the natural environment of the St. Elias Mountains of Alaska and Yukon Territory. Its approach to the task is truly geographical, within the widely accepted current meaning of geography as an integrator among the scientific disciplines. Not only is the project multi-disciplinary in its area of research, but it is also interdisciplinary in its approach to its objectives." Active participants who took part in the organization and leadership of the field work, as well as serving as co-editors of the volumes on scientific results, were Richard H. Ragle and Melvin G. Marcus (*Icefield Ranges Research Project: Scientific Results* vols. 1-4, 1969-1974.)

The wealth of information about the area and its vast glaciers is most impressive as revealed in the four volumes of scientific results cited above. The entire effort from its beginning in the middle of the 1930s, represents one of the longest and well-coordinated interdisciplinary projects which has been active in the field. The list of authors in the reports, which included well known scientists as well as junior members and graduate students, provides a good example of the scope and quality of the project. The entire effort represents one of the more significant milestones in the century-old history of U.S. and Canadian environmental studies of an alpine area and its glaciology.

Since the Hubbard Glacier and the Seward-Malaspina complex were the first to be studied in this area by I.C. Russell's National Geographic Society parties in 1890 and 1892 (Russell 1892 and 1893) and appear to be the second and third longest glaciers outside the Polar Regions, it seems appropriate to discuss them first.

Hubbard Glacier

Hubbard Glacier, exceeded in length only by the Bering, terminates in the most spectacular and active ice front in Alaska and probably anywhere else outside the polar regions. The terminus is 7 to 8 km in width. Moraines both above and below sea level show that in the tenth to thirteenth centuries Hubbard Glacier had advanced some 60 km from its present position to the mouth of Yakutat Bay (G. Plafker and D.J. Miller 1958). After a retreat, another advance took place in the 18th century to a point some 23 km in advance of the 1980s position. After that a further retreat ensued until glaciological observations were begun in 1890. During these earlier advances the entrance of what is now Russell Fiord had been blocked, forming an ice-dammed lake, referred to as Russell Lake, which lasted until it was drained and again became an arm of the sea.

Russell Fiord is about 50 km long with a 19 km side extension of Nunatak Fiord, altogether forming a basin of nearly 200 km^2. When mapped by the Canadian Boundary Survey in 1895, the Hubbard terminus was still about 2.6 km from the point where such a dam would form. This distance was narrowed to 1.5 km by 1959 (AGS survey) and the gap was closed beginning May 29, 1986 by a dam composed of ice, as well as moraine and outwash. This latest episode attracted much attention from the scientific community and the media. There were two aspects of special concern. First, if the ice dam held and the lake water level should reach 39 to 40 m above sea level as it had in the past, the overflow would be over a low ridge at the southern end of Russell Fiord into Situk River, a major source of salmon and steelheads fishing for the people of Yakutat. Second, was the likelihood that the marine life in the new Russell Lake would be endangered by a change from salt to fresh water. Efforts were made to rescue the porpoises, seals, and other marine animals trapped in the lake, but this effort was not generally successful.

The dam lasted over four months until October 7, when the lake level had reached a height of 25.1 m. The dam burst suddenly and Russell Lake drained in a tremendous outpouring during most of the next two days at an hourly average rate of 3,700,000 ft^3 per second or about three times the peak flow of the Yukon River (Mayo, 1986).

Intensive observations at Hubbard Glacier were begun when the danger of an ice dam being formed became apparent. These observations are still being continued by the Geological Survey, the Forest Service, the Fish and Wildlife Service, and other public and private groups. Survey and water-level gauging stations have been established, as there is a general expectation that as the glacier is still advancing, the gap may again be closed in the next few years and another Russell Lake will come into existence.

Malaspina Glacier

North and west of Yakutat Bay is the great piedmont lobe of Malaspina Glacier which with its principal source, Seward Glacier, totals about 113 km in length. The view across Malaspina Glacier from a ship or aircraft to Mount St. Elias and its neighbors, Mounts Logan and Vancouver, which enclose the basin of Seward Glacier, is one of the most awe-inspiring mountain views in the world.

Malaspina Glacier deserves special comment as it is a true piedmont glacier formed by the coelescing of several glaciers flowing from some of the highest peaks and névés in the St. Elias Mountains. The glacier has a lobate terminus almost 90 km wide, with an east-west dimension of about 70 km and 45 km north to south. At the base of the mountains, where the Seward and Agassiz glaciers enter it, the altitude of its surface is around 2000 ft (610 m). From there it slopes gradually to the terminus just above sea level which drains into several rivers and terminal lakes. In one area of the glacier, seismic soundings made in 1951 by C. R. Allen and G. I. Smith of Robert P. Sharp's party from California Institute of Technology reported that "Seismic reflections obtained from bedrock . . . along a ten-mile profile indicate ice thicknesses ranging from 1130 to 2050 ft. The base of the ice is 700 ft. below sea level . . . " (Alled and Smith, 1953, p. 755 and Sharp, 1953).

Seward-Malaspina Glacier Complex

The Seward-Malaspina Glacier Complex has been traversed by various mountaineering parties since Russell's expedition of 1890 (Russell 1891). The modern era of observations may be said to have begun with the introduction of aerial observations and photography.

The pattern of moraines on the surface of Malaspina Glacier has intrigued observers since the late 19th century. Then as aerial observations and photography became possible, these features and what they indicate of the dynamics of glacier flow became far more apparent than when seen from the surface of the ice. An interesting report on these complex moraines, which are the first, or at least one of the first, observations on Alaskan glaciers based largely on aerial observations, was published by Bradford Washburn following his and Richard Goldthwait's photographic flight over the Malaspina in 1933 and a follow-up flight in 1934 (Washburn, 1935). Even at that time he could write: "It is hard to overestimate the value of the airplane in Alaskan glacier work" (ibid p. 1880).

The next year, 1935, Walter A. Wood began his long term investigations of the Icefield Ranges which were largely based on the use of aircraft (Wood 1936, 1942 and 1948). This led to the establishment of a research station on Seward Glacier and detailed regimen studies under Robert Sharp's leadership on Seward Glacier in 1949 and 1951 (Sharp 1951, 1953 and 1958). The use of helicopters was begun by IRRP in 1966.

In addition to aerial photography by Austin Post beginning in 1960 a USGS party from the Tacoma office operated two camps on Malaspina Glacier in 1971 (*ICE* No. 38, 1972, p.13).

Surging Glaciers

Surges in the glaciers have been noted as of special interest since R.S. Tarr reported the dramatic advances in the Yakutat Bay area in 1905 and 1906 (Tarr, 1909). These studies were continued by him and Lawrence Martin in 1909, 1910, and 1911 (Tarr and Martin 1914). At the time they wrote of these glaciers: "From a state of stagnation a number of them have sprung into sudden activity and then, with almost equal abruptness, have relapsed again into a state of stagnation." (Tarr and Martin, (1914, p. 168) Since then these phenomena have become known as surges. After a lapse of some years the investigation of surging glaciers and the mechanics involved again became a subject of great interest, in part due to their being found on photo flights over large areas (Post 1969) and being seen while carrying out other field work. As most of Tarr and Martin's observations of sudden spasmodic advances were in Yakutat Bay, we can begin with the series of studies carried out at Variegated Glacier, which is just east of the Hubbard and discharges into the lower end of Russell Fiord; then consider the research efforts at Steele Glacier on the opposite side of the Icefield Range and its near neighbor, the Trapridge; and more briefly the aerial observations at several other glaciers in the Icefield Ranges that have surged in the last few decades.

Variegated Glacier

The work at Variegated Glacier was carried out from 1973 to 1985 by teams of scientists from three institutions led by Charles F. Raymond of the University of Washington; Will D. Harrison of the University of Alaska and Barclay Kamb of the California Institute of Technology. Other agencies such as the U.S. Geological survey also contributed personnel.

The study began in 1972 (Harrison 1972, pp. 455-456) following the observed surges in earlier years as reported in 1906 (Tarr 1909, p. 51), in the 1940s and in 1964-65 (Post 1969, p. 235). There followed six years of observations (Bindschadler et al 1977, pp. 181-194) before the next surge in 1982-83. Observations were continued throughout this more recent surge as discussed by Raymond and Harrison (1988) and various other authors in technical papers in *The Journal of Glaciology*, vols. 32-34, 1986-1987.

Steele Glacier

About 135 km due north of Yakutat Bay is Steele Glacier, formerly known as the Wolf Creek. Studies of the glacier were initiated by Walter Wood in 1935 with both aerial observations and the establishment of a network of survey-photo stations along the margins of the lower part of the glacier (Wood 1936). These observations were continued in 1936, 1939, and 1941. On the latter trip Sharp reviewed all the glaciers in the Steele Glacier drainage basin (Sharp 1947). Maps were greatly improved by those issued from aerial surveys by the Canadian Government in 1951 and 1956 and from a detailed survey by The Ohio State University Foundation in 1962 (*ICE*, No.11, 1963).

Thus an unusual amount of information about all these glaciers existed when the dramatic surge took place in 1965-1966. Its progress was recorded in considerable detail by various institutions including scientists from the Universities of British Columbia and Alberta (Wood 1967, 1972; Thomson 1972; and Stanley, 1969). At that time it could be said: "The 1965-66 surge of Steele Glacier, . . . is one of the best documented surge advances of a large glacier." (Clarke and Jarvis, 1974, p. 261).

Some observations on Steele Glacier have continued in the 1970s (Clarke and Jarvis, 1976).

Glaciers of Hazard Creek

In the 1960s several small glaciers at the head of Hazard Creek, tributary of Steele Creek, were identified as surge-type glaciers by Austin Post on one of his photo flights. With the increasing interest in surging glaciers these became objects of inquiry in the late 1960s and since then a great deal of research has been done there. All the scientists involved and their reports are too numerous to mention here. However, some comments are in order.

First of all the names of the glaciers and other features have been changed so that there can be some confusion between reports prior to 1972 and those published since then. What is now Hazard Creek had been originally called

PLATE 27

Photos by Bradford Washburn

Hubbard Glacier looking northeast at top. Bottom photo shows Hubbard advancing on Osier Island with Disenchantment Bay on left and Russell Fiord on right. When the glacier reached the island, for a few months Russell Fiord became Russell Lake. Photos on July 16, 1966.

North Fork River, tributary of Wolf Creek on Sharp's report of his work in 1941 (Sharp 1947) and now these features are officially known as Hazard Creek, tributary of Steele Creek. The first glacier on the north side of Hazard Creek, was then known as North Fork Glacier; now it is Hazard Glacier. The three other small glaciers unofficially referred to by Post as Fox, Jackal, and Hyena were officially named by the Canadian Government in 1972, respectively, as Rusty, Backe and Trapridge glaciers (Clarke 1972).

At the time of the surge of Steele Glacier in 1965-66, Hazard Creek became blocked and an ice-dammed lake was formed, now known as Hazard Lake. As part of the Icefield Ranges Research Project, studies were begun in 1967 of the whole drainage basin and of the glaciers in their pre-surge, surge, and post-surge conditions. Rusty Glacier was known to have surged in 1945, and another surge was expected in the 1960s. One reason for the interest in these small glaciers was, as seen elsewhere, that small glaciers lend themselves to research efforts where many of the parameters can be measured more effectively than at the larger and more complicated glacier systems.

Beginning 1967, scientists have been active in this area in all but possibly two years up to 1986. Although mentioned by Meier and Post (1969) on the basis of aerial observations, the first detailed studies were undertaken from 1967 to 1970 (Collins 1972) supported by the Arctic Institute of North America, the National Science Foundation, the Canadian Department of Energy, Mines and Resources, the Explorers Club, and the American Geographical Society. The next year Garry K.C. Clarke and David J. Crossley of the Department of Geophysics, University of Vancouver, British Columbia, began their studies (Crossley and Clarke 1970). Clarke was to continue and lead the work until 1986.

Rusty Glacier was one of the Canadian glaciers selected for special study during the International Hydrological Decade, 1965-1974.

Space does not permit additional references, but the reader will find articles not mentioned above on these glaciers in the *Journal of Glaciology*, Nos. 63, 70, 71, 74, 91, and 98, issued from 1972 to 1982; in *Icefield Ranges Research Project: Scientific Results*, vol. 3, 1972 and vol. 4, 1974; and in *ICE* from No. 33, 1970, to No. 85, 1987.

From the inception of IRRP there had been an objective of determining the thickness of the icefield up to one of its highest areas of over 8500 ft (2591 m) on the divide between the south-flowing Hubbard and the east-flowing Kaskawulsh glaciers. In 1963 a team from the University of Toronto, headed by Garry K.C. Clarke, carried out seismic depth studies along a profile (Clarke, IRRP vol. 1, 1972). This was followed up by radar soundings from an aircraft by Donald E. Nelsen of the Massachusetts Institute of Technology, over the same area and then extended along the entire Kaskawulsh Glacier and in the upper Donjek Glacier to an altitude of 12,500 ft (3810 m) (Nelsen, IRRP vol. 1, 1972).

Other observations were carried out over the years on these high névés on various aspects of glacial-meteorology, the general features of the climate, and the characteristics of the snow at various levels (Marcus 1965, Marcus & Ragle, 1970). Observations were also made of the glacial geology in the area and the history of glacier fluctuations in the Neoglacial period, roughly the last 10,000 years.

Throughout the period of the activities of the research on the Icefield Ranges, studies were carried out on various features of Kaskawulsh and Donjek glaciers.

High Mountain Environment Project

A related activity of IRRP was the High Mountain Environment Project which largely based its research efforts from 1966 to 1969 in the Chitistone Pass area which is between the St. Elias and Wrangell Mountains, and from 1967 to 1970 on the Mount Logan massif, the highest in the Icefield Ranges. An outline of the program appears in the first article in *IRRP Scientific Results*, Vol. 4, 1974, pp.1-11 by Melvin G. Marcus. Other accounts appear in succeeding articles in this same volume. The primary granting agency was the Army Research Office, Durham; and others were: U.S. Army Natick Laboratories; Institute of Aviation Medicine, Canadian Forces, Toronto; the University of Michigan; the Canadian Meteorological Service; and the National Science Foundation.

The Chitistone research objectives were outlined by Marcus who was principal investigator, including studies in climatology, geomorphology, glaciology, meteorology, and botany. Several glaciers around Chitistone Pass were examined. Logistical operations were handled by light aircraft based at Gulkana Airfield near Glenallen, Alaska.

The Mount Logan research was based on a station established in 1967 by a party led by Barry Bishop on the high summit plateau at 5360 m (17,586 ft) which is less than 700 m below the summit. It was serviced by the IRRP ski-wheeled Helio-Courier aircraft. In IRRP vol. 2 are articles by C.M. Keeler, and D. Alford and Keeler on the snow at that high level and in vol. 4 are observations of the climate by M.G. Marcus and J.P. LaBelle.

In closing this chapter on the glaciers of the Icefield Ranges, the writer must confess to having been overwhelmed by the amount and scope of the activity which has been going on since the 1930s. In an attempted summary it seems virtually impossible to cover all the work related to the glaciers and the glacial environment that has taken place in the last half century. Probably the worst casualty of this effort is the omission of the names of most of the participants who have done the work and the many government and private institutions in both Canada and the United States that made the effort possible.

In recent years much of the area of the Icefield Ranges in both Alaska and Yukon Territory has been included in the newly-established Wrangell-St. Elias National Park in Alaska and the adjacent Kluane National Park in the Yukon.

Historic Journeys Across the Icefields

The Icefield Ranges have such extensive névés that the early efforts to reach and climb the principal peaks required long journeys over the glaciers. Mount St. Elias was the first to be attempted in 1888 and the mountain itself was reached in 1890 and 1891 by the I.C. Russell party from the south and east across the Malaspina, and up Seward and Agassiz glaciers. After several other serious attempts, the summit was finally reached by the Duke of Abruzzi's party in July 1897.

An interesting record of late 19th century glacier travel was the attempt by prospectors to reach the interior by avoiding the dangerous passage past the glaciers along the lower Alsek River. This took place in the area east of Yakutat Bay, starting at Nunatak Glacier at the head of Russell Fiord. It required a trek of 80 to 90 km over the vast icefields which now are parts of Battle, Vern Ritchie, Tweedmuir, Fisher, and Lowell glaciers to the Alsek River, above the threatening glaciers from where the route to the interior was reasonably clear. According to Tarr and Martin (1914, p. 135), "in 1898 some 300 prospectors passed over the Nunatak Glacier highway to the Alsek Valley, and some returned by this route."

Other long journeys across the ice before the days of aerial support were made by U.S. and Canadian parties surveying the boundary between Alaska and Canada. In 1913, a party of U.S. and Canadian surveyors trekked up Logan Glacier from the Chitina Valley, then headed south up its tributary, the Baldwin, and continued across névés which now make up the head of Bagley Icefield and Columbus Glacier to the St. Elias massif. They then climbed the west shoulder to an altitude of 13,500 ft (4115 m) to establish a survey station almost exactly on the 141st meridian. This was 85 to 90 km from where they had first started up the ice. Their return journey was along the same route to the head of Chitina River (Green, 1982, pp. 168-172).

Twelve years later, in 1925, a joint Canadian-United States expedition climbed Mount Logan, again travelling up Logan Glacier, and turned up its tributary, the Ogilvie, which led directly to the western end of the massif. The route over the ice was at least 160 km round-trip. This was probably the last large mountaineering expedition in North America that required many days of glacier travel, before the advent of aircraft for reconnaissance, supply missions, and glacier landings.

Needless to say, the projects already referred to, such as the Juneau Ice Field Research Project in the Coast Mountains and the Project Snow Cornice and Icefield Ranges Research Project in the St. Elias, have depended heavily on aerial support as have almost all other such undertakings over the last forty years.

The Chugach Mountains

In this article the Chugach Mountains are considered to extend as the coastal range westward from the slopes of Mount St. Elias. What we refer to as the

Eastern Chugach extend from Mount St. Elias for about 210 km to the Copper River, which bisects the range. To the west of Copper River the Western Chugach form an arc around the head of Prince William Sound for a distance of some 270 km, ending at Portage Pass at the northwestern end of Prince William Sound, where the Kenai Mountains continue this coastal system to the southwest, ending at Cook Inlet.

The Eastern Chugach

The crest of the mountains are covered along most of their length by a huge névé called the Bagley Icefield which forms part of Bering Glacier, and smaller interconnected névés to the north, south, and west. They drain southward into Icy Bay and other rivers on the coastal plain, westward into the valley of Copper River, and northward into Tana and Chitina rivers, both eastern tributaries of the Copper.

The glaciers of this area will be considered beginning at Mount St. Elias and proceeding around the range; first, west along the coast, then up Copper River, and eastward along its tributary, the Chitina.

The first group of glaciers in the eastern Chugach drain into Icy Bay, which is immediately west of Malaspina Glacier and within 35 km of Mount St. Elias. Three glacier systems drain into it. The first is the Tyndall (c. 25 km), whose sources are on the southwestern slopes of Mount St. Elias; the second, the Yahtse (c. 60 km), which drains from Barkley Ridge, which forms part of the backbone of the Eastern Chugach; and the third is the Guyot (almost 30 km), which drains the eastern part of the Robinson Mountains. All three of these glaciers and some as yet unnamed tongues on the west side, discharge directly into tidewater. These are the only tidal glaciers of the eastern Chugach.

The glaciers of this bay have a history of oscillations. Geologists have determined that the bay existed between 1400 and 1700; again probably in the early 19th century. At other times it was occupied by an advance of the three glaciers. Since around 1900 another retreat has occurred which amounted to 17 km by 1965. As in Glacier Bay, it is an area of wide fluctuations, but in this instance the fluctuations are apparently over shorter periods of less than a century.

To the west of Icy Bay are the Robinson Mountains from which two glaciers, the Yakataga (24 km) and the Leeper (20 km), drain toward the Gulf but do not reach tidewater. Next to the west is Bering Glacier (203 km), which drains into the Gulf of Alaska by way of several short rivers. Its length of over 200 km and area estimated to be 5800 km^2 (Meier et al, 1966, p.8) rank it as the largest valley glacier outside the polar regions. Some 50 kilometers above the terminus it is 14 km across, then widens even more to a terminal area fully 45 km across and 80 km along the periphery of its lobate terminus which is fronted by a series of lakes less than 200 ft (60 m) above sea level. Most of this glacier is in Alaska, except for a small part of its upper source in Columbus Glacier in the Icefield Ranges of

Yukon Territory, which occupies the trench north of Mount St. Elias and between it and King Peak at the western end of the Logan massif.

West of the Bering is Martin River Glacier (48 km), which drains into the Copper River Delta.

Northwest of the Bering, there are four large glaciers that drain westward into Copper River: the Miles (52 km), Wernicke (33 km), Fan (34 km), and Bremner (44 km). On the northern side of the Eastern Chugach is the northward-flowing Tana Glacier (68 km), which drains into Tana River, a southern tributary of the Chitina, the main eastern tributary of the Copper; and three unnamed glaciers, the first (21 km) draining into Granite Creek, tributary of the Tana; the second (26 km) into Goat Creek, tributary of the Chitina; and the third (24 km), which flows into the head of the Chitina.

The Western Chugach

The extension of the Chugach Mountains west of Copper River is unofficially referred to as the Western Chugach. Here the range trending west bends around the head of Prince William Sound and turns southwesterly to end at Portage Pass, about 75 km southeast of the city of Anchorage. This part of the Chugach includes a series of high interconnected névés along the crest of the range, with several peaks rising between 10,000 ft (3048 m) and culminating in Marcus Baker, 13,176 ft (4016 m). The only break in this part of the range is Thompson Pass which is ice-free and now traversed by the Trans-Alaska Pipeline and the Richardson Highway, linking the town of Valdez with the interior highway system.

The glaciers can be listed in a clockwise direction beginning at the divide in the north between the westward-flowing Matanuska River, and the eastward-flowing Nelchina River, tributary of the Copper. The longest glaciers flowing northward into Nelchina River are the Nelchina (39 km) and Tazlina (47 km). Draining northeastward into Tasnuna River, tributary of the Copper, are the Woodworth and Schwan (both 23 km); then draining eastward directly into Copper River are Allen Glacier (31 km) and the Childs (19km). The southward-flowing glaciers draining into the flats near Cordova and west of Copper River are the Sherman (13 km), to be mentioned later, and the Sheridan and Scott (both 24 km). The southward-flowing glaciers draining into Prince William Sound are the Valdez (34 km), Columbia (c. 64 km), Meares (25 km), Yale (35 km), Harvard (39 km) and Barry (24 km). The glaciers flowing westward into the Cook Inlet drainage are the Lake George (24 km), Colony (29 km), the Knik (49 km), Marcus Baker (39 km); and at the western end of the Chugach, the Matanuska (46 km) and an unnamed (28 km).

The glaciers which presently reach tidewater in Prince William Sound are from east to west, the Shoup, Columbia, and Meares in the northeastern inlets; the Yale, Harvard, Smith, Bryn Mawr, and Wellesley in College Fiord; the

PLATE 28

Photos by Bradford Washburn

Looking north across Malaspina Glacier to Mount St. Elias. August 31, 1938 (at top). Lower photo shows Logan Glacier and Mount Logan. August 6, 1938.

Coxe, Barry, and Cascade in Barry Arm; and the Surprise and Harriman in Harriman Fiord.

Columbia Glacier

The most prominent and largest glacier in the Western Chugach is the Columbia, named for Columbia University, by the Harriman Expedition. It has attracted considerable attention since it was first visited by the geologist, G.K. Gilbert, and the geographer, Henry Gannett, of that party. Since its terminus is situated near the regular routes of commercial vessels, tourist ships, ferries, and local excursion boats, it has been visited by hundreds, even perhaps thousands, of people each year over most of this century.

The glacier has been of special interest because of its spectacular, active, main terminus at the head of Columbia Bay, some 3.8 km wide and 60 to 90 m high; and because in 1980 the terminus, unlike most tidal termini, had not changed its net position substantially since first mapped in 1899. However, in the 1970s, there was considerable evidence of widespread thinning in the lower end of the glacier, which if sustained might cause a massive recession which could increase the discharge of icebergs. The glacier was already calving icebergs only 8½ km (5½ miles) of open water from the ship channel, which since the 1970s was being used by oil tankers serving the southern terminus of the Trans-Alaska Pipeline at Valdez. An occasional berg had been known to float into the ship channel, so it was feared that a massive retreat might pose a more serious threat to this vital route of communication. Accordingly, in 1974 the U.S. Geological Survey began a long-term study of the glacier under the direction of Mark F. Meier. The lower part was mapped in detail and soundings were taken to determine the depths of water at the terminus and the thickness of the glacier in the lower 30 km. It was found that the bed of the glacier was below sea level for most of this distance. If the terminus were to recede to the head of the fiord, as tidal glaciers in retreat tend to do, a new fiord would be opened up of perhaps 30 km in length (*ICE*, No. 49, 1975, p. 14).

As expected and forecast in the models which had been constructed, the terminus began to recede in 1981 and continued each year until by 1987 it had broken back an average of about 3 km from its position in the 1970s. It turned out that a submerged moraine-shoal had been formed across the whole inlet where the terminus had been anchored since possibly the 18th century. This shoal had not been seen and its existence had not even been suspected until the 1960s. However, its existence helped to explain the unusual stability of the terminus in that area decade after decade. The shoal was entirely submerged to within 10 to 20 m of the surface where the main ice front had rested. After the retreat began, the shoal had the effect of blocking the large icebergs from floating out into Columbia Bay and into the ship channel in Port Valdez, but small bergs could still float over the bar. These were the bergs that were seen and were being avoided on March 24, 1989 by the tanker *Exxon Valdez* when it wandered off course and through a serious miscalculation on the part of those in the pilot house rammed into a reef and caused the worst oil spill in U.S. history.

The Geological Survey observations also recorded interesting and unusual rates of flow in the lower part of the glacier. From 1984 to 1986 the velocity of the ice a kilometer above the terminus averaged nearly 9 m per day with a maximum of up to twice that amount.

The likelihood is that the glacier will continue, with interruptions, to recede until some form of equilibrium between ice supply and loss can be attained. Many believe that under present climatic conditions this won't occur until the glacier has receded up through the area of deep water, in places over 400 m, to the head of the inlet, which as shown by the soundings through the ice, is some 25 to 30 km above the present 1987 termninus.

Between the present receding terminus and the moraine shoal, marking its position until 1981, the bay is choked with icebergs which have been calved, but are of too deep a draft to float over the bar. Therefore, in the last few years it has been virtually impossible for vessels to get past the shoal and close enough for a good view of the receding terminus. This now requires observations from aircraft or nearby ridges.

Glaciers West of Columbia Glacier

Other points of special interest in the Prince William Sound area of the Western Chugach are the magnificent fiord scenery and interesting glaciers in Unakwik Inlet, College Fiord, and Harriman Fiord.

Meares Glacier at the head of Unakwik Inlet has been advancing fairly steadily since first visited by a scientific party in 1905. It is one of the few in Alaska which are invading a forest over a century old.

Next to the west is Port Wells which opens up into College Fiord, Barry Arm and Harriman Fiord. These were first thoroughly explored and the glaciers named by the Harriman Alaska Expedition of 1899. Having named the first unnamed glacier they encountered in Prince William Sound for Columbia University, they continued this nomenclature in what they named College Fiord. Here the names, Amherst, Yale, Harvard, Radcliffe, Smith, Bryn Mawr, Vassar and Wellesley were applied. Since then several other glaciers in this fiord have been named for various other institutions. To a visitor in the 1980s who might refer to the pictures taken in 1899, the principal and obvious changes would only be a considerable recession of 2 to 3 km at Yale Glacier and an advance of nearly 2 km at the Harvard. This advance is not into forest, but a single tree with 246 annual rings was found in front of the terminus in 1935 and has since then been overrun. This proves that the glacier had not been farther forward since at least the late 17th century. College Fiord is now one of the most interesting and accessible fiords in western Prince William Sound and is now visited by an occasional cruise ship.

Barry Arm is headed by Coxe and the joint Barry and Cascade glaciers, which all discharge into tidewater. In Harriman Fiord are two tidal glaciers, the

Surprise and Harriman. The Surprise has not changed appreciably over the last few decades but the Harriman, after first retreating from 1899 to 1909 then readvanced about three-quarters of a kilometer by 1976.

At the western end of the Chugach Mountains is Eklutna Lake, 40 km northeast of Anchorage, which is fed primarily by Eklutna Glacier. For many years the runoff of Eklutna Lake has been used to generate electricity for the city of Anchorage. More recently a plan has been developed to begin using the lake for part of the Anchorage water supply system. To measure the volume and variations of the supply of water, the Anchorage office of the Geological Survey began studies of Eklutna Glacier in 1985 to determine its regime as the principal source of supply for this proposed reservoir. (*ICE* No. 86, 1988, p. 3)

About 55 km east of Anchorage and a little over 20 km southeast of Eklutna Lake is the Lake George complex, now consisting of the Lower, Inner, and Upper lakes, which occupy a basin some 20 km long with an outlet which flows through a gorge for some 6½ km between Knik Glacier and a 5755 ft (1755 m) mountain on the west. The lakes are fed by Lake George, Colony, and Knik glaciers and several others that are unnamed.

Knik Glacier is believed to have advanced within the last two or three centuries and formed an ice dam which blocked the outlet of Lake George and raised its level by as much as 160 ft (50 m). Prior to 1914 the dam may have remained intact for years at a time, as legends and local history suggest. Annual records were kept for many years because of the contruction of a bridge for the Alaska Railroad across Knik River, 27 km below the glacier. The ice dam formed each fall or winter from 1914 to 1962 and burst during the following warm season causing floods in the lower Knik River. Some of these caused considerable damage to settlements, the bridges of the Alaska Railroad and the Glenn Highway which links the city of Anchorage with the highways in the rest of Alaska. Since 1962, the dam formed occasionally in the early years and not at all since 1967 due to the recession of Knik Glacier.

As reported by Mayo and Trabant, of the USGS, who have studied the glacier: "A minor climatic change or flow instability could reform Lake George and renew the cycle of outburst flooding onto a flood plain that is subject to economic development." (*ICE*, No. 64, 1980, p. 3)

Farther to the east, the northward flowing Matanuska Glacier forms the main source of Matanuska River about 138 km north-northeast of Anchorage. It drains the extensive névés at elevations of 6000 to 12,000 ft (1829-3658 m) on the northern slopes of the Chugach Mountains along the divide with the Harvard Glacier system draining southward into College Fiord of Prince William Sound. The Matanuska lobate terminus is some 8 km long and extends to within 1 km of Glacier Highway where there is a tourist lookout for a view of the whole lower part of the glacier. Part of the terminus was studied in 1974 and 1975 by D.E. Lawson for the University of Illinois and in 1977 for the Cold Regions Research and Engineering Laboratory, U.S. Army.

Effects of the 1964 Earthquake

The March 1964 earthquake had its epicenter in the western Chugach between Unakwik Inlet and College Fiord. What appeared to be the most likely long-term effect on the glaciers in the Chugach Mountains were the rock slides which were triggered and fell on the glaciers, covering enough of their surfaces to affect their regimes. Seven slides were judged as likely to have a major impact on the glaciers (Ragle et al, 1965). Of these, two have received some detailed study. These were Sherman Glacier, east of the foreland between Cordova and the Copper River delta where aerial pictures and detailed terrestrial observations have been carried out, beginning in the summer of 1964 and up to at least 1987 by parties from the USGS, AGS, Institute of Polar Studies of The Ohio State University, and Muskingum College. The principal participants in the order of publication of results were: A.S. Post, 1965; W.O. Field, 1966; K.L. Shreve, 1966 and 1968; C. Bull and C. Marangunik, 1967 and 1968; G. Plafker, 1968; S.J. Tuthill et al, 1968; Bull, 1969; Marangunik, 1972, and Field, 1975.

The other slide that received attention was on a small glacier then unofficially referred to as Sioux Glacier, now named the Slide, which was studied by S.J. Tuthill of Muskingum College and John R. Reid of the University of North Dakota in 1965 and 1966 (Tuthill, 1966 and Reid, 1969).

The effects of the earthquake on iced-dammed lakes such as at Columbia, Nelchina, Tazlina, and Knik glaciers in the Chugach and Excelsior Glacier in the Kenai Mountains is discussed by M.G. Marcus (1968). Although he concluded that: ". . . ice-dammed lakes did not respond significantly to the earthquake", the article provides useful information on the location and characteristics of these lakes.

Travel Across the Chugach Mountains

The difficulty of travel across the Chugach Mountains has been a major problem since the days in the late 1890s when miners were trying to get from the coast to the goldfields in the interior. These difficulties continued as efforts were made to build railroads and later highways across these mountains. There were only two possible ice-free routes across the Chugach: (1) up Copper River past several large glaciers 25 to 70 km above its mouth; and (2) the route from Valdez up Lowe River through Keystone Canyon, over Thompson Pass, and down the Tsina and Klutina rivers to Copper Center. Once across the mountains there were reasonably good routes to the interior. Another possible route was to cross by way of the glaciers. As Tarr and Martin (1914, pp. 240-241) reported: "The ice pass sought was one formerly (1850-60) used by the Copper River natives on their way to Prince William Sound." It is not known for certain which glaciers had been followed, but by 1898 a route over Valdez and Klutina glaciers was in use. This required a trek over the ice of some 30 km up Valdez Glacier to the summit at about 1465 m and then 9 to 10 km down Klutina Glacier to its terminus at the head of Klutina River. Martin (1914) reported that "during February,

March and April of that year three thousand people landed at Valdez, and one or two thousand more came during the summer. . . . Mr. Charles Simonstad of Valdez, who crossed the glacier in 1898, states that 5000 men landed that year, that 4500 crossed the glacier pass, and that all but two or three hundred of them returned that fall by the same route. . . . In April and May 1898, some of the army detachments crossed the glacier pass several times. These men and the many prospectors encountered great hardships, being unprepared for glacier travel; . . . Nevertheless, it was quite an amazing feat to transport thousands of pounds of provisions and outfit, and even to take pack animals over the twenty-four miles of ice, twenty-three horses and mules being used by a single one of the army parties, and fourteen by another." (Tarr & Martin, 1914, p. 241) Few prospectors crossed the glacier pass in 1899 and it fell into disuse after the trail from Valdez up Lowe River, through Keystone Canyon and over Thompson Pass, was built. This route was followed decades later in the construction of the Richardson Highway connecting Valdez with the interior.

North of the summit of the pass, the highway crosses the moraines of Worthington Glacier, which from vegetation studies are now known to date from an advance that culminated in the middle of the 19th century. In 1976 the Alaska Pipeline from Prudhoe Bay to Valdez was built at this point next to the highway and only some 700 m from the Worthington Glacier terminus. It is not likely that the glacier will readvance that far, but a threat by ice or washouts remains.

Some 80 km to the south in Cordova, the construction of the Copper River and Northwestern Railroad up Copper River to the Kennicott Copper Mines was begun about 1907. At a point about 50 km up the Copper River it became necessary to erect a 430 m steel bridge, generally known as the Million Dollar Bridge, across the river between Childs and Miles glaciers. Childs Glacier discharges in a spectacular ice cliff directly into Copper River, while Miles Glacier across the valley, forms another ice cliff on the east side of Miles Lake which is part of the river. At that time the distance between the Childs and Miles termini was about 4 km. During the construction of the bridge both glaciers began to advance and by 1910 and 1911 the distance between the two glaciers was reduced by almost a kilometer. The Childs was surging. Lawrence Martin, reporting on his and the bridge-engineers' measurements, calculated that in the middle of the summer of 1910, the flow of ice at the terminus was "not less than 30 to 40 feet a day . . . and may well have been several times that amount." (Tarr and Martin, 1914, p.408) However, because of the undercutting of the advancing ice cliff by the swiftly-flowing river, the actual net daily advance was about 6½ feet (2 m). Even this was threatening, for the distance of the ice cliff to the bridge site had been reduced from 1000 m in 1909 to 450 m in 1911. As Martin pointed out there would have been no way to save the bridge if the advance had continued. Fortunately both glaciers ended their advance by 1911 and there have been no further serious threats since then.

At another point farther up the river, Allen Glacier ends in a great lobate terminus at the edge of the river. As another river crossing involving construction of two more bridges was deemed impractical, the tracks were laid along the river bank over the edge of the glacier. Martin reported: "Nowhere else in the world, so far as we know, is a railway built for 5½ miles upon the end of a living glacier . . . the level railway grade, which had been produced in 1909 by blasting out a shelf in the glacier ice and levelling it up with morainic ballast, was seriously modified in 1910. The slumping of the grade, due to melting of the ice beneath, amounted to two or three feet in many places and, at the maximum, amounted to over seven feet. Slumping at the water's edge showed that in 1910 the ice still extended out beneath Copper River." (Tarr and Martin, 1914, pp. 444-445) Martin also spoke of the "frequent breaking out of new streams, calling for new trestles, and in one case the shifting of a bridge support" and pointed out that "these difficulties will recur every summer." A quarter of a century later when we visited this stretch of track, washouts still occurred and disrupted traffic, although by then it was believed that there no longer was any ice immediately below the track.

Since this period of construction, the Kennicott Mine has been shut down and the railroad has been abandoned. What is known as the Copper River Highway was being built along the railroad right-of-way to connect Cordova with the Richardson Highway at Thompson Pass. By the late 1950s construction had reached the Million Dollar Bridge. Then in March 1964, the great earthquake knocked the northern section off its support and it fell partly into the river, where it remains. A new roadway has been built across the damaged span and construction has presumably been resumed farther up Copper River Valley.

Mining has also been carried out at a number of places in the Western Chugach. Several mines were operated in the first quarter of this century along the sides of Valdez Glacier. Access to and from these operations were on foot and by pack trains. Later the difficulties of operation were increased by the recession of the glacier in which the surface level at the mine sites were lowered so much as to leave these operations well above the glacier margins and difficult to reach. It then became impractical to continue.

Similarly, at Columbia Glacier a prospect was located some 12 to 13 km up the west side of the glacier. To reach it required travel up the glacier. One of the obstacles was to reach its surface from Columbia Bay to a point above the terminus. A road was built up through the woods around the western end of the ice cliff. Then the project had to be abandoned when the surface level was lowered 30 m or so in the 1920s, leaving a vertical cliff where the road issued from the forest onto the ice. Another mine on a nunatak on the east side of Columbia Glacier was operated successfully for a number of years in the second decade of this century, but in the end had to close because of the difficulties involved.

The Kenai Mountains

The Kenai Mountains are structually a continuation of the Chugach coastal mountains extending southwest onto the Kenai Peninsula from Portage Pass.

This mountain group is divided into two sections, separated by an ice-free pass through which the Alaska Railroad runs between the port of Seward at the head of Resurrection Bay and town of Portage at the head of Turnagain Arm, an eastward extension of Cook Inlet. These two sections will be referred to as northeastern and southwestern parts. Each is dominated by a large and a small icefield from which outlet glaciers radiate in various directions. The northwestern part is dominated by Sargent Icefield. The southwestern part is dominated by the extensive Harding Icefield which is an interesting example of an icecap where the névé is the dominant feature rather than the surrounding peaks which here rise only a few hundred meters above it.

The Kenai Mountains are lower than the other ranges discussed so far. Only a few peaks in both the northeastern and southwestern sections attain altitudes over 6000 ft (1829 m). The highest peaks seem to be 6532 ft (1991 m) on the edge of Sargent Icefield and 6316 ft (1926 m) overlooking Harding Icefield. Although lower than most parts of the coastal mountains which rim the Gulf of Alaska, these are so near the ocean that they receive a huge amount of snow which provides nourishment for the glaciers and cloudy summer months which result in cooler temperatures and a reduced rate of ablation.

Northeastern Section

The northeastern section is dominated by two groups of glaciers flowing outward from the two icefields, separated from each other by an ice-free valley. The northern and smaller one is situated between the valleys of Trail Creek and Placer River on the west and Nellie Juan River and Kings Bay, at the head of Port Nellie Juan, a western inlet of Prince William Sound, on the east. It is the source of glaciers draining into Trail Creek, Placer River, Portage Creek, Blackstone Bay, Kings Bay, and Nellie Juan River. None of these glaciers exceeds 20 km in length, but two on the northeastern side, the Blackstone and Beloit glaciers, reach tidewater and actively discharge icebergs into Blackstone Bay. Spencer Glacier, flowing westward, drains into Placer River within two kilometers of the tracks of the Alaska Railroad.

The southern of the two névés is known as the Sargent Icefield and is much the larger. Its area above 3000 ft (915 m) elevation is roughly 20 km in a northwest-southeast direction and 30 km in a northeast-southwest direction. Its longest outlet glaciers are the Chenega (22 km), Excelsior (24 km) and Ellsworth (27 km). Three glaciers, the Nellie Juan of Port Nellie Juan and the Chenega and Tiger of Icy Bay, discharge into tidewater.

Portage Glacier at the head of Portage Lake, which drains into Turnagain Arm by way of Portage Creek, is the site of a Forest Service Tourist Center within the Chugach National Forest. It is reached by a 80 km highway from Anchorage and is visited by thousands of tourists each year. In the 18th and early 19th centuries, Portage Glacier was recessed so that an ice-free pass existed from the head of Turnagain Arm on the Cook Inlet side to the head of Passage Canal on Prince William Sound and provided the only feasible low-level route across

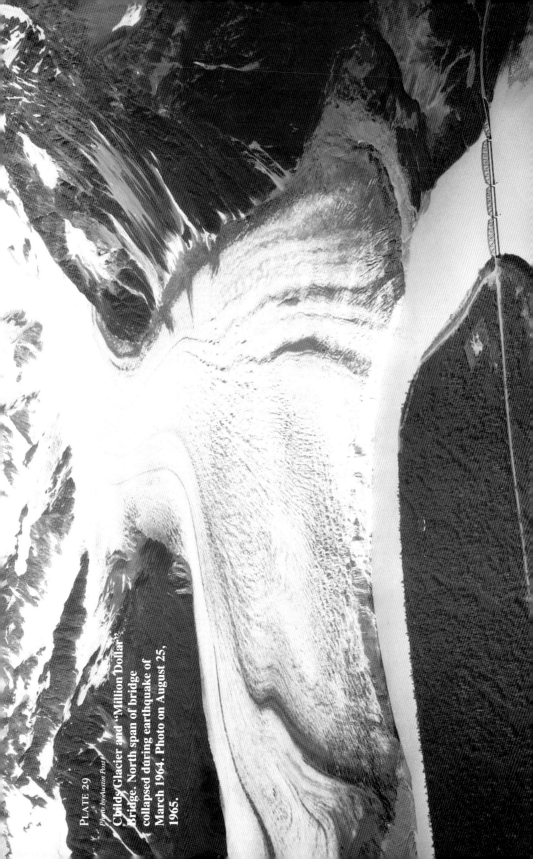

PLATE 29

Photo by Austin Post

Childs Glacier and "Million Dollar" Bridge. North span of bridge collapsed during earthquake of March 1964. Photo on August 25, 1965.

the coastal mountains between Copper River and Cook Inlet. From the head of Passage Canal the route was overland to the crest of the pass at slightly under 1000 ft in altitude, then down the valley to the head of Portage Creek which apparently presented no serious difficulties. To quote Tarr and Martin (1914, p. 362) "It is of particular interest because it occupies a low pass across the Kenai Mountains which was habitually crossed by the Alaskan natives and by the Russians previous to the explorations of Vancouver and Whidby in 1794, and probably later." The glacier then apparently advanced between 1794 and 1880, as suggested by Tarr and Martin (1914, pp. 364-365) blocking the ice-free route, but still remained passable despite the need to traverse the glacier for about 5 km. By 1912 Martin reports: "The glacier now fills this pass but it has, nevertheless, been used as a highway by a number of United States Army parties, and in 1898 by many prospectors." Since around 1914, the glacier has receded to near the pass, but in place of the outwash plain of the 18th century, is Portage Lake some 3 to 4 km long, which fills the valley from one steep rock wall to the other. Related to the advance of Portage Glacier in the 19th century and the subsequent recession in this century was the determination of the route of a spur of the Alaska Railroad to provide access from its main line at Portage to the new port of Whittier at the head of Passage Canal, which was established during World War II for a year-round ice-free port with access to Anchorage and the railroad.

Because of the lake and glacier blocking the route from Turnagain Arm to Portage Pass, it was necessary to reach Whittier by two tunnels one of which was 1.6 km long northeast of Portage Creek and the longer one 4.5 km between Bear Valley and the head of Passage Canal. The latter passes under the 4000-ft glacier-covered mountain on the northwest side of Portage Lake.

There are two features of some glaciological interest in the mountains of the northeastern section. One is the presence of an ice-dammed lake 7 to 8 km above the terminus of the large unnamed glacier at the head of Snow River. This lake occupies a depression on the margin of the glacier at an altitude of around 2700 ft (823 m) which is about 1000 ft (305 m) higher than the terminus. This lake drains out during some summer seasons, causing a flood down the valley of Snow River threatening the highway and railroad bridges and raising the water level of Kenai Lake enough to damage the docks and other installations along the lake front. When this ice-dammed lake seemed to be filled and about to drain, it was checked from the air so that adequate warning could be given to the people in the valley below.

Aside from observations of the fluctuations of the glaciers of this part of the Kenai Mountains and of the ice-dammed lake mentioned above, the only glaciological research has been undertaken at Wolverine Glacier. This is a relatively small hanging glacier, 8 km long, which drains into Nellie Juan River from a 5600 ft (1707 m) massif to the north. This glacier was selected by the Geological Survey for long term glacial-meteorological investigations as part of the detailed glacier basin studies of the International Hydrological Decade, 1965-1974. Observations have been continued up to the present.

Southwestern Section

As in the northeastern section, this one also has two névés, the northeastern one is Harding Icefield which is much the larger of the two. The southwestern one is separated from it by ice-free valleys on the peninsula extending southwest between Nuka Passage, an arm of the Gulf of Alaska, to Kachemak Bay at the mouth of Cook Inlet, on the west.

Harding Icefield

Harding Icefield is quite an extraordinary feature covering the crest of the Kenai Mountains southwest of Seward. Its undulating surface ranges from around 4000 ft (1220 m) to 5270 ft (1607 m) and is pierced in a few places by nunataks reaching from the 5000-ft (1524 m) elevation to a maximum of 6197 ft (1889 m). The icefield has 16 outlet glaciers which measure over 8 km in length. These have a total area of about 1380 km^2 so one can estimate that the névé is around 1200 to 1300 km^2. Its southeastern margin at the head of the outlet glaciers reaches within 10 km of tidewater and 30 km of the outer coast on the Gulf of Alaska. Mountaineers with skis have crossed the icefield, but the writer is not aware of any glaciological studies in the névé area.

Four glaciers flowing from Harding Icefield exceed 20 km in length, namely the Bear (27 km) of Resurrection Bay, Tustamena (32 km) flowing west into the upper end of Tustamena Lake, the Skilak (34 km) flowing northwest via Skilak River into Skilak Lake, and an unnamed (29 km) flowing north also into the Skilak basin. On the southwest side several glaciers plunge down steep slopes to discharge into tidewater. These are from northeast to southwest, the Aialik, Holgate, Northwestern, and McCarthy. Southwest of Harding Icefield and separated from it by the ice-free valley of the south-flowing Nuka River and the northerly-flowing Kachemak Creek and Bradley River, is an unnamed névé. For convenience it can be referred to as the Grewingk Icefield after its largest glacier, the Grewingk, which drains northwest into Kachemak Bay. This complex has no tidal glaciers and only four glaciers which attain lengths of 14 to 19 km.

In the last few years the Kenai Fiords National Park has been formed which includes the fiords between Resurrection Bay and Nuka Bay with its rugged coastal scenery, tidal glaciers, and varied bird and marine life. The area can be reached by excursion vessels from the port of Seward, which is the southern terminus of the Alaska Railroad and the Seward-Anchorage Highway.

In recent years a road has been built from Seward up Resurrection River for 12 km to the terminus of Exit Glacier, a rather dramatic ice stream which drains the northeastern part of Harding Icefield with a steep gradient dropping from 3000 ft (915 m) to 400 ft (120 m) in 4½ kilometers. Fronting its terminus is an interesting series of recessional moraines on which vegetation has taken hold and should provide a means of dating the recent fluctuations of this glacier.

The Alaska Railroad crosses the Kenai mountains on its scenic route between Seward and Portage. This section of the railroad is said to be the most difficult to maintain in winter of any part of the line between Seward and Fairbanks because of the excessively deep snow accumulation in this area, especially on the 1060 ft (323 m) divide between the head of Trail Creek and Placer River.

Along Placer River the railroad passes within a few hundred meters of both Bartlett and Spencer glaciers. When the railroad was being built in the early years of this century, Bartlett Glacier extended out into the valley blocking the only feasible route for the railroad to maintain an acceptable gradient. To get past this obstacle the tracks had to be laid on a wooden trestle over two kilometers long, including two loops, to cover the extra distance required to obtain the required gradient. The trestle was in use until the 1940s. By then, the glacier had receded far enough to allow the trestle to be abandoned and it became possible for a new right-of-way to be built on the terrain directly in front of the terminus from which the glacier had receded.

Another series of problems arose in passing in front of Spencer Glacier, which is over 18 km long and is one of the principal outlets of what we informally refer to as the Spencer-Blackstone Icefield. To circumvent the glacier the rails were laid along the crest of a late 19th century terminal moraine crossing Placer River by a steel bridge which at the time was within 200 ft (61 m) of the terminus (Viereck 1967, p.193). Another problem in building the railroad past Spencer Glacier was the threat of washouts at various points on the terminus. This required digging and blasting special drainage channels in the ice and over the outwash plain (Tarr and Martin, 1912). Their remains are still visible.

The first observations of the tidal glaciers at the heads of the fiords were made by U.S. Grant and D.F. Higgins of the Geological Survey in 1919. Two of the glaciers, the Northwestern at the head of Harris Bay and McCarty Glacier at the head of the east arm of Nuka Bay were then close to a maximum position marked by a trimline of old trees. Since then and up to 1968 the Northwestern has receded about 25 km and the McCarthy about 20 km. These instances of recession are only exceeded by the Muir in Glacier Bay and the Guyot in Icy Bay near Mount St. Elias.

The Wrangell Mountains

The Wrangell Mountains form a huge volcanic mass with six volcanoes over 12,000 ft in elevation which culminate in Mounts Blackburn (16,573 ft, 5052 m), Sanford (16,237 ft, 4949 m), and Wrangell (14,005 ft, 4269 m). The range lies northwest of the Icefield Ranges of the St. Elias Mountains and separated from it by two ice-free passes, the Chitistone (5822 ft, 1775 m) and the Scolai (4665 ft, 1422 m). The dimensions of the range are approximately 150 km from southeast to northwest and 125 km from northeast to southwest with an area of ice cover of 4195 km^2 (Denton, *Mountain Glaciers*, vol. 2, 1975, p. 552).

The crest of the range is covered by an extensive icefield which drains from the summits of both Mounts Blackburn and Wrangell to form Nabesna Glacier, 87 km long, with an area of 819 km^2.

Three-quarters of the drainage from these mountains is into Copper River either through small tributaries or via its principal eastern tributary, the Chitina. The rest of the drainage is from two glaciers on the north and northeast, the Nabesna and Chisana, which drain into Tanana River, and several smaller tongues into White River, both tributaries of Yukon River.

The glaciers 20 km or more in length beginning at Chitistone Pass and proceeding clockwise around the range are as follows: Nizina (51 km), Kennicott (44 km), Kuskulana (25 km), Kluvesna (22 km), Long (39 km), Sanford (27 km), two unnamed (20 and 21 km respectively), Drop (24 km), an unnamed (23 km), Copper (29 km), Nabesna (87 km) and Chisana (39 km).

In the early days there were various routes across the glaciers used by prospectors to reach the mining regions in the interior. H.F. Reid reported (1911 p. 89) in 1909: "The Nizina Glacier was formerly crossed by prospectors going to the White River region, but it has become so crevassed as to be practically impassable." Andy Taylor, who had been on the successful climb of Mount Logan in 1925, used to recall his winter trips with a dogsled carrying the mail over the glaciers to Chisana and other localities in the interior.

The biggest mining development in the area was the Kennicott Copper Mine which operated on the slopes 5 km above the terminus of Kennicott Glacier. According to Janson, (1975, pp. 145-155) work began in 1907 and reached full production when the Copper River and Northwestern Railroad was completed in 1911. By 1915, 750 tons of ore were being mined each day and over the years it constituted an estimated 90% of the total Alaska output of copper. Janson wrote: "By the 1920s the golden dream had faded. Still riding high on Kennicott copper, Cordova remained the 'Premier Copper Port of the World,' with still a million dollars a month of the red metal coming from the Wrangell Range" (p.155). This all ended during the great depression when the price of copper tumbled and by the mid 1930s little copper was mined at all. The last train ran on November 11, 1938 and shortly thereafter the rails were removed along with some segments on the route. Parts of this right of way have now been converted to what is called the Copper River Highway.

Aside from mountaineering efforts to climb the highest peaks and to cross the range to the interior, the summit of Mount Wrangell has been the scene of some interesting scientific studies sponsored by the University of Alaska. Mount Wrangell is not only the highest active volcano in Alaska, but is also the farthest north active volcano along the Pacific rim. This project deserves a full chapter but must be covered here in a few sentences.

The first effort was the establishment of a station for cosmic ray observations in 1953 in cooperation with New York University (Korff 1953). The party was flown to a base camp at 8500 ft on the west side of the mountain from where the scientists walked to the summit. Terris Moore in a Piper Super Cub made 30 landings and take-offs on the summit plateau.

In 1961 scientists led by Carl S. Benson of the University of Alaska continued the research work on Mount Wrangell (Benson, 1961). These studies of the summit conditions and the effects of the mountain's internal heat on the snow and ice cover of this still active volcano have continued ever since. In 1982 a team let by G.K.C. Clarke of the University of British Columbia joined Benson's group and carried out an airborne radar sounding survey of the glacier in the Mount Wrangell caldera. This indicated an ice thickness of 900 m (Narod et al, 1988 and Clarke, 1989). This led to a proposal to carry out an ice core drilling program in this caldera from which to determine the volcanic history of the mountain since as far back as, perhaps, the 7th century A.D.

For further notes on this interesting project, see *ICE* Nos. 28, 1968; 44, 1974; 49, 1975; 64, 1980; 72-73, 1983; and 77, 1985. Related to these studies were those made on the volcanoes of the Tordrillo and Chigmit Mountains in the southwestern part of the Alaska Range, to be mentioned in that chapter.

The Alaska Range

The Alaska Range is the longest mountain mass in Alaska and in the adjacent parts of Canada. The heavily glacierized area extends for roughly 950 km from Mentasta Pass at the eastern end to the depression at the head of Kamishak Bay on the western side of Cook Inlet. Except in some areas where there are few glaciers, such as around Rainy Pass at the head of Skwentna River, there are glaciers over 20 km long from one end of the range to the other. The range is bisected by rivers or ice-free passes at a number of places which provide a basis for dividing the area into the following groups, named after the dominant mountain in each. East of Mentasta Pass are the eastern outliers of the range in the Mentasta Mountains which lie northeast of the Wrangell Mountains and extend eastward to Nabesna River. A few small glaciers exist around the highest peaks, notably Noyes Mountain, (8235 ft, 2511 m).

Beginning at Mentasta Pass and extending westward about 160 km to Delta River, is an area dominated by Mount Kimball (10,300 ft, 3140 m). Delta River rises south of the range and flows north into the Tanana-Yukon drainage. Here is Gakona Glacier (32 km), draining south into the Copper River drainage. The northern drainage into Delta River from west to east are the Canwell (24 km) and the Castner (20 km). To the east draining into Tanana River are Gerstle Glacier (24 km), the Johnson (33 km), an unnamed (24 km) and the Robertson (22 km). Both the Canwell and Castner glaciers terminate within 3 km of the Richardson Highway which crosses the range along the valley of Delta River.

The next group extends westward from Delta River to the valley of Nenana River, which rises at Broad Pass south of the main range, and flows northward to Tanana River. This pass is the route of the Alaska Railroad and the George Parks and Denali highways. The highest peak in this group is Mount Hayes (13,832 ft, 4216 m), and several mountains rise to over 11,000 ft (3353 m). The longest glaciers on the south side are the Susitna (36 km) and the West Fork (41 km), which flow southward into Susitna River of the Cook Inlet drainage. Those in the north, draining into Nenana and Delta rivers, tributaries of the Tanana, are from west to east the Yanert (35 km), the Gillam (25 km), Hayes (20 km), Trident

(28 km) and Black Rapids (40 km). The last mentioned terminates on the flats bordering Delta River within 2 km of the Richardson Highway. It has commanded considerable attention during surges since the 1930s when it was feared it might endanger the highway (Matthes 1942, pp. 199-200).

The next group to the west extends southwesterly from Nenana River to Rainy Pass which is between the basin of Skwentna River of the Cook Inlet drainage and the headwaters of Kuskokwim River which flows into Bering Sea. The two dominant peaks of this area are Mount McKinley (Denali) (20,320 ft, 6193 m) and Mount Foraker (17,400 ft, 5303 m). The glaciers of the southern drainage all flow into the Susitna River system. From east to west they are the Eldridge (48 km), Buckskin (23 km), Ruth (63 km), Tokositna (44 km), Kahiltna (76 km), Yentna (51 km), and Dall (35 km).

The northern drainage at the western end is Chedotlothna Glacier (27 km), which flows into Kuskokwim River. To the east all in the Yukon River drainage are from west to east; Herron Glacier (25 km), Foraker (25 km), Straightaway (22 km), Peters (27 km), and Muldrow (61 km). All of these glaciers drain from the slopes of the main peaks from Mount Mather (12,123 ft, 3696 m) on the east, to Mount Russell (11,670 ft, 3557 m) on the west. All these peaks are included in the original Mount McKinley National Park, now known also as the Denali National Park and Preserve. Several of these glaciers, including the Muldrow, have had surges in recent decades.

From Dall Glacier to Rainy Pass the peaks are somewhat lower and apparently receive less moisture, so the glaciers are much smaller. Although there are several ice-free passes across the range in this area, the only established route is a trail through Rainy Pass.

In the general area of Rainy Pass, the range divides with a spur heading south-southwest and the highest ridge trending south some 140 km to Merrill Pass which marks an ice-free valley through the range west of Chakachamna Lake. This ice-covered mountain group is dominated by Mounts Gerdine (11,258 ft, 3432 m), Torbert (11,413 ft, 3479 m), and Spurr, an active volcano (11,070 ft, 3375 m). These mountains are also called the Tordrillo Mountains.

There are four glaciers over 20 km long in this section and all drain from these same peaks into Cook Inlet by either the Skwentna River, tributary of the Susitna, or the Beluga River. These glaciers are from north to south, the Hayes (48 km), Trimble (33 km), Triumvirate (45 km), and Capps (42 km).

On the ridges west of the massifs of Mounts Gerdine and Spurr are many small glaciers which extend out to the edge of the range and flow either into the Skwentna River drainage of the Cook Inlet drainage or into various tributaries of Kuskokwim River which empties into Bering Sea.

The next mountain group and the southernmost of the Alaska Range extends from Merrill Pass 225 km south to the lowland between Illiamna Lake on the west and Illiamna Bay on the west side of lower Cook Inlet. This mountain group is dominated by two active volcanoes, Redoubt Volcano (10,197 ft, 3108 m) and Mount Illiamna (10,016 ft, 3053 m). The most recent eruption has been that of Redoubt in December 1989. This group of mountains is also referred to as the

Chigmit Mountains and by some authorities is considered part of the Aleutian Range.

The largest glaciers in this area all drain into Cook Inlet. From north to south they are Shamrock (26 km), Blockade (44 km), unnamed (30 km), Double (26 km), unnamed (20 km), Tuxedni (25 km), and unnamed (27 km).

West of the main ridge, of which Redoubt Volcano and Mount Illiamna are the main peaks, are many ridges with smaller glaciers which drain into Stony River, tributary of the Kuskokwim, the Mulchatna-Nushagak river system, and into the Lake Clark drainage, both of which drain into Bristol Bay of Bering Sea.

The writer knows of only a few detailed glaciological studies in the Alaska Range. In the Mount Hayes group, observations have been made at Gulkana Glacier by members of the University of Alaska since the early 1960s. Two small glaciers, the Polychrome in Mount McKinley National Park and the West Gulkana in the Mount Hayes Group were surveyed by the American Geographical Society and the U.S. Navy Heavy Photographic Squadron as part of the International Geophysical Year program in 1957 and 1958. The two maps were published by the AGS in its publication *Nine Glacier Maps*, in 1960. The survey of the West Gulknan was repeated by a party from Arizona State University led by M.G. Marcus, in a cooperative undertaking with the U.S. Military Academy at West Point in 1987-1988. Adams Carter in 1958 and Carter and David Atherton in 1960 did glaciological studies on the Eldridge Glacier as reported in *AAJ, 1959 and 1961*.

Another important detailed survey of the lower 37 km of Muldrow Glacier in the Mount McKinley area was carried out by Bradford Washburn in 1976 and 1977 in cooperation with the Museum of Science in Boston, and the Swiss Foundation for Alpine Research in Zurich. The map has been published in five sections on a scale of 1:10,000 with 10 meter contours on the glacier and 20 m elsewhere.

Observations have also been carried out on Black Rapids Glacier by University of Alaska and U.S.G.S. parties in the Mount Hayes group which terminates within 2 km of Delta River and the Richardson Highway which follows along the east bank of the river.

In addition to traverses of glaciers to reach the principal summits in the Mounts Hayes and McKinley groups, aerial landings for the ascent of Mount McKinley have been made for years on Ruth Glacier, providing access to the western and southern ridges of Mount McKinley and the other high peaks in that area.

Another unusual activity has been the training of U.S. Army mountain troops from Fort Wainwright in Fairbanks on Gulkana Glacier on the southern slopes of the Mount Hayes group. This glacier is about 10 km long and only 7 to 8 km from the Richardson Highway, so access can be handled by both surface vehicles and helicopters.

Another activity connected with the glaciers has been the use of their drainage as a source of water for gold-mining activities. Instances of this were reported in the early days of this century in the headwaters of the Chistochina

River, tributary of the Copper, on the south side of the Mount Hayes group. (Mendenhall, 1905, p. 106)

In the Alaska Range are two large areas set aside as National Parks. Foremost is Mount McKinley National Park (now Denali National Park and Preserve), established in 1917, which includes the highest peaks and longest glaciers around Mounts McKinley and Foraker. About 170 km to the south-southwest, at the southern end of the Alaska Range, is the recently established Lake Clark National Park and Preserve. Its glaciers, although smaller than those around Mount McKinley, are of no less scientific interest because of their positions in the subsidiary ridges west of the high glacier-covered peaks between Mount Gerdine and Illiamna Volcano, and fronting on the drier and lower ridges at the heads of the eastern tributaries of the Kuskokwim and Mulchatna rivers of the Bering Sea drainage. In 1987 the Park Service initiated a long-term monitoring program of the glaciers in this park in what was described as a climatically sensitive zone (Matthew Sturm, personal communication).

Other Glacierized Areas

In earlier pages we have pointed out the scientific significance of the smaller glaciers in both the principal mountain ranges and in the more remote, generally lower, outlying ranges. These, although far less spectacular than the larger ones and those that discharge into tidewater, are important as useful recorders of any slight changes in climate. They are the first to show from superficial observations any growth or decrease in size and in some areas they may double in size or disappear within a few decades, whereas in long glaciers changes in length and other easily detectable signs may not be evident for many years or even decades.

The ranges which have not yet been discussed as they do not have glaciers of 20 km or more in length are mostly in somewhat different climatic zones or have generally lower elevations. These include the glaciers of the following areas listed in the order to be considered: the islands of the Alexander Archipelago of southeastern Alaska; the islands of Prince William Sound; Kodiak Island off the Alaska Peninsula; the Talkeetna Mountains lying between the Chugach and the Alaska Ranges; the Aleutian Range of the Alaska Peninsula; the Aleutian Islands; The Brooks Range of Arctic Alaska; and the small isolated mountain groups north of the Aleutian Range in the Bristol Bay area and on Seward Peninsula in western Alaska.

The Alexander Archipelago

Four of the islands of the Alexander Archipelago definitely have glaciers, while one island is believed to have one or two small cirque glaciers which are not shown on existing maps.

The largest concentration of glaciers is on Baranof Island on the main ridge east of Sitka at 4000 to around 5300 ft (1220-1616 m). Most are summit and cirque glaciers, but there may also be a few small valley glaciers. Chichagof, Admiralty, and Prince of Wales Islands each have one or more small glaciers, and one massif between 3000 and 4000 ft (915-1220 m) in height on Kupreanof Island has been reported to have one or two small cirque glaciers, possibly already in remnant stage.

The Islands of Prince William Sound

Of the many islands in Prince William Sound only Montague Island has a series of conspicuous and well-mapped glaciers along its principal ridge where the highest peaks range from 2500 to just under 3000 ft (762-914 m). One or two small cirque glaciers have been reported on Knight Island in the vicinity of a 3104 ft (946 m) peak, but they are not shown on maps and may be in a relict stage.

Kodiak Island

Kodiak Island which lies off the southern coast west of Cook Inlet has mountains reaching up to 3491 ft (1064 m). Wahrhaftig (p. 40) reports: "There are 40 cirque glaciers, all less than 2 miles long. . . ."

Talkeetna Mountains

The Talkeetna Mountains lie north of the Western Chugach and extend about 160 km north to south and 130 east to west. Drainage is into the Gulf of Alaska via tributaries of the Matanuska, Susitna, and Copper rivers. Glaciers are restricted to the highest peaks and ridges where elevations range from 6000 to 8800 ft (1829-2683 m). Only seven glaciers exceed 8 km in length and four of these are over 10 km. The two largest are an unnamed glacier (17 km) at the head of Sheep Creek, and the Chickaloon (14 km) at the head of Chickaloon River. The total area of ice in this range is estimated to be about 300 km^2 and a few glaciers appear to be virtually stagnant and reaching the relict state. (Collins, MGNH)

The Aleutian Range

This range forms the backbone of the Alaska Peninsula for about 750 km from the lowland between Lake Illiamna and Kamishak Bay to the tip of the Peninsula at False Pass. The whole Aleutian Range as well as the southern end of the Alaska Range are made up of a series of volcanoes some of which are active and most of which have glaciers on their summits and flanks.

Although there are no glaciers over 20 km in length in the Aleutian Range, there is one glacier of 19 km and 26 others which are over 8 km long. Many of them are unnamed.

Photos by Austin Post

PLATE 30

Sherman Glacier on August 16, 1963 at top. Bottom photo shows debris from earthquake of March 1964 as it appeared on August 25, 1965. The lower end of the slide reached the terminus in the early 1980s.

The first group of glaciers south of Kamishak Bay mantle the massifs of Mount Douglas (7064 ft, 2154 m) and Fourpeaked Mountain (6903 ft, 2105 m). These give rise to seven glaciers ranging from 8 to 14 km in length. The next group about 25 km to the southwest are around Mount Katmai and entirely in Katmai National Park and Preserve. This group consists of some nine ice-covered volcanoes, extending for about 75 km from Mount Denison (7600 ft, 2317 m) in the northeast to Martin Mountain (6050 ft, 1845 m) on the southwest. These peaks give rise to numerous glaciers of which 13 range from 9 km to the longest in the Aleutian Range, Hallo Glacier (19 km), which flows from sources on Mount Denison, Kukak Volcano and Mount Steller, ranging from 6700 ft to 7606 ft (2043-2319 m).

The top of Mount Katmai (now 6715 ft, 2047 m) blew off in the great eruption of 1912, decapitating its glaciers and leaving in its place a lake and ice-filled crater some 2 km in diameter.

About 120 km southwest of the Katmai Group are the small glaciers of Icy Peak and 30 km beyond that, those of Mount Chiginagak, an active volcano around 7000 ft (2134 m) high. Although some maps show no glaciers on Mount Chiginagak, the upper 1200 m of the mountain were reported to be covered with snowfields and glaciers by Smith and Baker (1924, p. 156).

Another 80 km southwest of Mount Chiginagak is Aniakchak Crater, with a caldera 9.6 km in diameter and glaciers lining its southern perimeter. The whole area is now included in Aniakchak National Monument.

Another huge caldera, Mount Veniaminof, rises 110 km farther to the southwest. Its highest point is 8225 ft (2508 m) and the crater is 8½ km across. It is described as ". . . filled with a great circular glacier, 8 to 10 km in diameter which overflows in three directions." (Knappen 1929, p. 180).

Some 200 km southwest of Veniaminof is the group dominated by the active Pavlov Volcano (8905 ft, 2715 m). Here, as in other volcanic peaks, the glaciers are mixed in with old lava flows and a covering of ash which makes it difficult to define the exact limits of the present ice cover.

The Aleutian Islands

The Aleutian Islands extend westward some 1900 km from False Pass at the southern end of the Alaska Peninsula to the westernmost island in the chain. Wahrhaftig estimated that there are 57 volcanoes on these islands of which 27 are reported as active. He adds: "Most high volcanoes bear icecaps or small glaciers and there are a few cirque glaciers on the mountainous islands." (1965, p. 23). At least seven of the islands are reported to have glaciers.

The easternmost and the largest of these islands is Unimak, with two of the highest peaks in the Aleutians: the active and unusually spectacular Shishaldin Volcano (9372 ft, 2812 m) and Isanotski Peaks (8025 ft, 2447 m) and its neighbor Roundtop Mountain (6140 ft, 1872 m), all sharing the same ice cover. To the southwest at the far end of the island is Progromni Volcano (6568 ft,

2002 m) and its two neighbors, each over 5000 ft (1524 m) with a reported 26 km^2 of glacier ice.

According to Wahrhaftig (1965, p. 33) west of Unimak Island the firn line on the glaciers rises from about 3000 ft (915 m) to about 4500 ft (1372 m), so that the mountains rising higher than that are likely to have glaciers.

Unalaska Island, the next west of Unimak, is said to have the heaviest ice cover of the Aleutian chain on its highest peak, Makushin Volcano (6680 ft, 2004 m) (Sharp 1956, pp. 101-102).

West of Unalaska, glaciers are reported on Mount Vsevidof (6920 ft, 2076 m), Mount Recheschnoi (6510 ft, 1953 m), and in Okmok Caldera (3400 ft, 1037 m) on Umnak Island; at Korovin Volcano (4852 ft, 1456 m) on Atka Island; at Great Sitkin Volcano (5740 ft, 1722 m) on Great Sitkin Island; at Tanaga Volcano (5925 ft, 1806 m) on Tanaga Island; at Mount Gareloi (5160 ft, 5173 m) on Gareloi Island. At Kiska Volcano (3996 ft, 1199 m) on Kiska Island a small glacier, possibly in a relict stage, was reported by William L. Putnam as being in existence in 1943. (Henderson and Putnam 1947, p. 32)

The Brooks Range

The Brooks Range extends some 900 km from the De Long Mountains east of Point Hope in the Chukchi Sea to the Alaska-Yukon Boundary. All of it is above the Arctic Circle, so the glaciers are primarily of the sub-polar type, with ice temperatures below freezing except for a surface layer during the summer months.

Small glaciers occur mostly in the central and eastern Brooks Range over a distance of some 650 km. The largest concentration of ice is in the Franklin and Romanzof Mountains at the eastern end.

According to Wahrhaftig (1965, p. 22): "Small cirque glaciers are common in the higher parts of the range, in the Schwatka Mountains and the mountains around Mount Doonerak. The firn line is at an altitude of about 6000 ft in north-facing cirques and about 8000 ft in south-facing cirques." Mount Doonerak is one of the dominant peaks in the central Brooks Range with its height shown in various sources ranging from 7610 ft (2320 m) to 8800 ft (2683 m). The lower figure is the most likely to be correct. In the Philip Smith Mountains east of Mount Doonerak are many small, mostly cirque, glaciers and there are several glaciers in the spectacular granite Arrigetch Peaks, 6000-7200 ft (1829-2195 m) in the western part of the Brooks Range.

The glaciers in the Franklin and Romanzof Mountains of the eastern Brooks Range have commanded the most attention, in part because they appear to be the only valley glaciers in Arctic Alaska. This area is dominated by Mount Chamberlin (9020 ft, 2750 m) and Mount Michelson (8855 ft, 2699 m), probably the highest in the Brooks Range, and by far the source of the greatest concentration of glaciers. The Romanzof Mountains have the largest glaciers with some 260 km^2 of ice cover and one glacier, the McCall, almost 8 km in length.

Detailed glaciological studies were carried out at McCall and Chamberlin glaciers in the International Geophysical Year 1957-1958. The Arctic Institute of North America carried out the work at the McCall, and the Air Force Cambridge Research Center at Chamberlin Glacier in 1958. Since then occasional studies have been continued at McCall Glacier.

The McCall was also surveyed by a party from the American Geographical Society (AGS) with the cooperation of the Arctic Institute and the U.S. Air Force. The resulting map on a scale of 1:10,000 with 5 m contours on the glacier and 25 m elsewhere was published in the report, *Nine Glacier Maps: Northwestern North America*, by the AGS in 1960.

The glaciers of the Brooks Range are of great interest climatically. Hamilton (1986, p.10) states: "The climate . . . ranges from arctic in the northern valleys to subarctic in the south and from continental in the eastern and central areas to maritime in the west. . . . Modern glaciers in the Brooks Range are nourished by precipitation derived from the Bering Sea to the west, the North Pacific Ocean to the south, and the Arctic Ocean to the north. Past changes in those moisture sources should have been reflected in the relative extents of ice advances in different sectors of the range, as well as in the extent of Brooks Range glaciation relative to that farther south in Alaska."

This adds significance to the need of maintaining a record of glacier fluctuations in the Brooks Range which may be important in assessing whatever climatic changes may occur during the next century, due to such factors as changes in the ice cover of the Arctic Ocean, temperatures of the world's oceans, and in the direction of prevailing moisture-laden winds in northern and central Alaska.

The Small Isolated Glacierized Mountain Groups in Western Alaska

The principal glacierized area in western Alaska north of the Alaska Peninsula, is in the Kilbuck Mountains at the southwestern end of the Kuskokwim Mountains, north of Bristol Bay and between the Kuskokwim and Nushagak rivers. These mountains are also called the Tikchik and Wood River Mountains. The highest elevations are around 5000 ft (1525 m) with the highest prominent peak, Mount Waskey (5026 ft, 1532 m). The largest glacier in the area, which has been named the Chikuminuk is about 5 km long with sources in mountains ranging from 4430 to 4595 ft (1350 to 1400 m). It was surveyed by an AGS party in cooperation with the Institute of Geodesy, Photogrammetry and Cartography at the Ohio State University and the U.S. Navy in 1958-1959 and published on a scale of 1:10,000 with 5 m contours on the glacier and 25 m contours elsewhere. (Map No. 8 in *Nine Glacier Maps, 1960*)

In regard to the Seward Peninsula, which is the westernmost part of Alaska, forming the east side of Bering Strait, there is a general concept, reported by Wahrhaftig (1965, p. 31) that "The Seward Peninsula has no glaciers." Yet there have been reports of small, probably relict, ice masses in cirques in the Kigluaik

Mountains on the Seward Peninsula, north of Nome, where the dominant peak seems to be Mount Osborn (4714 ft, 1437 m).

In the 1955 to 1957 period, when the volumes entitled *Geographic Study of Mountain Glaciation in the Northern Hemisphere* were being researched, there was an exchange of letters with David M. Hopkins of the USGS who had been working on the geology of the Seward Peninsula and on developments during the Pleistocene glaciation when, due to a lowered sea level, a land bridge existed across Bering Strait. He reported in 1956 that "living glaciers are found on Seward Peninsula only in the Kigluaik Mountains. . . . Glaciers were reported in three locations in early Geological Survey publications . . . , but these glaciers have all disappeared." From aerial pictures taken in 1949 and 1950 he located three previously unknown glaciers in the same area. He continued: "The largest glacier on Seward Peninsula . . . lies at the head of the middle fork of Grand Union Creek. It is about a mile long. . . . Smaller cirque glaciers are found at the head of the unnamed tributary of the Pilgrim (Kruzgamapa) River next above Grand Union Creek and at the head of the east fork of the valley of Glacial Lake. . . ." (Hopkins 1956, personal communication cited by Camilla McCauley, MGNH). So far as the writer knows there has been no more recent information since then. These glaciers may well be relict and on the verge of extinction, but nevertheless merit some attention to determine if they still exist and their present status.

The Longest Valley Glaciers Outside the Polar Regions

The question often arises as to which are the longest valley glaciers outside the Polar Regions. Unlike the heights of mountains, the length of glaciers not only vary as their termini advance or retreat, but the exact upper limits of their drainage basins are often difficult to determine, as many maps presently available have contour lines often too far apart to determine the point where the down-valley flow begins. Therefore, the determination of glacier lengths measured along the flow line is to some extent subject to differences in methods of measurement and may vary by one or two kilometers, and different researchers could quite easily arrive at somewhat different results.

The glaciers in Table 2 are listed in order of length according to what appear to be the most reliable data. In some cases they may not reflect unusual advances or recessions that have occurred in the last decade or two or in any recent corrections made on the maps from which they are taken. Many of these data were compiled in the late 1960s and the early 1970s for two reports compiled from literature surveys undertaken at the AGS. (See references)

In Alaska, the lengths were determined mostly from the USGS 1:63,360 series (Topographic) and in the Yukon from the sheets of the National Topographic System of Canada on a scale of 1:250,000. In other parts of the world lengths were determined from the literature and maps available at the time at the AGS. When the exact location of the upper sources of a glacier is in doubt the length is given as approximate, but is thought to be accurate within one or two kilometers.

All the glaciers listed which are in North America are either in Alaska (U.S.) or the Yukon (Canada). A number of the glaciers are in both, so the nation in which the terminus is located is shown first and the one which includes the source area second.

The sources referred to, listed alphabetically, are:

Kremmel, Robert M. (1987) *Columbia Glacier in 1986: 800 Meter Retreat.* U.S. Geological Survey Open-file Report 87-207, p. 2.

Meier, Mark F. et al. (1966) "Field Work; USA." U.S. Geological Survey, Tacoma, Washington in *ICE*, No. 22, pp. 7-8.

Mercer, John H. *Southern Hemisphere Glacier Atlas* (SHGA), sponsored by the Office of the Chief of Research and Development, Dept. of Army; issued in June 1967.

Mountain Glaciers of the Northern Hemisphere, (MGNH), William O. Field, Editor, with chapters by various authors, two volumes of text and one consisting of an Atlas; prepared under contract with U.S. Army Engineer Topographic Laboratories, and issued in June 1975 by Corps of Engineers, U.S. Army, Cold Regions Research and Engineering Laboratories, Hanover, NH. The contributors to the chapters cited in this report, other than the editor, were Sam G. Collins, George H. Denton, Rosemary Fitch, Eva Horvath, Barbara Kiteme, and John H. Mercer.

Table 2

Glacier	Length (kms)	Mtn. Range	Nation	Sources
1. Bering	205	Chugach	US/Canada	Meier et al, (1966)
2. Hubbard	125	St. Elias	US/Canada	Collins & Field (MGNH) (Other estimates vary from 130 to 150 km.)
3. Malaspina-Seward	113	St. Elias	US/Canada	Field & Collins (MGNH)
4. Klutlan	c. 88	St. Elias	Canada/U.S.	Field & Collins (MHNH)
5. Chitina	c. 88	St. Elias	US/Canada	Field & Collins (MHNH)
6. Nabesna	87	Wrangell	US	Denton (MGNH)
7. Kahiltna	76	Alaska	US	Denton (MGNH)
8. Kaskawulsh	75	St. Elias	Canada	Field & Collins (MGNH)
9. Lowell	73	St. Elias	Canada	Field & Collins (MGNH)
10. Siachen	73	Karakoram	Pakistan	Mercer (MGNH)
11. Fedchenko	71.2	Pamir	USSR	Horvath (MGNH)
12. Tana	68	Chugach	US	Field (MGNH)
13. Donjek	c. 65	St. Elias	Canada	Field (MGNH)
14. Columbia	64	Chugach	US	Krimmel (1987)
15. Tweedsmuir	64	St. Elias	Canada	Field (MGNH)
16. Ruth	63	Alaska	US	Denton (MGNH)
17. Hispar	62	Karakoram	Pakistan	Mercer (MGNH)

Glacier	Length (kms)	Mtn. Range	Nation	Sources
18. Yahtse	62	Chugach	US	Field (MGNH)
19. Muldrow	61	Alaska	US	Denton (MGNH)
20. Upsala	60	So. Andes	Argentina	Mercer (SHGA)
21. Yuzhniy Inyl'chik	59.8	Tian Shan	USSR	Horvath, Kiteme & Fitch (MGNH)
22. Biafo	59	Karakoram	Pakistan	Mercer (MGNH)
23. Batura	57	Karakoram	Pakistan	Mercer (MGNH)
24. Baltoro	57	Karakoram	Pakistan	Mercer (MGNH)
25. Dusty	54	St. Elias	Canada	Field & Collins (MGNH)
26. Barnard	54	St. Elias	US	Field & Collins (MGNH)
27. Rongbuk	52	Himalaya	Tibet	Mercer (MGNH)
28. Miles	52	Chugach	US	Field (MGNH)
29. Nizina	51	Wrangells	US	Denton (MGNH)
30. Yentna	51	Alaska	US	Denton (MGNH)
31. Chogo Lungma	50	Karakoram	Pakistan	Mercer (MGNH)

Two decades later there are bound to be changes in these figures determined from more recent surveys or from satellite imagery which would alter the figures and add or eliminate some of the 31 glaciers listed. This compilation should therefore be considered as an initial effort, and subject to change. More recent data and corrections to this table would be welcomed, especially from glaciologists on other continents.

Addendum

This report has depended heavily on the following sources listed below. The writer is deeply indebted to the various authors cited in the text as well as others in The AGS Department of Exploration and Field Research who, although not mentioned, helped assemble much of these data from 1946 to 1980.

U.S. Geological Survey topographic maps.

Canadian topographic maps issued by the Department of Mines and Technical Surveys and the Army Survey Establishment R.C.E.

Wahrhaftig, Clyde: (1965) *Physiographic Divisions of Alaska*, U.S. Geological Survey Professional Paper 482.

Mountain Glaciers of the Northern Hemisphere, (MGNA) (1975) William O. Field, Editor, three volumes with individual chapters by various authors compiled at The American Geographical Society (AGS) from 1968 to 1971. Corps of Engineers, U.S. Army Technical Information Analysis Center, Cold Regions Research and Engineering Laboratory (CRREL) Hanover, New Hampshire, USA.

Orth, Donald J. (1967) *Dictionary of Alaska Place Names*. U.S. Geological Survey Professional Paper 567.

PLATE 31

Photo by Austin Post

Harvard Glacier at head of College Fiord has advanced two kilometers since 1899. Radcliffe Glacier is first tributary on left. Photo on August 24, 1968.

REFERENCES:

Allen, Clarence R. and Geroge I. Smith (1953) "Seismic and Gravity Investigations on the Malaspina Glacier, Alaska," *Trans. Amer. Geophys. Union,* vol. 34, No. 5, pp. 755-760.

American Geographical Society (1960) *Nine Glacier Maps, Northwestern North America.* Special Publ. No. 34, Amer. Geog. Soc., N.Y., 37 pp., plus maps.

Anderson, P.J.; R.P. Goldthwait, G.D. McKenzie, Editors (1986) "Observed Processes of Glacial Deposition in Glacier Bay, Alaska." *Miscellaneous Publication No. 236 of the Institute of Polar Studies,* the Ohio State University, 167 pp.

Bengtson, K.B. (1962) "Recent History of the Brady Glacier, Glacier Bay National Monument, Alaska, U.S.A.," pp. 78-87 in: *Symposium of Obergurgl: Variations of the Regime of Existing Glaciers.* Publ. No. 58, Int'l. Ass'n. Sci. Hyd., Int'l. Union Geodesy and Geophys., Gentbrugge, 312 pp.

Benson, Carl S. (1966) *ICE* No. 22, p. 6.

Bindschadler, R. and W.D. Harrison, C.F. Raymond, and R. Crosson (1977) *Journ. Glac.* vol. 18, No. 79, pp. 181-194.

Blake, W.P. (1867) "The Glaciers of Alaska, Russian America," *Amer. Jour. Sci.,* 2nd Ser., vol. 44, pp. 96-101.

Brooks, Alfred H. (1911) *The Mount McKinley Region, Alaska.* U.S.G.S. Prof. Paper 70, pp. 1-136.

Burroughs, John, John Muir and George Bird Grinnell (1901) "Narrative, Glaciers, Natives." *Harriman Alaska Expedition* vol. 1, pp. XXXVII, 183.

Caldwell, Francis E. (1986) *Land of the Ocean Mists: The Wild Ocean Coast West of Glacier Bay.* Alaska Northwest Publishing Co., Edmonds, WA, 223 pp.

Carter, H. Adams (1959) "East of Mount McKinley," *Amer. Alp. Journ.* vol. 11, No. 2, Issue 33, pp. 201-207.

Carter, H. Adams and David L. Atherton (1961) "Milton Mount McKinley Range Expedition," *Amer. Alp. Journ.* vol. 12, No. 2, Issue 35, pp. 291-296.

Catalogue of United States Contributions to the International Hydrological Decade 1965-1974. National Academy of Sciences, 1975, pp. XVI, 255.

Clarke, Garry K.C. and Gary T. Jarvis (1976) "Post-Surge Temperatures in Steele Glacier, Yukon Territory, Canada." *Journ. Glac.* vol. 16, No. 74, pp. 261-268.

Cooper, Wm. S. (1937) "The Problem of Glacier Bay, Alaska: A Study of Glacier Variations," *Geog. Review,* vol. 27, pp. 37-62.

Cooper, Wm. S. (1956) *A Contribution to the History of Glacier Bay National Monument.* Dept. of Botany, Univ. Minnesota, 36 pp.

Dall, William H. and Charles Keeler, Henry Gannett, William H. Brewer, C. Hart Merriam, George Bird Grinnell, and M.L. Washburn (1901) "History, Geography, Resources," *Harriman Alaska Expedition,* vol. 2, pp. 185-383.

Davis, T. Neil and Norman K. Sanders (1960) "Alaska Earthquake of July 10, 1958: Intensity Distribution and Field Investigation of Northern Epicentral Region," *Bull. Seis. Soc. Amer.,* vol. 50, No. 2, pp. 221-252, incl. map.

Derksen, Stephen J. (1976) "Glacial Geology of the Brady Glacier Region, Alaska," *Institute of Polar Studies Report* No. 60, The Ohio State University, XII, 97 pp.

Field, William O. (1926) "The Fairweather Range: Mountaineering and Glacier Studies," *Appalachia,* vol. 16, pp. 460-472, plus map.

Gilbert, Grove Karl (1903) "Glaciers and Glaciation," *Harriman Alaska Expedition,* vol. 3, pp. XII, 231 pp.

Goldthwait, Richard P. (1936) Seismic Sounding on South Crillon and Klooch Glaciers, *The Geog. Journ.,* vol. 87, No. 6, pp. 496-517.

Goldthwait, Richard P. (1966) Glacial History, Abstract, pp. XVI and XVII; Part 1, pp. 1-18 in Soil Development and Ecological Succession in a Deglaciated Area of Muir Inlet, Southeast Alaska, by R.P. Goldthwait et al, edited by Arthur Mirsky, *Institute of Polar Studies Report,* No. 20, 1966. The Ohio State University Research Foundation.

Green, Lewis (1982) *The Boundary Hunters; Surveying the 141st Meridian and the Alaska Panhandle,* University of British Columbia Press, Vancouver and London, 214 pp.

Hamilton, Thomas D. (1986) "Late Cenozoic Glaciation of the Central Brooks Range," pp. 9-49, in *Glaciation in Alaska,* edited by T.D. Hamilton, K.M. Reed, and R.M. Thorson, Alaska Geological Society.

Harriman Alaska Expedition of 1899. See under Burroughs et al (1901); Dall et al (1901); and Gilbert (1903).

Harrison, W.D. (1972) "Reconnaissance of Variegated Glacier: Thermal Regime and Surge Behavior," *Journ. Glac.,* vol. 11, No. 63, pp. 455-456.

Hazelton, G. M. (1966) *Glacial Geology of Muir Inlet, Southeast Alaska,* Rept. No. 18, Inst. Polar Studies, Ohio State Univ., 34 pp.

Haumann, Dieter (1960) "Photogrammetric and Glaciological Studies of Salmon Glacier," *Arctic,* vol. 13, No. 2, pp. 74-110, plus map.

Henderson, K.A. and W.L. Putnam (1947) "Aleutian Mountaineering," *Harvard Mountaineering,* No. 8, pp. 27-32.

Heusser, Calvin J. and Melvin G. Marcus (1960) *Glaciological and Related Studies of Lemon Creek Glacier, Alaska.* Juneau Ice Field Research Project, Final Rept. Amer. Geog. Soc., N.Y., 30 pp. incl. photos, diagr., map.

IRRP Scientific Results, vol. 1 (1969), vol. 2 (1970), vol. 3 (1972), edited by Vivian C. Bushnell and Richard H. Ragle; vol. 4 (1974), edited by Bushnell and Melvin G. Marcus.

Kindle, E.D. (1953) *Dezadeash Map-Area, Yukon Territory,* Geol. Survey Memoir 268, Dept. of Mines and Tech. Surveys, Ottawa, 68 pp. plus map.

Knappen, R.S. (1929) "Geology and Mineral Resources of the Aniakchak District," *U.S.G.S. Bull.,* 797-F, pp. 161-223.

Korff, Serge A. (1953) "Mount Wrangell Expedition of 1953," *Explorers Jour.,* vol. 31, No. 4, p. 39.

Lawrence, D.B. and Elizabeth G.Lawrence (1949) "Some Glaciers of Southeastern Alaska," *Mazama,* vol. 31, No. 13, pp. 24-30.

Lawrence, D.B. (1950) "Glacier Fluctuation for Six Centuries in Southeastern Alaska and its Relations to Solar Activity," *Geog. Review,* vol. 40, pp. 191-223.

Lawrence, Donald B. (1958) "Glaciers and Vegetation in Southeastern Alaska," *Amer. Sci.,* vol. 46, No. 2, pp. 89-122.

Marcus, Melvin G. (1960) "Periodic Drainage of Glacier-Dammed Tulsequah Lake, British Columbia," *Geog. Review,* vol. 50, pp. 89-106, incl. photos, figs., maps.

Matthes, F.E. (1942) Chapter on Glaciers in Hydrology, *Physics of the Earth,* vol. IX, Dover Publ., N.Y., pp. 149-219.

Mayo, Lawrence R. (U.S.G.S. Fairbanks, Alaska); Mark F. Meier and Wendell V. Tangborn, (USGS Tacoma, WA) (1972) "A System to Combine Stratigraphic and Annual Mass-Balance Systems: A Contribution to the International Hydrological Decade," *Journ. of Glac.,* vol. 11, No. 61, pp. 3-14.

Mayo, Lawrence R. (1986) "Hubbard Glacier Near Yakutat, Alaska—The Ice Damming and Breakout of Russell Fiord/Lake," pp. 42-49, *National Water Summary 1986 —Ground-water Quality: Hydrologic Conditions and Events.*

McKenzie, Garry D. (1970) "Glacial Geology of Adams Inlet, Southeastern Alaska," *Institute of Polar Studies Report No. 25,* The Ohio State University Research Foundation.

Meier, Mark F. and William J. Campbell, Wendell V. Tangborn, and Austin Post. Note on Bering Glacier, *ICE,* No. 22, Dec. 1966, p. 8.

Mendenhall, W.C. (1905) "Geology of the Central Copper River Region, Alaska," *U.S. Geol. Surv. Prof. Paper No. 41,* 133 pp.

Mickelson, David M. (1971) "Glacial Geology of the Burroughs Glacier Area, Southeastern Alaska," *Institute of Polar Studies Report No. 40,* pp. XIII, 149 pp. The Ohio State University Research Foundation.

Miller, Don J. (1960) "Giant Waves in Lituya Bay, Alaska," *U.S. Geol. Survey Prof. Paper 354-c,* 86 pp., plus map.

Miller, Maynard M., Foundation for Glacier Research (1963), *Taku Evaluation Study,* conducted for the State of Alaska Department of Highways in cooperation with the U.S. Department of Commerce, Bureau of Public Roads. 200 pp. plus appendices.

Miller, Maynard M. and Research Affiliates of the Juneau Icefield Research Program (1975) *Mountain and Glacier Terrain Study and Related Investigations in the Juneau Icefield Region, Alaska-Canada,* Final Report, U.S. Army Research Office, Durham, Foundation for Glacier and Environmental Research, Pacific Science Center, Seattle, WA 98109, 136 pp. plus extensive appendices.

Molnia, B.F. (1986) "Glacial History of the Northeastern Gulf of Alaska—A Synthesis," Chapter on Glaciation in Alaska; *The Geologic Record,* pp. 219-235. Edited by T.D. Hamilton, K.M. Reed, and R.M. Thorson, Alaska Geological Society.

Morse, Fremont (1906) "Evidence of Recent Volcanic Action in Southern Alaska," *National Geographic Magazine,* vol. 17, No. 3, pp. 173-176.

Muir, John (1895) "The Discovery of Glacier Bay," *Century,* vol. 50, No. 2, pp. 234-247.

Muir, John (1915) *Travels in Alaska,* Houghton Mifflin Co., Boston, 327 pp.

Ostrem, Gunnar; Nils Haakensen, Tommy Eriksson (1981). *Geografiska Annaler,* vol. 63, Ser. A., pp. 251-260.

Peterson, Donald N. (1970) "Glaciological Investigations on the Casement Glacier, Southeast Alaska," *Institute of Polar Studies Report No. 36,* The Ohio State University Research Foundation.

Péwé, Troy L. (1975) "Quaternary Geology of Alaska," *U.S.G.S. Prof. Paper 835*, V, 145 pp.

Plafker, George and Don J. Miller (1958) *Glacial Features and Surficial Deposits of the Malaspina District, Alaska*, U.S. Geol. Survey Misc. Geol. Invest. Map I-271.

Post, A.S., (1969) "Distribution of Surging Glaciers in Western North America," *Jour. Glac.*, vol. 8, No. 53, pp. 229-240, incl. map.

Post, A.S. and Lawrence R. Mayo (1971) *Glacier Dammed Lakes and Outburst Floods in Alaska*, Hydrologic Invest. Atlas HA-455, U.S. Geol. Survey, 9 pp., plus maps and photos.

Raymond, C.F. and W.D. Harrison (1988) "Evolution of Variegated Glacier, Alaska, USA," *Journ. Glac.*, vol. 34, No. 117, pp. 154-169.

Reid, Harry F. (1892) "Studies of Muir Glacier, Alaska," *Nat'l. Geog. Mag.*, vol. 4, pp. 19-84, plus map.

Reid, Harry F. (1896) *Glacier Bay and Its Glaciers*, U.S. Geol. Survey, pp. 421-461, incl. photos, figs., and maps. (Extract from the 16th Annual Report of the Survey, 1894-95, Part I.)

Reid, Harry Fielding (1911) "The Variations of Glaciers XV," *Journ. Geology*, vol. 19, No. 1, pp. 83-89.

Russell, I.C. (1891) "An Expedition to Mount St. Elias, Alaska," *Nat'l. Geog. Mag.*, vol. 3, pp. 53-204, incl. map.

Russell, I.C. (1892) "Mt. St. Elias and Its Glaciers," *Amer. Jour. Sci.*, 3rd Ser., vol. 43, pp. 169-182.

Russell, I.C. (1893) "Second Expedition to Mount Saint Elias, in 1891," *U.S. Geol. Survey 13th Annual Rept., Part 2 — Geology*, pp. 1-91.

Russell, I.C. (1897) *Glaciers of North America*, Ginn and Co., Boston and London, 210 pp., incl. photos and maps.

Scidmore, E. Ruhamah (1885) *Alaska; Its Southern Coast and the Sitkan Archipelago*, pp. 131-152, D. Lothrop and Co., Boston.

Sharp, Robert P. (1947) "The Wolf Creek Glaciers, St. Elias Range, Yukon Territory," *Geog. Rev.*, vol. 37, No. 1, pp. 24-52.

Sharp, R.P. (1948) "Project 'Snow Cornice'," *Engineering and Sci. Monthly*, vol. 12, No. 2, pp. 6-10.

Sharp, Robert P. (1951) "Accumulation and Ablation on the Seward-Malaspina Glacier System, Canada-Alaska," *Bull. Geol. Soc. America*, vol. 62, pp. 725-744.

Sharp, Robert P. (1953) "Deformation of Bore Hole in Malaspina Glacier. Alaska," *Bull. Geol. Soc. America*, vol. 64, pp. 97-100.

Sharp, Robert P. (1956) "Glaciers in the Arctic," *Arctic*, vol. 9, Nos. 1 and 2, pp. 101-102.

Sharp, Robert P. (1958) "Malaspina Glacier, Alaska," *Bull. Geol. Soc. of America*, vol. 69, pp. 617-646.

Stanley, A.D. (1969) "Observations of the Surge of Steele Glacier, Yukon Territory, Canada," *Canadian Jour. Earth Sci.*, vol. 6, No. 4, pp. 819-830, incl. maps.

Tarr, Ralph S. (1909) *The Yakutat Bay Region, Alaska: Part I, Physiography and Glacial Geology*, U.S. Geol. Survey Prof. Paper 64, pp. 11-144.

Tarr, Ralph S. and Lawrence Martin (1912) "An Effort to Control a Glacial Stream," *Annals of Assoc. Amer. Geog.*, vol. 2, pp. 25-40.

Tarr, Ralph S. and Lawrence Martin (1914) *Alaskan Glacier Studies*, Nat'l. Geog. Soc., Washington, D.C., 498 pp., plus maps.

Taylor, Lawrence D. (1962) *Ice Structures, Burroughs Glacier, Southeast Alaska*, Rept. No.3, Inst. Polar Studies, Ohio State Univ., 106 pp.

Thomson, S. (1972) "Movement Observations on the Terminus Area of the Steele Glacier," pp. 29-37, *IRRP Scientific Results*, vol. 3, AGS and AINA.

Viereck, L.A. (1967) "Botanical Dating of Recent Glacial Activity in Western North America," pp. 189-204 in *Arctic and Alpine Environments*, eds., H.E. Wright, Jr. and W.H. Osburn, Indiana University Press.

Wahrhaftig, Clyde (1965) *Physiographic Divisions of Alaska*, U.S. Geol. Survey Prof. Paper 482, 52 pp., plus maps.

Washburn, Bradford (1935) "Morainic Bandings of Malaspina and Other Alaskan Glaciers," *Bull. Geol. Soc. Amer.*, vol. 46, pp. 1879-1889.

Wood, Walter A. (1936) "The Wood Yukon Expedition of 1935: An Experiment in Photographic Mapping," *Geog. Review*, vol. 26, pp. 228-246.

Wood, Walter A. (1942) "The Parachuting of Expedition Supplies: An Experiment by the Wood Yukon Expedition of 1941," *Geog. Review*, vol. 32, pp. 36-55.

Wood, Walter A. (1948) "Project 'Snow Cornice'," *Arctic*, vol. 1, No. 2, pp. 107-112.

Wood, Walter A. (1967) "Steele Glacier Surge," *Amer. Alpine Jour.*, vol. 15, No. 2, pp. 279-281.

Wood, Walter A. (1969) *Icefield Ranges Research Project: Scientific Results*, vol. 1, pp. 3-13, Editors Vivian C. Bushnell and Richard H. Ragle, AGS and AINA.

Wood, Walter A. (1972) *Steele Glacier 1935-1968. Icefield Ranges Research Project: Scientific Results*, vol. 3, pp. 1-8, AGS and AINA.

World Glacier Monitoring Service (1989). World Glacier Inventory, Status 1988. A Contribution to the Global Environment Monitoring System (GEMS) and the International Hydrological Programme. IAHS (ICSI)-UNEP-UNESCO. Canada, Stikine River. Page C75.

Wright, G.F. (1887) "The Muir Glacier," *Amer. Jour. Sci.*, 3rd Ser., vol. 33, pp. 1-18.

PLATE 32

Photo by Bradford Washburn

The Unclimbed East Face of MOUNT McKINLEY at the head of the Traleika Glacier.

Climbs and Expeditions, 1989

The Editorial Board is extremely grateful to the many people who have done so much to make this section possible. Among those who have been very helpful, we should like to thank in particular Kamal K. Guha, Hari Dang, Harish Kapadia, H.C. Sarin, Józef Nyka, Jerzy Wala, Tsunemichi Ikeda, Sadao Tambe, Hanif Raza, Zafarullah Siddiqui, Trevor Braham, Luciano Ghigo, César Morales Arnao, Vojslav Arko, Franci Savenc, Bernard Newman, Paul Nunn, José Manuel Anglada, Jordi Pons, Josep Paytubi, Elmar Landes, Robert Renzler, Colin Monteath, Annie Bertholet, Fridebert Widder, Silvia Metzeltin Buscaini, Zhou Zheng, Ying Dao Shin, Karchung Wangchuk, Dolfi Rotovnik, Robert Seibert, Lloyd Freese and Tom Eliot. We mourn the untimely death of Soli Mehta, Editor of the Himalayan Journal.

METERS TO FEET

Unfortunately the American public seems still to be resisting the change from feet to meters. To assist readers from the more enlightened countries, where meters are universally used, we give the following conversion chart:

meters	feet	meters	feet	meters	feet	meters	feet
3300	10,827	4700	15,420	6100	20,013	7500	24,607
3400	11,155	4800	15,748	6200	20,342	7600	24,935
3500	11,483	4900	16,076	6300	20,670	7700	25,263
3600	11,811	5000	16,404	6400	20,998	7800	25,591
3700	12,139	5100	16,733	6500	21,326	7900	25,919
3800	12,467	5200	17,061	6600	21,654	8000	26,247
3900	12,795	5300	17,389	6700	21,982	8100	26,575
4000	13,124	5400	17,717	6800	22,310	8200	26,903
4100	13,452	5500	18,045	6900	22,638	8300	27,231
4200	13,780	5600	18,373	7000	22,966	8400	27,560
4300	14,108	5700	18,701	7100	23,294	8500	27,888
4400	14,436	5800	19,029	7200	23,622	8600	28,216
4500	14,764	5900	19,357	7300	23,951	8700	28,544
4600	15,092	6000	19,685	7400	24,279	8800	28,872

NOTE: All dates in this section refer to 1989 unless otherwise stated. Normally, accounts signed by a name alone (no Club) indicate membership in the American Alpine Club.

UNITED STATES

Alaska

Denali National Park and Preserve Mountaineering Summary, 1989. For the fourth consecutive year, a new record was set for the number of mountaineers attempting to climb Mount McKinley. In 1989, 1009 persons registered to climb the mountain. It was the first time that more than 1000 people had done so in a single year. There were winter attempts by three separate expeditions, including one soloist. One of the groups, three Austrian guides, succeeded on the West Buttress route on February 20. The second winter attempt, a few days later on the West Buttress, was unsuccessful and resulted in the death of three experienced Japanese climbers who were apparently caught above a high camp in a severe storm. The soloist, Alaskan resident and McKinley guide Dave Staeheli, completed the first solo winter ascent of the West Rib. (See his article.) Temperatures were relatively mild during the mountaineering season, but April through mid June was consistently stormy. Exceptionally good weather from mid June through mid July salvaged what would otherwise have been a dismal year for success-rate statistics. Beyond mid July, summer storms dumped heavy snowfalls at all elevations, making travel both difficult and hazardous.

The Denali Medical Research Project received funding and was in full operation this season. The team continued research into the causes and treatment of high-altitude illnesses. The staff designed and had constructed an aluminum pressure chamber which was capable of sleeping two persons. They continued studies comparing oxygen breathing in association with pressurization as a treatment for High-Altitude Pulmonary Edema (HAPE). They also extended 1988 studies of pulmonary vasodilation drugs for the treatment of HAPE. Results from the 1989 investigations suggest limitations to the usefulness of pulmonary vasodilation drugs in the field treatment of HAPE. At the end of the season, Dr. Peter Hackett announced that the Denali Medical Research Project would not operate during the 1990 season, but that they planned to return to continue in 1991. Despite the record number of climbers on the mountain, there were only five search and rescue incidents in which the National Park Service was involved, including one rescue in the Ruth Glacier area. This is the lowest number since 1975 when 362 persons registered to climb McKinley. The National Park Service conducted three three-week patrols on McKinley, as well as numerous patrols in other parts of the Alaska Range. We continue to staff a ranger station in the town of Takleetna where mountaineers register for their expeditions. A strong emphasis is placed on the importance of environmentally sound expeditionary climbing and sanitation techniques. Additionally, climbers are encouraged to remain self-sufficient and to conduct their own evacuations whenever possible.

Interesting Statistics: *Record Number of Climbers on Mount McKinley:* In 1989, new all-time records were set for the number of persons attempting to climb Mount McKinley: 1979=533, 1980=659, 1981=612, 1982=696, 1983=709, 1984=695, 1985=645, 1986=755, 1987=817, 1988=916, 1989=1009. *Success Rate:* 524 (52%) of those attempting the summit of McKinley were successful. This figure includes 14 who successfully climbed to the north summit. For the first time in three years, climbing teams reached the summit of Mount Foraker. Five out of 13 climbers (38%) attempting Foraker got to the summit. Eight out of 24 climbers (33%) attempting Mount Hunter reached the summit. *Record Number of Climbers on McKinley in a Given Week:* A new all-time high of 367 climbers were on the slopes of McKinley for the week ending May 13. *New Altitude for Mount McKinley?* Also establishing four stations at lower altitude, on June 21 and 24 a team of researchers and support climbers reached the summit of Mount McKinley. They carried a Global Positioning System receiver that when used in conjunction with Global Positioning Satellites can measure heights. Preliminary indications show the elevation of Mount McKinley to be 14 feet lower than the height previously measured by more traditional survey methods. The newly computed height of 20,306 feet is not yet official. For the time being, the previous height of 20,320 feet remains the official height. *Acute Mountain Sickness:* 95 (9%) had symptoms, of which 39 (4%) were mild, 33 (3%) moderate and 23 (2%) severe. *Frostbite:* 54 (5%) reported some degree of frostbite. Of these, three (0.3) required hospitalization. *West Buttress Route:* 854 (85%) of the climbers on McKinley were on the popular West Buttress route. This is exactly the same percentage as during 1988. *Soloists:* 19 persons registered for solo climbs this year, two more than in 1988. A number of these were able to team up with other groups once they got to the mountain, at least to traverse the heavily crevassed portions of the lower glaciers. *Mountain Guiding:* 265 (26%) of the climbers on McKinley traveled with one of the authorized guiding companies. The overall success rate of the guided groups was 43%. Most were on the West Buttress, but other guided trips attempted the Muldrow Glacier, West Rib and South Buttress. *Foreign Climbers:* 360 (36%) of the McKinley climbers were from foreign countries. 27 nationalities were represented: Austria 27, Australia 3, Belgium 2, Canada 5, Chile 8, Czechoslovakia 6, France 29, Germany 47, Great Britain 41, Iceland 6, Kenya 1, Indonesia 4, Italy 26, Japan 39, Korea 24, Luxembourg 1, Mexico 8, New Zealand 6, Northern Ireland 4, Poland 17, Romania 1, Russia 1, South Africa 2, Spain 7, Sweden 1, Switzerland 42, Taiwan 2. *New Low Temperature Reading:* The National Park Service maintains a minimum recording thermometer, supplied by the National Weather Service, at 17,200 feet on the West Buttress. The winter of 1988-9's coldest temperature was −77° F (61.5° C).

Accidents: The following are the more significant accidents or incidents that occurred in 1989. *Winter attempt, multiple hypothermia fatalities, ground and helicopter evacuation by own support group:* On February 16, a very experienced, four-person Japanese team flew to the southeast fork of the Kahiltna Glacier to attempt a winter ascent of the West Buttress. The leader, Noboru Yamada, was on a quest to become the first person to climb to the summit of the highest mountain on each of the seven continents in the winter. Teruo Saegusa,

DENALI NATIONAL PARK AND PRESERVE
1988 MOUNTAINEERING SUMMARY

	Expeditions	Climbers	Successful Climbers
Mount McKinley			
West Buttress	176	625	329
West Buttress (guided)	28	229	115
Muldrow	10	34	20
Muldrow (guided)	1	15	11
West Rib	15	38	9
West Rib (guided)	3	13	6
Messner Couloir	1	2	2
Cassin	10	28	22
Cassin (guided)	0	0	0
South Buttress	2	6	0
South Buttress (guided)	1	8	4
American Direct	1	3	0
Reality Ridge	1	2	0
Northwest Buttress	1	6	6
Pioneer Ridge	0	0	0
Wickersham Wall	0	0	0
	(250)	(1,009)	(524)
Mount Foraker	5	13	5
Mount Hunter	11	24	8
Mount Huntington	2	4	2
Kahiltna Dome	1	8	0
Kahiltna Dome (guided)	1	6	6
E. Kahiltna Peak	0	0	0
Mount Russell	1	2	2
Mount Russell (guided)	1	6	0
Mount Brooks	3	9	2
Mount Brooks (guided)	2	24	10
Mount Silverthrone	0	0	0
Little Switzerland	4	12	N/A
Little Switzerland (guided)	1	14	N/A
Gorge Peaks	7	15	2
Mount Dickey (guided)	1	5	0
Mount Barrille	1	2	0
Mooses Tooth	5	10	2
Mooses Tooth (guided)	1	3	0
Mount Dan Beard	1	1	0
Mount Francis	1	3	3
Rooster Comb	1	2	0
	50	163	N/A

NOTE: Since registration is required only for Mount McKinley and Mount Foraker climbs, statistics for other climbs represent those climbers who voluntarily checked in with the Mountaineering Rangers. Other climbs, especially in the Ruth Glacier area, are likely to have occurred.

Kozo Komatsu and Shunzo Sato were the other team members. Sato became ill early in the climb and returned to Base Camp to wait for the others. The remaining three reached the 17,200-foot high camp on February 20, the same day that a team of three Austrians returned to the high camp from a successful summit climb. On February 21, neither team could move because of severe weather. On the 22nd, there was a short break in the weather and the Austrians began their descent. The Japanese team was still in their camp. They were not seen alive or heard from again. Weather soon deteriorated and an extremely severe wind storm enveloped the upper mountain. Wind speeds were estimated to be 200 mph and they continued through February 26. Winds then decreased somewhat through March 9 to from 60 to 90 mph. On March 10, search flights located three bodies below Denali Pass. Search efforts were terminated on March 11. It is believed that the three climbers tried for the summit during the brief lull and were caught near Denali Pass as the winds again increased. The bodies were recovered later in March by a 17-person team of Japanese climbers who came to Alaska for that purpose. *Fall with injuries, survival epic, helicopter evacuation:* On March 14, Anchorage climbers Jim Sweeney and David Nyman flew to the Ruth Glacier. They did not take a radio. They eventually decided to climb a couloir known as the Elevator Shaft on the north face of Mount Johnson. On March 19, the first day of their climb, Sweeney began leading the fourth pitch. He placed an anchor and climbed 40 feet above it, where he encountered an ice window. He grabbed under the window and leaned out for a better look at his options. Suddenly, the entire formation on which he was climbing collapsed. Sweeney and the 15-foot-wide, 35-foot-high and 6-foot-thick ice formation fell down the couloir. His anchor held, but his hip was fractured by the resulting 80-foot fall and avalanche. The events of the next seven days are too involved to be recorded here but proved to be a test of endurance and of their will to survive. During this time, either one or both of the men were hit by eight different avalanches. Weather deteriorated and prevented all access to the mountains by rescue teams. The two men were eventually rescued on March 26 by military helicopter. *Fall, triple fatalities, ground and helicopter recovery:* On May 15, three British climbers, Chris Massey, John Lang and Julian Dixon, began their summit attempt of McKinley from a 16,500-foot camp on the West Rib. As the day progressed, the weather began to deteriorate. The three men were seen by other parties who turned back but the British team indicated that they planned to continue on. Early the next day, a National Park Mountaineering Ranger camped at the 14,200-foot basin on the West Buttress noticed what appeared to be bodies at the base of the Orient Express, a couloir which cuts across the upper West Rib. The rescue team discovered that all three Britons had died in a fall. It appears that the men were probably descending the West Rib, roped together, in extremely poor weather when one of them slipped and pulled the others down the couloir. Tent with occupants blown from ridge, injuries, *helicopter evacuation:* On May 27, a guided group from Genet Expeditions was camped at 16,400 feet on the West Buttress. For the previous three days, the weather had been intermittently windy. Winds increased during the evening. One especially violent gust tore one of the tents, with three occupants, from its anchors. The tent and occupants began a tumbling fall toward the Peters Glacier. One occupant, John Richards, the assistant guide, was ejected early in the fall and came to rest 300 feet below the ridge campsite. The other two occupants, Jim Johnson and Howard Tuthill, fell 1000 feet and came to rest on a small ledge, dressed only in polypro underwear. All clothing and equipment was lost in the fall. The assistant guide was able to ascend to the camp and alert the others of the accident. The chief guide, Dave Staeheli, was able to descend and provide survival equipment to Johnson and Tuthill. Others on the mountain, including the Denali Medical Project personnel and private mountaineers, organized a difficult and dangerous rescue effort, eventually stabilizing the two men, who were flown off the mountain the following day via helicopter. Johnson suffered a compression fracture of lumbar vertebrae and Tuthill frostbit his fingers. Both suffered from hypothermia. The lives of these two men were saved by the rescue efforts. *Tent and occupant blown from ridge, equipment lost, no injuries:* In a very similar incident to the one previously described, a Rainier Mountaineering Inc. guided expedition was camped at 16,100 feet on the West Buttress during an extended storm. Chief guide Curt Hewitt was alone in the tent when a severe gust ripped the tent from its anchors and lifted it and Hewitt over three-foot snow walls. The tent began a tumbling fall. Hewitt was able to escape through the entry tunnel and climb back to the campsite, but the tent and equipment were lost. No rescue was needed or injuries sustained, but the expedition had to retreat. *High- altitude pulmonary edema, ground evacuation:* A Genet Expedition trip led by Dave Staeheli reached the 17,200-foot camp on June 21. They waited there for three days for the weather to improve. One of the clients, John Michel, had been feeling poorly earlier on the trip. At High Camp, he lacked energy and spent most of the three days sleeping. It was decided he was not to attempt the summit. On June 24, all but Michel left for a summit attempt. No other parties were at High Camp. Late that afternoon, another Genet team arrived and discovered Michel to be suffering from HAPE. They evacuated him to the 14,200-foot camp where Michel received treatment and recovered. There were other incidents of altitude illness and frostbite. Most were treated at the Denali Medical Project camp at 14,200 feet on the West Buttress. *Perforated ulcer, peritonitis, ground evacuation to Base Camp:* On May 25, Japanese climber Tetsumi Inoue developed severe abdominal pain while at 9800 feet on the West Buttress. He was evacuated to Base Camp, was flown to Talkeetna and then transported by ambulance to Valley Hospital. There he underwent surgery for a perforated ulcer and peritonitis resulting from gastric emptying.

Trends and Items of Special Concern: *Percentage of foreigners requiring rescues:* Foreigners accounted for 36% of the total number of climbers on Mount McKinley. Fourteen persons required some sort of organized rescue or recovery effort this year. Seven (50%) were from foreign nations. All six of the fatalities during 1989 were foreigners. *Sanitation:* With increasing use, it is more important than ever for climbers properly to dispose of their human waste to prevent the contamination of snow that might be melted and used for drinking or cooking water by future expeditions. We suggest the use of plastic bags as latrines. When moving camp, tie the bags off and toss them into a deep crevasse. The use of biodegradable plastic bags is recommended. This season, a new latrine was installed at the 17,200-foot camp on the West Buttress. It seemed to be successful in concentrating human waste in the pits below the latrine. Unfortunately, the latrine had to be moved four times as the pit filled. The snow-and-ice pack at the High Camp moves slowly. This causes concern for the eventual proliferation of waste-filled pits. For 1990, the latrine will be moved further out in the 17,000-foot basin, where there is greater movement of the glacier. *Trash:* Many expeditions are hauling their trash to Base Camp where it is flown off the mountain. Still others continue to crevasse their trash. Trash accumulation on other popular mountains of the world has recently received considerable publicity. Mountaineers from all nations must take the responsibility for, and the initiative in, preserving the quality of the world's mountain environments. A combination of education, leading by example and peer pressure is probably the most effective way that can be brought to bear against less considerate climbers. *Looking ahead to 1990:* Since the Denali Medical Research Project will not operate during 1990, the National Park Service will staff a small weather port at the 14,200-foot basin on the West Buttress. The camp will serve primarily as a communication and coordination base for rescue incidents. A new German translation of the Mountaineering Brochure is now available for distribution. For more information or to request mountaineering information and/or registration forms, please contact me: Robert Seibert, South District Mountaineering Ranger, Talkeetna Ranger Station, PO Box 588, Talkeetna, Alaska 99676. Telephone: 907-733-2231.

ROBERT SEIBERT, *Denali National Park and Preserve*

Mount McKinley Winter Attempt and Tragedy. Japanese Noburo Yamada, Teruo Saegusa and Kozo Komatsu attempted to make a winter ascent of McKinley. They were last seen on February 22 by Austrians when they were pitching camp at 17,000 feet. An aerial search in mid March revealed their bodies below Denali Pass. Yamada had climbed nine 8000-meter peaks. He had ascended Everest three times. He was also trying to make the winter ascent of the highest point of each of the continents. He had already done Everest, Aconcagua, Kilimanjaro and Mont Blanc in winter. Saegusa had ascended four 8000ers, including Everest twice. Komatsu had climbed Dhaulagiri I, II, III, IV and V between 1975 and 1982.

Alaskan Climbs Appearing as Full Articles. Aside from the climbs reported here, the following are covered in complete articles: the east face of Mount

Russell, Foraker's Infinite Spur, the northwest face of Mount Hunter, the Eroica route on Hunter and the west rib of the south face of Mount McKinley in winter. Foraker, Sultana Ridge. Todd Miner, Gordy Vernon and I were the first to visit the summit of Foraker in three years when we reached there on June 16 after a 6000-foot summit day up the northeast ridge. We spent a total of 18 days on the Sultana Ridge, much of it in wind. Only one of our five camps was exposed enough to require triple-thick walls. The most useful gear turned out to be wands, not the ice-and-snow gear we carried since the route was not difficult technically. The length of the ridge has probably kept people away, but it is safer than the more popular, avalanche-prone southeast ridge.

WILLY HERSMAN

Hunter, Southwest Ridge to South Summit. After encountering chest-deep snow on the Lowe-Kennedy route, Andy Jenson, Cory Brettmann, Dave Karl and I had Jim Okonek fly us to the south side of Mount Hunter. We had our eyes set on the southwest ridge first climbed by Alan Kearney and company in 1979 and apparently not yet seconded. The first 2500 vertical feet were in a couloir with perfect conditions; we raced up unroped in two hours. We then placed our first camp on a bench 3/4 of a mile from the top of the couloir and fixed two lines through some moderate mixed terrain. The next day was a long one with 11 pitches of hard 65° to 70° ice that ended at 11,600 feet for our high camp. Two days of storm and an avalanche that nearly did Jenson and Brettmann in came close to turning us around, but never-the-less, on May 27 we headed for the summit, only to be stopped 100 feet shy by an overhanging bergschrund which seemed to encircle the summit cone. Off with the crampons, and 6-foot-8 Cory and 6-foot-4 Andy boosted me up over the final obstacle. Two days more of storm passed without food in wet bags before we descended. After rappelling the steep ice, we glissaded the 2500-foot initial couloir in 15 minutes, although it nearly ended in tragedy when I sailed over the schrund.

CHRIS HAALAND

Mount Brooks, South Summit, East Ridge. Scott Gill and I climbed the east ridge of Mount Brooks to the south summit on June 29. This is a new route. The climb consisted of endless hours of post-holing in soft, unconsolidated snow. The final 75 meters, however, were a knife-edged ridge with spectacular exposure on both sides. It took 9½ hours to reach the summit from our camp at 6300 feet on the Brooks Glacier.

DOUGLAS CHABOT

Crown Jewell, Throne and "Plunger", Little Switzerland. In August, Rob Heineman and I spent four days on the Pika Glacier between bouts of heavy rain.

On August 4 we warmed up with a climb of the south face of the Throne. The following day, Heineman and I joined with Britons Bill Whitfield and Andy Garland and climbed what we believe was the first complete ascent of the attractive, prominent pinnacle on the divide extending south from the Throne, which has come to be called the "Plunger" (c. 6300 feet). A pitch on the east face leads to a platform splitting the upper pinnacle. A second pitch follows a beautiful overhanging hand-crack to the airy top (5.9, A2). On August 6, Heineman and I established a new route on the west ridge of Crown Jewell (IV, 5.8). A 400-foot, 50° snow slope at the foot of the ridge leads to a third- and fourth-class scramble along the ridge to a headwall. Four pitches of good granite were a joy to climb. Alternating pitches of 45° ice, fourth-class rock and a steep, sharp, airy ridge brought us to the summit. Five minutes after returning to our tent, a deluge of rain started and continued for four days. We then had a three-day wet slog out to the Petersville Road. Although Little Switzerland offers outstanding granite, sharp edges are a threat to rope and rappel anchors.

JAMES LITCH, *National Park Service*

P 7400, East Side of the Ruth Gorge. Doug Klewin and I climbed the southwest face of P 7400. The first eight pitches were 5.9 or 5.10 with an occasional aid move. After that, it was easier, 5.8 or so. The route was 22 pitches in all and included roofs, slabs, pendulums and cracks, all on excellent granite. The climb took 28 hours, including the descent by rappel. We then attempted the south face of Mount Dickey via a previously attempted route but retreated, having done the lower third in two days, because of bad rock and excessive rockfall.

TODD BIBLER

"Naglishlamina Peak," Tordrillo Mountains. The last unclimbed Anchorage skyline peak exceeding 10,000 feet was finally ascended on April 5 in a seven-day expedition under perfect early-spring conditions. "Naglishlamina" is one of the five prominent Tordrillo peaks due west of Anchorage across Cook Inlet. The others are Mount Spurr, "Chickantna Point," Mount Torbert and Mount Gerdine. Our "mature" group (average age 45 years) consisted of Dr. James Sprott, Daniel Blake, David Johnston and me. On April 2, Lowell Thomas Jr. ferried us by bush plane to the north side of the Tordrillos, landing at 2300 feet on the Nagishlamina River below the snout of the Pothole Glacier. The lake which we recalled at this spot from two previous approaches up the Pothole to Mount Spurr had mysteriously disappeared, leaving a rough landing zone of ice ridges and wind hummocks. A fairly easy march with skis and sleds led us to Camp I at 3300 feet on the main Pothole Glacier. While the main Pothole had been the access to Spurr on at least two earlier expeditions, we think that we were the first to use the northeast branch to gain the Spurr plateau. This tributary is relatively crevasse-free and straightforward up to 6500 feet. Camp II at 6200

feet was below a prominent icefall with steep walls capped by hanging glaciers rising before us, an inspiring sight. The fine weather inexplicably improved with each passing day. On day three, we climbed fairly steep firm snow on the northern margin of the glacier to reach a prominent rock ridge at 7850 feet, where we placed Camp III. The terrain fell away on all sides of this spectacular location with Spurr and "Naglishlamina" right above us and the ice plateau of the Chigmits to the southwest, bounded on its far side by abrupt, unclimbed pickets in the Revelation Mountains. Our summit day, April 5, dawned nearly unclouded and windless with temperatures slightly above zero. The ridge required rock-and-snow scrambling to a subsidiary peak of 10,175 feet, over-looking the Harpoon Glacier. From there, we dropped to a gradual saddle and then climbed to the rounded summit of "Naglishlamina" (3373 meters, 11,068 feet), which we reached at 2:30 with cloudless skies and −5° F. The descent on April 6 took us from Camp III all the way to the landing zone. On the 7th, Johnston soloed P 6740 by its southwest ridge. The following morning, Lowell Thomas slipped in ahead of foul weather and returned us to the comforts and cares of civilization.

THOMAS MEACHAM, *Mountaineering Club of Alaska*

"Bounty Peak," P 7240 and P 7265, Western Chugach. Beautiful, remote "Bounty Peak" had not been climbed since 1969. (See *AAJ, 1970,* page 113.) Jim Sayler, Randy Howell and I did a new route on July 4, going up the east ridge, a non-technical ascent. Our one-day approach and climb was from a camp above the East Fork Eklutna drainage, seven miles away. A steep ice-and-snow gully and a wide snow band on the north face form a perfect cross, visible for miles, leading straight to the summit, which would make an esthetic new route. Sayler, Jeff McCarthy and I spent five days in the Hunter Creek drainage, fighting brush and mud to reach the remote Hunter Creek Glacier and do some climbing. We made the first ascents of P 7240 ("Devil's Club Peak") on July 26 and P 7265 ("Mountaineer's Peak") on July 28, both from the glacier. These were the last unclimbed 7000-foot peaks in the western Chugach. Nothing new had been attempted in the Hunter Creek area for 19 years, which attests to the undesirable alders and devil's club found there. (See *AAJ, 1971,* page 334.)

WILLY HERSMAN

P 7455, P 7420, P 6600, Thompson Ridge, Chugach Mountains. On June 7, a six-man joint St. Elias Guides and American Alpine Institute expedition flew to the Thompson Ridge area near the headwaters of Granite Creek. On the 9th, we attempted P 7455 but turned back at 6800 feet due to the approach of daytime and softening snow. After moving camp higher on the 10th, we climbed P 6600 on the evening of June 11 via an icefall on its north side. On the 12th, three of us ascended P 7455 via its northeast ridge up steep snow, ice and rock. On the 13th, four of us climbed P 7420 via 5th-class rock on the southwest ridge after crossing an unnamed glacier to get to the base of the ridge. We believe these were all first ascents.

Danny W. Kost, *St. Elias Guides*

P 7254, P 6842, P 5651, P 7724, P 7138, Chugach Mountains. On June 19, Conner Hough, Kelley Miller-Pluckebaum, Bob Pluckebaum, Bob Schindler and I flew to an iceberg-choked lake west of the Tana Glacier and north of the Bagley Icefield, one of the most spectacular spots within the Wrangell-St. Elias National Park. We established Base Camp above the lake with views of the calving glacier at its upper end. On June 20, we ascended P 6842 by the glacier and then a snow gully on its south face. The 21st saw us ascend pretty, flat-topped P 5651, due south of P 6842. On June 22, we moved camp to 3000 feet at the base of P 7254. The weather turned bad and we were unable to attempt the peak until the 25th. That evening we ascended the peak through an icefall on its northeast side. It involved tricky, steep climbing through crevasses and séracs, the last 100 feet being directly up the west face to the summit. We hiked back to the calving glacier and were flown out to McCarthy on June 27. From July 4 to 13, Shawn Dorsch, Ray DiStacio and I climbed in the Bagley Icefield region. We were landed on the same lake we had been at a week before. July 5 and 6 were spent moving to Base Camp at 3700 feet at the toe of the icefall flowing off P 7348. On July 7, we ascended the mountain via the icefall and a 45° to 50° gully on its east face. The summit involved balancing on a knife-edged ridge to reach the highest point. On July 8, we moved camp to 4500 feet on a rock-and-alpine-flowered island between two glaciers. We climbed P 7138 on the 10th via a glacier on its southern flank and then a 50° to 60° snow-and-ice gully for about 400 feet which gave access to the easier upper slopes. From the summit we dropped down the southwestern slopes to attain the south face of P 7724. We ascended 50° ice for 800 feet to reach the summit. The snow conditions were deteriorating and so we decided to spend the day waiting on a rock ridge at 6700 feet. The snow hardened enough for safe travel at 10:30 P.M. We headed down and arrived at Base Camp early the next morning. On July 12, we descended to the airstrip. I believe these were all first ascents.

Danny W. Kost, *St. Elias Alpine Guides*

P 7401 and P 6283, Thompson Ridge Area, 1988. Austrian Thomas Schranz and I were flown to a sandbank in a river bed in the Thompson Ridge area. We found the rock terribly rotten and tried to keep as much as possible on snow and ice. After climbing a 50° ice slope, we ascended the loose rock of the north face of P 7401 on August 1, 1988. After that we made an exhausting route across moraine and boulders to P 6283. We then climbed a 1700-foot-high ice slope (up to 60°) which led to a 1000-foot-high narrow ridge of rotten rock. Bad weather discouraged further climbs.

Eduard Birnbacher, *Deutscher Alpenverein*

Photo by Bradford Washburn

MOUNT FAIRWEATHER from the Southeast. The new route started up the ridge at the right where the two shadows nearly meet.

Frederika Mountain, Wrangell Mountains. Frederika is a beautiful, snow cone just east of Mount Regal. The mountain was first named Mount Abercrombie but was later given its present name in honor of Frederick Schwatka, an early USGS explorer to the region. On September 4, Sean Ragain and Steve Mulholland flew to Skolai Creek to meet me for an attempt on unclimbed Frederika Mountain. I had just completed an eight-day hike up the Chitistone Canyon. We hiked to the toe of the Frederika Glacier that day at 3700 feet. For two days, it rained and the wind howled. Finally on the 7th, we were able to move up a glacier on Frederika's southwestern flank to camp at 6700 feet. September 8 started out rainy and foggy. September 9 was beautiful. We ascended the icefall to an upper basin at 8000 feet. Then we went up 50° snow and ice to the west ridge at 9000 feet. From there we ascended the west face up 45° snow and ice to the summit (10,356 feet). The view to Mounts Sanford, Tom White, Logan, Bona and the rest of the Wrangell and St. Elias Mountains was spectacular.

DANNY W. KOST, *St. Elias Guides*

Caliban, Xanadu, The Maidens and Shot Tower, Arrigetch Peaks, Brooks Range. In Late June and early July, Bob McGregor, Yan Marrand, Gary Brill and I flew to Circle Lake from Bettles and then hiked to an airdrop site near the head of Arrigetch Creek. We all pioneered a fine route on excellent granite (5.8) on the south buttress of Caliban Peak. We then made a foray into the deep cirque walls to the west. Poor snow-and-ice conditions and massive and exfoliated flakes made routes impractical. McGregor and Marrand did a new route on the east rib of the south peak of Xanadu. During unsettled weather, McGregor, Marrand and Brill made the second ascent of the impressive north buttress of the central peak of the Maidens (V, 5.9). This climb, perhaps the most impressive ever done in the Arrigetch, was first climbed by John Markel and Bob Duggan in 1982, but it was never reported in the climbing literature. Marrand and Brill made a marathon hike to Shot Tower, just managing to make the ascent and get back to the lake for the float plane. In a tragic aftermath to the expedition, several weeks later Bob McGregor died from injuries suffered when a snow bridge in the Tantalus Range of British Columbia collapsed on him.

FRED BECKEY

Mount Fairweather, East-Southeast Ridge and "Sabine." Gaping crevasses made it impossible to land near our chosen objective. A snap, mid-air decision left us at the base of an ideal consolation prize, the unclimbed east-southeast ridge of Fairweather. (This is clearly seen on the photograph on page 33 of *AAJ, 1981.*) With the weather unusually fair, Jim and Kevin Haberl, Alastair Foreman and I began climbing almost immediately. The first day took us up gullies, shattered rock, cornices and occasional towers over the summit (8860 feet) of the sub-peak which rises on the lower arm of the east-southeast ridge. On Day 2, we followed a spiny ridge leveling onto a hanging glacier, which then reared up onto a 1500-foot-high, 50° snow-and-ice face. Again established on the ridge, we found a fragile perch for the evening tucked into the lee of a rock tower at 11,300 feet with vistas of chaotic ice swirling below. Day 3 was Alaska at its finest: delicate climbing and breath-taking exposure as we threaded our way up pinnacles and cornices in blustery weather to a roomy bergschrund bivouac at 12,300 feet. From here, a short ice step opened up to broader slopes leading to the 13,820-foot sub-peak. Near here, we joined the route which had been descended by Jim Wickwire, Greg Markov and Dusan Jagersky in 1973. Not far beyond P 13,820, we turned back in a blizzard. The wind still howled on the morning of Day 5, but the sky had cleared. On May 20, in a few hours from camp we reached the point where the southeast ridge abuts into the Carpé Ridge, which we followed up its impressive ice nose to ripping wind on the summit, the highest point in British Columbia, an important point for us from Vancouver. We took another two days to descend the Carpé, including a final half-day of scouting a way through bewildering and dangerous ice cliffs that guard the bottom of the route. Spent, we arrived back in Base Camp just as huge lenticular clouds heralded the collapse of weather for almost two weeks. In a quick non-stop dash just before pick-up time, Foreman and the Haberl brothers climbed the beautiful and sharp southeast spur of "Sabine" (3172 meters, 10,405 feet) in a 28-hour return-trip. This was probably the third ascent of the peak.

MICHAEL DOWN, *Alpine Club of Canada*

Washington—Cascade Mountains

Chablis Spire, Lichen Bouquet. The Wine Spires are a tight cluster of granite needles east of Washington Pass with sheer walls and tiny summits. During 1952 and 1953, Fred Beckey and partners scaled the four pinnacles and even today, Burgundy Spire is thought to be one of the most difficult climbs in the state. On October 8, Mark Houston and I scrambled up a long gully to the base of Chablis' west face. Decomposed blank rock prompted us to climb the gully higher and begin the route on the southwest side. We started the climb by crossing a ramp and ledge and then climbing a corner system to join the west face. Once on the face, we climbed four pitches up cracks and face to just below the tilted summit needle. A short off-width crack lured me from more sensible climbing and I executed the final moves amid small clouds of lichen dust. The wire brush was a useful item. (II, 5.9.)

ALAN KEARNEY

Lexington Spire, East Face, Right Side, "Tooth and Claw." This seven-pitch route ascends slabs, roofs and discontinuous systems to the right of the standard east-face route. On June 24, Dave Tower and I scrambled to the highest ledge at the base of the face and climbed easily to bolted friction climbing. From here, the route is fairly obvious. The third pitch shares a belay with the standard route, but instead of following the open-book to the left, we climbed directly up to the small roofs above. The first five leads are all difficult, with the crux friction slab on the fifth pitch. A little loose rock is found on the last pitch, but otherwise the climb is solid and well protected. (IV, 5.11d.)

STEVEN C. RISSE

Washington Pass Overlook. On June 25, Brian Burdo, Dave Tower and I did the first free ascents of two routes on the cliff below the Washington Pass Overlook. *Bridal Flight* follows the obvious open-book in the middle of the cliff. At an overhang, an awkward exit right leads to a belay stance and easier climbing. (I, 5.10d.) *Over the Edge* is a spectacular three-pitch climb starting 40 feet left of Bridal Flight. Bolted face- and thin crack-climbing led right up to the overlook guard rail. (II, 5.11b/c.)

STEVEN C. RISSE

North Early Winter Spire, West Face, "Labor Pains." On Labor Day, Donna McBain and I did this fun six-pitch route on slabs and crack systems beginning just right of the large cave on the bottom of the west face. The middle pitches ascend through roofs with bolt- and fixed-pin protection. The fifth pitch ends next to the standard west-face route, which is followed to the summit. (III, 5.11a.)

STEVEN C. RISSE

Chimney Rock, North Peak, North Ridge. From an approach on the Overcoat Glacier, Donna McBain and I did this route on August 14. The first four pitches follow steep, lichen-covered rock, just east of the ridge crest, to the base of a large tower blocking the ridge. This is bypassed by easy fifth-class climbing to the west. From there, about 400 feet of fourth-class climbing reach the summit. (III, 5.7.)

STEVEN C. RISSE

Mount Index, North Peak, Supercouloir. On February 8, Jim Nelson and I hiked from Lake Serene through a 1360-foot pass to Anderson Creek. Within two hours we were at the base of the west face of the north peak of Index. A couloir, visible from the road, forks at about half height; we chose the right fork but were unprepared for what we found: a partially melted 200-foot tier of blue ice. A third of the way up the 4000-foot route, a large free-standing pillar of ice hung off the second snowfield. We bypassed both of these features to the left through cedar trees. Excellent névé and an occasional belayed ice bulge led to a bivouac in a forest of large trees below the west-face gendarmes. On the second day, we faced the crux: a steep, narrow, 300-foot-high ice smear which drained a hanging couloir above. We used rock protection almost exclusively here, except for two ice screws near the top. More névé with one short step led almost directly to the summit.

MARK BEBIE

Dragontail Peak, Northeast Buttress, Stuart Range. During a stormy July weekend, Wayne Wallace and I climbed the northeast buttress of Dragontail Peak. After approaching via Cold Chuck Lake, we proceeded on white granite up the toe of the northeast buttress. We leap-frogged six pitches of up to 5.11 and left our ropes fixed. We climbed down a terrifying 200-foot weakness of the Dragonfly route. Near the toe of the buttress we bivouacked without bivy sacks. A storm dumped sleet on us for six hours, robbing us of sleep. In the morning, black clouds billowed over us as we climbed unroped on damp rocks to our ropes. After prusiking up them, we decided to go for it. Wayne re-led a super 5.11c crack. After two pitches of moderate climbing to 5.10c, I led the crux of cracks up an overhanging corner. We then cruised the fearsomely exposed headwall on three pitches of 5.11b on thin hand cracks. Yoyoing through three roofs, we jammed upward as our ropes floated in space. We were ecstatic as we topped the beautiful white granite on the headwall. We then soloed 1000 meters up to 5.9+. We reached the top near the triple couloir as the sun set.

ROBERT MCGOWN

Dumbbell Mountain, Northeast Face, 1988. On September 5, 1988, I climbed this new route. I started at the high point of the snowfield between the main and northeast peaks of Dumbbell where an obvious steep, narrow gully divides the smooth faces. I followed the gully up and generally right (class 3 and 4). At the high point of the face on the right, a ledge led rightward to easy slopes north-northeast of the summit.

DAVID G. BRIGGS

Beacon Rock, Final Curtain, 1988. In July of 1988, Tim Olson and I climbed a discontinuous six-pitch arch, slab and dyhedral system up the central east face of Beacon Rock. Tim had attempted the route four times previously with Greg Lyons, Celil Colley, Wayne Wallace and me. On this ascent, we mostly free-climbed the wall, using some A3+ pins and a tension traverse. The second aid pitch was fixed from a previous attempt. In August, Tim and Wayne returned to free-climb the wall after Tim rappelled the route, cleaning dangerous exfoliated flakes and lichen. Neal Olson and Jim Davis free-climbed the route one week later, enjoying the second ascent.

ROBERT MCGOWN

Beacon Rock, East Face Closure. The southeast face of Beacon Rock was closed in July of 1989. The Washington State Park Ranger, Steve Johnson, caught two climbers climbing near the east central buttress. As they were ascending a new route, the ranger demanded that they come down and waited for their arrival. He was adamant about the east and southeast face closure. Previously, informally Beacon Rock's east face was closed due to traffic jams as cars stopped to watch climbers. Ranger Johnson threatened to cite the climbers for "mining without a permit" in a Washington State Park. There was also some rockfall from new-route activity near the trail. The closing of the southeast face is a loss to the climbing community. Long climbs, like Pacific Rim and Final Curtain, have gained popularity and kept the south face from overcrowding. The south face is more dangerous than the east face since there are many scree fields above the south face. The trails can be relocated away from the rock on the east and south faces. Beacon Rock State Park is a multi-use facility. Hikers have as much right to the south-face trails as climbers, although 85% of trail use is climber oriented. A petition is being circulated to reopen the southeast face to the central buttress. Negotiations with the park service are under way.

ROBERT McGOWN

Lithuanian-American Exchange. In August, a team of Lithuanian mountaineers arrived in the United States to climb in the Cascades, despite some last-minute complications in Moscow. They were Dainius Makauskas, Rimvydas Simutis, Vilius Saduikis, Keskutis Baleisis and Juazas Daugvila. While in the Northwest, they were generously hosted by various American friends and Lithuanian families. In the mountains they were accompanied by local climbers and second-generation Lithuanians. Despite unusually bad weather, they climbed the following summits: Cutthroat Peak by south buttress, Mount Rainier by Liberty Ridge, North Early Mountain Spire by northwest corner, Lexington Tower by east face, Snow Creek Wall by various routes, Ingalls Peak by south face, Mount Stuart by north ridge, Forbidden Peak by west ridge traverse and Mount Shuksan by north face. On September 10, the team departed for visits to Chicago, New York and Washington before returning home. The Lithuanians have invited an American team to climb in the Tien Shan Mountains of the USSR in August of 1990, two of the best known of which are Pik Pobedy and Khan Tengri. Climbers interested should contact me at 2226 Third Avenue, Seattle, Washington 98121. A spin-off from these activities is an invitation for Makauskas and Simutis to join Carlos Buhler and Michael Kennedy in their attempt this fall to climb the great east face of Dhaulagiri. It is a very exciting opportunity for Lithuanians to reach the summit of an 8000er. Contributions to make the trip possible may be sent to the Seattle Lithuanian Alpine Society, 2226 Third Avenue, Seattle, Washington 98121. For tax deductibility, make the check out to "American Mountain Foundation."

ALEX BERTULIS

California—Yosemite

Bunnell Point, Little Yosemite, "The Golden Bear." In June, Richard Swayze and I climbed two-and-a-half pitches on this large formation before retreating due to a lack of bolts. Mike Jauregui and I returned the following month to complete the climb. The route basically follows a huge dike that starts near the center of the wall and slants up and left for hundreds of feet. Two pitches follow the dike up and over a roof to a belay at the higher of two ledges. The third and fourth pitches (both 5.10) follow bolts left into a right-facing open-book, then up the book to a belay at a flake. The route climbs dikes over the book past two bolts to another belay. Several more dike pitches lead up and left to a ledge just east of an open-book with a squatty pine. Face climbing leads through a small but prominent white scar to a series of small corners which face right, then left higher up. Enjoyable climbing up these corners brought us to a solitary summit pine. Take a good selection of RPs and stoppers and one of each Friend of size 0 to 3½. We placed 15 bolts in 19 pitches. (V, 5.10b.)

BART O'BRIEN

El Capitan Climbed by a Paraplegic. Mark Wellman, whose fall on another Yosemite climb in 1982 rendered him a paraplegic with paralyzed legs, completed the climb of the Nose on El Capitan with Mike Corbett on July 26. He had to inch himself up with the use only of his arms. The pair had temperatures up to 100° F and very strong gusts of wind. They took nine days on the climb, starting on July 18. They climbed 300 feet on the last day from Chickehead Ledge.

California—Sierra Nevada

Moro Rock, East Face, Sequoia National Park, "Pièce de Renaissance." In mid April during a spell of clear weather, Jon Gatti, John Vargas and I completed this 9-pitch route just left of the climbs, Moro Oro and Full Metal Jacket. Fantastic face climbing on steep knobs characterizes this route for its entire distance, with the exception of three aid rivets at a blank headwall. A light selection of hardware from tiny to 3″ is recommended. (IV, 5.10, A1.)

EDWIN C. JOE

Angel Wings, South Face, "Hell on Wings." In July, Richard Leversee, Kim Grandfield and I climbed this route, located on the same pillar as the Rowell-Jones route. It follows a bold crack system just left of the aforementioned route and consists of several wide grooves. Most of the climb went free with some aid near the end of the third pitch and on the fifth pitch. Both sections involved minimal nailing, nutting and some serious hooking. After fixing the first three pitches, we completed the final seven (including "miles" of scrambling on the second day. (V, 5.10, A3.)

EDWIN C. JOE

Ruby Lake Wall, "Technical Knockout." It is somewhat confusing to describe routes on this wall. Basically, there is a series of four dihedrals in a row near the middle of the wall. The farthest left corner, which Kim Miller, Roanne Miller and I climbed in July, is one of the most striking lines on the face. It is very clean and steep, has a large roof halfway up on the left and is split high on the left side by a wide (3- to 8-inch) crack that looks like something straight out of the Utah desert. This high-quality route climbs those cracks for four steep, spectacular pitches. We descended via the gully below with several rappels. Take a double set of protection from ½″ to 5″. (III/IV, 5.11.)

RICHARD LEVERSEE

King's Canyon, Buck Rock. Old bolts give evidence of people climbing at Buck Rock for years. Below the lookout, there are some short, very overhanging faces. These short routes are both classics. *Mowin' the Yawn* (5.10a), a candidate for the steepest 5.10a in the state, ascends the left side of the southeast face (toward the road). *Temporary Insanity* (5.11+) is the obvious beautiful, very overhanging face directly below the lookout stairs. Access is via the Buck Rock Lookout road and a 200-yard walk on road and trail to the lookout. Both were climbed by Ron Carson, Jon Allen, Brian Hodges and me in November.

RICHARD LEVERSEE

Patricia Bowl, Rock Creek Area. Paticia Bowl is a high bowl directly above (northwest) of Rock Creek Lodge. Access is via the trail from just above Rock Creek Lake. On the right (north) side of the bowl is a series of towers on the ridge. *E-Ticket* (5.10b) climbs the obvious crack system on the large, clean, rectangular tower on the left for two pitches. *Diamond Star Tower* (5.10, two pitches) ascends the south side of the beautiful tower on the far right. The tower is visible from Rock Creek Lodge. *Templo del Sol* (5.11/12, four pitches) is on the longest continuous section of good-quality rock near the head of the bowl on its left side. The formation looks like a temple halfway up with vertical pillars on each side. The route ascends an obvious crack/corner system to the left side of the ledge, then up a very thin finger crack on the wall above. Two rappels got us down. Take a double set of protection from tiny to 3½″. All routes were done by Todd Vogel, Pat Kent and me.

RICHARD LEVERSEE

Mount Russell, West Chimney, The west face of Mount Russell is one of the finest big walls in the Sierra Nevada. In early September, after descending from another route on the peak, Steve Porcella and I stood under this face and spotted a steep chimney. It is left of the main west face but right of the west couloir. It

PLATE 34

Photo by Cameron Burns

**Steve Porcella on the First Ascent of
the West Chimney of Mount Russell,
California.**

was, in fact, the most noticeable unclimbed line on the mountain. Although late in the day, we eagerly started up. We climbed three pitches, including a 5.9 overhang on the second pitch, before traversing left and rappelling into the west couloir in total blackness. The next day, we quickly regained our highpoint and continued for five more pitches of chimneys and sometimes loose, poorly-protected climbing. Steve led the seventh and crux pitch, a shallow dihedral culminating in unprotected 5.10 face moves. (III, 5.10.)

CAMERON M. BURNS, *Los Alamos Mountaineers*

Mount Tyndall, Northeast Arête. The east face of Mount Tyndall is one of the most impressive walls in the Sierra Nevada. In early June, after spending two days watching avalanches sweep down the left side of the face, Cameron Burns and I decided to try what we believe was the unclimbed northeast arête. At its base is a large broken crack that ascends vertically for about two pitches, then splits, giving the appearance of a large "Y". Cameron took the first pitch, climbing a difficult bulge a short way up; however, the crux was higher on the pitch, a difficult face step off a sloping triangular block on the left side of the crack. On a ledge at the end of the fifth pitch, we were surprised to find the remains of a deer carcass, obviously dead from exposure. Class 4 and 5 slabs and a short headwall took us from there to the summit. (III, 5.9.)

STEVE PORCELLA, *Unaffiliated*

Mount Williamson, Direct South Arête. The south face of Mount Williamson is a complex wall of chutes, ribs and faces. The easiest approach to the face is via George Creek. However, this is closed for ten months of the year as a bighorn sheep preserve. The alternative is a strenuous hike through the Williamson-Trojan Peak saddle, which is closed for only five months of the year, from July 15 to December 15. On June 13, Steve Porcella and I made the strenuous hike and established camp near the massive face. The next day we climbed the most prominent arête on the face. We started on the right side of an enormous triangular tower in the center of the south face and followed a large dihedral for the first three pitches. At that point, the dihedral disappeared and the arête rises to the left as a wildly exposed knife-edge. Three pitches up the arête took us to a large flat ledge. Above the ledge was the crux, a right-facing corner. An exposed class-4 pitch took us to the top of the tower, where we unroped for the remaining 1500 feet to the summit. Most of this is class-4 with an occasional fifth-class move. The rock is excellent throughout the climb. (IV, 5.8.)

CAMERON M. BURNS, *Los Alamos Mountaineers*

North Palisade, Putterman Couloir. On July 2, Cameron Burns and I ascended what we believe to be a previously unclimbed couloir on the west side of North Palisade. On this face are three distinctive white cliffs. The original

COLOR PLATE 4

Photo by Paul Fehlau

Cameron Burns on the LEANING
TOWER, Jemez Mountains, New
Mexico.

PLATE 36

Photo by Steve Porcella

Cameron Burns in the West Chimney of Mount Russell, California.

west-side route, first climbed by LeConte in 1903, takes the gully between the two southernmost cliffs. Our route ascended between the two northern cliffs on the left. Loose third-or fourth-class climbing led to a steeper section up loose blocks and an orange headwall on the left, which was the crux. From there we traversed left, coming out on top of the northernmost cliff. This loose, dangerous route has nothing to recommend it. It is named for the Colorado mountaineer, Ethan Putterman. (II, 5.5.)

STEVE PORCELLA, *Unaffiliated*

North Palisade, "The White Ship." After climbing the Putterman Couloir, Steve Porcella and I ascended a route up the center of the northernmost cliff on North Palisade's west side. It starts in the center of the face, just left of a small black water-stain. The first pitch goes up a dihedral with a difficult mantle move. A blocky pitch follows and leads to a huge ledge. Another difficult dihedral and then two easier pitches took us to the top of the cliff. The rock is clean, very solid and of a beautiful white color. (II, 5.9.)

CAMERON M. BURNS, *Los Alamos Mountaineers*

North Palisade, "Es lässt sich nicht lesen." The day after climbing the previous two routes, Cameron Burns and I attempted to climb the west-face route on this peak. Unfortunately, we got lost trying to follow the description in the guidebook. We followed what we thought was the "wide chute" until it narrowed. Then we followed a white band to the right for several hundred feet, dropping down at one point to avoid a difficult unprotected traverse. At that point we had entered a steep, snow-filled couloir. Roping up, I led the first pitch, which involved 5.10 face moves on the right side of the couloir. The next pitch ascended left-facing corners to a large flat area. Two easy leads took us left across this flat area into an easy chimney system. The last pitch, also easy, gained the summit ridge behind a tower. We then dropped down onto the regular route and scrambled to the summit. (III, 5.10.)

STEVE PORCELLA, *Unaffiliated*

Middle Palisade, "Smoke Blanchard Memorial Route." On July 10, Steve Porcella and I climbed a new route on the west side of Middle Palisade. In the center of the face is a steep buttress, easily recognized by the two deep gullies on either side. We ascended the center of the buttress for eleven easy pitches, with a 5.9 headwall on the tenth pitch. At this point, there are several possibilities, all 5.9 or harder, leading to the top of the buttress. From there, a rappel is necessary. A class-3 ridge and class -4 chimneys led us to the top. This 14-pitch route boasts high-quality rock and is named for a long-time AAC member, Smoke Blanchard, who died in a car accident in early 1989. (IV,5.9, A1.)

CAMERON M. BURNS, *Los Alamos Mountaineers*

Split Mountain, "Horseshoe Arête." While climbing Middle Palisade, Cameron Burns and I noticed a massive ridge coming off P 13,803, curving west, northwest and finally north, encircling Lake 11,599 and forming a huge north-facing bowl. In late August, we established a camp under the west side of Split Mountain and started up the arête without ropes or hardware. The first mile was class-3 and then it steepened to sections of class-4. About halfway up the ridge, just past the junction of the Cardinal-Split ridge, we came to a precipitous notch. Deciding that the opposite wall looked too steep for soloing, we returned to camp and moved to Cardinal Lake. The next day, we returned to the notch and ascended a couloir to our previous highpoint. Cameron led the pitch on the opposite side of the notch, which was the crux of the climb. From there, we climbed mostly unroped, sometimes dropping to either side of the ridge to avoid loose blocks and towers. We finally reached the north summit late in the day and descended the south-side route. The route is 3.5 miles long and varies from superb to dangerously exposed on fractured rock. (IV, 5.6.)

STEVE PORCELLA, *Unaffiliated*

Utah

Cottontail Tower, East Face, Fisher Towers. This is an area known for soft, dirty rock and aid routes with long bolt ladders. Mine was the first major route without bolts and other drilled protection. There were long run-outs of A4, with potential multi-pitch rips. The route features extensive hooking and bashies with a crux pitch of thin, rotten expanding rock, looking at the big death fall. The last pitch goes all free at 5.10 and I got to the summit via an unprotected arête. I spent one night and nine days doing this 900-foot route. (VI, 5.10, A6.)

JAMES BEYER

New Mexico

"Leaning Tower," Jemez Mountains. Though they appear relatively gentle from the distance, the Jemez Mountains have many canyons, towers and crags and offer many climbing possibilities. In the Las Conchas area, rhyolite crags rise as high as 200 feet. Their warped and convoluted walls present challenges of route finding and protection. In September, I made reconnaissance hikes from the road at Las Conchas along the east fork of the Jemez River. I found a 170-foot rhyolite tower, whose east face overhung for the entire height. In 1978, George Rinker and Chris Foster attempted this east face, but, according to Rinker, he made it to within a few feet of the top before he ran out of gear. He downclimbed on direct aid to a point halfway up the tower. From there he was lowered to the ground. In October, I returned to the tower with Mike Schillaci and Paul Fehlau and began climbing a thin crack on the east face. After two

hours of awkward direct-aid climbing, in which I had gained only 80 feet, I lowered off the rock. I took a half-hour break. Realizing that the tower could be done in one pitch, I reascended to my high point and continued nailing. After passing Rinker's old pins, I continued on to the top, pulling over the edge just before sundown. I came back two days later to clean the route. (III, A2.)

CAMERON M. BURNS, *Los Alamos Mountaineers*

Idaho

P 10,240, Lemhi Mountains. For the most part, the Lemhi Mountains are rounded peaks of rotten sedimentary rock which offer little opportunity for interesting technical climbing. Fortunately, there is an exception. Located at the end of the Bear Valley Lakes trail is Bear Valley Lake (9135 feet) and P 10,240. On September 3, Jeannie Meyer-Tyson, Scott Tyson and I climbed the obvious crack-and-chimney system splitting the 900-foot-high northeast face on solid quartzite. The crux of this six-pitch climb (II, 5.7) comes at the slight overhang on the fifth pitch. The relatively easy access to the peak, the good fishing in the lakes of the Bear Creek valley and the large amount of virgin rock on the northeast face make this a worthwhile objective for any alpinist.

PATRICK M. LANG

Wyoming—Wind River Range

Wolverine Peak, North Buttress, 1988. James and Franciska Garrett and I climbed a new route at the head of the northeast cirque of seldom-visited Wolverine Peak on July 14, 1988. The buttress is spectacular with sound rock and good pitches. There was a rappel from a tower about midway up the climb. (III, 5.8.) The Garretts spent two days on the east face of Wolverine but cracks eventually bottomed out and became very moss-filled.

FRED BECKEY

CANADA

Yukon Territory

Mount Logan and Mount Kennedy, Icefield Ranges. A number of expeditions were on Mount Logan in 1989. Coloradans Peter Smith, JoAnn Metzler, Timothy Lofgren, Larz Onsrud and Ed Cupp were on the mountain in April and three of them reached the summit via the King Trench route. Also successful on the King Trench route were Bob Jonas, Reid Dowdle, Scott Smith and James McClatchy from Idaho. In May, Dave Williams, Timothy Franklin Booth, Greg Stattles, Darlene Anderson and Brian Waddington also reached the summit. An Austrian group in May failed. Mount Kennedy was climbed in May via the

Cathedral Glacier by Canadians Juri Peepre, Alan Jones, Joe Pilippone and Patrick Egan.

RON CHAMBERS, *Kluane National Park Reserve*

Mount Logan Research. A glaciological expedition led by me spent 42 days, from June 1 to July 13, on Mount Logan, carrying out a snow-pit sampling traverse and resurveying the snow saddle (5320 meters) between Russell Peak and Prospectors' Peak (5630 meters). This col will be a future new ice-core site for paleoclimatic and atmospheric environmental studies. The automatic weather station that we installed in 1988 was still recording temperature, but was missing the anemometer. We used the King Trench route to simplify the logistics, which involved helicopter lifts of equipment and supplies to 4800 meters on the edge of the "football field." Evacuation of equipment and samples was from the same point. The snow-pit stable isotope data show a vertical profile that can be interpreted in terms of tropospheric structure from 1780 meters on the Seward Glacier to 5920 meters on the West Peak. The main summit (5951 meters, 19,525 feet) was climbed on July 7 by R. Campbell, S. Chambers, J. Josephson and S. Richie. As usual, Andrew Williams provided air support from Kluane to the Quintino Sella Glacier.

GERRY HOLDSWORTH, *Arctic Institute of North America*

Mounts Wood and Queen Mary, Icefield Ranges, 1988. During the spring of 1988, the wardens of Kluane National Park made two training exercises. From April 22 to May 6, Rick Staley, Bruce Sundbo, Andrew Lawrence, Evan Manners, John Nidrie and I climbed Mount Wood (4842 meters, 15,885 feet) from the east. Three members also climbed a 10,000-foot peak to the east of Wood. From May 9 to 16, Ron Chambers, Ray Breneman, Lorne Laroque, Jeff Meir, Steve Oates and Dr. Roger Mitchell climbed Mount Queen Mary and skied out the Kluane Glacier.

LLOYD FREESE, *Kluane National Park Reserve*

McArthur Peak, Central Spur of South Face, 1988. From May 22, 1988 through May 26, Tim Friesen, Ken Wallator and I climbed a new line on a very prominent spur on the south face of McArthur Peak. The 7000-foot route offered excellent climbing on steep snow and ice and reasonably solid granite. We reached the 14,000-foot summit early on May 26 in $-30°$ temperatures. I cracked a bone in my foot in a short fall into a crevasse on the summit ridge but could complete the climb. We descended the west ridge for a short way and then dropped straight back down the south face to the Hubbard Glacier. Following this climb, Wallator and Friesen climbed the east ridge of Mount Logan in a remarkable six-day effort.

CHARLES SCOTT, *Alpine Club of Canada*

British Columbia Coast Range

Heartstone Peak, North Buttress. In late July, from a fine camp on a tiny outcrop at the edge of the Cataract Glacier icefall, Carl Diedrich, Greg Collum and I spent a beautiful day ascending this unclimbed buttress. The route was entirely snow and ice, the first part taking a traverse to the eastern part of the glacier, beneath the Four Horsemen. The untechnical ascent of the lower glacier, keeping close to the lower northern buttress, took several hours of weaving through crevasses. From the final col, where the striking narrow snow-and-ice crest of the upper buttress begins, we followed the crest. A pitch of rock completed the climb. We descended to the Tellot Glacier and then down the narrow, crevassed Cataract Glacier.

FRED BECKEY

Mount Styx, Bella Coola Range, British Columbia, 1988. On August 28, 1988, Fred Beckey, Stimson Bullitt and I made the first ascent of Mount Styx (2713 meters, 8900 feet). The biggest obstacle to successful ascents in this region is the weather. Storms from the Pacific move in quickly and frequently. Our first attempt on this remarkably beautiful peak took place the year before, in 1987. We flew to Bella Coola from Vancouver. Veteran mountaineer and local resident, Frank Cook, generously provided transportation to the back country. After a bumpy, two-hour ride over old logging roads, we arrived at Purgatory Lake. Since the river was too deep and swift for a safe crossing, we paddled across the lake in two rubber rafts, carefully avoiding floating chunks of ice spewed by the hanging glacier nearby. After a short bushwhack, we proceeded up the forested north flank of the mountain. Traversing upward across slabby rock, interspersed with waterfalls and brush, we reached the north shoulder just before sundown and established our high camp. We planned to climb the remaining 3000 feet of glacier and steep rock the next day. That night, the weather broke. The descent was wet and unpleasant in the whiteout the next morning. On August 27, 1988, during a predicted "window" of good weather, the same team of three drove from Seattle to Vancouver and caught the plane for Bella Coola. We transferred our gear to a waiting helicopter and flew to the north shoulder of Mount Styx by midday. There were several hours of daylight left and so Bullitt and I proceeded up the glacier to reconnoiter a route through the crevasses and icefall. Beckey remained to set up camp. Early the next morning, we retraced our steps from the day before. The crux of the climb was crossing a rather complex bergschrund onto the imposing northwest face. This entailed a pitch of steep ice. The face was uncomplicated and allowed for quick upward movement via 40° snowfields and broken ribs of rock. The summit was reached early in the afternoon, just as another storm arrived from the Pacific.

ALEX BERTULIS

Selkirks

Moby Dick, 1988. The very prominent steep and crevassed north glacier of Moby Dick was climbed for the second time on July 24, 1988 by Dave Pollari, Jim Ruch and me. During a 1986 trip into the Battle Range we had contemplated the route, but wide-open crevasses and threatening séracs made us opt for rock routes. In 1988, as in 1978, the conditions were excellent with a few short steep snow-and-ice sections amid moderate glacier runouts. One crevasse was a problem on the ascent but quite jumpable on the descent. (Grade III.) On July 25, 1988, Pollari and Ruch climbed a prominent curved dihedral on the major rock buttress left (east) of the north glacier, which they called *The Boomerang.* There were a number of wet, polished slabs and mixed ice-and-rock pitches. The route was more committing than the north glacier and ended on the summit ridge east of the top. They descended the north glacier. (Grade IV.)

FRED BECKEY

Gimli, Valhalla Group, 1988. On August 12, 1988, Cliff Leight, Peter Jewett, Dan Waters and I climbed a new line on Gimli on the right edge of the northwest buttress. The rock is excellent quartzite with incut holds on a steep and exposed corner (II or III, 5.8).

FRED BECKEY

Ahab, 1986. Ronald Van Horssen, Steve Drake and I climbed the striking pillar on the lower southwest face of Ahab in August 1986. We ascended the striking pillar, which has several spectacular towers, and ends on the south summit of Ahab (II, 5.8). That same August, we climbed the upper south buttress directly (5.7). The rock is blocky granite, reminiscent of the Bugaboos.

FRED BECKEY

Canadian Arctic

Climbs in Auyuttuq National Park, Baffin Island. On August 7, Willard Moulton, Bill Morris, Jim Osborne, Dr. Douglas Halliday, Dr. Michael Parker and I were boated to the Overlord Camp at the head of Pangnirtung Fiord. We carried our too-heavy loads up the Weasel Valley in misty weather, turning east up the Tiroka Glacier to set up Base Camp below Mount Sif on August 11. Eight inches of fresh snow on the glacier made sled hauling and ski approaches possible. We enjoyed five days of unusually clear, warm weather. On the 12th, Morris, Parker and I made the second ascent of the Sandcastle Ridge. Meanwhile, Moulton, Osborne and Halliday made a ski ascent of a subsidiary peak (reference 404550) three miles due east of Mount Sif. On August 13, Parker and I skied over a col and descended north to the base of a double-peaked mountain (reference 403550). A first ascent of the south summit was made via the east-face snowfields and a short summit rock scramble. That same day, Moulton, Morris and Osborne climbed a subsidiary buttress of Mount Sif behind Base Camp. On the 14th, Moulton, Morris and I climbed a solitary triangular peak immediately south of the Park boundary (reference 491500). The northwest-face route included initial rock scrambling to a steepening snow face and a short pitch up the summit block. The final climb, on August 15, was the first ascent of the north peak of a prow-shaped mountain due east of Mount Sig (reference 403500). Parker, Halliday and Moulton ascended on skis via a col and south slopes, finishing with a rock scramble. On the 16th, in worsening weather, we carried all the way to Overlord.

JAMES VERMEULEN

Borup Fiord, Ellesmere Island, 1988. Although the primary aims of the expedition were scientific, there was mountaineering activity. Most peaks over 3000 feet in the area were climbed. Mount Leith (3822 feet; 80° 51′ 30″ N, 81° 36′ 20″ W) was climbed on May 17, 1988. It was a good alpine walk or scramble. P 3500+ (80° 56′ N, 81° 25′ W) and Mount Burrill (80° 56′ N, 81° 26′ W) were climbed on May 30 and June 10. Five peaks on the Ellmerson Peninsula were climbed on June 13 and 14: P 3500+ (80° 44′ 10″ N, 81° W), P 3500+ (80° 44′ 50″ N. 80° 55′ W), P 3500+ (80° 45′ 30″ N, 80° 55′ W), P 3860+ (80° 46′ 30″ N, 80° 52′ 30″ W) and 3500+ (80° 55′ N, 82° W). On June 14 and July 4, other parties climbed P 3500+ (81° 01′ 50″ N, 82° W) and P 3500+ (81° 01′ 50″ N, 81° 45′ 10″ W) flanking the Base Camp valley. On July 14, Mount Schuchert (3855 feet, 80° 46′ N, 84° 45′ W) was climbed, a fine alpine peak with a pointed snow-capped summit. On August 9, P 5300+ and P 5000+ (81° 03′ 30″ N, 80° 55′ 30′ W and 81° 04′ 30″ N, 80° 59′ 20″ W) were climbed; they were 20 miles from Base Camp. On the return trip, five peaks of 4500+ feet were traversed; the coordinates of the first and fifth are 81° 02′ 10″ N, 81° 00′ 30″ W and 81° 00′ 45″ N, 80° 58′ 30″. Whilst making a traverse of the Neil Peninsula, its high-point (3250+ feet; 80° 50′ N, 82° 10′ W) was climbed on August 15.

CORPORAL DAVID WALKER,
Royal Air Force, Joint Services Expedition

GREENLAND

Gunnbjørns Fjeld, Dome and Cone, 1988. Our expedition consisted of Lars Ogenhag and me, Sweden; Peter Herzog, Austria; Mark Jenkins, USA; and Helge Bardseth, Norway. We flew to the region from Isafjördur, Iceland. Except for Bardseth, we all climbed to the summit of Gunnbjørns Fjeld (3708 meters, 12,166 feet) on July 3, 1988. From the top we saw two other high peaks about ten kilometers to the south. Excellent weather made it possible to climb both. We skied and pulled sleds to the south, skirting the eastern side of Gunnbjørns Fjeld and establishing two more camps. The Dome was ascended on July 6 by Herzog and Jenkins and again on the 7th by Herzog and me and the Cone on July 7 by Jenkins and Ogenhag. Our aneroid barometer readings showed that the former is 3790 meters and the latter 3780 meters high.

INGEMAR OLSSON, *Major, Marine Reserve, Sweden*

Note on the Altitudes of Gunnbjørns Fjeld, Dome and Cone. Although Major Olsson has made the claim that both Dome and Cone are higher than Gunnbjørns Fjeld and has suggested that Dome be named "Ingemars Fjeld" and Cone "Lars Fjeld," the Danish Geodaetisk Institut has informed us that Ingemar Olsson's surveying methods were very primitive and that further control has proved that Gunnbjørns Fjeld is the highest mountain in Greenland. The Institute further informed us that it will not accept the names of Ingemars Fjeld and Lars Fjeld as mountains cannot be named for living persons.

Gunnbjørns Fjeld. A Mountain Travel expedition made another ascent of Gunnbjørns Fjeld. On June 26, Americans Jim Williams, Jerry Corr, Robert Hoffman and I and Dane Gunnar Jensen climbed to the summit. An original objective of measuring neighboring peaks by triangulation was not possible because of the weight of carrying the theodolite to the top in soft snow.

LEO LE BON

Previous History of Gunnbjørns Fjeld. James Lowther has been kind enough to supply us with further data about Gunnbjørns Fjeld. After Gino Watkins' expedition of 1930-31 had spotted the peak, Martin Lindsay fixed its position in 1934 during his remarkable crossing of Greenland from the west coast. In 1935 Augustine Courtauld succeeded in getting to the peak from the east coast and climbing it. His route followed the Sorgenfri Glacier from Jakobsen's Fjord and crossed the Christian IV Glacier from Icefall Pass. The party took aneroid barometer readings on the summit, which gave a height of 12,200 feet (3718 meters). In 1984, the Geodaetsik Institut determined the height to be 3708.53 meters, using a Global Positioning System, a difference of only 10 meters. Before 1988, the region was visited again only twice. In 1971, Alistair Allen's expedition approached from the Rosenborg and then the Korridoren Glacier. (See *AAJ*, 1972, pages 151-2.) In 1987, Woolley's expedition roughly followed Courtauld's route from Sødalen. (See *AAJ*, 1988, p. 153.) On all three ascents of Gunnbjørns Fjeld, two mountains were noted, which resembled a cone and a dome, probably the second and third highest mountains in the Arctic. We apologize for previous misspellings of Gunnbjørns Fjeld. Mr. Lowther has given us more details about the peaks climbed by his group and also of the 1986 expedition, in which he participated.

Gunnbjørns Fjeld, 1988, More Details. (This will help complete the report given in *AAJ*, 1989, page 164.) In addition to Greg Englefield, Nick Hulton,

Lewis Jones and me, we were also accompanied by a film crew, Allen Jewhurst and Jan Pester. After we landed to the north of Gunnbjørns Fjeld, we did not appreciate that Cone and Dome were very close to Gunnbjørns Fjeld; otherwise we would have skied straight there since they were our primary objectives. We chose instead to head into the unexplored part of the Watkins Mountains, southeast of the peak. We ascended a glacier north of the Rosenborg Glacier, roughly parallel to it, just north of the main chain of the Watkins Bjerge. We made the first ascent of six of the highest and most attractive peaks in the southeastern part of the range. These were P 3600 (68° 47.7′ N, 29° 36′ W) on June 30 by Hulton, Lowther; P 3190 (68° 48.2′ N, 29° 17.5′ W) on July 3 by Englefield, Jones, Jewhurst; P 3330 (68° 49.7′ N, 29° 10.5′ W) on July 4 by Hulton, Pester, Lowther; P 3550 (68° 46.1′ N, 29° 24′ W) on July 6 by Hulton Pester, Lowther; P 3500 (68° 48.4′ N, 29° 32′ W) on July 7 by Englefield, Jones, Hulton, Jewhurst by two different routes; P 3400 (68° 49.4′ N, 29° 30′ W) on July 7 by Lowther, Hulton. We then placed our third climbing camp at 3400 meters on the col between Gunnbjørns Fjeld and Cone with the base of the former some 800 meters away. Cone lay four kilometers away across a small icecap and beyond that, with a glacier in between, was Dome. After some bad weather, on July 12 we all made the fifth ascent of Gunnbjørns Fjeld, climbing the south-southwest ridge in an hour and a half. On July 13 Jones and I ascended Cone, skiing three kilometers to the base of the mountain and climbing the east ridge. Hulton, Englefield and Pester repeated the climb the next day. On July 14, I climbed Dome. The following are our conclusions on the height of Cone and Dome. Having set both our Thommen altimeters on the summit of Gunnbjørns Fjeld, we determined the height of our camp to be 370 meters beneath the summit. From there, we made two ascents of Cone in about an hour and 15 minutes. On both occasions, we recorded with both altimeters a height of 3670 meters, 38 meters less than Gunnbjørns Fjeld. I took five hours to climb Dome and did not return to camp to check if there had been a change of atmospheric pressure. However, the height of 3650 meters would seem to be very logical. It has already been noted that on July 17 Jones and I made the first ascent of P 3080 (69° 10.6′ N, 29° 33′ W), probably the highest mountain in Knud Rasmussen Land.

JAMES LOWTHER, *Royal Geographical Society*

Mont Forel and Schweizerland, 1986. On the evening of July 9, 1986, Duncan Bond, Greg Englefield, Jim Lowther and I departed by boat from Angmagssalik to the head of Tasilaq Fjord where our Base Camp was to be located a few kilometers up the valley. On July 14, we pulled away with loaded pulks at snowline. The first three days as far as Conniats Pass were trouble-free over smooth snowfields. The fourth day brought our first serious obstacle, the crevasses of Midgaårdgletscher. We could finally use skis again from the top of Midgaårdgletscher onto the Glacier de France and into the Femstjernen. Crevasses there forced us to leave the pulks there and to push forward to Mont Forel backpacking. We progressed up the Paris Gletscher and onto Bjørnegletscher until at the end of Day 10 we were camped beneath the bulk of Forel's southern flank. Good weather enabled us on July 25 and 26, 1986 to make the first British ascent of the mountain (the eighth in all) from the south, using Roch's 1938 first-ascent route. We then skied along the edge of the icecap before descending through Døren down the length of the Paris Gletscher to recover our pulks and continue into unexplored Schweizerland. Our initial route lay down the chaotic Franche Conté Gletscher, where we were forced to continue backpacking. After the difficulties of the Franche Comté, we found a relatively easy route taking us further west into Schweizerland. After a three-day storm, we made five first ascents in this virgin area before commencing our return to the coast. The ascents there follow: P 1950 (66° 32' 40" N, 36° 59' 20" W) on August 6, 1986 by Englefield, Jones, Lowther; P 2100 (66° 33' 10" N, 37° 15' 00" W) on August 11 by Englefield Jones; P 2050 (66° 31' 25" N, 37° 06' 00" W) on August 12 by Jones, Lowther; P 1910 (66° 32' 00" N, 36° 05' 00"W) on August 13 by Bond, Lowther; P 2250 (66° 32' 20" N, 37° 01' 30" W) on August 14 by Bond, Englefield, Jones, Lowther.

LEWIS JONES, *Royal Geographical Society*

Milne Island, Scorseby Sound, East Greenland. From July 29 to August 18, Michael Garrett, Pamela Glanville, Margaret Graham, Philip Nixon, John Shrewsbury, Belinda Swift, Christopher Whitford and I explored the area around the Korridoren Glacier and climbed seven unclimbed peaks, including the highest on the island, P 1867 (6109 feet). We were landed by Twin Otter plane on the delta of the Korridoren River, where we had also been landed in 1986, when we had made one of the first visits to the island. We moved up the Korridoren Glacier to Advance Base close to an icefall coming from a side glacier that we needed to climb to reach our main objective, P 1867. We worked our way up the icefall to a high glacier plateau. We ascended three unclimbed mountains, including P 1867, in perfect weather. We progressed up the Korridoren Glacier to its summit and watershed. After two days, the party split, five members going back down to Base Camp for study along the coast of plant, bird and animal life. The remaining three members at the high glacier camp, climbed another four unascended mountains.

MALCOLM SALES, *Royal Geographical Society*

Peaks Above Fenrisgletscher, Schweizerland, East Greenland. Elziro Molin, Gastone Lorenzini and I as leader were helicoptered from Tasiilaq on June 26 to a 1050-meter-high Base Camp in an unexplored region near the head of the Fenrisgletscher just below the Inland Icecap. In beautiful weather, we ascended the next day a side glacier to the east and climbed the principal peak in 11 hours on slopes up to 55°. After a period of rest, Molin and Lorenzini climbed P 2080 (6,824 feet) from the south and then traversed south to the top of P 2180 (7,153 feet). Meanwhile, I crossed the Fenrisgletscher solo to the western edge of the glacier and entered a cirque opposite Base Camp. I climbed a steep icefall with pitches up to 85° where I had access to the summits of four peaks, three along the western wall of the glacier and P 2010 (6595 feet). I was back in Base Camp after 25 hours. Thus, in ten days we explored the region and made seven first ascents.

GIANNI PAIS BECHER, *Club Alpino Italiano*

P 2100, Kap Farvel, 1974 and 1986. Beyond Kangikitsoq on the right bank of the fjord rises imposing P 2100 (6890 feet). At the beginning of August in 1974, Claude Aulard, Alan Douglas and I climbed a difficult 1200-meter-high route up the great couloir on the west face. We bivouacked once. This was a second ascent although a new route. We followed a British party led by Richard Hoare; David Cornell and Tim Hurrell discovered a straight snow route to the summit up the southeast ridge. The British route was repeated in 1977. From July 30 to August 3, 1986, Jean-Paul Bouquier, Gérard Creton and Christian Veronese made a third new route on rock on the southwest buttress which rose 900 meters in 40 pitches (UIAA VI, A1).

BERNARD DOMENECH, *Club Alpin Français*

SOUTH AMERICA

Ecuador

Sangay. Although Sangay (5323 meters, 17,463 feet) was no first ascent, it will be useful to give information for anyone who decides to go there. Jim Velie, my brother Dana and I set off from Quito to Riobamba by bus, where for about $8 we hired a taxi that took us three and food and equipment in two hours to Alao, a tiny village. There we met up with Casimiro Lema Quillay, an excellent guide. He had hired four porters for $4 a day. One must inquire a week in advance to hire Casimiro, whom we highly recommend. The next morning we set out up the valley to an obvious notch in the southern side of the valley. We were in ankle-to knee-deep mud, which was to be our daily companion. The Amazon jungle air mixes with the cool mountain air to produce constant moisture, from fog to drizzle. I recommend knee-high rubber boots for the mud and numerous stream crossing. They are available in Quito up to about size 9. Porters should carry all your gear since the mud takes getting used to. On our first day we gained 3000 feet to the cloud-shrouded pass and then descended a long, steep-sided ridge to drop 4000 feet to the Río Culebrillas. If you are lucky, the clouds will part and give you a spectacular view. In the evening it tends to be clearer and the view of Sangay becomes spectacular. The bright red lava constantly weeps, flowing and bouncing down a 4000-foot wall from the northwest crater. After a rest day, we set off in the rain for Yana Yaku, where we entered a dense temperate rain forest on a trail, if you can call it that. It wanders up and down badlands. Vertical mud steps with only grass to cling to require leather gloves to prevent the grass from cutting hands. On that day, we crossed

33 rivers and streams and wallowed in mud in constant drizzle. The next day we found that the best terrain feature to follow was ridge crests that usually are no wider than a foot with steep sides you wouldn't want to fall down. It finally brought us to an ancient lava flow, a welcome relief from the arduous trail. We camped in La Playa, an area already showing signs of too many campsites. From here when the weather is clear, Sangay is awesome with reverberating booms of eruptions, huge glowing rocks cascading down and plumes of volcanic ash and gas soaring thousands of feet into the atmosphere. At night the show was even more outstanding. Luckily we had ten straight hours of clear skies. The next morning it was drizzling again as we set off through sulphur steam and vegetation that made you wonder if a dinosaur might not appear. The forest gave way to grasslands, then to petrified lava towers covered with moisture-weeping mosses and lichens and finally to barren lava scree and boulders. Casimiro went no further and warned us of cannonballs of stone even on the safest route. We changed rubber boots for mountain shoes. We stuck to thin waves of snow that gave better footing than the lava scree. We climbed unroped to be able to play dodgeball when the rocks flew. Lava scree and snow finally gave way to sand-like black ash. The sulphur smell and gasses made our eyes water and our high-altitude breathing painful. Finally, we arrived on the saddle next to the middle crater, inactive at the moment. We could hardly see in the impenetrable ground fog created by the vapor and steam. I explored toward the lava-spewing north crater, feeling my way and leaning on lava towers for support. The heat became unbearable and my gloves sizzled on the rocks I leaned on. I returned to the others and we started up the last hundred feet toward the true summit which is the lip of the third crater. When we were not more than three feet away from it, a huge eruption occurred. Ash, small rocks and noxious gases nearly overwhelmed us. Yet we kept our cameras going. In the 45 minutes we spent on the summit, we witnessed another eruption. We did some fantastic giant-step glissading in the lava scree on the descent. It took us three days to return to Alao. Casimiro and the porters agilely ran on slime mud downhill with heavy packs. Some hints: Use rubber boots. Buy food in Quito where the variety is great. Take lightweight, ventable rain gear. Plastic bags are a must. Cotton clothes never dry; use polypro. No technical gear is needed other than a good helmet. You'll never find your way in without a good guide.

STEVE UNTCH

Cayambe, North Side, Cotopaxi, Yanasacha Wall and Tungurahua, South-west Flank and South Ridge. A new route on the north side of Cayambe (5789 meters, 18,993 feet) was completed on August 9, 1988 by four residents of Quito, some of them foreign: Luis Gonano, Eric Lawrie, David Purdy and Phil Townsend. They started from Lago San Marcos, ascended the glacier, the north face and the north buttress. They bivouacked 100 meters below the summit. The last part was extremely steep with crevasses and séracs. They descended the normal route. Although it is only some 350 feet high, the Yanasacha rock wall provided a direct ascent up the north side of Cotopaxi (5997 meters, 19,345 feet). It is a fairly difficult climb because of the unstable volcanic rock. On May 1, 1989, Emilio Salgado, Jorge Peñafiel, Eduardo Agama and Danilo Mayorga climbed this new route. After the wall, they encountered only ice. On February 26, Pablo Catalán and Alfredo Mensi climbed Volcán Tungurahua (5005 meters, 16,420 feet) for the first time by its southwest flank and south ridge.

FREDDY LANDÁZURI, *Editor, Campo Abierto, Quito*

Peru

Notable Ascents in the Cordillera Blanca, 1989. I feel that the international press has exaggerated the danger to climbers in the Cordillera Blanca. Despite many fewer climbers, many have visited the region safely during the past year. Among other climbs made in the region, I note the following. *Taulliraju:* From July 5 to 10, New Zealanders Peter Sykes and Lionel Clay made the second ascent of the English Fowler-Watts route on the southwest face with a variation at the beginning, where they went further left on the spur. *Huantsán Oeste, Southwest Face and South Ridge; Santa Cruz; Huandoy Sur and Norte:* Frenchmen Daniel Bianchi, Emmanuel Beguin, Jean Philippe Floras and Eric Brochot climbed a new route on the southwest face of Huantsán Oeste from July 20 to 25. They reached the summit on July 23 and went on to attempt the main summit, but they gave up 50 meters from the top because of the exposure, 60° to 70° ice and unstable séracs. In the final part, they joined the Italian route of 1973; the Italians also failed to climb from the western foresummit to the main summit. At the end of July they moved to the Llanganuco valley, where they climbed Huandoy Sur by the southwest ridge and on to Huandoy Norte the next day. Joined by Sylvie Tubiana and Marie-Claire Mandon, between June 28 and July 6, they climbed Santa Cruz by the northeast face and north ridge, the original 1948 route. Catalans Toni Casa, Jordi Sunyer and Joan Amils carried out a remarkable program in June and July. See below. *Ocshapalca:* On July 26, Catalans Olivier Cantet, Víctor Domenech and Albert Castellet repeated the route on Ocshapalca done shortly before by Casa, Sunyer, Amils and Obregón. *Aguja Nevada, Ocshapalca, Vallunaraju Sur, Maparaju and Cayesh.* On June 21, Gianni Calcagno, M. Giovale and Roberto Piombo climbed the Aguja Nevada by its northwest face. On the 28th, Calcagno and Piomba made still another new route on the south face of Ocshapalca. The same pair climbed a new rock route on the southeast face of Vallunaraju Sur on June 30. These two then ascended Maparaju by the west face on July 6 and Cayesh by the 1986 English route in a single day from Base Camp, on July 7.

WALTER SILVERIO,
Asociación de Guías de Montaña del Perú

Quitaraju, Alpamayo, Tsurup, Pisco, Ocshapalca, Cayesh. For acclimatization Joan Amils and I climbed the north face of Quitaraju on June 16 and the southwest face of Alpamayo. On June 28, we repeated the 1982 Spanish route on the southwest face of Tsurup, a fine, difficult ice route. Jordi Sunyer then joined

PLATE 37

Photo by H. Adams Carter

**HUANTSÁN, Cordillera Blanca,
from the Southwest.**

us and we did Pisco for his acclimatization. We three, joined by Amandi Obregón, did a route, possibly a new one, on the south face of Ocshapalca on July 11. It ascended one of the flutes to the right of Grassi's and emerged on the rock ridge to the right of the summit. It averaged 60° to 70° with 85° to 90° in the last two pitches. Our last climb was the northwest face of Cayesh, where Amils, Sunyer and I on July 19 to 20 climbed the 1986 British route with a bivouac on the face.

TONI CASAS, *Barcelona, Spain*

Tocllaraju, Southwest Face. The expedition of our newly founded Club de Montañeros Américo Tordoya placed a Base Camp in the Quebrada Ishinca. While we climbed Urus and Tocllaraju by the normal routes, Mario Masuelos and Gonzalo Menacho headed for the unclimbed southwest face of Tocllaraju (6032 meters, 20,795 feet). On July 21, they left their high camp at 5350 meters and climbed 50° slopes that gradually steepened to 60°. They emerged on the ridge and got to the summit at 7:25 P.M. almost in total darkness. They rappelled down the same route.

WALTER LAZO, *Club de Montañeros Américo Tordoya, Lima, Perú*

Huandoy, Correction. In *AAJ, 1988,* page 158, the climb given as Huascarán Norte was actually of Huandoy Norte. The same error appears in the caption of Plate 34.

Colque Cruz V and Other Peaks, Cordillera Vilcanota. Our expedition was composed of Jon Morgan, James Hall, Charles Halstead, Tim Dickinson and me as leader. In Malma we hired eight horses for the 16-kilometer trek to our 4825-meter-high Base Camp. On July 15, we established a bivouac site at 5050 meters on the glacier below Chuchillo and Kiru. The following day, we all made the second ascent of Kiru (5700 meters, 18,701 feet) by the north ridge. On July 17, we attempted Chuchillo but turned back at 5500 meters because of avalanche danger and altitude problems. On July 21, we all plodded up to 5520 meters on the northeast face of Colque Cruz IV and dug a snow hole. The next day, we climbed up and over a spur coming down from Colque Cruz IV, but only Dickinson and Hall carried on. They climbed up steep ground to reach the col between Colque Cruz V and VI, having bivouacked on the face. After a third bivouac on the 5800-meter col, they attempted the southeast ridge of Colque Cruz V. Poor conditions, cornices and snow mushrooms forced them back. On July 25, Morgan and I set off from Base Camp to climb Colque Cruz VI by its northeast face, a new direct line. Initially it was up relatively easy rock, ice and snow. The final 100 meters were 70° to 90° ice flutings to the summit (5980 meters, 19,620 feet). We reached the top two hours after sunset and had seven unenviable hours abseiling to a 5300-meter bivouac on the glacier. On July 28, we five set off for a second attempt on unclimbed Colque Cruz V. We bivouacked

at 5300 meters on the glacier below the north face. The next day, we made good progress up fairly easy snow to a rock band that proved to be the crux. A short pitch of difficult rock led to a rock gully system that allowed us to reach the final 50 meters of steep ice before the ridge. From there it was a 20-meter wallow through powder snow to the summit (5965 meters, 19,570 feet). We got to the top at sundown and had five hours of exhausting abseiling to reach the bivouac site. Morgan and I made an attempt on Colque Cruz I and II but were turned back at 5650 meters by heavy snow at the start of a three-day storm.

SIMON COOKE, *Sheffield University Mountaineering Club, England*

Tacusiri, Ausangate and Other Peaks, Cordillera Vilcanota. Because of terrorism in the Cordillera Huayhuash, we changed our objective to the Vilcanota. On June 13, Bruce Jardine, Andy Bunnage, John Lyall and I established Base Camp on the banks of Jatun Pucacocha. To the north, the icefalls of Ausangate tumbled into the turquoise lake. The spectacular rock spires of the Surimani group rose to the south. During our stay, all four climbed Tacusiri by the northeast ridge and Ausangate (6372 meters, 20,905 feet) from the southeast. We made the first ascents of three peaks which lie west of Señal Nevado Extremo Ausangate. Lyall and I in 9½ hours climbed an obvious couloir directly up the center of the triangular south face of P 5300 (17,389 feet; Grid Reference 545745), an excellent 650 meters of steep ice and mixed climbing. The other two peaks lie east of the first. From a snow hole south of a col between them, Jardine, Bunnage and I climbed P 5370 (17,618 feet; GR 550750) and P 5400 (17,717 feet; GR 555745). Perhaps the most difficult route was Lyall and Bunnage's on Tacurani, the spectacular spire southwest of Base Camp. A couloir led to the notch south of the summit and was followed by steep mixed ground on the south face, 400 meters of very technical climbing. They descended the northeast ridge. At the same time, Jardine and I climbed the south peak of Jatunhuma. We failed to climb new routes on the north side of Ausangate and the impressive southwest face of Mariposa because of delicate snow conditions.

STEVEN AISTHORPE, *Scotland*

Bolivia

Iscacuchu, Cololo, Huelancalloc and Other Peaks, Northern Pupuya Group, Cordillera Apolobamba. Steve Hillen, leader, Ian Burgess, Ian Diamond, David Lister, Tim and Kathy Mather, Ian Woolgar and I visited the southern Cordillera Apolobamba. This region had been previously visited by Germans in 1957 (*AAJ, 1958*, p. 102) and by Japanese in 1961 (*AAJ, 1962*, p. 254) and 1965 (*AAJ, 1966*, pp. 182-3). On July 28, we drove from La Paz to Paso Osipal between the Pupuya and the Cololo groups and the next day set up Base Camp two kilometers southeast of the pass at 4900 meters in a pasture below the glacier of Iscacuchu. During the next three weeks, we climbed most of the peaks near the pass. The triple-summited peak of Iscacuchu (5665 meters, 18,586 feet) was climbed several times: direct north faces of the southwest (Diamond, Hillen; August 1) and central (Burgess, Lister; August 3) summits, and complete traverses both southwest-northeast (Burgess, Lister, T. Mather; August 10) and northeast-southwest (Shellabear, Woolgar; August 14). Huerancalloc (5836 meters, 19,145 feet) was traversed by Diamond, Hillen, Woolgar and me on August 10; we ascended the west ridge from a cave bivouac at 5000 meters and descended the north ridge. Cololo (5915 meters, 19,405 feet) was climbed on the second attempt via the west ridge by Burgess, Hillen, Lister, T. and K. Mather on August 13. The following peaks were also ascended; Mita (5465 meters, 17,930 feet) via north ridge on July 31 by Burgess, Lister and on August 17 by Diamond, Hillen, Shellabear, Woolgar; Wellencamp (5185 meters, 17,011 feet; assumed to be the rock peak northeast of the Iscacuchu group) via northwest ridge by Diamond, Shellabear on August 13 and by T. and K. Mather on August 16; twin-summited P 5375 (17,634 feet; just north of Iscacuchu) via north-south traverse by Hillen, Woolgar on August 6; Posnansky (5385 meters, 17,667 feet) via southwest ridge of the south summit by Shellabear, Woolgar on August 7; Cunuareya (5370 meters, 17,618 feet; rock peak two kilometers north of Paso Osipal) via northeast ridge by Burgess, Lister, K. Mather on August 5 and by Diamond, Hillen on August 8; Sunchuli (5305 meters, 17,405 feet; snow peak one kilometer southeast of Posnansky) via west flank by T. Mather, Shellabear on August 4 and by Diamond, Woolgar on August 15. The last two names were given us by local shepherds.

MICHAEL SHELLABEAR,
Loughborough Students Mountaineering Club, UK

Cololo, Palomani Grande, Huanacuni and Nubi, Cordillera Apolobamba. David Tyson, Pamela Holt and I climbed on both sides of the Peruvian-Bolivian border during August. We had Base Camp for two weeks at the head of Lago Nubi, from which we climbed Cololo (5915 meters, 19,405 feet) by the north ridge, a new route, and descended the west ridge. We placed a high camp at 18,000 feet on the snowfield below the north and west ridges. We got to the summit on August 9 after 15 hours on the north ridge. We had mixed climbing mostly on the eastern side of the ridge just below the crest. The shattered rock was very steep in sections and required care. The final 250 meters were corniced to the west and we had to traverse 70° snow on the eastern side. We failed on Huanacuni (5705 meters, 18,717 feet) after underestimating the difficulties. The long, horizontal ridge from Cololo to Huanacuni looked as if it would be easy, but access proved more difficult than expected. Once on the ridge, we encountered a steep, knife-edged section with poor snow and so abandoned the route. We did climb Nubi (5710 meters, 18,734 feet) on August 14. This is a preliminary peak on the ridge south of Huanacuni. Our second Base Camp was established just north of Lago Suches about two miles over the frontier into Peru. From there we made the first ascent of the southwest ridge of Palomani Grande (5677 meters, 18,924 feet). The lower two-thirds of this ridge was a scramble over shattered slate with two pitches over harder, steeper rock. We camped at the base of the snow spur leading to the final summit slopes. On August 24, we climbed the snow spur in three 70° pitches. The final summit slopes had séracs and a few wide crevasses.

DAVID WOODCOCK, *Bath University, England*

Pico del Norte, Illampu Group. In the middle of August, Spaniards Alvaro Fernández and Miguel Merlo climbed what they believe is a variant on the German route. They began to the right of the German route, then joined it and left it to the right near the top.

Chachacomani, Chearoco and Other Peaks, 1984 to 1989. The American Alpine Institute has conducted a number of expeditions into the Chachacomani-Chearoco massif over the past few years. We normally approached from the east into the Echsococho valley. A number of ascents of Chachacomani (6066 meters, 19,902 feet) were made. Usually we ascended the east face to the middle of the northeast ridge, which was then followed to the summit. However, on August 1, 1989, John Culberson, Geof Bartram, Larry Hall and Matt Koehler climbed a new route on the southeast buttress. This is the most difficult route we have done on Chachocamani. There was 70° ice and 5.7 rock. On August 5, Culberson, Bartram, Hall, Koehler, Mark Adams and Richard Reidy ascended the southeast face of Chearoco. It is probably the route by which the British Reading University Expedition made the first ascent of the peak in 1962. In 1985, Germans Georg and Josef Seifried climbed the southeast face, which they gained from the south. Our climbers have also ascended a number of the 17,000- and 18,000-foot peaks northeast and east of Chachacomani near Achapampa. An unnamed one just south of Achapampa was climbed in September 1985 by Bartram, Bolivian Mario Clemente and me via the west ridge and an ice couloir. Clemente is a llama-packer, who knows this region well and has been an enormous help to us. In 1986, the peak southeast of Achapampa, Cerro Wampa, was climbed by Bartram, Chris Copeland and eight clients up its rather gentle eastern face. The second ascent was made on July 30, 1989 by Bartram, Culberson, Koehler, Hall and Adams, who climbed the 65° to 70° south face. The same team, plus Reidy, then made the first ascent of Coco Rico, which lies southeast of Cerro Wampa.

DUNHAM GOODING

Chachacomani. Our expedition was composed of Eddie Boulton, Peter Delmissier, Steve Norris, Kevin Spooner, Bill Bays, Bill Wolf and me as leader. With five herdsmen from the Janko Khota region and 49 llamas, we approached the Chachacomani-Chearoco massif from the east in a strenuous three-day trek that took us over three passes that averaged 15,000 feet in altitude. We crossed

PLATE 39

Photo by Erich Gatt

The West Face of HUAYNA POTOSÍ.

PLATE 40

Photo by Erich Gatt

Traversing into the Summit Wall on HUAYNA POTOSÍ.

PLATE 41

Photo by Erich Gatt

**Mixed Climbing on Huayna
Potosi's West Face.**

PLATE 42

Photo by Erich Gatt

On HUAYNA POTOSÍ's West Face.

into and ascended westward to its head below Chearoco a valley that rises from the town of Amaguaya. The natives informed us that they call it Chekap Kuchu, which means "Valley's End" in Aymara. Base Camp was at 14,100 feet. We placed one of our three high camps at 16,400 feet two miles north-northeast of Chachacomani. Our first attempt on the northeast ridge failed, but two days later, on June 6, Boulton, Delmissier, Norris, Spooner and I climbed the entire northeast ridge to the main northeast summit of Chachacomani (6066 meters, 19,902 feet). We also traversed on to the slightly lower southwest summit. From camp, we crossed the crazily broken northeastern icefall, about two miles of weaving crevasse work in a maze of ice pillars, and then traversed the ridge over a couple of tricky ice pitches on the north face and on to the summit. Delmissier skied down the northeastern slopes. On June 11, Delmissier, Norris and I by a new route made the second ascent of a peak first climbed in 1962 by the British Reading University Expedition, which they called Dome 2 (5706 meters, 18,781 feet). Our attempt on the northeast face of Chearoco failed.

JOHN HESSBURG

Huayna Potosí, Probable New Route on the West Face, Cordillera Real. Martin Wolf and I camped at the foot of the west face of Huayna Potosí and on July 28 started at 5100 meters up a relatively objectively safe spur on the right side of the face. After climbing about 400 meters, we left the spur and traversed upward to the left to ascend the summit wall to the highest point (6088 meters, 19,975 feet). The rock was granite of UIAA IV+ difficulty. There was mixed climbing in the upper part of the spur. We left the safe rock of the spur at 5500 meters and diagonaled left up a steep ice couloir. Since this is in the shade during the whole day, the ice is extremely hard and brittle. It is the crux and the most dangerous part as there is falling ice and rock. There were other blank ice sections on the summit wall so that at dark we had to bivouac in a bergschrund at 5950 meters with a −25°C temperature. We climbed the last 100 meters of the face on the morning of July 29 and found a gap in the summit cornice, which allowed us to emerge on the sunny summit at nine A.M.

ERICH GATT, *Österreichischer Alpenverein*

Condoriri and Huayna Potosí, Cordillera Real. From September 7 to October 4, Patrick Gabarrou and I made new routes, climbing ice gullies. The conditions were poor, with warm, unstable weather, little ice in the gullies and the rainy season two months ahead of time. On September 10, we succeeded in climbing on the west face a very difficult ice route to the top of the southern spur (5520 meters, 18,111 feet) of Condoriri, accompanied by Yvan Estienne. This was in the northernmost couloir, the farthest one to the left. Two days later, we two climbed another route farther left amid séracs and rock to the top of the southern spur and continued on also by a new route onto the 5700-meter

(18,701-foot) southeast spur of Condoriri. On September 19, we made a direct route in the center of the west face of Huayna Potosí.

YVES ASTIER, *Club Alpin Français*

Pirámide Blanca, Southwest Face, 1988. Geoffrey Bartram, Nevin White-law and David Peltier made a new route, the southwest face, on Pirámide Blanca (5230 meters, 17,159 feet) in the Cordillera Real in August, 1988.

DAVID MARSHALL

Quimsa Cruz. From May 28 to June 30, I carried out a solo reconnaissance of the Cordillera de Quimsa Cruz, south of Illimani. In a first campaign, I entered from Pongo by truck and explored the valleys of Pusi Cota, Coricampana and El Aguila at the southeast end of the range. I made two first ascents. Three different mountains all bear the same name of Coricampana. On June 2, I climbed by its west ridge the southernmost (5200 meters, 17,061 feet), a bold granodioritic pyramid east of Nevado San Juan. Three days later, I ascended the fine ice dome, P 5460 (17,914 feet) by its south ridge and glacier. This lies north of San Juan. I named it Anco Collo (Aimara for "White Peak"). In my second campaign, I circumambulated the entire range. From Pongo and the Argentina mine, I marched north along the eastern side past big Chatamarca lake to the Salvadora Apecheta (pass) in the extreme north. Along the way, I explored Bengala and Corichuyma valleys. From the Viloco mine, I walked south along the western side of the range, entering the Casarata, Jisca Coquecota, Choque-cota and Atoromachuma valleys. In the last I climbed the rock peak, Ñuñu Collo (5215 meters, 17,108 feet), by its northeast gully and found a surveyor's cairn on the top.

EVELIO ECHEVARRÍA

Chile

Volcán Juriques, 1987. In September, 1987, nine women led by Julia Meza made a 12-day trip to the Licancabur district. On the 16th, all nine climbed Volcán Juriques (5704 meters, 18,713 feet) on the Chilean-Bolivian border.

EVELIO ECHEVARRÍA

Umarata and Other Peaks, 1984 and 1985. Important climbs have been belatedly filed with the Federación de Andinismo de Chile. In August 1984, 30 climbers, including four women, climbed in the Nevados de Quimsachata, in Lauca National Park on the Chilean-Bolivian border. Acontango (6052 meters, 19,855 feet) received its second, third and fourth ascents on August 11, 12 and 13, 1984, Capurata (5990 meters, 19,653 feet) its second on August 12, Guallatiri, an active volcano, (6071 meters, 19,918 feet) its fourth on August 13 and Umarata (5717 meters, 18,758 feet) its first and second on August 13 and 14. The leader was Edmundo Lagos. In 1985, two university groups were active in the same region. On August 4, 1985, 37 mountaineers from the Catholic University of Santiago, led by Renato Campodónico, crossed the frontier into Bolivia and placed a camp on the slopes of Sajama (6520 or 6546 meters, 21,391 or 21,463 feet). Twelve reached the summit, including Julieta Mery, one of the first women to have climbed the highest mountain in Bolivia. At the same time a University of Chile group of 38, led by Claudio Gálvez, camped below the frontier massif of Larancagua. On August 5, 1985, 18 climbers ascended Cerro Guaneguane (5100 meters, 16,733 feet). On the 7th, six made the first ascent of Nevado Larancagua (5433 meters, 17,824) while six others made the first ascent of Nevado Condoriri (c. 5250 meters, 17,225 feet). An attempt on Sajama failed.

EVELIO ECHEVARRÍA

Nevados de Arhuelles, 1985. A belated report comes of climbs made in the Nevados de Arhuelles, eastern sources of the Maipo river. Between February 2 and 9, 1985, nine climbers led by Ramón Medina including four women made the first ascents of Torreón Antu Pirén (4830 meters, 15,847 feet), an imposing rock tower, and Alto del Pamir (c. 4500 meters, 14,764 feet) and the second ascent of Centinela del Pamir (c. 4700 meters, 15,420 feet).

EVELIO ECHEVARRÍA

Argentina

Nacimiento Massif and Other Peaks, 1986 and 1988. Our club has sent four expeditions into the region south of the Ojos del Salado in 1976, 1986, 1987 and 1988. In 1986 and 1988, we made first ascents. Our 1986 group had seven climbers. In January, 1986, I ascended alone P 6175 (20,258 feet), situated wholly in Argentina some ten kilometers south of Nevado del Muerto on the international border. I named it Cerro Medusa, since it rises above the lake of the same name. In 1988, Orlando Bravo, leader, Antonio Fons, Jorge Madozzo, Marcelino and Sergio Muntaner, Luis Salinas and I returned to the same area, approaching through Cazadero Grande and El Chorro. From the later, Salinas and I ascended P 4650 (15,256 feet), which we named Cerro Chango. We found wood scattered over the summit, perhaps left by pre-Columbian Indians. We continued the approach march along the Cazadero valley to Real del Rasguido. P 6660, which the Chileans call Nevado del Cazadero, was attempted but the snow was too deep. Salinas and I traversed to the Arenal valley and on January 12, 1988 ascended P 6050 (19,849 feet), ten kilometers south of Cerro Medusa. We named it Cerro Gendarme Argentino. A day later, Fons and Muntaner repeated the ascent. On January 14, O. Bravo and Madozzo climbed the impressive volcano (6200 meters, 20,342 feet) north of the Nacimiento massif. It seems to be the peak called Volcán del Viento by the Poles when Justyn

Wojsznis climbed it on February 10, 1937. Salinas and I then climbed the northeast peak of the Nacimiento massif, or Cerro Nacimiento II (6460 meters, 21,195 feet), while Fons and Madozzo reached the summit of Nacimiento V (c. 6320 meters, 10,735 feet), north of Nacimiento I. The Poles climbed Nacimiento II. Nacimiento V is a first ascent.

CLAUDIO BRAVO, *Club Andino Tucumán, Argentina*

Alma Negra District. In mid April, near the Alma Negra pass over to Chile, east of the city of San Juan, Argentines Antonio Beorchia, Antonio Mastellaro, Mario Muñoz and Edgardo Yacante made the first ascent of Cerro Mirador del Olivares (c. 4800 meters, 15,748 feet.) After southern winter had started, Humberto Campodónico, Roberto Pereyra, Juan Sanz and I set out to do the first ascent of the big unnamed peak at the source of the Pismanta River. We approached the unknown mountain from the Quebrada de las Trancas and then followed the long, winding east ridge. We placed two camps, the higher at 14,000 feet. On June 1, we set out for the summit, but Sanz, aged 14, had to descend before reaching it. We have named it Nevado de Pismanta. Contour lines in the official maps indicate it is somewhat higher than 5400 meters (17,717 feet). On September 21, the first day of Argentine spring, we set out for the mountain settlements of Las Flores and Peñasquitos, south of the Agua Negra road and north of the Olivares massif. After transportation difficulties, we reached our destination. We marched up the Pismanta valley and camped at 13,000 feet. On September 23, we set out for P 5036 (16,622 feet), which we reached in the afternoon. We continued along the southeast ridge to the main summit (5100 meters, 16,733 feet). We named the massif Nevado de Bauchaceta. On the main summit were Miguel Beorchia, Maricio Manzi and I.

MARCELO SCANU, *Centro de Investigaciones Arqueológicas de Alta*
Montaña, San Juan, Argentina

Cerro Negro Aspero. In the winter of 1989, in August, we attempted this massive mountain but a blizzard drove us back. At the beginning of the southern summer Humberto Campodónico, Roberto Pereyra and I made a successful second try. On November 18, we walked up the valley from the post of Guardia Vieja to camp at 4325 meters. The next day unstable weather and mountain sickness stopped our attempt. Therefore, we placed a camp at 5400 meters, only 100 meters below the top. After a trying night due to *siroche*, wind and cold, we set out for the summit (5500 meters, 18,045 feet), which we reached at a very early hour. Cerro Negro Aspero was one of the more important yet unclimbed peaks in the Agua Negra district.

MARCELO SCANU, *Centro de Investigaciones Arqueológicas de Alta*
Montaña, San Juan, Argentina

New Altitude Measurements for Aconcagua and the Ojos del Salado. In February, a team of Italian scientists from the University of Padua and Italian climbers, supported by the Argentine Institute of Glaciology and Nivology and Argentine climbers, made new measurements of the two highest peaks in the Americas, Aconcagua, which lies entirely in Argentina, and the Ojos del Salado, which is farther north on the Chilean-Argentine frontier. The project was under the direction of Francesco Santon. The surveyors employed GPS (Global Positioning System). This uses a constellation of earth-orbiting satellites and portable receivers. The receivers track and record the positions of many of the satellites simultaneously. In addition to a receiver being placed in an "unknown" location, such as a mountain summit, other receivers are placed at "known" positions, such as benchmarks. When all receivers are switched on, they record the positions of the overhead satellites, forming mathematical triangles. Using a form of triangulation, the position of the "unknown" receiver can be determined based on the "known" positions of the other receivers and the satellites. For the measurements of Aconcagua, the surveyors set up stations at Mendoza, Potrerillos, Punta de Vacas, Cristo Redentor, Puente del Inca and Plaza de Mulas. For the Ojos del Salado, the stations were all in Argentina, at Cuesta de Reyes, Fiambalá, Cuesta de Loro Huasi, Chaschuli, Cazaderos Grandes, Aguas Calientes and Laguna Negro Pass. The height obtained for Aconcagua was 6962 meters (22,841 feet), which is 2.3 meters higher than the previous official altitude. They determined the altitude of the Ojos del Salado to be 6900 meters (22,628 feet), with a possible error of 5 meters. This is 15 meters higher than the previous official altitude of 6885 meters. It is not known by us if the respective governments have accepted the new altitudes as being official. As we go to press, Francesco Santon has been kind enough to inform us that he left Italy for the Andes on January 15, 1990 in order to refine the measurements of the Ojos del Salado.

Aconcagua, the 1988-1989 Season. Although Aconcagua is ascended all year round, most mountaineering, particularly for foreigners, takes place in December and January. In this summer season of 1988-1989, 211 expeditions were registered: 52 from the United States, 33 from Argentina, 21 from Germany, 20 from Spain, 16 from France, 11 from Japan and other parts of Europe and Latin America. The most common route was from the northwest, taken by 159 expeditions. The Polish route on the east was chosen by 41 groups and the south face by 9. Of the 792 climbers, 72 were women. In contrast, only five groups visited Aconcagua in the peak of winter. The speed record—Plaza de Mulas to the summit—that had been established by German Michael Dacher in 1988 was broken on January 12, 1989 by American Marty Schmidt, who accomplished the ascent in 6 hours, 13 minutes; that is two minutes shorter than Dacher.

LUIS ALBERTO PARRA, *Club Andinista Mendoza*

Aconcagua, South Face, Ascent by First Argentine Woman and Twins. Probably the youngest two climbers to ascend the south face of Aconcagua were the twins Carolina and Horacio Codo. She is also the first Argentine woman to have made the climb. In order to acclimatize, they first ascended the route of the Glaciar de los Polacos, reaching the summit on January 22 on the second day of their ascent. They then took five days to climb the Messner route on the south face, reaching the summit on February 1.

ALBERTO TARDITTI, *Club Andino Córdoba, Argentina*

Peaks in Las Cuevas Valley. During a folklore-collection trip along the valley of Las Cuevas in the hinterland of Mendoza, I managed several climbs. I entered the hitherto unexplored lateral valleys of Los Gemelos (south of the international highway to Chile) and Los Chorrillos (north of the village of Las Cuevas). In the former, on December 24 I made the first ascent of Cerro Negro (4432 meters, 14,500 feet). Since there are so many Andean peaks of the same name, I rechristened it Cerro Negro del Inca, being close to Puente del Inca. On December 30, I also made the first ascent of a 4200-meter (13,780-foot) peak on the north rim of the Chorrillos valley. I suggest it be called Cerro Peñas Colorados (Red Crags). I also explored access to border peaks P 4596 and P 4764. Bad rock prevented my reaching higher than 4000 meters on both.

EVELIO ECHEVARRÍA

Pico de la Plata. This massive mountain (5850 meters, 19,193 feet) has two summits: Cerro and Pico. The latter is some 150 meters lower. The Cerro's steep east face has been climbed in both summer and winter, whereas no winter ascent had been made of the east face of the Pico. On September 12, Mendoza climbers José Luis Arboleda and Eduardo Ferllén worked their way up the east buttress of the Pico, using six days for the whole expedition from Mendoza and back. The 3200-foot-high face averaged 50°.

LUIS ALBERTO PARRA, *Club Andinista Mendoza*

Argentine and Chilean Patagonia

San Valentin, First Winter Ascent. The correct altitude of San Valentin has not been determined with complete accuracy. It is given either as 4058 or 3876 meters (13,314 or 12,716 feet). It is surely the highest of the Patagonian Andes. The first winter ascent was made on August 7 by Italians Casimiro Ferrari, Egidio Spreafico, Carlo Buzzi and Giuliano Maresi. They climbed the west ridge. That same day Dino Piazza and Giorgio Sacerdoti climbed Cerro Fierro (3300 meters, 10,872 feet). The expedition was flown to Laguna San Rafael. They ascended to the Northern Patagonian Icecap and skied for five days to reach the mountain. They were back on August 11 at the lake, having had a difficult descent in bad weather.

SILVIA METZELTIN BUSCAINI, *Club Alpino Italiano*

Patagonia

Patagonian Climbing, 1989–1990 Summer. At the end of the season (February 23, 1990), I have little to report. At the end of January, 1990, Italians Paolo Grippa and Eliana de Zordo were avalanche victims and swept into a crevasse below the Torre Egger. At the beginning of February Argentines Sebastián Pavesi and Eduardo Osal made a fatal fall into a crevasse on the Aguja Poincenot. For a long time the weather was very bad and little could be done. There followed two weeks of good weather, an extraordinary period in the south, when most were occupied with the accidents and rescue attempts. Cerro Torre was climbed by Swiss, Austrians, Germans and Czechoslovaks. Fitz Roy was ascended by Argentine Alberto del Castillo and two Brazilians, by two Swiss and by four Koreans. Argentines and a Spaniard climbed the Aguja Guillaumet and Swiss and Czechs, Poincenot.

VOJSLAV ARKO, *Club Andino Bariloche*

Cerro Torre, Fitz Roy, Aguja Poincenot and Aguja Guillaumet in the 1988-1989 Season. There were three ascents of Cerro Torre, all by the Maestri bolt route: on November 10, 1988 by Americans Brad Schilling and Mike Clifford and by Spanish Catalans Toni Torà Borredà and Joan Javer García and on January 5 by Poles Marek Olszyk and Krzysztof Djiubek. A winter ascent of Fitz Roy was made on August 8, 1988 by Italians Paolo Crippa, Danilo Valsecchi and Dario Spreafico, who climbed the Franco-Argentine route. This was not the first winter ascent as they reported; the first winter ascent was made on July 27, 1986 by Argentines. On January 9, Austrians Thomas Bonaface and Gerold Dünser completed an ascent of Fitz Roy's Supercanaleta. All other Fitz Roy ascents were by the Franco-Argentine route: on November 7, 1988 by Spaniards César Tome Ondicol and Eladio Lantada Zarzosa and by Italians Fabrizio Defancesco and Paolo Borgonovo; on January 12 by Swiss Thomas Ulrich and Georg Hödle; and on February 14 by Swiss Michael Schwitter and Brazilian Luis Makoto Ishibe. All Aguja Poincenot ascents were by the Whillans route: on November 7, 1988 by Spaniards Vicente Lagunilla and Angel Villán; on November 30, 1988 by Spanish Basques Guillermo Bañales and Ion Laskano and by Italians Diego Zanesco and Mauro Bernardi; on December 27, 1988 by Spaniards Antonio Ramos Villar, César Aorta Orduña, Miguel Ortega, Juanjo Ruiz and Iñaki Vicente; on January 6 by Swiss Michael Schwitter and German Joseph Heine; and on March 3 by Argentine Jorge and Mariano Tarditti. There were ascents of Aguja Guillaumet: on October 2, 1988 by Argentines Pato Seuflejer and Marcelo Venere; on December 27, 1988 by Argentines José Váquez, Marcos Aprile, Fernando Ferios and Marciano Tarditti; on January 2 by Alfredo Flury and Pablo Alvarez; and on February 23 by Swiss Michael Schwitter, Brazilian Luis Makoto Ishibe and Canadian Alex Fried.

ALBERT TARDITTI, *Club Andino Córdoba, Argentina*

Paragliding from Fitz Roy and Cerro Torre, 1988. Four German climbers led by Matthias Pinn made a number of unsuccessful attempts on Cerro Torre in August 1988 before turning to Fitz Roy, which they climbed by the Supercouloir. After a bivouac on the summit, they paraglided back to Base Camp. Finally, they managed to climb the Maestri bolt route on Cerro Torre, but the wind was so strong that the only sensible thing was to climb back down. Some days later, they were helicoptered back to Cerro Torre's summit and they completed paraglider descents from there.

Aguja de la Silla, East Spur, and Aguja Bífida, North Face. On February 21, Swiss Peter Lüthi and Argentine Horacio Bresba made the first ascent of the Aguja de la Silla (2978 meters, 9770 feet) by its eastern spur. They approached via the Paso Superior, the Brecha de la Italianos and the Silla Americana. They climbed ten mixed or ice pitches and five pure rock pitches. Some of the ice was 60°. From the col, after a 50-meter pitch on the north face, they climbed beautiful cracks to a recess on the eastern crest. They then kept somewhat to the left (south) of the crest to the summit blocks. They climbed the first block up a chimney on its east and then north and the second up a wide crack on its south side. (UIAA VI+, A1.) The same pair did one of the most interesting climbs of the 1988-9 season when they ascended the north face of the Aguja Bífida (2450 meters, 7956 feet). The climb had been attempted by climbers from Buenos Aires, who failed because of technical difficulties. The wall rises some 750 meters, was of sustained UIAA VI+ and had places of A1. They climbed 22 rope-lengths in a single day, March 2, and had to make several pendulums. There was much rotten rock in the upper half. They rappelled down the same route. They found signs of the previous attempt to within 120 meters of the summit.

VOJSLAV ARKO, *Club Andino Bariloche*

Torre Innominata. On January 5, Argentine Carlos Domínguez de San Juan and I completed the second or third ascent of the first-ascent route of the Torre Innominata (Rafael; 2501 meters, 8205 feet) in 2½ days. We climbed ten mixed pitches and four on rock with UIAA difficulty of VI and V and A1. There was some avalanche danger but the rock on the ascent was good. We descended the south spur with many rappels.

PETER LÜTHI, *Schweizer Alpen Club*

El Mocho, East Buttress; Torre Innominata, North Spur; Aguja Poincenot, East Face; Aguja Guillaumet, Southeast Face; and Other Climbs. Michel Piola and I arrived at Chaltén on December 6, 1988. Our first intention had been to try

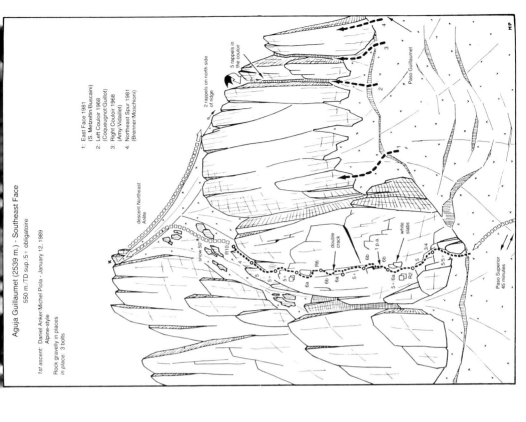

Aguja Guillaumet (2539 m.) - Southeast Face

550 m./TD sup.- 5+ obligatoire

1st ascent: Daniel Anker/Michel Piola - January 12. 1989

Alpine-style

Rock gravelly in places
in place: 3 bolts

1: East Face 1981
   (S. Metzeltin/Buscaini)
2: Left Couloir 1968
   (Coqueugniot/Guillot)
3: Right Couloir 1968
   (Amy/Vidailet)
4: Northeast Spur 1981
   (Brenner/Moschioni)

5 rappels in the couloir

2 rappels on north side of ridge

descent Northeast Arête

double crack

white slabs

Paso Guillaumet

Paso Superior 45 minutes

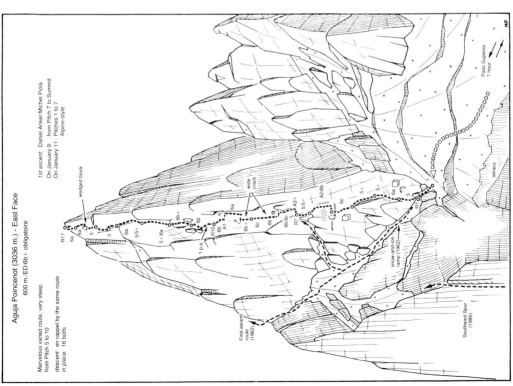

Aguja Poincenot (3036 m.) - East Face

600 m./ED/6b+ obligatoire

Marvelous varied route, very steep

descent: en rappel by the same route
in place: 16 bolts

1st ascent: Daniel Anker/Michel Piola
On January 9: from Pitch 7 to Summit
On January 11: Pitches 1 to 7
Alpine-style

wedged block

wide crack

snow-and-ice ramp (1962)

First-ascent route (1962)

Southeast Spur (1986)

séracs

Paso Superior 1 hour

a new route on the impressive west face of Pier Giorgio. We set up our tent on the Marconi Glacier, three hours from the wall. Up there, some hours beyond the last habitation at Piedra del Fraile, we spent first five days and then eleven days waiting for good weather. The conditions were so bad that we decided to do a shorter climb, the 600-meter-high west buttress of Cerro Pollone (2396 meters, 7860 feet). In two half-days with better weather, we fixed 200 meters of rope. Then, on December 28, 1988, we set out at three A.M. to try to climb to the summit. In the afternoon the next snowstorm began. Still 100 meters below the foresummit, some 13 pitches up, we decided to rappel off. During the first part of January, the weather was better whenever it was windy. We went to the Cerro Torre Base Camp. On January 4, we walked to the base of El Mocho (1980 meters, 6496 feet) and made a new route on the left of the east buttress. This 500-meter-high climb was interesting and principally free. We rappelled down the same route. We came down late at night and had a rest day. On January 6, we made the first ascent of the north spur of the Torre Innominata (2501 meters, 8205 feet). This 400-meter-high beautiful ascent was mainly in cracks. We climbed five pitches on the west flank of the ridge and the last six on the east side. The incredibly strong west wind nearly blew us off the normal east-ridge route on the descent. We got back to the Cerro Torre Base Camp at 1:30 A.M. The next afternoon we returned to Chaltén. The following day, we went up to the Paso Superior. On January 9, we first started up the snow-and-ice ramp on the Aguja Poincenot (3036 meters, 9961 feet) on which the first-ascent route begins; this route was originally climbed in 1962 by Don Whillans and Frank Cochrane and is now the normal route up the needle. Halfway up the ramp, we turned to the right and regained the rock of the east face. After a difficult climb of 10 pitches, we reached the summit at eight P. M. We finished our descent to the Paso Superior at two A.M. Fortunately, it began to snow and so we had a forced rest day. On the 11th, we climbed straight up seven pitches to where we had begun our rock climb on the 9th; we had rappelled down this section on the previous descent. Thus we completed all 17 pitches of this 600-meter-high climb in two efforts. Finally, on January 12, we climbed a new route on the southeast face of the Aguja Guillaumet (2539 meters, 8330 feet). Part of the rock was gravelly. Again the wind was very strong on the top and during the descent. That evening we returned to Chaltén and left the national park the day after. (Our routes may be followed on the accompanying drawings, all done by my companion, Michel Piola. "R" followed by a number indicates a belay stance; "pa" indicates direct aide.)

DANIEL ANKER, *Schweizer Alpen Club*

Aguja Mermoz, East Buttress. Italians Vanni Spinelli, Ezio Tanzi, Antonio Colombo, Giulio Maggioni, Danilo Galbiati, Giorgio Confalonieri and Davide Corbetta climbed the 700-meter-high east buttress of the Aguja Mermoz. They set up Base Camp at the Piedra del Fraile on October 19. Bad weather delayed them but on October 24, they got to the Paso del Cuadrado. The next day, they

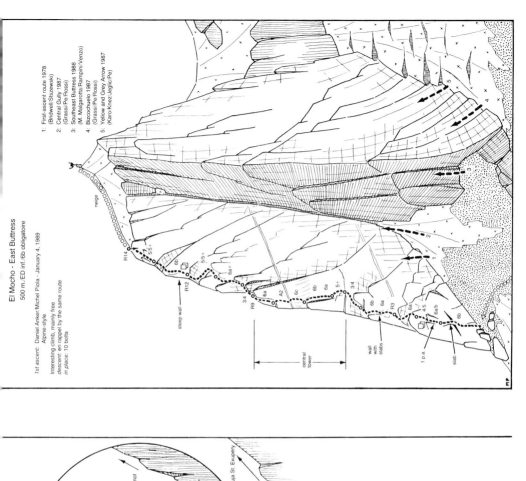

El Mocho - East Buttress

500 m./ED inf./6b obligatoire

1st ascent: Daniel Anker/Michel Piola - January 4, 1989
Alpine-style

Interesting climb, mainly free
descent: en rappel by the same route
in place: 10 bolts

1: First-ascent route 1978
   (Bridwell/Stszewski)
2. Central Gully 1987
   (Grassi/Pe/Rossi)
3. Southeast Buttress 1988
   (M. Malgarotta/Rampini/Venzo)
4. Bizcochuelo 1987
   (Grassi/Pe/Rossi)
5. Yellow and Grey Arrow 1987
   (Karo/Knez/Jeglic/Pe)

neige

R14
5.5+
6b
5.5+
6a+
R12
steep wall
3.4
R9
6a
A2
6c
6b
6a
5+
3.4
R3
6b
6a
6a
45
6a/b
1 p.a.
6a/b
slab
6b

central tower

wall with slabs

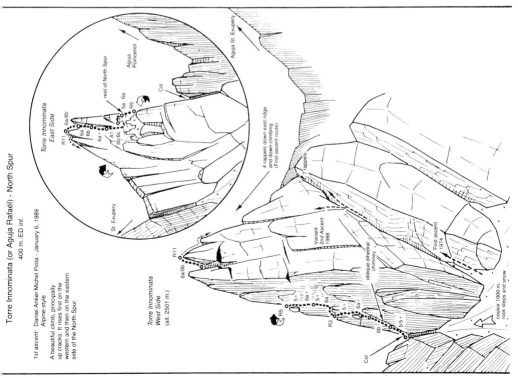

Torre Innominata (or Aguja Rafaël) - North Spur

400 m./ED inf.

1st ascent: Daniel Anker/Michel Piola - January 6, 1989
Alpine-style

A beautiful climb, principally
up cracks. It rises first on the
western and then on the eastern
side of the North Spur.

Torre Innominata
East Side

rest of North Spur

R11
6a 6b
6a
6b
6a
6b/6c
6a
A1
5a 6a
R5
Col
Aguja
Poincenot

St. Exupery

Aguja St. Exupery

Torre Innominata
West Side
(alt. 2501 m.)

R11
6a 6b
R5
5.5+
5+
6a+
6a
6b
5.5+
R3

oblique dihedral
chimney

Variant
2nd Ascent
1988

First ascent
1974

4 rappels down east ridge
and down-climbing
(First-ascent route)

7 rappels

couloir 1000 m.
rock steps and snow

Col

fixed rope on snow-covered slabs. More storms followed. On the 28th, they began working up a 300-meter-high dihedral. Finally, on October 31, those who had been preparing the route were joined by all the others, who ascended the fixed ropes. Together, they climbed the whole day, getting to the summit at ten P.M. They then made several attempts on Fitz Roy and Cerro Torre, all frustrated by bad weather. Finally, Spinelli and Maggioni made a 120-kilometer crossing of the Southern Continental Icecap.

Cerro Stanhardt, West Face. Italians Maurizio Giarolli, Ermanno Salvaterra and Elio Orlandi climbed a very difficult new route on the west face of Cerro Stanhardt. It rises 1200 meters. On September 21, they attacked the west face from the Bifida-Stanhardt col. The first 500 meters were slabs that diagonalled up to the right. They bivouacked at the base of the vertical climbing. On September 22, they climbed straight up very difficult rock and finally through ice mushrooms. They reached the summit at four P.M. in dense fog. They descended the east face, bivouacking on the wall.

Aguja del S. A 4-man Bulgarian party led by Alexandr Ruevski had hoped to climb Fitz Roy but could not because of bad weather. Miroslav Sevilevski and Valentin Trenev took advantage of a calm day to make a new route on the east-southeast face of the Aguja del S in the St. Exupéry ridge. After four hours of climbing up to UIAA V-, they reached the top.

JÓZEF NYKA, *Editor, Taternik, Poland*

Punta Negra, Tridente and Cerro Norte del Paine. Ian Burgess, David Lister, David Tyson and I arrived on September 30 for a six-week stay in the Paine region. We set up Base Camp high in the Río de los Perros valley. On October 19, we all made the first ascent of Punta Negra (2100 meters, 6890 feet), a sedimentary rock peak which lies north of Catedral and southwest of the Mellizos. Starting from the Olguin Glacier, the route followed the northwest face via two long snow gullies onto the hanging glacier. We then climbed a steep mixed gully to a notch in the north ridge, which provided six pitches of very loose rock to the summit. This was our second attempt on the peak. The ascent took nearly 24 hours non-stop. On October 27, from a high camp under the north face of the Escudo, we followed two easy snow gullies and a short rock step to ascend the minor peak, Tridente (1900 meters, 6234 feet) via the apparently previously unclimbed northwest face. This was a fantastic viewpoint for the Towers of Paine. On November 7, we made an ascent of the North Tower of Paine by the normal Col Bich route. We took 22 hours, starting from the Japanese camp in the Río Ascensio valley. We had problems with fresh snow and the cold. The fixed rope on the 100 meters of mixed ground leading to the Col Bich was removed that same day by its American owners.

STEPHEN HILLEN, *Loughborough University, England*

Central Paine Tower, Winter Attempt. Spaniards José Luis Gallego and Raúl García were in the Paine Towers from May 1 to June 6. They attempted to climb the east face of the Torre Central despite low temperatures and high winds. They climbed 1100 meters of the wall but could not finish the climb. Gallego had already attempted the same route in the summer of 1966, when he and his brother managed to get up the first 500 meters.

Tierra del Fuego

Roncagli, Cordillera Darwin, Tierra del Fuego, 1990. On January 14, 1990, Julian Mathias, John Mothersele and I made the first ascent of magnificent Roncagli (2300 meters, 7046 feet) by its northwest ridge to the north summit. We climbed 1200 vertical meters of sustained mixed climbing in a 20-hour push from an advanced glacial camp. This was the fifth British expedition to visit the area and attempt the peak. The line climbed had originally been attempted in 1988 by Iain Peters and me after we has spotted the possible route on this complex peak when we saw it during our ascent of Pico Ohi. This year, we also made the first ascent of Pico País de Galles to the east of the Stoppani Glacier.

DAVID HILLEBRANDT, *Alpine Club*

AFRICA

Kilimanjaro, Credner Glacier. What started out as a centennial commemoration of Hans Meyer's first ascent of Kilimanjaro 100 years ago evolved into an exploration of the westernmost ridge and a new route up the remote Credner Glacier. The team was composed of Norwegian Odd Eliassen, Swiss Christoph Jezler, Englishman Richard Palmer, Americans Lane Gregory, Rob Taylor, Timothy and Nicholas Wiedman and me as leader. We proceeded up the southeast route to the Mandara and Horombo Huts, tarried for three days of medical research on descending climbers and then continued due west. During three more days we traversed the Karanga valley past the Arrow Glacier cut-off to the Great Barranco under the Breach Wall. Continuing into the Shira Plateau, we camped at the base of the Lent Group at 4250 meters. Part of the team then elected to return through Machame to the standard route. The rest of us followed the southwest ridge leading to the bergschrund of the Credner Glacier to camp at 5150 meters. We ascended the Credner Glacier on crampons on 30° alternating blue ice and crust to its top at 5690 meters. A 30-meter abseil off the ice cliff at the crater rim took us to the crater floor. We traversed the crater to the southeast through sharp-knived *nieves penitentes* down to the standard route. We met the rest of the party at Horombo. With Timothy and Nicholas Wiedman and Lane Gregory, we all reascended the next day to Gillman's Point and Uhuru.

MICHAEL WIEDMAN, *M.D.*

EUROPE

The UIAA Mountain Medicine Centre, London. The UIAA Medical Medicine Commission, founded in 1980, has flourished as an international group which now meets annually and attracts delegates from 26 countries. One of its principal functions is to collect information for the climber members of the UIAA and advise them about mountain medicine and in particular about problems of high altitude. The Mountain Medicine Centre, initiated in 1981, is run on a voluntary basis by me, a neurologist at St. Bartholomew's Hospital in London, with the assistance of Mrs. Ann Tilley. We aim to provide information to climbers and trekkers about a wide range of topics and use a series of information sheets to tackle common problems. Difficult issues are handled personally and on occasion by formal consulation and investigation. Currently we receive about 800 enquiries per year. The Information Sheets cover the following topics: Acute Mountain Sickness, Pulmonary and Cerebral Edema; Problems of Climbing at Extreme Altitude; Frostbite; Medical Aspects of Avalanche Rescue; Oxygen Systems for use at High Altitude; Portable Compression Chambers; Rock-climbing Injuries and How to Prevent Them; The Causes of Death at Extreme Altitudes; First-Aid Kits for Expeditions. The Centre is funded by a small grant from the UIAA and contributions have been received from the Swiss Alpine Club, the Mount Everest Foundation, the German Alpine Club, the American Alpine Club, the Alpine Club of Canada and personal donations. A small charge is made to cover printing and postage. All enquiries should be made to the Mountain Medicine Centre, St. Bartholomew's Hospital, London EC1A 7BE, England.

CHARLES CLARKE, *M.D., Alpine Club*

ANTARCTICA

South Pole International Overland Expedition. During the austral summer of 1988-89, the first privately funded cross-country ski expedition to the South Pole took place. Eleven members representing five nations reached the South Pole on January 17, 1989. The journey took 50 days and covered a distance of 750 miles. This was 77 years to the day since George Fallon Scott's expedition had arrived at the pole. We had just finished the first overland crossing from the South American side. We started from Hercules Inlet off the Ronne Ice Shelf at 80° S, 80° W and paralleled the Ellsworth and Thiel Ranges. Supported by snowmobiles and pre-arranged caches, we averaged 15 miles a day with temperatures down to −35°. We navigated ten days in whiteout conditions with only a compass, resting only when the storms deteriorated into a summer blizzard. The members were Canadians Martyn Williams, leader, and Stuart Hamilton, Briton Mike Sharp, Chilean Alejo Contreras Staeding, Indian J.K. Bajaj, and Americans Victoria Murden, Jerry Corr, Sherly Metz, Ron Milnarek, Joseph E. Murphy Jr. and I.

JAMES WILLIAMS

Tyree, Shinn and the Vinson Massif. Mugs Stump made an impressive solo first ascent of the 8000-foot-high west face of Mount Tyree. He feels that it is "perhaps the hardest route yet accomplished by man." This was the second ascent of Tyree. On the same day, New Zealander Rob Hall repeated the Chouinard route on Mount Shinn, adding a direct line to the summit, solo, in eleven hours. Mugs Stump, Ed Stump and New Zealanders Hall and Paul Fitzgerald also repeated the standard route on Vinson in December. Their group was independent of mine. Officially they were in Antarctica to carry out geological research. Mugs Stump returned to Antarctica in January 1990 and guided several clients up the normal route on Vinson. I went to Antarctica with Canadian Rob Mitchell, German Klaus Wengen, American Ken Kammler and Netherlander Peter Kinchen. On December 9, we all ascended an unnamed mountain of about 12,000 feet at the head of the valley north of the standard Base Camp. On December 14, Wengen, Kammler and I climbed to the summit of Vinson by a variant of the normal route. We avoided the icefall below the col between Vinson and Shinn by following the very prominent first ridge to the north. Future parties should consider this slightly more difficult but much safer alternative. Unfortunately, Kinchin developed frostbite in his right foot and all further climbing objectives had to be abandoned. I have now climbed to the highest point of all seven continents. If Carstenz Pyramid counts as the highest point in Australasia, I am now the only American to have done so.

GEOFFREY TABIN, *M.D.*

ASIA

Nepal

Altitude Corrections. Buddhi Shrestha, Surveyor General of Nepal, has been kind enough to make the following corrections in the altitudes which were given in *AAJ, 1985* in the "Classification of the Himalaya." Nepal Peak is 7168 meters, 23,518 feet (not 6910 meters). Langtang Lirung is 7225 meters, 23,704 feet (not 7234 meters). Ganesh II is 7163 meters, 23,501 feet (not 7111 meters). Palta Thumba is 6157 meters, 20,200 feet (not 6126 meters).

Kangchenjunga Traverses. The second Soviet Himalayan expedition had 32 members, of whom 22 climbers spent two years of hard training and high-altitude acclimatization in the Caucasus, Pamir and Tien Shan. The leader was Eduard Myslovsky, who in 1982 made a new route with Vladimir Balyberdin and others on the southwest face of Everest. The expedition left Moscow on February 8 and arrived with 600 porters at their 5350-meter Base Camp below the normal route on March 4. The Soviet climbers with the help of Sherpas established five camps on the slopes of the main, central, south summits of Kangchenjunga and of Yalung Kang, which is the westernmost top of Kangchenjunga. On April 9, Vasily Yelagin, Vladimir Korotaev, Eugeny Klinezky and Alexander Sheinov ascended to the main summit, making its 27th ascent. On April 15, Sergei Bershov, Viktor Pastuk, Mikhail Turkevich and Rinat Chaibullin made the third ascent of the south summit. That same day, Balyberdin, Sergei Arsentiev, Anatoly Bukreev and Valery Khrishchaty made the fourth ascent of the central summit. On April 16, Kazbek Valiev, Viktor Dedy, Grigory Lunjakov, Vladimir Suviga, Zijnur Khalitov, Alexander Glushkovsky, Yuri Moiseev and Leonid Troshchinenko reached the main summit. On April 18, Eugeny Vinogradsky, Korotaev, Mikhail Mozaev and Alexander Pogorelov again got to the south summit. On April 29, Pastuk, Mozaev, Korotaev, Chaibullin and Sergei Bogomolov reached the main summit and Pastuk, Mozaev and Korotaev continued on over the south summit. On April 30, the traverse of the entire ridge began. The first group traversed from Yalung Kang to the main, central and south summits mainly, but not entirely, along the summit ridges. Bershov, Bukreev, Vinogradsky, Pogorelov and Turkevich made the 15th ascent of Yalung Kang and traversed to Camp V below the main summit. On May 1, they left Camp V at eight A.M. and were on the main summit at 10:10. After an hour's rest in mild, windless weather, they continued on to reach the central summit at 12:40 and the south summit at three P.M. All five used supplementary oxygen. This first group was accompanied to the summit of Yalung Kang on April 30 by Arsentiev, Klinezky, Suviga, Khrishchaty, Dedy and Sheinov. On May 1, a second group of five attacked the south summit first. The leader of the group Elagin, Lunyakov and Khalitov with oxygen got to the south summit at 12:10 P.M. but were obliged to wait for Balyberdin and Korotaev, who were without oxygen. It was decided that all should continue on oxygen. At 3:40 they reached the central summit and traversed to Camp V between the main summit and Yalung Kang. On May 2, they climbed to the main summit and then reached Yalung Kang at 2:10 P.M. This completed the traverse by ten climbers in opposite directions. On May 3, the main summit was ascended by Soviets Nikolai Cherny and Sergei Yefimov and Ang Babu Sherpa. In most cases the Soviets used supplementary oxygen for safety sake. However, Kazbek Valiev's group on April 16 climbed without it. The next day, while the group was descending, Dr. Karpenko examined Valiev, who was not feeling well, and found that he was being threatened by edema. (The Editor is very grateful to Dr. Kolev, who was not part of the Soviet team, for this information.)

SVETOSLAV KOLEV, *Bulgarian Mountaineering Federation*

Kangchenjunga from the North. Our expedition consisted of Lou Whittaker, leader, George Dunn, Phil Ershler, Jim Hamilton, Robert Link, Larry Nielsen, Dr. Howard Putter, John Roskelley, Eric Simonson, Craig Van Hoy, Ed Viesturs, Jim Wickwire, Skip Yowell and me. We also were joined by Nawang Gombu and six Sherpas. Four Indonesian climbers traveled to Base Camp as training for a future Himalayan expedition of their own. Political trouble between India and Nepal delayed the arrival of our gear until long after we got to Base Camp at Pang Pema at 16,500 feet at the north foot of Kangchenjunga. Outfitted with little more than the hope that our equipment would join us soon, we established Camp I three days later at 17,000 feet on the gently sloping Kangchenjunga Glacier. On April 13, we sited Camp II just above a small icefall at the head of the glacier below the Twins and at the foot of the 3000-foot wall leading to the north col. When our gear finally did arrive, it was only 75% complete but it renewed our enthusiasm. Choosing a line between Scott's and Messner's up the west wall, we established Camp III in the bergschrund at 21,500 feet on April 20. Steep ice and rock complicated by bad weather slowed progress. Not until May 10 could we place 24,000-foot Camp IV above the north col and along the north ridge. Seven days later, Camp V was established and occupied by Phil Ershler, Craig Van Hoy and Ed Viesturs. May 18 dawned beautiful and the three joined Scott's route and traversed the north face to the summit, which they reached in 8½ hours. Van Hoy and Viesturs climbed without oxygen. On May 21, Link, Nielsen and I repeated the ascent with Link leading strongly through deep snow deposited by the previous day's storm. Nielsen and I climbed without supplementary oxygen.

GREG WILSON

Kangchenjunga Solo Attempt. I was accompanied to Base Camp at 5050 meters at Pang Pema, which we reached on October 10, by Jean-Yves Goutte, Mlle Monique Loscos and Jean-Louis Teyssier. I attempted the 1980 Japanese route, placing Camps I and II at 6000 and 6850 meters on October 18 and 23. I encountered the principal technical difficulty on October 24, a very steep mixed zone above 7000 meters, some 200 meters in height, where I fixed 50 meters of rope. I got to about 7100 meters. The first summit try got me to Camps I and II on October 29 and 30, but was stopped by a 40-cm fall of snow. On the second summit attempt I climbed from Base Camp to Camp II on November 3. That camp was destroyed by high winds and I returned to Base Camp on the 4th. I stayed there until November 9, but the wind continued and I gave up the attempt.

ERIC MONIER, *Club Alpin Français*

Yalungkang Attempt, Winter, 1988-9. Our expedition was led by Józef Stepień of Wrocław and had as members Aleksander Lwow, Ewa Panejko-Pankiewicz, Bogdan Stefko, Zdzisław Jakubowski, Dr. Kazimierz Pichlak and me. We left Kathmandu on December 17, 1988 and ran into snow at 2000 meters. Further snowfall, especially above 4000 meters, slowed the approach and forced us on January 10 to make a Lower Base Camp, three days's march below actual Base Camp, which was established at 5600 meters finally on January 27. Only a few porters helped us carry from one Base Camp to the other. Above 5000 meters snow conditions were favorable but above 6500 meters was the zone of storms. We used the normal southeast-side route. Camps I and II were placed at 6200 and 6900 meters on February 1 and 7. We fixed 400 meters of rope. On February 12, the high point of 7150 meters was reached by Lwow and Jakubowski, who had to crawl on hands and knees in the high winds. More heavy snowfall in the next days forced abandoning the expedition.

WANDA RUTKIEWICZ, *Klub Wysokogórski Warszawa, Poland*

Yalungkang. Yalungkang was climbed via its southeast face by a Korean expedition led by Park Soo-Jo. On October 13, Sho Kang-Ho with Ang Dawa Tamang and Gombu Sherpa completed the 18th ascent of the peak.

ELIZABETH HAWLEY

Yalungkang Ascent and Tragedy. A Korean expedition led by Kim Teuk-Hee climbed the normal route on Yalungkang in winter but the summit climbers never returned. On December 20, Jin Kyo-Sup, Ang Dawa Sherpa and Tshering Tshemba Sherpa left Camp IV at 8100 meters on the southeast face at 4:30 A.M. At 2:30 P.M., Jin reported by walkie-talkie that it was cloudy and windy and they were worried about their ability to return safely to Camp IV after nightfall. It would have been dark even if they had turned back then, but they kept on for the top. They made radio contact again at 4:05 to say that they were on the summit (8501 meters, 27,891 feet) and were resting for a few minutes. At 4:14, one of the Sherpas with Jin tried to talk to a fellow Sherpa at Camp IV, who happened to be chatting to Base Camp. The two men who were talking to each other stopped their conversation and tried to speak with the summit, but now there was no reply. There was no reply all night. A search by the men in Camp IV the next day produced no trace of the summit party. The leader speculates that they probably fell down the mountain's great north face.

ELIZABETH HAWLEY

Kumbhakarna North Face. The solo ascent of this face by Tomo Česen is presented in a full article in the first part of this volume.

Kumbhakarna (Jannu) Attempt. On September 25, Rob Mahoney, Kevin O'Meara and I established Base Camp at 15,000 feet on the Yamatari Glacier on the south side of Kumbhakarna. On October 1, we moved to Camp I at 17,000 feet. Camp II was established five days later at 18,500 feet. In another five days, we fixed 1500 feet of rope to Camp III at 20,500 feet. We found our way to the hanging ice shelf above the Yamatari Icefall and Camp IV at 21,200 feet by October 25. On October 26, we placed an alpine-style bivouac at 23,125 feet, which proved to be our high point. We felt we were one day from the top. After waiting a full day for the very high winds to stop, we descended to another bivouac on October 28 and back to Base Camp on October 29. We left the mountain on the 30th.

HOOMAN APRIN, *Unaffiliated*

Kumbhakarna Attempt, 1990. Our expedition consisted of Stanisław Dudek, Kazimierz Kieszka, Andrzej Samolewicz, Ryszard Papaj, Adam Potoczek, Ryszard Knapczyk, Dr. Piotr Wojciechowski, Bogdan Stefko and me as leader. We hoped to climb Kumbhakarna by the southwest buttress. We established Base Camp and Advance Base at 4450 and 4850 meters on November 24 and 30. The icefall was much more difficult and dangerous than we had expected and we fixed 700 meters of rope. Despite cold and wind, we set up Camps I, II and III at 5350, 5800 and 6450 meters on December 5, 12 and 20. After December 15, the weather was bad and windy. Snow had been blown off the hard ice. On January 2, 1990, we reached the edge of the "Throne" and pitched Temporary Camp IV. Very steep, hard ice on the "Throne" made us fix 1000 meters of rope. Camp IV was set up on January 8 at 7200 meters. Following the direct French variant on the summit cone, Kiszka and Samolewicz reached a high point of 7360 meters on January 9 but were turned back by high winds. We cleared Base Camp on January 14.

JAN ORŁOWSKI, *Klub Wysokogórski Kraków, Poland*

Ohmi Kangri. The Nepalese-American Ohmi Kangri Expedition was the first American group to visit this area of northeastern Nepal on the Tibetan border. Our leaders were Rick Richards and Sangya Dorje. We left Basantipur on April 9. The first nine days of our trek to Base Camp went up the Tamur River past Yangma and continued north. Our first view of our mountain came only one hour below Base Camp at 5130 meters on April 21. It is easy to see why early maps confused Ohmi Kangri with Nupchu. Our original joint team comprised ten climbers: seven Americans and three Sherpas. Two weeks into the climb the strength was reduced to four, primarily due to illness. We ascended the west face to the southwest ridge. Between Camps I and II there was much more snow than the Swiss encountered when they climbed the peak previously and we fixed 300 feet of rope on a steep section approaching Camp II. From Camp II to III on a very difficult section with ice and rock faces, we placed 1500 feet of rope. On May 9, Dawa Nuru Sherpa, Jan Harris and Mingma Gyalzen Sherpa reached the summit. Dawa Nuru was also one of the first-ascent party in 1985; he reported that the route from Camp III to the summit this year was much more difficult than before with hard ice replacing what had been firm snow. The official altitude of 6829 meters or 22,405 has been controversial; our altimeter read 22,850 feet

(6964 meters). On May 13, the day after we removed the last gear from the mountain, the sunny weather we had been enjoying was replaced by blustery, snowy weather. It rained enough at lower altitudes during the trek back to wash out the road we had used in April. We walked an extra two days to Dhankuta, arriving there on May 28 and hired a bus for the first stage of our journey back to Kathmandu.

KEN ZAFREN

Makalu, West Buttress Attempt. Our expedition, composed of Atxo Apellaniz, Juan Oiarzabal, Kike de Pablo and me as leader, began our approach march from Hille, which was made difficult because of snowstorms on the Barun La. We set up Base Camp and Camp I at 5400 and 5950 meters on April 2 and 7. Much wind and ice obliged us to fix 1200 meters of rope toward Camp II, which we established on April 20 at 6550 meters. On May 4, we got to Camp III at 7350 meters. Having fixed the route to 7650 meters, we set out from Camp III on May 17. It took us three hours to surmount a difficult wall at 7700 meters and at sundown we got to the top of the buttress at 7800 meters, where we rested for several hours. We had only a bivouac tent and no sleeping bags. At one A.M. on the 8th, we headed for the summit and got to the sunny southeast ridge at six A.M. A bit later, at 8350 meters, the dangerous conditions and the lack of technical gear forced us to give up our attempt. We came across the body of the Czech climber, Karel Schubert, who died in 1976. We were back in Base Camp on May 19.

JOSÉ LUIS ZULOAGA, *Euskal Espedizioa, Spain*

Makalu Attempt. Belgian climbers led by Jos Dewint reached 7700 meters on the northwest side of Makalu on April 25 before having to give up the attempt.

ELIZABETH HAWLEY

Makalu S. Face. Pierre Beghin's remarkable climb of the S. face of Makalu is described in a full article starting on page 1 of this volume.

Makalu Traverse Attempt and Kangchungtse Attempt via West Face. Our expedition was composed of Mike Woolridge, leader, Rob Collister, Andy Fanshawe, Lindsay Griffin, Dr. Gill Irvine, Hamish Irvine and me, all British, and American Steve Sustad. We failed to complete our first objective: the traverse of Makalu. The southeast ridge was followed to 6800 meters and the normal northeast ridge to 7500 meters. The principal cause of failure was the short time between the end of the monsoon on September 29 and the onset of the high winds associated with winter, about three days later. These three days were the only window of opportunity on Makalu this autumn; the only person to take advantage, Pierre Beghin, had already committed himself irreversibly to the mountain. Our second objective was the previously unclimbed 1000-meter-high west face of Kangchungtse. It has a central snowfield, a rim of summit cliffs and granite slabs seamed with ice gullies in the lower half. The left side of the face has big black and red cliffs from which stonefall emanated. The right flank was guarded by a large sérac. Sustad and I left our tent at 6500 meters during the night of September 25 to 26 and followed a line through difficult mixed ground with particularly steep sections at 7000 and 7500 meters. The weather deteriorated. At 9:30 P.M. on the 26th, we reached the summit ridge at P 7600, 40 meters below and 300 meters from the summit of Kangchungtse. We descended without going to the summit. It cannot be said that we lost our way coming down; we never knew it. The map showed Makalu La as being south, but it did not show the cliff bands we nearly fell over. The descent was through 7400-meter Makalu La and thence via the normal Makalu route back to our tent, which we reached on the evening of September 27.

VICTOR SAUNDERS, *Alpine Climbing Group*

Makalu Attempt. George Austiguy, Dick Jackson, Brad Johnson, Scott Thorburn, Dave Wright and I had hoped to climb the Japanese Ridge on the northwest face of Makalu. We established Base Camp on September 17 at 5400 meters and set a staging camp at 5800 meters where the real climbing would begin. On September 28, a major snowstorm forced a retreat to Base Camp. On October 2, we broke trail back up to our staging camp only to find the avalanche danger on the Japanese Ridge to be extreme. We decided to switch to the safer normal route. Climbing alpine-style, we reached 7000 meters on October 4 but returned to Base Camp to rest for a summit attempt. Jackson and I returned to 7000 meters on October 9 for a first summit try, but heavy wind and snow forced us to descend the following day. Austiguy and Thorburn reached Makalu Col (7400 meters) on October 13 but descended because of high winds. On the 15th, Jackson, Johnson and I climbed to 7000 meters. Johnson continued on to 7600 meters and the following morning soloed to 8100 meters, but turned around because of dangerous windslab avalanche conditions. We abandoned the climb on October 25.

JOE FRANK, *Unaffiliated*

Makalu Post-Monsoon Attempts. Aside from the international expedition led by Michael Woolridge and the American one led by Joe Frank, there were three unsuccessful ones on the northwest side of Makalu in the post-monsoon period. Swiss Bruno Zaugg led a group of three Austrians and a German which got to 8000 meters on September 27. Spaniard Señora Ana Sese was the leader of five Spaniards who reached 8000 meters on the 28th. On October 15, seven Spaniards under the leadership of Pere Giro got to a high point of 8100 meters.

ELIZABETH HAWLEY

Baruntse Attempts. There was an unsuccessful British attempt on the southeast ridge of Baruntse led by Andrew Wigley. They reached 6860 meters on May

3. Spaniards led by Luis Miguel Montero got to 7100 meters on the same route, apparently less than 30 meters from the summit!

ELIZABETH HAWLEY

Baruntse Attempt. Our expedition had as members Gerd Krischer, Wolfgang Seul, Dr. Michael Hahn, Dr. Dieter Rebmann, Ingrid Weitzsch, Dieter and Hilde Müller, Wolfgang Grade, Wolf Wilfert, Werner Wilmes and me as leader. Our approach started on April 18 from Jiri, ascended the Khari Khola and Thuli Kharka, went over the Mera La into the uninhabited Hunku valley. Base Camp, high in that valley at 5350 meters on the easternmost of the Panch Pokhari, was reached on May 2. The approach was made more difficult for the porters by two snowstorms. Seul and I prepared the route to the west col up a 200-meter-high, 50° ice face south of the col. On May 6, we all occupied Camp I at 6135 meters on the west col. The next day we climbed to 6500 meters but could not pitch Camp II because of wind and so descended to Base Camp. On May 9, Wilfert, Wilmes and I and three Sherpas climbed to Camp I and the next day placed Camp II at 6500 meters. Wilmes and I reached 6900 meters on May 11, climbing in 6 inches of exhausting breakable crust. A high-altitude cough made me quit. On May 15 we crossed the Amphu Labtsa Pass. We erected a 300-meter lift to lower equipment into the Imja Dragka valley.

UDO SCHMIDT, *Deutscher Alpenverein*

Baruntse. A Swiss expedition of nine made the 21st ascent of Baruntse (7129 meters, 23,389 feet) when Michel Siegenthaler reached the top by the southeast ridge on October 23. The party was led by Jacques Grandjean.

ELIZABETH HAWLEY

Kusum Kanguru, East Face, 1988. On October 23, 1988, British climbers John Diploch, Julian Holmes and I and Sherpas Ang Jangbo, Kami Tsering, Dawa Nuru and Lhakpa Dorje stood on the summit (6367 meters, 20,889 feet) of Kusum Kanguru, having just made the first ascent of the east face. It was a mixed route similar in complexity to that of the north face of the Eiger. The most serious problem was rockfall, which started around nine A.M. after the sun had been on the face for a couple of hours. One of the Sherpas was hit in the face by rock, but fortunately it only broke his goggles and caused a small cut by his right eye. Base Camp was in the Hinku valley at 14,000 feet. We established Camp I at 16,000 feet just below the Lungsamba Glacier on October 10. Between Camps I and II we crossed a large boulder field and an ice ramp with some rockfall. The Lungsamba Glacier was complex. We established Camp II at 19,000 feet on October 14, having fixed 500 feet of rope between these two camps. There were two principal features on the wall. One was a rock buttress; the other a large rock-and-ice ramp near the top of the face. We placed 2500 feet of rope between Camps II and III. On the fifth day on the wall, we bivouacked at 20,000 feet rather than go back down the fixed rope to Camp II. The temperature dropped to $-37°$ and we had some minor frostbite. We established Camp III on a small col at 20,400 feet on October 22 and left there at five A.M. on the 23rd. The final 500 feet were on steep, soft snow and we reached the summit at 7:15 A.M. We had a new system of solar energy which supplied all power needs at Base Camp and all upper camps.

NICK MASON, *Royal Geographical Society*

Kusum Kanguru. Swiss climbers Ruedi and Urs Homberger and Christian Jaggi made a rapid ascent of Kusum Kanguru.

Thamserku Attempts, 1988 and 1989. In the winter of 1988, Dr. Ed Farrar, Canadian Dan Culver and I attempted the second ascent of the west ridge of Thamserku. Although previous sightings and photos had shown a frozen snow arête leading to the summit, we found very shattered and unstable rock gullies due to very dry conditions. After five days on dry, loose faces, we attempted the south ridge. Two days later, on December 7, 1988, we established Base Camp at 13,700 feet between the north face of Kusum Kanguru and the south ridge of Thamserku. Farrar left the expedition and Culver and I made a fast alpine attempt. From a small camp at 15,000 feet on the east ridge, we started up the east side of the south ridge with five days' supplies and minimal hardware. We bivouacked at 17,200 feet at the base of a 250-foot rock buttress on December 9. Medium-quality rock ended at a steep snow-and-ice face intercepted by bands of shattered rock. Above, good rock and three pitches of good snow led to our second bivy at 18,500 feet. Steep rock put us on a snow ridge which we climbed to bivouac for a third time at 19,500 feet. The great final tower would have required many more pitches of rock climbing. We had much more ice gear than rock anchors and barely enough to rappel down what we had already climbed. We ended our winter attempt at Bivouac III and descended on December 12 as a winter storm approached. Dan Culver and I returned in April of 1989. We fixed the lower section to Bivouac III (now Camp III) in ten days. We noticed that much more snow and ice had melted and the newly exposed rock was extremely dangerous. On April 13, we left Camp III, hoping to climb the rock tower alpine-style. To our surprise, the whole snow ridge leading to the tower had melted, leaving very bad rock. At midday, 200 feet up the tower we had run into so much loose rock that when a large flake that I was jamming behind broke off and shot down the west face, we decided that the route was too risky in these dry conditions. We returned to Base Camp on April 14.

HOOMAN APRIN, *Unaffiliated*

Kwangde Nup, North Buttress. In the pre-monsoon period, Alex Lowe and I climbed a new grade-VI route on Kwangde Nup to the right of the one done by

Jeff Lowe and David Breashears in 1982. Our route followed the north buttress, which is simply an extension of the ridge which divides the Hungo and Thame valleys. We took three days up and one day down. The first two days were mostly easy to moderate rock climbing with no pitch exceeding 5.9. The third day involved the steep upper headwall which had several difficult mixed pitches, although they were mostly rock. Lowe led one very hard pitch that he rated 5.10. We rappelled the route on the descent.

STEVEN SWENSON

Kwangde Central Northeast Face. Alan Kearney's full article on this ascent appears earlier in this volume.

Ama Dablam Attempt. Our commercial group consisted of Americans Dwain Stranahan and Craig Selsman and Britons Alan Lees and me. Since the Nepalese give more than one permit for the same route at the same time and since there is not much room for tents, we opted to go early, in March rather than in April. Camp I was established at the usual site at 19,000 feet. We spent the next three days fixing rope along the south ridge, generally on good rock. Do not count on fixed ropes remaining below the Yellow Tower; Sherpas from Pang-boche tend to remove them. The Yellow Tower offers the most technical rock climbing (5.8). Camp II was sited on the top of a second subsidiary tower. From there, we were forced to retreat by a storm and it was ten days before we could return. Our time was running low and a Colorado group was on its way to Base Camp. We spent two days climbing the true second tower, which was quite difficult. In the upper section leading to the Mushroom Ridge, the ice was fantastically hard and bottle green. We had much rockfall and two fixed ropes were chopped. At the foot of this tower, we found the body of Canadian Charles Eckenfelder, who was killed in 1988; we were unable to bury him. Our final dump was made at the end of the Mushroom Ridge on April 12. We had run out of time.

WILLIAM O'CONNOR, *England*

Ama Dablam Attempt. Our expedition was made up of Masashi Tatsuta, Mrs. Joshimi Tatsuta, Seisuke Kurokawa, Miss Harumi Ichimura, Miss Kyoko Horikawa and I as leader. After climbing Imjatse, we attempted the north ridge of Ama Dablam. Mr. and Mrs. Tatsuta established Base Camp at 4950 meters on April 12. We three men placed Camp I at 5600 meters on April 20. Rockfall cut a rope we had fixed at 5500 meters. On April 23 to 25 we pushed the route to 5900 meters and went down to Base Camp for a rest. In Base Camp we discovered the kerosene was gone and we were unwilling to face the rockfall; so we gave up the climb. On April 30 we retrieved our deposit from 5900 meters but left the fixed ropes in place.

TEIJIRO NAMBA, *Hyogo Mountaineering Association, Japan*

Ama Dablam Attempt. Our members were Edward Ramey, Austin Weiss, Chuck Hanaway, Fred Sralam, Clyde Soles and I as leader. We established Base Camp, Camps I and II on April 5, 14 and 16 at 16,000, 19,000 and 19,800 feet on the southwest ridge of Ama Dablam. The party progressed to 21,400 feet (6520 meters) on April 20 but was turned back by heavy, dangerous rockfall.

WENDY L. OSTGAARD, *D.V.M., Colorado Mountain Club*

Ama Dablam Attempts. An Australian-New Zealand expedition of six climbers led by Michael Groom failed in two tries on Ama Dablam. They got to 5700 meters on the northeast spur on April 26 and to 6740 meters on May 11 on the southwest route.

ELIZABETH HAWLEY

Ama Dablam, Post-Monsoon Ascents and Attempt. German Günther Härter led an expedition of six Germans, 4 Austrians and an Italian which climbed Ama Dablam by its southwest ridge. The summit was reached on October 22 by Härter, Austrian Peter Konzert and German Karl Dehn and on October 24 by Germans Lothar Reiser, Dieter Porsche, Austrians Klaus Gürtler, Wolf Dieter Jarisch and Italian Miss Hildegard Wolfsgruber. These were the 67th and 68th ascents of the peak. An American expedition placed all its members on the summit by the southwest ridge. On October 26, leader Gary Ruggera, James Nowack, Gilbert McCormick and Dr. John Woodland got to the top. An eight-member French party led by Jean-Pierre Frachon was also successful on the southwest ridge. The summit was reached on November 1 by Frachon and Wongel Sherpa, on November 6 by Frachon and Wongel again, Bernard Madeuf and Danu Sherpa and on November 8 by Vincent Protopopoff, Georges Favre and Kami Tenzing Sherpa. Slovenian Yugoslavs Bojan Počkar and Vanja Furlan were driven back on the north face and north ridge by bad weather. They got to 6030 meters on October 28.

ELIZABETH HAWLEY

Lhotse Shar. A Korean expedition was composed of Han Gwang-Geol, leader, Cha Jae-Woo, Kim Young-Soo, Ma Jong-Ho, Kang Sung-Do, Chun Young-Ho, Ahn Seung-Ho, Kwon Chun-Sik, Lee Young-Hak, Park Jae-Wook and Jung Yuong-Jin. They climbed the normal southeast ridge. They reached Base Camp at 5200 meters on the Lhotse Shar Glacier east of Imjatse (Island Peak) on August 21. Camps I, II, III, IV and V were established at 5700, 6100, 7000, 7700 amd 8100 meters on September 4, 9, 17, 14 and October 3. On October 4, Kwon Chun-Sik and Sherpas Rinji and Dawa Wangchu reached the summit.

ELIZABETH HAWLEY

Lhotse South Face Attempt. Our expedition, led by Reinhold Messner, was international. The members were Italians Hans Kammerlander and Roland Losso, French Bruno Cormier, Christophe Profit, Sylvianne Tavernier, Michel Arizzi, Spaniard Enric Lucas, Swiss Fulvio Mariani and Poles Artur Hajzer and I. We set up Base Camp a little too late, on April 9. The wall was in unusual condition. Due to some very dry months, there was less ice and snow and the wall seemed more dangerous. We decided to take the Austrian route on Lhotse Shar to 7100 meters and then to make a long traverse on the highest sérac barrier to the Czech-Polish line on the main face. We placed Camps I, II and III on April 11, 21 and 27 at 5800, 6700 and 7100 meters, the latter in the middle of the traverse. It was apparent that it was too late to extend the line of camps. After we were acclimatized up to 7100 meters, we decided to carry out different plans. Hajzer and I tried to climb alpine-style the Czech-Polish line, which we had already tried in 1985 and 1987. From May 11 to May 14, we climbed to 7100 meters, where bad weather stopped us. We spent three nights there and on May 17, having finished our food and fuel and with no improvement in the weather, we made a long traverse to the right to Camp III, from which we descended to Base Camp on May 18. Profit and Lucas were also thinking about the central couloir, but they again attempted the prepared route. Due to ever worsening weather, they abandoned too. On May 20, all members were back in Base Camp.

KRZYSZTOF WIELICKI, *Klub Wysokogórski Tychy, Poland*

Lhotse Ascent and Everest Ascent and Tragedy. A Macedonian expedition led by Jovan Poposki was joined by Slovene Viktor Grošelj and Croat Stipe Božić on April 15. The Macedonians were already at Camp III at 7400 meters. While the latter continued to work on the South Col route, Grošelj and Božić left Camp III on April 30 for Lhotse. At the Yellow Band, Božić turned back fearing frostbitten feet, but after warming his feet at Camp III set out again. Grošelj kept on and reached the summit at 2:30 P.M. in very bad weather. He met Božić at 8200 meters and together they descended to Camp III. On May 7, the same pair left Base Camp and reached the Macedonian summit party, Dimitar Ilijevski, Borče Jovčevski and Sherpas Sonam Tsering and Agiwa. On May 8 and 9 they climbed to Camps III and IV. On May 10 at four A.M., Ilijevski, Božić, Grošelj and the two Sherpas left the South Col in good weather. All but Grošelj reached the summit at 5:30 P.M. This was the second time that Božić, Sonam Tsering and Agiwa had stood on Everest's summit; Božić had made the first ascent of the entire West Ridge 1979. On the way down, they met Grošelj on the Hillary Step. He reached the top at 7:30 P.M. in the dark; this was his ninth 8000er. On the way back to the South Col, they missed Ilijevski. Although Božić waited for him a full day, he did not appear and it is presumed that he is dead.

FRANCI SAVENC, *Planinska zveza Slovenije, Yugoslavia*

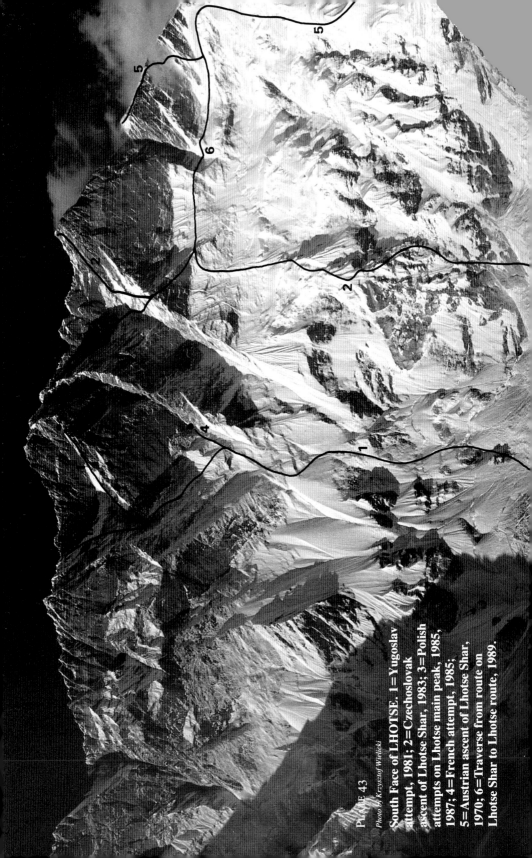

PLATE 43

Photo by Krzysztof Wielicki

South Face of LHOTSE. 1=Yugoslav attempt, 1981; 2=Czechoslovak ascent of Lhotse Shar, 1983; 3=Polish attempts on Lhotse main peak, 1985, 1987; 4=French attempt, 1985; 5=Austrian ascent of Lhotse Shar, 1970; 6=Traverse from route on Lhotse Shar to Lhotse route, 1989.

Lhotse South Face Tragedy. Although two expeditions from Katowice, Poland had already tried this tremendous wall, both times they had lacked luck—one or two windless days when the attacking teams were high. This year we managed to organize a team strong enough to climb the face. Our expedition was composed of Jerzy Kukuczka, leader, Ryszard Pawłowski, Macij Pawlikowski, Przemysław Piasecki, Tomasz Kopyś, Michał Kulej, Elżbieta Piętak, Witold Oklek, Leszek Czech and me, Poles, Frenchman Yves Ballu, Swiss Fulvio Mariani and Italian Floriano Castelnuovo. Our plan was to fix rope to Camp II while climbers acclimatized on neighboring 6000ers and on the normal route on Lhotse. The climbers on Lhotse's normal route would also establish a camp at 7400 meters to protect the descent from the summit. However, nature changed our ambitious plans as the monsoon lasted until the first days of October. There was no alternative but to try only the Polish route on the south face of Lhotse. Luckily we had several kilometers of rope which were carefully fixed on the wall. Camps I, II, III, IV, V and VI were placed at 5800, 6200, 6800, 7100, 7450 and 7800 meters on September 13, 18, 28, October 5, 8 and 21. During the whole period while the rope was being fixed, the weather was bad and there was a great danger of avalanches. The climbers suffered from the high moisture and sharp cold, and most had painful coughs. Not until October 5 did the weather improve enough pitch the higher camps. As traditionally is the case, in the middle of October strong winds blew in from Tibet. On October 18 Kukuczka and Pawłowski set out from Base Camp hoping to reach the summit. The next day, the wind stopped blowing. Taking advantage of the good weather, they reached Camp VI on October 21. On the following day, they continued, bivouacking first at 8000 and then at 8300 meters. The weather was still excellent. Just after sunrise on the 23rd, Kukuczka began to climb toward the ridge crest which he could already see. Just as he was about to reach it on the final obstacle, he suddenly fell off. The rope could not hold the fall of more than 100 meters and broke and he fell the whole length of the face to his death. Pawłowski could not inform Base Camp about the accident because Kukuczka had the radio in his rucksack. He spent the night on a rock ledge at 8100 meters. The next day he met the support team of Kopyś and Pawlikowski. All three returned to Base Camp on October 26.

RYSZARD WARECKI, *Klub Wysokogórski Katowice, Poland*

Lhotse. A two-man Korean expedition completed the 20th ascent of Lhotse. Leader Heo Young-Ho reached the summit via the west face on October 14.

ELIZABETH HAWLEY

Lhotse South Face, Solo Winter Attempts. There were two separate unsuccessful attempts made by Frenchmen to climb the south face of Lhotse in winter. On November 29, Marc Batard reached 7000 meters before giving up. Accompanied by Catalán Enric Lucas, Christophe Profit reached 6700 meters on December 18, but after two bivouacs there, the pair had to descend in bad weather. Lucas then returned to Spain. Profit made a solo attempt on January 13 and 14, 1990, which reached 7150 meters, where his tent was destroyed by the wind. A final attempt from January 19 and 21, 1990 failed at 7600 meters.

ELIZABETH HAWLEY

Nuptse, Joint Attempt by the Left Buttress of the Central Part of the South Face. Our expedition was composed of Italians Kurt Walde, Alberto Guelpa and me. On April 14, we placed Base Camp on the Lhotse Nup Glacier. The next day, four Canadians set up camp next to ours. We all had the same objective; the route attempted in 1986 by Jeff Lowe and Marc Twight. A few days later, our group headed for Camp II on the normal Everest route both for acclimatization and to scan the 1961 British route on Nuptse, which we hoped to use on the descent. The Canadians also spent some days acclimatizing. In early May, we were all back in Base Camp, but two Canadians and Guelpa had to withdraw for health reasons. That left Canadians Jim Elzinga, Peter Abril, Kurt Walde and me, who joined forces. Starting on May 7, it took us seven days of very difficult climbing to reach the top of the buttress at 6917 meters. The weather was clear and cold on the first four days and unstable during the last three. We bivouacked at 5600, 6100, 6300, 6550, 6750 and twice at 6900 meters. On the eighth day, we were holed up in an ice cave at 6900 meters. On the evening of May 15, Peter and Jim headed up for the summit of Nuptse. Kurt had a badly infected throat and possibly frostbitten feet. We two began the descent of the 1961 British route. The Canadians had meanwhile gained 200 meters more, but they too began the descent. With another bivouac at 6100 meters on the descent we got down. The Canadians returned the next day.

ENRICO ROSSO, *Club Alpino Italiano*

Nuptse, Northwest Summit. A five-person German expedition to Nuptse was led by Ralf Dujmovits. On November 2, they climbed the northwest ridge to the northwest summit (7742 meters, 25,400 feet), still about 400 feet short of the true summit.

ELIZABETH HAWLEY

Everest, Polish Ascent and Tragedy. An expedition led by Eugeniusz Chrobak climbed Mount Everest up the western side from Nepal. The 19-member team included 10 Poles, 4 Americans, 3 Mexicans, a Canadian and a Briton. They established five camps along the west ridge and Hornbein Couloir. Rather than to climb directly to the Lho La, they went over the south summit of Khumbutse (6408 meters), west of the pass, and dropped down to Camp I at 6000 meters at the head of the West Rongbuk Glacier. On May 22, nearly two months after reaching Base Camp, Mirosław Dąsal and Mirosław Gardzielewski reached the top of the Hornbein Couloir in an unsuccessful try for the summit. They retired to Camp IV to support the next summit team and help evacuate the camps. On May 24, Chrobak and Andrzej Marciniak left Camp IV at the foot of the Hornbein Couloir at one A.M. and reached the summit of

Everest late in the afternoon. In deteriorating weather during the descent the next day, they were supported by the two other Poles. On the Lho La (6026 meters),

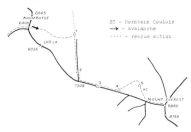

a third pair, Zygmunt Andrzej Heinrich and Wacław Otręba, arrived from Base Camp. The weather worsened with heavy snowfall. After the night of May 26 at 6000-meter Camp I, they decided to continue the descent despite the avalanche danger. The descent route from the Lho La used the Lwow-Karolczak variation, described above, which goes via the south summit of Khumbutse. The rocky face of this peak was fixed with rope and seemed safe enough. On May 27, all six climbed via the steep slope using the fixed ropes. Fresh snow up to a meter deep made progress slow and arduous and they often changed the lead. At about one P.M. an avalanche hit them and dragged them downward. The fixed ropes broke and they fell 200 to 300 meters back to the Lho La. Only Marciniak escaped relatively unhurt. Dąsal, Gardzielewski and Otręba were dead. Heinrich died soon after. Chrobak was alive but not fully conscious; he expired during the night. Marciniak remained alone, fortunately with radio communication with Janusz Majer in Base Camp on the Khumbu Glacier. He decided to go back the kilometer and a half to Camp I. In the fall with the avalanche, he had lost his sun glasses and became snow-blind. On the way to the camp, he fell into a crevasse and injured himself. Thanks to radio communication between Base Camp and Kathmandu, a rescue operation could be organized by Artur Hajzer, who was on the way home from the Lhotse south-face expedition. Simultaneously from Warsaw, diplomatic contacts with China and other countries were arranged. A rescue operation from the Khumbu side was not possible because of snowfall and acute avalanche danger. An international team composed of Pole Hajzer, Sherpas Zangbu and Shiwa and New Zealanders Rob Hall and Gary Ball was brought to the north foot of Everest. Via the Rongbuk Glacier, they managed to reach Marciniak at Camp I on June 1. Marciniak related about the moment of rescue: "When I first heard shouts, I thought it was music. I was sure I was dreaming or hallucinating when I heard the voices, but soon I saw figures approaching through the mist and realized they were people." "It was a moving moment," Ball added. The effective rescue operation was possible because of perfect radio contact, helpful collaboration of the authorities of Nepal, China and other countries as well as by the international mountaineering fraternity. The Polish Alpine Association warmly thanks all who helped to save the life of the only survivor of the tragedy. All five victims were experienced Himalayan climbers. Chrobak and Heinrich had had 30 years of mountaineering experience and had made such first ascents as Kunyang Chhish, the southeast buttress of

Nanga Parbat and Kangchenjunga South and Middle. This was the greatest catastrophe in the 50-year-long history of Polish Himalayan climbing.

JÓZEF NYKA, *Editor, Taternik, Poland*

Everest Attempt and Rescue of Andrzej Marciniak. We were Rob Hall, Apa Sherpa, Pincho Norbu Sherpa and I. We established Base Camp on March 17 and then spent 17 days along with McConnell's team opening the Khumbu Icefall before the arrival of the other expeditions. Camps I and II were set up on April 4 and 8. From Camp II we all returned to Base Camp with a severe viral infection. Upon our recovery, we returned to the south buttress but retreated when Hall and Pincho Norbu had a near miss during continuous rockfall. With Ministry permission, we made a brief foray onto the South Col route. Pincho Norbu returned to Base Camp with thrombosis and Hall retreated ill from 7500 meters. On May 17, our 62nd day on the mountain, Apa reached 8000 meters and I got to 8200 meters. On this last stretch, I accompanied Peter Hillary and Roddy McKenzie. Our return to the south buttress was abandoned because of illness and pulmonary edema. When we got back to Kathmandu, we were involved in the rescue of Pole Andrzej Marciniak; his five companions had been killed in an avalanche on the west ridge. He could not be reached from his own Base Camp on the Nepalese side because of avalanche danger. We hurried overland into Tibet, trucking to the Rongbuk Base Camp and racing up the West Rongbuk Glacier to the Lho La and a relieved Andrzej. We had reached him in 55 hours from Kathmandu. We all returned to Kathmandu the same way.

GARY BALL, *New Zealand Alpine Club*

Everest Funeral Expedition. As noted above, on May 26 five Polish mountaineers were killed in a tragic avalanche accident. In the late autumn, a special burial expedition was arranged by the Polski Związek Alpinismu (Polish Alpine Association). On December 1, Professor Jan Serafin, Stefan Heinrich, Zenon Stoń (priest) Chuldim Dorje Sherpa and I crossed the Tibetan border at Kodari. On December 4, we climbed to the Lho La but found no trace of the five bodies or their Camp I. The priest said a funeral mass with the usual ceremonies and we descended to the Rongbuk monastery. Two commemorative tablets were fixed, one at the Khumbu Everest Base Camp and the other on the moraine of the Rongbuk Glacier.

ZIEMOWIT J. WIRSKI, *Polski Związek Alpinismu*

Everest, First Mexican Ascent and Tragedy. Our expedition was made up of Americans Scott Fischer, Robert Reynolds, Wally Berg, Bill Butler, Pat Howard, Tim Thorne, Ken Frick, Scott Moore, Dick Moran, Sheri Henderson, Peter Jamieson and me as leader and Mexicans Sergio Watkins Fitch and Ricardo Torres Nava. Our route was the normal South-Col route. We established Base Camp, Camps I, II, III, and IV at 17,500, 19,500, 21,000, 23,500 and 26,000 feet on March 11, April 4, 7, 15 and 24. It took 19 days to fix the icefall route due to hazardous conditions and one snowstorm. The traditional right-side approach was not feasible and the route was placed under the shoulder of the west ridge. We coordinated fixing the route with five other expeditions. We made three summit attempts: May 2 by Fischer, Berg and Jamieson to 28,000 feet thwarted by deep snow and exhaustion; May 13 by the same team turned back at 28,000 feet by storm; and May 16 to the summit by Torres, Phu Dorje Sherpa and Ang Danu Sherpa. I had to return from 27,000 feet. Oxygen was used above the South Col. Phu Dorje disappeared during the descent. His body was spotted several days later by other expedition members. Base Camp was a virtual city with considerable environmental impact and requiring expertise in international diplomacy.

WALTER McCONNELL, M.D., *Unaffiliated*

Everest. Our expedition had Karen Fellerhoff and Peter Athans as logistical leaders. The other members were Americans Jeff and Kellie Erwin Rhoads, Andy Lapkiss, Glenn Porzak and Tom Whittaker, Swedes Carl Johan Lager and Mikael Reuterswärd, New Zealander Peter Hillary, Belgians Rudy Van Snick and Nick Tettelin, Australian Roddy McKenzie, Britons Alan Burgess and I and 12 Sherpas. Porzak, Lapkiss, Al Burgess and I got to Base Camp on March 30, but most members did not arrive until April 12 because of supply problems in Kathmandu and illness in the Khumbu. On April 10, we established Camp I, a little higher than usual because of bad conditions in the icefall. Camp II was placed at 21,000 feet on April 17. Platforms for Camp III were dug at 23,500 feet on April 22 but the camp was not occupied until April 24. Porzak, the two Belgians, Reuterswärd and two Sherpas made the first summit attempt from Camp IV on the South Col on May 4. However, bad weather stopped this group as well as the next four summit attempts. The idea was that because of the considerable experience of the group we should all have the opportunity to make a summit bid. Actually twelve of the Westerners did go to Camp IV on the South Col without oxygen, spent the night there and either made a summit bid or descended, thwarted by bad weather. Finally on May 24 Lhakpa Nuru Sherpa, Sonam Dendu Sherpa, Roddy McKenzie and I left the South Col at midnight and reached the summit at seven A.M. We were back at the South Col at ten o'clock and at Camp II at two P.M. Two bottles of oxygen were carried by all four climbers. The snow conditions were very good, hard snow-ice. The weather was perfect until late afternoon when it quickly deteriorated. A final summit bid on May 25 was foiled by bad weather. There were two accidents and deaths on the South Col route this spring, involving other teams. The Nepalese government is now allowing a number of expeditions on this route at the same time. It would appear that the capability of teams ranges from very experienced to wildly incompetent. The main cause of accidents is because climbers are taking so long on the final day that they do not arrive at the summit until after four P.M. Then, tired from their efforts, they must descend in failing light and with failing strength. Teams should decide on a reasonably early turn-around time, such as two P.M., and then adhere to it.

ADRIAN BURGESS

Everest Attempt. The members of our expedition were French Annie Dubois, Jean François Rouys, Americans Alain Hirsch, Jay Sieger and I as leader. We tried the South Col route. We established Base Camp, Camps I, II, III and IV at 5400, 6000, 6450, 7200 and 7978 meters on April 11, 12, 14, 28 and 29. Wind aborted several summit attempts. On May 16, Annie Dubois, three Sherpas and I got to the South Col. On May 19, Jay Sieger got to 8500 meters with Austrian Kurt Stüwe.

KARL HUYBERECHTS, *Club Alpin Belge*

Everest Attempt by Austrians. Kurt Stüwe and Sepp Hassler were to have been members of an Austrian expedition to the Tibetan side of Mount Everest, but when the permission for that was withdrawn, they applied for the South Col route. They arrived at Base Camp only late in April to find many climbers on the mountain and a beaten path to the South Col. Apparently there were many difficulties between the two climbers and much of the time they operated separately. On April 30, Stüwe climbed the Khumbu Icefall to Camp I, followed the next day by Hassler. The latter fell into a crevasse, extricated himself and was escorted to Camp I. It took them ten days to get established at Camp II, where they say there was a small city with some 50 tents! Stüve joined two Americans and after two nights on the South Col made an unsuccessful try on May 14 to 8200 meters. When they descended, they found Hassler at Camp III. He had unsuccessfully tried to reach the South Col and had had to turn back at the Yellow Band. He descended to Base Camp and did not make any further attempts. Stüwe teamed up with American Jay Sieger; they reached the South Col again on May 18. There was deep new snow. They set out at midnight and almost immediately one of Stüwe's crampons broke. Nonetheless, he carried on. The pair got to 8500 meters at three P.M.on the 19th, but wisely gave up the attempt there.

Everest Post-Monsoon Ascents by a Mexican, Japanese and Koreans. On October 13, Mexican Carlos Carsolio, leader of a four-man team, reached the summit of Everest by the South Col route. That same day and by the same route, Japanese Toichiro Mitani, Hiroshi Ohnishi and Atsushi Yamamoto with Sherpas Chuldin Dorje and Tshering Thebe Lama also got to the top. The leader of this expedition was Ken Kanazawa. Also on the 13th, Cho Kwang-Je climbed to the summit via the south buttress and the southeast ridge. He was a member of a 16-person Korean expedition led by Kim In-Tae. On October 23, Chung Sang-Yong and Sherpas Nima Rita and Nuru Jangbu made the 99th successful ascent of Everest, climbing the west ridge from the Nepalese side. This expedition of 11 Koreans was led by Lee Suk-Woo.

ELIZABETH HAWLEY

Everest Post-Monsoon Attempt. The members of a French expedition to Everest were Jean-Franck Charlet, leader, René Ghilini, Jacques Fouques, Guy

Abert, Michel Flouret and Bruno Gouvy. They attempted to climb the south buttress but could reach only a high point of 8450 meters on September 25.

ELIZABETH HAWLEY

Everest Winter Attempt and Tragedy. A large Korean expedition led by Kim Ha-Kyung with 25 members attempted to climb Everest by the South Col route in winter. They apparently reached the South Col on December 29 but could go no higher. There was an unusual tragedy. One of their porters died from high-altitude sickness, an unusual cause of death among the Sherpas, who are born and live at altitudes well above sea level.

ELIZABETH HAWLEY

Pumori. The members of our expedition were Masayoshi Utsumi, Toshiaki Kobayashi, Toshiyuki Hayakawa, Hisao Tatsukawa, Yongjong An, Mrs. Suzue Terasaki, Miss Ritsuko Sakai and I as leader. This was the second time I had climbed the mountain, having made the first ascent of this route in 1973. We established Base Camp, Camps I, II and III at 5320, 5800, 6120 and 6650 meters on the southwest ridge on April 9, 13, 18 and 20. On April 21, Utsumi, Kobayashi and I reached the summit.

TATSUJI SHIGENO, *Japan*

Pumori, Women's Expedition. We were seven women, Diane Taliaferro, Sue Giller, Lucy Smith, Carol Snetsinger, Kathy Phibbs, Lynne Wolfe and I, and one man, Steve Lawrence. We climbed the southwest ridge. Through a series of events, we ended at a Base Camp on the west side of Kala Patar, and so may have pioneered a new route on the first 2000 feet. From Base Camp we worked around the right of the triangular glacier and up a thousand vertical feet to the Kala Patar ridge through sections of rock and 60° to 70° ice. Camp I was placed on April 7 at 19,600 feet on the first bit of flat ground. The route was unusually dry this season. We encountered mostly loose rock and mushroom ice between Camps I and II. The latter was occupied on April 13 at 20,400 feet. We intersected the regular route there. We traversed under rock towers through very loose rock and along sun-cupped ice and water ice before moving vertically onto better rock back to the ridge. We placed Camp III at 21,500 feet on April 23. The route was littered with old fixed rope and hardware, some of which we cleaned. On April 25, Lucy Smith, Carol Snetsinger and Kathy Phibbs summited. Three days later, Diane Taliaferro and I also reached the summit.

SHARI KEARNEY, *National Outdoor Leadership School*

Pumori Post-Monsoon Ascents and Attempt. Many climbers reached the summit of Pumori (7161 meters, 23,494 feet) in the post-monsoon period. All ascended

PLATE 45

Photo by Shari Kearney

Lucy Smith in the abandoned fixed ropes on PUMORI.

the normal southeast face and ridge route. On September 18, Italian Marino Giacometti, leader, Oswald Santin and Giampietro Verza got to the top. West Germans Sigi Hupfauer and his wife Gaby made the ascent on October 12. A large international expedition led by South Tyrolean Josef Holzer put 14 climbers onto the summit: Swiss Heinz Bosshard, Austrian Bruno Gruber, Germans Helmut Buntrock, Fräulein Ottilie Dörrich, Horst Gimbel, Wolfgang Pauer and Horst-Werner Riches on October 13; Austrians Gottfried Baier, Christian Haas, Frau Helga Heisler and Pemba Tharke Sherpa on October 15; and Germans Rolf Haas, Kurt Wildensinn and Ang Dawa Sherpa on October 15. Members of a four-person French group led by François Duthil joined with the previous party. On October 13, Etienne Bertrand, Michel Roy and Lhakpa Nuru Sherpa summited, followed on the 15th by Mlle Hélène Hardy. On October 16, Americans Randal Harrington, Evan Kaplan and Briton Callum MacKay got to the top. Canadian Jan Neuspiel, leader of a Canadian-Irish expedition, reached the summit solo. Michel Richard's Swiss-French expedition reached only 6400 meters on November 1.

ELIZABETH HAWLEY

Pumori. After acclimatizing on nearby Lobuche, Briton Callum MacKay, Americans Evan Kaplan and I reached the summit of Pumori on October 16 from Camp I at 20,500 feet on the southeast ridge, thus completing the 47th ascent of the mountain. The fourth member of the team, Jim Springer, was forced to descend from just below the summit because of cold feet.

RANDAL R. HARRINGTON

Pumori Tragedy. Our 7-member expedition established Base Camp on September 16 at the foot of the southeast ridge of Pumori. From the 17th until October 3, we worked at placing camps on the mountain, having many difficulties because of the weather. Camps I and II were at 5750 and 6200 meters. The accident happened at 6400 meters on October 3, probably between 3:30 and 4:00 A.M., when an enormous avalanche swept down. I was in Camp I at the time and climbed up to look for them. The victims were Francisco Salgado, Antonio Luis Galea, Pablo de Miguel and Jóse de Miguel.

ADOLFO GARCÍA, *Spain*

Pumori Tragedy. An expedition of eight Americans and Australians hoped to make the winter ascent of Pumori by its southeast face. Australian George Curry fell and was killed on the first day of the attempt, December 28, when he was still only at 5800 meters, some 400 meters above Base Camp. They gave up the attempt.

ELIZABETH HAWLEY

Pumori, Winter Attempt, 1990. South Tiroleans led by Anton Stocker attempted to climb Pumori by the normal southeast face route but they could get no higher than 6750 meters, which they reached on January 22, 1990.

ELIZABETH HAWLEY

Tawoche, Lobuje East and Pokalde, Winter Ascents. A four-man British-German expedition was led by David Etherington. Two unsuccessful attempts were made on Tawoche before it was climbed: the northeast buttress to 5500 meters on December 4 and the north face to 5350 meters on the 6th. On December 11, Etherington and German Jörg Schneider completed the seventh ascent of Tawoche (6501 meters, 21,329 feet) and the first winter ascent, climbing the east ridge. They descended the southeast face. On December 18, Britons Roger Chippendale and Richard Emerson climbed the southeast face to the summit. That same day, Etherington and Schneider climbed Lobuje East (6119 meters, 20,075 feet) via its east face. On December 22, Etherington soloed Pokalde (5806 meters, 19,040 feet) by its north ridge.

ELIZABETH HAWLEY

Cho Oyu. On March 5, Martín Zabaleta, a Spanish Basque living in the United States, Americans Alan Kearney and I, our staff and four "family" trekking members set off in a hired bus for Jiri, the beginning of our walk to the mountain. An approach on foot would increase our enjoyment and decrease the risk of altitude problems. In spite of our slow pace, Alan Kearney came down with a cough the day before arriving at Base Camp. He and his wife remained behind to recuperate while on March 19 the rest of us established Base Camp at a site at 5290 meters known as Kangshung. Unfortunately, Alan had to drop out, as he explains in his article on Kwangde. Martín and I proceeded with our acclimatization. We used the clear periods between storms to reconnoiter possible routes on Cho Oyu's south and southwest sides. Eventually we placed a tent at 5800 meters, about four hours' walk from the foot of the west ridge, first climbed by Poles in 1986. The ridge seemed both technically interesting and yet feasible for a quick ascent. Unfortunately, a heavy storm deposited a half a meter of snow on the glacier, even at Base Camp. After the skies cleared, we still could not move for two days. However, we believed that high winds might sweep the mountain clean of fresh snow by the time we reached high on the mountain eight or ten days later. We set off from Base Camp on April 2. We spent the nights of April 2 and 3 at 5800 and 6150 meters. I quote from my journal, "*April 6*: These last two days have involved some great climbing. From the beginning of the ridge at 6150 meters, it has never been too difficult but never has it allowed us to lose our concentration. We came up a much exposed, knife-edged ridge mixed with short 45° to 55° slopes of snow and ice. The 200-meter-high rock pyramid was a mystery until we got close to it. At first, I was sure we should have to find a way around it, but as we came nearer, we could see that it was not as steep as we thought. Nevertheless, it was a spectacular 200 meters with a ramp system leading around the steep upper wall. In the last hour of light, we emerged from the rock onto a knife-edged ridge which led us to the broad shoulder at 7000 meters. Luckily, the enormous snow slope above has been swept clean of fresh snow. Otherwise, we couldn't make it; it's a perfect angle for avalanches. *April*

7: The winds kept us pinned until midday. We climbed the broad slope in four hours and set up the tent at 7450 meters after another hour's climbing." We managed to get to the summit on April 8 despite very windy conditions. I had trouble keeping my toes warm. Martín found it difficult to keep food down. We found a sheltered spot on the lee of the ridge at 7800 meters and got a little warmer. Several times we were forced to find shelter on the southwest side of the ridge. Finally we swung back left to the northeast and braced ourselves with our ski poles. Once off the last rock steps, Martín began veering toward a snowy mound on our left. At the same time, I realized that the top must be far to the southeast side of this immense plateau. We pressed on over the nearly level plateau, gaining only a few meters for every hundred that we crossed. Though the winds were still high, the midday sun seemed to bring some decrease in their intensity. We were still gaining altitude. Suddenly, after three-quarters of an hour, we were rewarded with a view to the east of Everest, Lhotse, Nuptse and the entire Khumbu valley. The scenery was breath-taking. This is why I love to climb. Only two or three hundred meters remained until the plateau began to drop off to the south. There were jumbles of large ice blocks, wedged up from glacial pressure. As we reached this mound, we hugged each other roughly. We shot a few photos as Martín clung tightly to his Basque flag and I to my American one. This was our second high summit together. This forges bonds that will last a lifetime. Then we began descending the 700 meters back to our bivouac tent.

CARLOS BUHLER

Cho Oyu Attempts. Seven Swiss climbers led by Karl Kobler failed to climb Cho Oyu. They got to 6200 meters on the southwest ridge on April 28. Seven Koreans led by Chi Yoon-Soo reached 6600 meters on the same ridge on May 9 but could not complete the climb.

ELIZABETH HAWLEY

Cho Oyu. A Korean expedition led by Park Sang-Yeol crossed to the west ridge and west face of Cho Oyu from the south. On September 2, Hong Kyung-Pyo, Lee Dong-Yeon and Wangel Sherpa reached the summit.

ELIZABETH HAWLEY

Cho Oyu, Southeast Face Attempt and Assault. Our Belgian expedition, consisting of Louis Lange, Régis Maincent, Michel Brent and me as leader, attempted to make a winter ascent of the southeast face of Cho Oyu. We established Base Camp, Camps I and II at 5250, 6100 and 6800 meters on November 24, December 4 and 10. After two unsuccessful alpine-style attempts for the summit which reached 7200 meters, we gave up because of the constant threat of falling séracs sweeping the upper part of the face. Twice we were nearly overwhelmed. The snow and ice conditions were very good. The wind was strong and it was cold, but the sérac danger was too great. There is a very grave matter to report. There was a Korean expedition with which we never succeeded in communicating which despite a permission only for the southwest ridge came to the southeast face. When we removed our fixed ropes, they attacked us with extreme violence. The liaison officers were four days' march below us. Except for the intervention of the Koreans' Sherpas, we would not have escaped with our lives, as attested to by our open wounds.

ALAIN HUBERT, *Club Alpin Belge*

Cho Oyu Attempt, Tragedy and Assault. An expedition of seven Koreans apparently had permission for the southwest ridge of Cho Oyu but turned instead to the southeast face. They reached 7800 meters before abandoning their effort. Ang Lhakpa (also known as Lhakpa Nuru) had scaled Everest twice as well as two other 8000ers. He fell and was killed on this expedition. Tragically, he was one of five Sherpas who died as they accompanied climbers on winter expeditions this year. The Sherpa climber's death rate was three times that of the foreigners who perished this winter. Since the Koreans were on the same route as the Belgians, there happened what possibly was bound to happen sooner or later when more than one team is on the same route on the same mountain at the same time. They came to blows. Alain Hubert and Régis Maincent were attacked with fists and sticks, according to them, by three of the Korean party and six Sherpas. The Korean leader Lee Ho-Sang denies that any Koreans took part in the fracas, but he does agree that in the hour-long fight Maincent received a head wound that bled badly and that a rope was tied around Maincent's neck and his arms were pinned behind his back. The Europeans fled into the night, hobbling away with the aid of their ski poles.

ELIZABETH HAWLEY

Dorje Lhakpa Attempt. Our expedition consisted of M. Paolucci, D. Morandotti, F. Cella, L. Zarpellon, L. Lehner, Dr. M. Dell'Oca and me as leader. We approached from the south. We hoped to climb the ridge system used by the Germans for their descent in 1986. On October 5, we set up Base Camp at 4300 meters near the moraine of the glacier that comes down the south face of Dorje Lhakpa. We placed Camp I at 5300 meters on the lower part of the west ridge on October 8. On the 10th and 11th, Zarpellon, Morandotti, Cella and a Sherpa tried to climb to the site of Camp II but because of avalanche danger they gave up at 5650 meters.

EZIO GOGGI, *Amici del Contrin, Italy*

Langsisa Ri. Koreans Oh In-Hwan and Park Young-Seok and Nima Tamang composed this small expedition. They approached via the Langtang Khola and set up Base Camp at 4300 meters on April 12. They put Advance Base at 4700 meters on the 13th and Camp I the next day at 5450 meters on the west face of the mountain's southwest peak. On April 16, Park and Nima Tamang stood atop the southwest peak (6154 meters, 20,190 feet), having thought they were headed for the highest summit. On April 18, the same pair were back in Camp I and the next day pitched Camp II at 5800 meters on the south face of the main peak (6327, 21,086 feet). On April 20, the two left at 3:30, were on top at 11:30 A.M and back in Base Camp at 11:30 P.M.

ELIZABETH HAWLEY

Langsisa Ri in Winter. A Korean expedition led by Lee Dong-Myung made the sixth ascent of Langsisa Ri, climbing its south face. On December 14, Kim Bo-Youl and Dawa Tshering Sherpa reached the summit.

ELIZABETH HAWLEY

Langtang Ri Winter Ascent. An expedition of three Koreans made the sixth ascent of Langtang Ri (7205 meters, 23,638 feet). On December 9, leader Park Young-Seok, Youn Tae-Young and Nepali Bir Bahadur Tamang reached the summit via the southwest ridge.

ELIZABETH HAWLEY

Langtang Lirung Tragedy. An eight-member Japanese expedition from Hosei University in Tokyo attempting Langtang Lirung via the southeast ridge ended in tragedy. On March 29, four climbers ascending to Camp I at 5600 meters were struck by a huge avalanche at 4900 meters and carried down 600 meters. Noruo Matsumoto was miraculously able to free himself from the debris and was not even injured. The three others were killed. The survivors and two Sherpas seached for them, finding the bodies of Noriyuki Futami and Yasuhisa Kuwashina. The body of Masahiro Hisamoto could not be found.

Langtang Lirung, Swiss-West German and British-Irish Ascents. There were two successful expeditions on Langtang Lirung (7234 meters, 23,734 feet), both by the southeast ridge. On November 10, Swiss Markus Baumann, Frau Dorothee Landolt, Martin Lochstampfer and Fritz Mauer reached the summit, followed the next day by the Swiss leader Hans Berger, German Fräulein Barbara Leitz and Swiss Liselotte Schmidt. On November 12, Irishman Declan MacMahon got to the top, completing the 12th ascent of the peak. He was a member of the expedition led by Briton Andrew Creigh.

ELIZABETH HAWLEY

Ganesh IV (Pabil) Attempt. Our expedition to Ganesh IV or Pabil (7052 meters, 23,136 feet) was composed of Dr. Pedro Rossi, Miguel A. Vidal, José

PLATE 46

Photo by Benoît Chamoux

Ladder on Buttress of MANASLU.

María Martín. Félix García, Javier Delgado, Luis Alberto Agüero and me as leader. Our approach march was complicated by bad weather for the last three days where we had to open a path in the jungle and construct bridges. We set up Base Camp and Camp I at 4400 and 5000 meters on September 11 and 18. We fixed 800 meters of rope before getting to Camp II at 5600 meters. The weather was very bad. On October 2, we abandoned the normal route and turned to the 1980 French route on the southwest spur. We gave up our attempt at 6100 meters on October 7.

FAUSTINO GARCÍA, *Avila, Spain*

Manaslu. The Esprit d'Equipe expedition led by Benoît Chamoux hoped to carry out its program by climbing a new route on the south face of Manaslu. After an eight-day approach, we established temporary Base Camp on April 5 at the end of Thulagi Lake at 3800 meters. Three days later we were able to place our real Base Camp at 4250 meters up the Thulagi Glacier. To gain access to the glacial Butterfly Valley at the foot of the summit pyramid, we ascended a rocky, 800-meter-high buttress squeezed between two avalanche zones. Difficult walls, overhangs, chimneys made up the climbing on rock of good quality. It took several days to fix ropes and ladders. Because of the verticality of the route, we had to make a kind of aerial tramway to raise our gear. After the buttress, we continued on mixed terrain and then glacier to place Camp I at 5500 meters in the Butterfly Valley on April 18. Our progress was seriously hindered by violent winds and daily fresh snow. On April 23 we succeeded in setting up two tents in the bergschrund of the Pungen (South) Col at 6500 meters, but intensified bad weather forced us back to Base Camp for a relatively long time. On May 2, after several unsuccessful tries to move up the south ridge beyond 7000 meters, we changed our strategy and route, heading for the west ridge, the route pioneered by Messner in 1972. The gale winds and windslabs gave us no hope to complete the still unclimbed ridge. For that reason, we established a new Camp II on the Butterfly Col at 6300 meters on May 3. The next day Italian Soro Dorotei and Czech Josef Rakoncaj placed a tent at 7400 meters before descending. A new start from Base Camp on May 6 allowed the installation of a second tent at 7400 meters. After waiting there for two days and nights, Chamoux and Pierre Royer managed to struggle against the wind and cold and get to the summit of Manaslu (8163 meters, 16,780 feet) on May 9. They were followed on May 10 by Dorotei and Rakoncaj, on May 11 by Frenchmen Yves Detry and me, and on May 12 by Italian Mauro Rossi, Briton Alan Hinkes and Tamang Tirta.

FRÉDÉRIC VALET, *l'Esprit d'Equipe*

Manaslu Attempt. A six-man Italian expedition led by Oscar Piazza got up to 7300 meters on the east ridge of Manaslu on May 1 but had to give up there.

ELIZABETH HAWLEY

Manaslu Attempt and Tragedy. In March, China cancelled my Shisha Pangma permission and I obtained a permit for the northeast face of Manaslu. We were Jim Sutton and I from the United States and Spaniards Javier Iraola, Albino Quinteiro, José Melón and Santiago Suárez. Having departed on April 4 from the roadhead town of Gurkha, we arrived on April 10 at Base Camp at 3850 meters. Camp I was established on April 14 at 5000 meters on the glacial snowfield below Manaslu's northeast face and the north peak. Camp II was placed on April 17 at 5500 meters on the lower north peak slopes and Camp III on May 1 just past the avalanche-prone traverse of the mid-height north-peak slopes. On May 6 and 7, Camps IV and V were set up at 6300 and 7280 meters just above Naike Col and at the lower edge of the great summit plateau. On May 7, Iraola, Quinteiro and Suárez were traversing under the plateau at 7100 meters when Suárez fell to his death. After locating and burying the body at 6400 meters, the surviving Spaniards and I descended to Base Camp. No further summit attempts were made.

KEITH BROWN

Manaslu Attempt. We were Americans Andy Lapkass, Peter Nichols, Chris Treese, Jim McEachern, Ken Thorp, Steve and Ron Matous and Pete Athans, Britons Paul Moores, Alan Burgess and I, although I live in the United States, and Sherpas Dawa Nuru and Pinzo. We climbed in small independent groups of two or three at the speed and rate of ascent which suited the particular individuals. On September 30, we set up Base Camp at 14,300 feet. This is a low Base Camp; Spaniards, Austrians and Japanese all had theirs at 16,300 feet, where we erected a large tent for a storage dump on the way to Camp I on Naike Col at 18,300 feet. There is no real climbing to this point, just a straightforward glacier; it took between 3½ to 4 hours from Base Camp. The route above the col steepens and then crosses a 600-foot-wide open gully, which, although threatened from above by crumbling ice cliffs, only avalanched once in any proportions. The route then follows a series of four step-like bumps up to Camp II at 20,500 feet. One step involved 250 feet of steep snow-and-ice climbing, but the Spaniards had already fixed rope on it. There was a 15-foot aluminum ladder spanning a small crevasse, which opened at an alarming rate of eight inches per day. By the end of the expedition, it spanned a 16-foot hole. The weather during the whole of September had been horrible. We were told it snowed for 23 out of 26 days, building up a dangerous windslab above Camp II. We approached it warily—but not warily enough. Three Sherpas working for the Austrians, tailed by Andy Lapkass, broke a deep trough to 22,000 feet. Andy returned a little in advance of the others and saw them cut a 500-foot-wide slab which carried them 1000 feet. Luckily the threesome came to rest on top of the debris and were only shaken. Andy then went back up and effected a rescue back down to Camp II. Although the weather had cleared, we had very high winds above 22,000 feet. During the third week of October, Paul Moores, Lapkass, my twin Alan and I went up to Camp III at 23,150 feet, sandwiched above and below ice cliffs. After a foul, windy night, we were forced to descend. A few days later, Dawa, Nichols and Treese went to Camp III but given the ferocity of the wind, they decided not to sleep there. Nobody went back to that height again. After another week of waiting in Camp II, we abandoned the attempt. We left Base Camp on November 6.

ADRIAN BURGESS

Manaslu Attempts via the Northeast Face in the Post-Monsoon. Two Austrians, a Swiss and a German led by Austrian Horst Frankhauser reached 7300 meters on October 10 with bad weather and threatening avalanches. Spaniards Carles Gel, Víctor Marín, Joan Colet and Ong Chu Sherpa were also unsuccessful. They established Base Camp at 4750 meters on September 5. Between September 19 and 29, they made three alpine-style attempts, but their high point was 6000 meters. Bad weather and avalanche danger kept them from climbing higher. On October 4, four Japanese led by Masaaki Fukushima turned back in high winds at 7350 meters.

ELIZABETH HAWLEY

Manaslu Attempt. A six-man British team led by Mark Dixon attempted the southwest face of Manaslu. They gave up on October 20, after reaching 7000 meters.

KAMAL K. GUHA, *Editor, Himavanta, India*

Himalchuli West. Ours was a commercial expedition operated jointly by Himalayan Kingdoms Limited (England) and High Country Expeditions (New Zealand). It comprised nine clients, British Mark Vallance, Graham Hoyland, Bill Bennett, Norwegians Jon Gangdal, Bjarne Schmidt, Australians Philip Segal, Campbell Mercer, New Zealander Chas Turner and from Hong Kong K.K. Woo, and guides Australian Paul Bayne, New Zealander Russell Brice and me. Himalchuli West (7540 meters, 24,738 feet) was booked at very short notice following the closure of the Tibetan border, which prevented access to Changtse, our original objective. It was selected on account of its comparable height with Changtse and its supposedly low technical difficulty. The latter was incorrect and we encountered considerable difficulties both on rock and ice on a long and arduous route. We were also hindered by a good deal of bad weather. We succeeded in climbing the whole southwest ridge and making the second ascent of Himalchuli West. Base Camp was established at Meme Pokhari at 4600 meters on May 9. Two or so hours above Base Camp we reached the ridge crest at 5400 meters. The ridge runs for three kilometers until it abuts the main mass of Himalchuli. Along its length lay eleven pinnacles of varying size and difficulty. Camp I was placed on the ridge at 5500 meters on May 16 and Camp II at its end at 5700 meters on May 25. The climbing proved increasingly difficult as we proceeded along the ridge. Much rope was fixed. On May 27, Brice, Vallance and Hoyland fixed most of the route above Camp III, a long, winding route between steep ice cliffs and gaping crevasses. The next day, they established Camp III at 6400 meters below a huge ice cliff. On May 29, Brice made a superb 300-foot lead up the cliff. The three were joined by Bayne and Gangdal from Camp II. The first three returned to Camp III from 7000 meters, but Bayne and Gangdal found a crevasse and sat in it without sleeping bags for the first part of the night. At 1:30 A.M. on May 30, they left for the summit, which they reached eight hours later. Brice and Mercer left Camp III shortly after midnight on May 31, jümared up the ropes and plodded briskly to the summit, getting to it in a biting wind at 7:30.

STEPHEN BELL, *Himalayan Kingdoms Limited, England*

Himalchuli Attempt. A nine-man Korean expedition attempted to climb Himalchuli by the southwest ridge but got only to 6250 meters, which was reached on September 9. The leader Chung Chai-Hong died of illness and his place was taken by Han Seung-Kwon.

ELIZABETH HAWLEY

Chulu East, South Buttress, 1988. On November 25, 1988, Sara Ballantyne, Nuru Wangchu and I stood on the summit of Chulu East. We believe we had made the first ascent of the triangular-shaped south buttress, 2000 feet of 60° ice. Approach camps were at 13,000 feet, where a yak was killed by a snow leopard one evening, Base Camp at 15,000 feet and High Camp at 17,200 feet at the col between Chulu Far East and Chulu East. This appears to be the most direct and classic line on the mountain.

CHRIS HAALAND

Tilitso. Our expedition consisted of Max Jeanpierre, Michel Laurent, Roger Laot, Denis Jeanvoine, Dominique Moutel and me as leader. I give a word on our approach and return. We followed the classic route to Manang in seven days. It takes a couple of difficult days from Manang to the eastern end of Tilitso Lake at 4800 meters. On the second day it was dangerous for the porters for whom we had to cut steps in the "rock pudding." We finally needed another day to Base Camp at 4900 meters at the northern end of the lake, but we wasted a week in that section, first trying to skirt the lake on the western side, which is subject to avalanches. At last we went around the lake on the northeastern side and over a rock barrier. We also had to send to Manang for new porters with good footgear because of the snow. We finally got to Base Camp on April 15. On the return, we crossed the Mesokanto, a 5100-meter-high col in two days, which gave access to the Kali Gandaki. We did fix rope on a 40° snow slope for the porters, but this was much easier, safer and not longer. We placed Camp I dug into a 50° slope at

5850 meters on the east spur on April 18. On April 20, we set up Camp II at 6250 meters where the spur meets the slopes north of the summit. There was a 50-meter-high section of 80° ice below Camp II. On the 21st, Jeanpierre, Jeanvoine, Laurent and one of two Sherpas were driven back by the wind at 6300 meters. That same night, Laot left Camp I and got to 6800 meters, where he bivouacked before returning to Camp II. On April 23, Laot, our other Sherpa and I set out from Camp II. Ongel and I turned back in the summit rocks at 6920 meters in bad weather, but Laot reached the summit (7134 meters, 23,405 feet) at ten A.M. The storm made the descent for us three to Base Camp difficult and we were glad for the fixed ropes.

CHRISTIAN BAILLET, *Club Alpin Français*

Tilitso, Winter Attempt. J.C. Laverne, Don Adamson, Chris Macknie, Martin Lurtz and I as leader started our trek from Dumre on November 15. From Manang we cut across in four days to the Tilitso Base Camp on the shore of the lake at 5000 meters. Continuing cold and bad weather forced us to wait out even another storm. On December 1, four climbers and the Sherpas reached the foot of the northeast ridge. Laverne, one Sherpa and I kept on to Camp I at 5500 meters, which we hacked out of ice on the ridge. The Sherpa was forced back the next morning by the cold. We two kept on to 6100 meters at which point we decided to abort the climb. Because of the cold, the new snow was so dry that it provided no secure base for footing. Under the snow was loose rock.

STEVE ADAMSON, *Alpine Club of Canada*

Lamjung Attempt. Eight Japanese climbers led by Yoshiaki Sugiyama failed to climb 6983-meter (22,910-foot) Lamjung via the southeast ridge. On April 22, they reached their high point of 5950 meters.

ELIZABETH HAWLEY

Annapurna, Bulgarian Attempt on South Face, Winter 1988-9. A Bulgarian expedition was led by Metodi Savov and composed of Ivan Vlchev, Arso Arsov, Dino Tomov, Dimitr Nachev, Kostas Kandidis and Liubomir Ilyev. After a difficult approach complicated by snowfalls, Base Camp was established from November 6 to 10, 1988. They acclimatized on lower summits. Advance Base was at 5100 meters. Between December 1 and 12, three camps were placed along the 1981 Polish route on Annapurna's south face, the highest at 6500 meters. The leading team reached a high point of 6800 meters. Ang Kami Sherpa was injured in a crevasse fall between Camps II and III. Heavy snowfalls between December 16 and 27 interrupted climbing. On December 30, a new attempt was made. However, it began to snow heavily again and on January 6, they decided to abandon the climb. This was the second unsuccessful Bulgarian winter attempt. In 1985-6, they got to 7000 meters.

JÓZEF NYKA, *Editor, Taternik, Poland*

Annapurna and Everest Solo Attempts. I made an unsuccessful attempt on the south face of Annapurna, which reached 5800 meters on April 6, but there was too much snow, which hid dangerous crevasses, and falling séracs. I then got to 7800 meters on the Bonington route on Everest on April 20. I put in eleven hours non-stop from Base Camp to reach that point at three A.M. but had to halt my ascent because of very strong winds and clouds on the summits of Lhotse and Everest. I was also experiencing severe pain in my left knee, for which it has been necessary to return to France for an operation.

MARC BATARD, *Club Alpin Français*

Annapurna Solo Attempt. South Tyrolean Reinhard Patscheider hoped to make a solo ascent of Annapurna by the northwest face, which he knew from having been a member of Messner's successful expedition on it in the spring of 1985; Patscheider did not get to the summit that year either. This year he got only to the foot of the face, where he placed a tent at 5200 meters on April 22. Heavy snowfall, winds and avalanching prevented him from ever sleeping in this tent. When he went back to it a week later, he found it ruined by an avalanche. He retreated immediately. His retreat was by paraglider, but after he had been airborne for only about a minute, the wind sent him to a crash landing at 5000 meters and gave him a dislocated shoulder. When he went back up after another snowstorm to retrieve his gear, a piton came loose on a short roped traverse and he fell 15 meters and bruised his back. (These were not his first accidents on the route; in 1985, he fell 600 meters and was lucky not to have been killed.) He says he will return sometime for another solo attempt on the same face.

ELIZABETH HAWLEY

Annapurna Attempt. Three Austrians led by Peter Wörgötter failed at 5800 meters on May 4 to climb the north side of Annapurna.

ELIZABETH HAWLEY

Annapurna Attempt. A 14-member Korean expedition led by Jang Bong-Wan attempted to climb the north face of Annapurna. On December 19, they reached 7300 meters before abandoning the attempt.

ELIZABETH HAWLEY

Annapurna Ascent and Tragedy in Autumn and Winter Attempt. A 19-man Bulgarian expedition led jointly by Todor Grigorov and Ivan Vylchev intended to climb Annapurna by the Messner route but switched to the Dutch route. They set up Base Camp at 4200 meters on September 21. On October 1, three climbers were swept down by an avalanche at 6200 meters. After a 600-meters fall, Vylchev and Veselin Chaushev suffered hand and rib fractures while porter Dawa Tamang was unhurt. They set up Camps II, III and IV at 5900, 6700 and 7400 meters. On October 26, Vylchev, Liubomir Iliev and Dimitr Nachev climbed to within 40 vertical meters of the top but were driven back by bad weather. On October 28, Milan Metkov, Ognian Stoykov, Liudmil Yanakiev and Petr Panayotov left Camp IV at 2:30 A.M. Three of them reached the summit at 11:30. During the descent, they met Metkov, still climbing uphill despite high, cold winds. Stoykov stopped and persuaded him to withdraw. Both thus dropped behind. The weather suddenly turned bad and they descended in mist and snowfall. The first pair took refuge in Camp IV. At 3:15 P.M., Metkov contacted Base Camp by radio, saying that he and Stoykov could not find Camp IV. Shortly thereafter, teams climbing to Camps II and III below the cloud cover saw "something falling." Apart from pieces of their equipment, no sign of the two climbers could be found despite searches in terrible weather. On October 30, three frostbitten members were evacuated by helicopter. Another Bulgarian party led by Metodi Savov attempted to climb Annapurna by the Polish route on the south face. They were unsuccessful, reaching 6600 meters on December 16.

JÓZEF NYKA, *Editor, Taternik, Poland*

Gangapurna North Face. A small Slovene team reached the summit of Gangapurna (7455 meters, 24,457 feet) in the Annapurna Himal by the previously unclimbed north face. Rok Kolar and Stanko Mihev completed a three-day push on October 1. The other members of the expedition were Andrej Gradišnik, Edi Krebs and I as leader. Base Camp was established at 5200 meters on September 8 and an equipment dump was made at the foot of the face. Although without great technical difficulties, bad weather was the main problem. Since the monsoon lasted so long this year, there were only five good days out of the 30 spent at Base Camp. Because of avalanche danger, the lower 800 meters of the 1600-meter-high face were fixed with rope. On September 24, four members climbed to bivouac 950 meters up the face at 6800 meters. We were driven back by deteriorating weather. The final push started on September 29. After a bivouac at 6800 meters, Kolar and Mihev spent the next day in the tent waiting for better weather. On October 1, they ascended the 400-meter crux, the ramp, with passages of 65° to 75°. Difficult snow and ice led them to the ridge and the summit. They descended the same route, rappelling down the ramp.

FRANC PUŠNIK, *Planinska zveza Slovenije, Yugoslavia*

Tarke Kang. A German expedition led by Adi Welsch failed to climb Tarke Kang (Glacier Dome; 7193 meters, 23,599 feet) by its south ridge. They reached 5400 meters on October 18 and 21.

ELIZABETH HAWLEY

PLATE 47

Photo by Franc Pušnik

North Face of GANGAPURNA.

Annapurna IV Ascent, Possible Ascent and Tragedy on Annapurna II. Our expedition had as members Park Duk-Woo, Chang Byung-Ho, Jeong Jae-Ho, Kim Yong-Kyu, Jeong Kab-Yong, Jeong Joon-Mo, Lee Su-Jin, Cho Won-Bae and me as leader. We set up Base Camp at 3600 meters north of the peaks on August 20 and Advance Base and Camps I, II and III at 5300, 6300, 7300 and 7400 meters on August 23, September 3, 11 and 20. Camp III was for Annapurna II only. On September 20, Cho Won-Bae, Jeong Joon-Mo and Dawa Gyalzen Sherpa climbed to the summit of Annapurna IV (7525 meters, 24,688 feet) via the east ridge. This was the 22nd ascent. On September 21, Kim Yong-Kyu and Jeong Kab-Yong were contacted by radio just below the rock face under the summit on the west ridge. They expected to complete the ascent of Annapurna II (7937 meters, 26,041 feet,) in a short time and bivouac high on the mountain that night. The other members waited for a radio call from them with the good news, but it never came. A search team ascended to Camp III but they could find no trace of them.

LEE DONG-MYUNG, *Yeungnam University Alpine Club, South Korea*

Annapurna Dakshin Attempt. Our expedition, composed of Martin Doyle, Lindsay Griffin, Dave Harries, Mike Woolridge, Katherine Slevin and me as leader, attempted the very difficult, unclimbed east buttress of Annapurna Dakshin (7919 meters, 23,683 feet). Base Camp was established on April 12 at 4180 meters in the Annapurna Sanctuary. Two or three meters of winter snow still lay at that altitude. Almost continuously bad weather hindered us for the next six weeks. Griffin and Tinker had the novel experience of clipping into a bolt left behind by Japanese on the only previous attempt on the buttress when all three Japanese died. On May 10, Doyle and Harries reached 6000 meters. Ropes were left in place, but further attempts were thwarted by illness. With little time left and the main difficulties still above, the route was abandoned. Griffin and Tinker made an unsuccessful attempt on the original east face-southeast ridge route but persistent snowfall dictated prudence.

JONATHAN GARRATT, *Captain, Grenadier Guards, British Army*

Dhampus. On October 15, Japanese Shigeyuki Baba, leader, and Kenichiro Kawaguchi and Gaja Bahadur Gurung climbed to the summit of Dhampus (6012 meters, 19,724 feet) by its southwest face and west ridge.

ELIZABETH HAWLEY

Dhaulagiri Attempt. Our group was composed of Italo Valle, Gino Casassa, Rodrigo Mújica, Giorgio Cattoni and me as doctor and leader. The permission for our original objective, Shisha Pangma, was cancelled. After a period of acclimatization near Everest, Mújica had to withdraw because of a recurrence of mononucleosis. The rest of us headed for Dhaulagiri. From Marpha, we crossed

Dampus and French Passes, despite difficulties for the porters caused by excessive snow on the passes. We got to Base Camp at 4700 meters on April 22, below the northeast ridge, also being attempted by other expeditions. The intense snowstorms increased the danger of avalanches between Base Camp and Camp II at 5700 meters, which we occupied on April 27. On April 30, Casassa and I headed for the southwest summit of Tukuche (6690 meters, 21,949 feet) and camped at 6300 meters. On May 1, we climbed to the summit in poor weather and returned that same day to Camp II on the northeast col of Dhaulagiri. Meanwhile, Valle and Ang Phurba Sherpa had established Camp III at 6600 meters, but they were trapped there by weather until they could descend to Camp II on May 4. Casassa and I ascended to Camp III on the 5th, but bad weather prevented further progress. Up till then we had had only two good days in 14. On May 10, Valle and Casassa established Camp IV at 7200 meters and descended to Camp II on the 11th. On May 14, they had hoped to climb to Camp IV and make a summit try, but the wind was so strong that they gave up the attempt.

> MAURICIO PURTO, M.D., *AAC and Chilean Section of the*
> *Club Alpino Italiano*

Dhaulagiri. Our expedition was composed of Graziano Bianchi, Dr. Elisabetta Castellaro, Fausto Destefani, Aristide Galbusera, Silvio Mondinelli, Claudio Schranz, Maurizio Simonetto, Lino Zani, Sergio Martini and me as leader. Our original plan of climbing the southwest side was impossible because of slides. On April 25, we moved to Base Camp at 4600 meters below the northeast ridge, having been allowed by the Chileans to try that route. After reconnaissance in bad weather, we all started for Camp I at 5700 meters on the northeast col on April 30. Zani fell into a crevasse halfway up and had to be helped back to Base Camp. He was evacuated by helicopter on May 3 at which time several members left. Camps II and III were established at 6400 and 7000 meters on May 2 and 3. The weather was very unstable. On May 10, Destefani and Martini placed Camp IV at 7500 meters and on the 11th reached the summit at 11:45 after a six-hour climb. This was the eighth 8000er for both. News that Tibet had been reopened reached us on May 12 and bad weather returned. For that reason, we quit to head for Everest, our previous objective.

> ORESTE FORNO, *Club Alpino Italiano*

Dhaulagiri. On April 23, Peter Rohrmoser, Erwin Reinthaler and I left Pokhara with our liaison officer and eight porters to cross the Ghorapani Pass to Tukuche and the Dhapa Pass to Hidden Valley. We had to wait there for some days because five of the porters were not prepared to go on to the Dhaulagiri Base Camp. Finally, on May 7, with three porters, we continued to Base Camp at 4600 meters. We reconnoitered and made a dump on the northeast col at 5750 meters on May 9. On the 12th, we climbed past the col to 6500 meters, where we set up a tent. After some bad weather, on May 15 we climbed to 6500 meters, where Reinthaler had to turn back and return to the col alone. Rohrmoser and I kept on to camp at 7000 meters. On the 16th, Rohrmoser had to return to the col because of stomach trouble. I spent the day in the tent. On May 17, I climbed alone to bivouac at 7500 meters. After a stormy night, I climbed to the summit, reaching it at 11:30 A.M.

SEPP INHÖGER, *Österreichischer Alpenverein*

Dhaulagiri Attempts. Argentines led by Raúl Uranga failed to climb Dhaulagiri by the northeast ridge, getting to 7100 meters on April 10. Catalans Carles Galàn, Jaume Ganges and Luis Giner also attempted to climb Dhaulagiri by the same ridge. Their high point was 7200 meters, reached on May 1. After their unsuccessful try on Makalu, the 10-member Belgian team led by Jos Dewint were turned back by high winds on the northeast ridge at 7600 meters on May 17.

ELIZABETH HAWLEY

Dhaulagiri Autumn Attempts. Five expeditions attempted to climb the northeast ridge of Dhaulagiri. None of them was successful. Six Spaniards led by Ignacio Olaizola reached 6500 meters on September 21. Three Frenchmen and a Spaniard led by Alain Bigey got to 6500 meters on September 25. A French military group failed; they lost two Sherpas in an avalanche. (See below.) Spaniard Jordi Magriñà and a companion had to give up at 6750 meters on September 26. French climber Christophe Profit and Spaniard Enric Lucas, accompanied by Sylvianne Tavernier, Ana Masip and Pierre-Louis Olland, were forced back by bad weather at 7800 meters on November 14.

ELIZABETH HAWLEY

Dhaulagiri Attempt and Tragedy. After our success on Indrasan in April, the Groupe Militaire de Haute Montagne hoped to climb Dhaulagiri in September and October, one group by the east face and the other by the normal route. In the second week of this climb, two members had to be evacuated, one with pulmonary edema and the other because of excessive fatigue. We decided to give up the east face try. Still present were Lieutenant Hubert Giot, Sergeants Bruno Prom, Eric Gramond, Dominique Gleizes and Philippe Renard, Adjutant Lionel Mailly, Captain Doctor Pierre Lavier and I as leader. We set up Camps I and II at 5700 and 6450 meters on September 14 and 18. The weather got worse and worse. On September 25, Giot, Gleizes and Sherpas Ajiba and Kami Sarki left Camp II for Camp III while it snowed lightly. When the weather worsened, they dropped their loads at 7100 meters at the base of the "Pear." They were overwhelmed by an avalanche. Giot and Gleizes were saved, being attached to a fixed rope. The Sherpas, 50 meters behind, disappeared over the north face, carried away by the avalanche. A long period of bad weather followed. On October 3, a team ascended to find Camp I completely destroyed. On October 11, climbers went up to Camp II but there was too much avalanche danger. On the 15th, it was decided to abandon the expedition.

ALAIN ESTÈVE, *Captain, Groupe Militaire de Haute Montagne*

Dhaulagiri Tragedy. Two Catalans, Andorran Francesc Dalmases and Spaniard Jordi Cañameras, hoped to climb the west face of Dhaulagiri in the post-monsoon season. This route is technically difficult and was particularly so in the bad weather. In late September, at about 7000 meters, Cañameras decided to descend and returned to Base Camp with badly frozen feet. Dalmases insisted on keeping on and since he did not return from the mountain, it must be assumed that he has perished.

ELIZABETH HAWLEY

Dhaulagiri Attempt. On September 16, Oscar Cardiach and I arrived at Base Camp at 4700 meters below the northeast ridge of Dhaulagiri after crossing Dhampus and French Passes. There we met two French expeditions, one civilian and one military, and a Basque one. We also talked with ill-fated Quicu Dalmases and Jordi Cañameras, who were to attempt the west face. On September 19, Cardiach and I set out for Camp I at 5650 meters on the northeast col. The first part is easy but exposed to avalanches and rockfall from the Eiger. The second part took us through a very broken sérac barrier, where we fixed some rope. We spent two nights there before returning to Base Camp. We were back on the 23rd with worsening weather. Finally on the 26th, we set up Camp II at 6750 meters. This stretch should have been easy but snow and windslabs made it dangerous and we descended to Base Camp. The French military lost two Sherpas in an avalanche on the 27th. Much more snow fell. On October 2, we reascended to Camp I but were forced back the next day. After much snowfall, we plowed our way back up to Camp I on the 9th. We tried unsuccessfully to get back to Camp II on the 10th. We left Base Camp on October 13.

JORDI MAGRIÑÁ, *AAEET de Valls, Spain*

Dhaulagiri Attempt. Our expedition was composed of Olivier Besson, Philippe Michaud, Guy Cousleix, Michel Beulné and me. We tried to climb the normal northeast ridge of Dhaulagiri. After an approach via the Mayagdi Khola we got to Base Camp on November 24. Six days of bad weather followed by sun still did not let us get to the north col despite four tries. The snow was belly-deep. We quit at 5200 meters. Then, Besson, Beulné and I climbed Tukuche Peak by the northeast ridge. When we returned to Base Camp, we learned that one of our approach porters, a lad of 17, had died in an avalanche. We called the attempt off on December 17.

LAURENT LUKIE, CLUB ALPIN FRANÇAIS

Dhaulagiri Tragedy. In December, three men disappeared on Dhaulagiri who were attempting a winter ascent by the normal northeast ridge. Four Americans and two Canadians, whose leader Timothy Brill did not even reach Base Camp, were apparently more a collection of people interested in scaling Dhaulagiri than a team. The climbing leader Jim Yoder left after some days of climbing. He went back to Kathmandu, not having been able to acclimatize. The rest pushed on to Camp II at 5800 meters. Three descended from there while three more presumably climbed to Camp III at 6400 meters. After those that descended had reached Base Camp, the two Canadians departed for home. While Joseph Cain stayed there, the two Americans still on the peak, Gregory Barber and Scott McGrath, and their only climbing Sherpa Nuru Wangchuk remained at Camp III at 6400 meters, determined to continue the climb. There followed a nine-day snowstorm. Cain waited out the snowstorm at Base Camp and then scanned the mountain for signs of the men above. Before the prolonged snowfall, he thought he had been able to see Camp III and the cache of equipment above it, but now he could see neither the camp, the cache nor any indication that there was anyone anywhere on the mountain. They had taken no radios with them and so could not communicate. Cain had to return home and when he left, only a Sherpa cook and helper remained there. They dismantled the camp a few days later and when Yoder and one of the Canadians came back from Kathmandu, they found absolutely no one.

ELIZABETH HAWLEY

Churen Himal, Central Summit. Our team consisted of Christopher Burt, Henry Chaplin and Roger Pyves and me as leader, as well as Sherpas Ang Jangbo and Lkakpa Gyalu. We completed the third ascent of the central summit of Churen Himal. There are three summits, all of which are given as having an altitude of 7371 meters (24,184 feet). Our 12-day walk to Base Camp started from Pokhara. We followed the Kali Gandaki north to Beni, where we branched off up the Myagdi Khola through Darbang. We proceeded through Sibang and Lulang over an 11,000-foot pass to Gurjakhani and finally up the Kaphe Khola to Base Camp, which we reached on October 1. From there we followed the Japanese first-ascent route on the southeast face. We established Advance Base on the Kaphe Glacier at 15,600 feet and Camp I at 16,700 feet. It took several days to fix rope up the wall above, but by October 10 we had Camp II at 19,200 feet on a spur of Ghustang North. Camp III was placed at 20,300 feet on the airy crest of a small ridge in front of the south face of Dhaulagiri VI. From Camp III we crossed a heavily crevassed bowl under the long ridge joining Churen's east peak to Dhaulagiri VI. A lower ramp led to a broad ridge and the central peak. Camps IV and V were established at 21,600 and 22,400 feet on October 19 and 25. On October 26, Burt and Sherpas Ang Jangbo and Lhakpa Gyalu were on the summit at 12:25 P.M. After an eternity of breaking through the crust and a delicate 50-yard traverse, Chaplin, Pyves and I got there a little later.

CHUCK EVANS, *England*

Gurja Himal Attempt. On October 7, my wife Danielle Fioggiaroli-Gendey, Dr. Dominique Ollier, Jacques Henry, Patrick Huard, Jean-Luc Le Floch and I left Pokhara with 60 porters, hoping to climb the 1969 Japanese route on Gurja Himal (7193 meters, 23,600 feet). After having gone around the Dhaulagiri massif, we got to Base Camp at 4100 meters on the Kaphe Glacier on October 18. We placed Camps I and II at 4700 and 5000 meters on October 20 and 23. A thousand meters of steep but easy rock led to the hanging plateau of the Kaphe Glacier. This part of the route was entirely fixed with rope by Chuck Evans' expedition to Churen Himal and by us. We placed Camp III at 5950 meters on the 28th. A big snowfall prevented placing Camp IV on the far side of the plateau until the 30th. The next day, Le Floch, Pemba Norbu Sherpa and Sonam Sherpa bivouacked on the ramp that leads to the shoulder at 6300 meters. On November 1, they made a summit try but had to give up because of high winds and avalanche danger.

PATRICK GENDEY, *Club Alpin Français*

Kande Hiunchuli. Eight British climbers led by Garry Kennard attempted the north ridge of Kande Hiunchuli (6627 meters, 21,742 feet), but they could not proceed beyond 5900 meters due to fresh snow. The expedition was abandoned on October 29.

KAMAL K. GUHA, *Editor, Himavanta, India*

P6380, Kanjeralwa Group. Four French climbers were led by Michel Thodoroff. They climbed the north face to the north ridge. On September 30, Michel Thodoroff, Vincent Dalmais and three Gurung porters Iman, Man Bahadur and Dunbar completed the first ascent of the peak (20,932 feet). On October 1, Cyril Thodoroff, Marc Bioret and for a second time Michel Thodoroff, Dalmais, Man Bahadur and Dunbar also reached the summit.

ELIZABETH HAWLEY

India—Kumaon

Chaudhara. On June 8, leader S.N. Dhar, Rabin Paul and Lhakpa Tsering Sherpa reached the summit of Chaudhara (6510 meters, 21,360 feet). This was probably the second ascent. We had set up three higher camps. We climbed the west face. The other members were R.S. Bhowmick, M. Bose, C. Chakraborty, P. Bej, Achintya Mukherjee, B.M. Bhattacharjee, S. Mukherjee, U. Sarkar, Tarchen Sherpa and I as deputy leader.

J.K. PAUL, *Diganta, Calcutta, India*

India—Garhwal

Nanda Kot. An Indian expedition led by Miss Chandra Prabha Aitwal climbed Nanda Kot (6861 meters, 22,510 feet). Details are missing.

Nanda Devi East Attempt. After a lapse of seven years, our joint Indo-Polish expedition was the first to climb on the Nanda Devi massif since the Nanda Devi Sanctuary was declared a Bio-Sphere Reserve and closed for all expeditions. We were permitted to attempt Nanda Devi East from outside the sanctuary via the Munshiyari and Lawan valleys to the east. The Polish Alpine Federation wanted to celebrate the 50th anniversary of the first ascent of Nanda Devi East by Jakub Bujak and Janusz Klarner in 1939. We were Poles Jan Kwaiton, co-leader, Ryszard Kowalewski, Jerzy Tillak, Wojciech Jedliński and Indians Thandup Sherpa, Fateh Singh, Attar Singh, Magan Bissa, Dr. Ling Raj, Bhoop Singh, Ratan Singh Bisht and I as co-leader. We established Base Camp at Shiama Kharak at 14,170 feet on September 4 despite blocked roads and heavy rains in the area. In a short spell of good weather, we placed Camps I and II on September 9 and 12 at 17,000 and 19,500 feet, the latter on Longstaff Col. Suddenly the weather turned bad. The team members still attempted to prepare the route up the south ridge, fixing rope over difficult gendarmes and knife edges, completely devoid of snow. The rock was rotten and dangerous. The winds were furious. Due to bad weather, the team was forced to withdraw three times to Base Camp. We prepared the route to Camp III at 21,000 feet. The weather did not improve and there was continuous snowfall. We were compelled to call off the attempt on September 30. The Poles joined with us in a real spirit of cooperation and international understanding.

S.P. CHAMOLI, *Indo-Tibetan Border Police*

Nanda Ghunti. A British expedition led by Dr. Ian Teasdale climbed Nanda Ghunti (6309 meters, 20,700 feet) in September. Details are missing.

Kamet and Abi Gamin. The climbers of our expedition were Miss Bachendri Pal, leader, Pritam Bhowmik, Robindra Kumar Bhuyan, Miss Manika Biswas, Mala Honati, Nabender Singh, Madan Singh Gosain, Parvaz Kapadia, Rajendra Singh Pal, Nirmal Pandey, A.K. Mehta, Utpal Sorkar, Miss Sumita Roy, Anil Thakur and I. Base Camp was set up at Vasundhara Tal near the Raikana Glacier at 15,500 feet on August 29. Five more camps were established, the highest in Meade's Col at 23,500 feet. The entire route on the East Kamet Glacier was hazardous and the last stages took a heavy toll of climbers. Rajendra Singh Pal contracted high fever, while Nabender Singh had to return because of altitude sickness. Anil Thakur sacrificed his chances for the summit in order to escort them down. Seven climbers were caught by an avalanche while ferrying loads to Camp III but were able to escape. A first summit attempt on Kamet on September 17 failed 500 feet short of the summit. On September 19, Madan Singh, Rabindra Kumar Bhuyan, Utpal Sorkar, Pasang Namgyal and Wangchu

Sherpa climbed to the summit of Kamet (7756 meters, 25,447 feet). On September 20, Nirmal Pandey and I climbed Abi Gamin (7355 meters, 24,130 feet).

AVINASH DEOSKAR, *Jamshedpur, India*

Kamet Attempts. Kamet continues to be the target for many Indian expeditions. In 1989, expeditions led by Manzoor Ahmed and V.G. Kelkar failed to reach the summit. We still have had no news of a joint Indo-Netherlands party led by N. Sherpa.

Abi Gamin, 1988. An Indian expedition led by Bilwanath Ghosh climbed Abi Gamin. Camp V was established at 22,400 feet on September 15, 1988. After a day confined to their tents by the weather, on the 17th, Miss Anita Sarkar and Sherpas Kami and Phurba climbed to the summit of Abi Gamin (7355 meters, 24,130 feet). They were accompanied as far as Meade's Col (23,600 feet) by Gopal Chandra Pal and Sherpas Lhakpa, Mingma and Pasang, who pitched Camp VI on the col. Their attempts on Kamet on the two successive days failed in bad weather.

KAMAL K. GUHA, *Editor, Himavanta, India*

Abi Gamin. A 20-member team from the Indian Army Armored Corps was led by Lieutenant Colonel B.S. Varma. Base Camp was set up at Vasudharatal on May 30. On July 1, Captains M.S. Dhami, R.A. Khan, V.K. Vaid, Lieutenants Parminder Singh, Sriram, M.B. Thapa and Swr Yellappa reached the summit of Abi Gamin (7355 meters, 24,130 feet). Another group had to turn back from Kamet because of a biting blizzard and exhaustion.

KAMAL K. GUHA, *Editor, Himavanta, India*

Mukut Parbat Attempt. I led a Paratroopers expedition to Mukut Parbat (7242 meters, 23,760 feet) on the Indo-Tibetan border. The mountain had been climbed only once before, by New Zealanders in 1951. They climbed the northwest ridge from the Dakhni Chamrao Glacier. We were 20 climbers, mostly youngsters. Among them were Rupinder Singh Dhillon, M.K. Sorab, Adapa, Umed Singh, Dharam Singh, Arvind Sharma, Ravi Misra, Dr. J.S. Cheema, Sorab Gandhi, Jagdish Sharma and Jai Singh. From the roadhead at Mana village, we walked up the Saraswati Gad to beyond Ghastoli and then up the Pachmi Kamet Glacier. One porter died due to natural causes during the approach. This and rough going up the boulders of the moraine made many problems before we got to Base Camp at 5100 meters on the glacier on August 28. This was two kilometers higher than the Indo-French Kamet Base Camp of 1985. Camp II was placed at 5500 meters on September 3. We fixed 1200 meters of rope in a very steep, narrow gully, where we were exposed to rockfall, to emerge on the west ridge at 6800 meters on September 15. The ridge was knife-edged and windy. We made three summit attempts from Camp II between September 18 and 27, all defeated by high winds. Sorab and I made another attempt along the route of the first ascent and camped at 6100 meters. After waiting for 48 hours for better weather, intense cold defeated us at 6900 meters. Two 6000-meter peaks north of Base Camp were ascended.

BALWANT SANDHU, *Colonel, Indian Army, and Himalayan Club*

Mandir Parbat. A 10-member team led by Shankar Biswas was composed of Subrata Banerjee, Debashish Biswas, Sanjoy Das, Dr. Sujit Guha, Ajoy Mondal, Bhaskar Mukherjee, Soumajit Roy, Shyamal Sarkar and Nishi Kanta Sen. The summit (6559 meters, 21,520 feet) was reached on September 20 by Sarkar and three porters, Nataraj, Tendi and Tharchen. The peak had been climbed only once before, by Indians, in 1981.

KAMAL K. GUHA, *Editor, Himavanta, India*

Kedarnath Dome, East Face Attempt. We originally planned to climb a buttress in the middle of the unclimbed east face of Kedarnath Dome. After our arrival, we discovered so much rockfall on the lower section that we changed our objective to the line attempted by the 1986 Polish expedition. This takes a ramp system leading to the left ridge of the face and up that ridge. Ian Dring and I arrived at Base Camp at Topovan on July 29 and Julian Mathias on August 6. We made an attempt on August 10 but on the second day, having climbed 1000 feet, we were hit by a storm and abseiled off. Until then, the weather was mainly dry with afternoon showers, but the second half of August had a series of storms culminating in a very bad, long storm at the end of the month.

DAVID FLETCHER, *England*

Rock Tower near South Face of Kedarnath. Stefano Righetti, leader, Gian Carlo Grassi and I hoped to ascend the unclimbed 6000-meter rock tower near the south face of Kedarnath. Our Base Camp was at 4000 meters a few walking hours above Kedarnath village. Another two hours took us to Advance Base at 4300 meters at the foot of the big rock-and-ice spur that led to the tower. On September 10, we placed a high camp at 5200 meters on a snow patch still an hour and a half below a crevassed hanging glacier and the base of the wall at 5350 meters. We remained at our high camp for seven days in terrible weather and in several attempts we got only 300 meters higher. On September 21, we decided to give up.

ROBERTA VITTORANGELI, M.D., *Club Alpino Italiano*

Kedarnath South Face Attempt. James Garrett, David Pollari, Mel Brown and I spent the month of September envisioning a new route on the south face of

Kedarnath to the western crest of the massif. We established Base Camp behind the southern lateral moraine of the Kedarnath Glacier and packed loads to a cache where the route begins at an avalanche-snow-laden couloir. From part way up the couloir, where one does not tarry, we traversed rightward onto a series of ledges, which by angling back and forth brought us to a spectacular campsite on the crest of the large lower rock buttress. A number of rock pitches, interspersed with heather scrambling, led to a second campsite, which proved to be our last. Three ropes were fixed on this long section. Pollari and Brown climbed moderately steep snow on slopes that again led to the buttress crest, but two weeks of poor weather followed. The high point was about 18,000 feet. Camps and equipment were cleared, a decision that tested us, for the new snow continued to fall daily.

FRED BECKEY

Kedarnath Dome, To the Top of the East Face. We believe that the east face of Kedarnath Dome had never before been successfully climbed. Our climbing members were Dr. Walter Kraft, Gábor Babcsán, Szabolcs Szebdrö, János Singer, Gábor Berecz and I as leader. We fixed 850 meters of rope on the 1300-meter-high wall and also used ropes left in place by a previous English party. The latter amounted to 500 meters on the lower third, mostly on snow. We had two camps on the wall. The lower was in a snow cave at 5400 meters, in which we stored equipment and food. This was totally covered by a heavy snowfall; we had to search for it for two-and-a-half days and luckily found it. The rock face was beautiful. In October, the days were cold and short. We moved quickly to ascend rock of UIAA difficulty from V to VII—to place a camp at 5800 meters. Because of an accident and health problems, above there the climbing party was reduced to two people. My partner was Szendrö. When he was younger, he lost his left knee in an accident and now climbs with a prosthesis. At 43 years, he did a fantastic performance during our four-day final attack. Above Camp II, the rock was excellent. We climbed free 90% of the wall. At the top of the wall, at 6200 meters, we bivouacked on October 20 without sleeping bags or food in a temperature of −20° C. We did not follow the snow ridge to Kedarnath Dome's summit (6831 meters, 22,410 feet), which would have taken us a full day without technical difficulties.

ATTILA OZSVÁTH, *Hungary*

Satopanth Attempt and Near Tragedy. Our expedition was composed of Michel Chamot, Denis Favre, Guy Bartschi, Jean-Pierre Susini, Patrick Gavard, Henri Gay-Balmaz, Gabriel Dubuis, Philippe and Elizabeth Beguin, Christine Sherwood and me as leader. My objective was to make the first "extreme ski descent" of the direct north face of Satopanth. The way up was the northeast ridge. We placed Base Camp, Advanced Base and Camps I and II at Nandanban at 4300 meters, at Vasuki Tal at 4800 meters, at 5300 and 6000 meters on May 10, 13, 17 and 19 respectively. On May 21, I was pushing myself

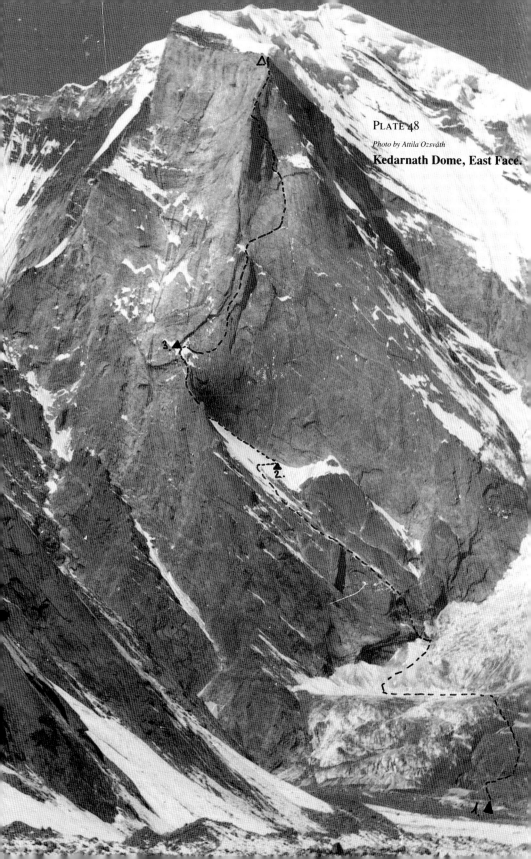

PLATE 48

Photo by Attila Ozsváth

Kedarnath Dome, East Face.

PLATE 49

Photo by Szabolcs Szebirõ

Ozsváth on the East Face of KEDARNATH DOME.

PLATE 50

Photo by Attila Ozsváth

**Camp on the East Face of
KEDARNATH DOME.**

too much at 6500 meters, carrying my ski equipment, when I suddenly fell unconscious with an apparent heart arrest and pulmonary edema. Luckily I received immediate medical assistance. I was in a coma for four hours and semi-conscious for the next three days while I was being evacuated on an improvised litter made from my skis. I was helicoptered from Base Camp by an Indian Army helicopter.

DOMINIQUE NEUENSCHWANDER, *Club Alpin Suisse*

Satopanth Attempt. Koldo Aldaz, Juanito Cebriain and I set up Base Camp on Vasuki Tal at 4950 meters and Camp I at 5300 meters on July 31 and August 4. I fell sick and had to abandon the climb. Another of us had an accident and had to be evacuated. The remaining member could not occupy Camp II until August 26 after much snowfall. In continuing bad weather, he joined a Polish team that fixed the route to 6200 meters. On August 28, it was still snowing and an avalanche swept the whole north face and destroyed Camp I. He gave up.

ALFREDO TORREBLANCA, *Pamplona, Spain*

Satopanth. Our team was made up of Gabriel Denamur, Mirosław Bukowski, Tomasz Samson, Dr. Tomasz Juda, Jadwiga Skawińska, Kazimierz Wszołek, Mirosław Konewka, Emil Witos, Bogdan Remplakowski, Władysław Janik and me as leader. Our original objective had been a 2000-meter-high new route on the east of Satopanth from the Suralaya Bamak. However, delays of our baggage reaching New Delhi kept us from having enough food and equipment and we had to use the Swiss route from the Sundar Glacier on the north-northeast. We set up Base Camp at Vasuki Tal at 4900 meters, Advance Base on the Sundar Glacier at 5300 meters and Camp I at 6000 meters on the saddle on August 30, September 4 and 7. A first summit try on the 8th had to turn back because of the late hour some 50 meters below the top. On September 10, Wszołek, Remplakowski, Konewka and Janik reached the summit (7075 meters, 23,212 feet). On September 18, I made a solo ascent in a 10-hour round-trip.

MIECZYSŁAW JAROSZ, *Klub Wysokogórski Jastrzebie, Poland*

Satopanth. Our group of nine Austrians and a Swiss had first hoped to climb Satopanth (7075 meters, 23,212 feet) by its northwest ridge. We failed when five members fell sick at the beginning of the climbing period. On September 14, Klaus Reininger, Peter Burgstaller, Ivan Exnar and I started up the normal route, the north ridge, but we failed at 6700 meters because of insufficient acclimatization. Ernst Gritzner, Paul Alf, Oswald Pletschko, Heinz Zimmermann and Franz Mischka reached the summit on September 18, followed on September 22 by Exnar and me.

PETER SCHIER, *Österreichischer Alpenklub*

Karchakund. Our expedition consisted of Daniele Turrini, Arnaldo Colombo, Luigi Gallo, Anna Rosa Guzzetti, Luigi Mascherini and me as leader. We got to Base Camp at Tapovan at 4350 meters on August 2. On August 6, we set up Advance Base at Sundanban at 4630 meters. We placed Camp I at 4800 meters on the Kirti Glacier on the 9th. The ascent began on the 13th. We climbed a 55° gully for 500 meters to reach the west ridge. Camp II was at 5650 meters. Turrini, Gallo and Lopsang Sherpa climbed snow-covered rock, steep snow gullies and ice slopes up to 60° for ten hours to place Camp III. On August 15, the three reached the summit of Karchakund (6632 meters, 21,758 feet). Meanwhile Anna Rosa Guzzetti and I occupied Camp III. On August 17, we two also reached the summit.

LUIGI CATTANEO, *Club Alpino Italiano*

Bhagirathi I, North Ridge. Our expedition was composed of Toshifumi Sakae, Mikiei Otake, Kenichi Saito, Miss Yuki Sato, Miss Noriko Hasegawa and me as leader. We set up Base Camp at Nandanban, Advance Base on the northeast side of Bhagirathi II and Camp I below the northeast spur of the north ridge of Bhagirathi I at 4400, 4800 and 5500 meters on August 15, 17 and 20. Bad weather set in for ten days. On September 5, we established Camp II on the northeast spur at 6000 meters. Camp III was placed at 6500 meters just below Schubert's Peak. Camp IV was established beyond Schubert's Peak in the col between it and P 6550 on September 16. On September 20, Sakae and Saito continued along the north ridge to the summit of Bhagirathi I (6856 meters, 22,493 feet), completing the new route. The two women made an attempt on September 22 but did not have enough time.

TAKEOMI SASAKI, *Aizuwakamatsu Alpine Club, Japan*

Bhagirathi III, Southwest Face. Our three-man expedition climbed the Allen Fyffe route on Bhagirathi III. We got to Base Camp at Nandanban of August 5 and acclimatized until August 15. Kwag Bong-Sin and Jang Hong-Youl set out from Advance Base at 5000 meters on the 16th. Not skilled in load-hauling, they climbed only two or three pitches a day. They continued until August 22, when they got to a good ledge at 5580 meters. They waited there in bad weather for three days. As they descended from the ledge, a pin pulled out and one of them fell 10 meters, but he only bruised a calf. More bad weather followed. On September 4, the pair got back up to 5400 meters and to the ledge on the 5th. The next day, they reached 5800 meters, the start of the snow. On September 7, they climbed the seven pitches of snow to the summit. They descended the north snow face, where they were helped by Indian and Japanese climbers.

BAE SEUNG-YOUL, *Korean Alpine Club*

Meru Attempt and Bhagirathi II Ascent. After a British group failed to climb the east ridge of Meru, Andrew MacNae and Gavin Thomas made a rapid ascent of Bhagirathi II (6512 meters, 21,365 feet) by its east face. Sudarshan Parbat Attempt and Thelu Ascent. After a three-day bus ride to Gangotri, James Cade, Mark Dale, Steven Steckmyer, Edward and Margaret Yoshida and I spent an easy six days getting to Base Camp on May 18 at 4500 meters at the junction of the Thelu and Raktvarn valleys. We established Camp I at the end of the Thelu Glacier at 5280 meters on May 21 and Camp II at 5715 meters at the head of the glacier on May 30. Thelu (6002 meters, 19,691 feet) was climbed by all of us and the liaison officer via fairly steep snow slopes and the northeast ridge, which connects it to Sudarshan Parbat. The route we attempted on the latter was the southwest ridge, first climbed by Japanese in 1985. We gained the ridge via a gully to the right of the Japanese route and placed Camp III at 5915 meters on June 9. That same day Dale and Steckmyer climbed to 6160 meters, our high point. That evening heavy snowfall began, which lasted for 48 hours. Thereafter the weather was poor with fog and more snowfall. We left Base Camp on June 17.

MICHAEL D. CLARKE

P 6702 or Vasuki Parbat South, 1988. Italians Massimo Marchegianni, Tiziano Cantalamessa and Marcello Ceci made the first ascent of P 6702 (21,988 feet), which lies just south of Vasuki Parbat. They climbed the east face alpine-style in four days and reached the summit on September 4, 1988. There were 1700 meters of difficult climbing. They rated the maximum difficulty of UIAA VI on the rock and ice up to 70°. They approached via Nandanban and the Chaturangi and Sundar Glaciers.

P 6352, Seta Glacier, 1988. On June 9, 1988, Mukul Mukhopadhay, Dilip Chakrabarty and I made the first ascent of P 6352 (20,840 feet) at the head of the Seta Glacier. We established Base Camp on Vasuki Tal in late May. Two camps were placed on the Chaturangi Glacier, a camp was made on June 5 on the Seta Glacier and a summit camp was established on June 8 on the north face of P 6352. We climbed the north face to the shoulder and traversed to gain the west ridge, which we climbed to the summit.

BIDYUT ROY, *Abhiyatrik, India*

Shivling West Summit. After establishing Base Camp at Tapovan on September 1, Dan Jenkins, Austin Weiss and I lazed about for nine days. On September 10, we hiked to the base of our route and bivouacked in a beautiful meadow. The next morning, we made a foray up the gully which gives access to the southeast ridge. At two A.M. on September 12, we headed back up the gully and moved quickly over a giant gendarme and traversed the ridge toward the snow basin.

After some postholing and slow going, we carved a ledge beneath a cliff and erected the tent at 4500 meters. The next day took us to a 700-meter diagonal traverse to the headwall, a 100-meter gully and another 100 meters of loose flakes to the ridge at 6000 meters. We could dig three trenches for a bivouac. From here the ridge steepened and became very demanding mixed climbing with poor protection. We made little headway that day, gaining only 150 meters, and returned to the airy bivy spot. In the morning the grey sky filled the air with snow. We spent a miserable day watching snow pile up on our sleeping bags. September 16 dawned with blue skies. We jümared to our high point but soon were engulfed in another storm. The conditions ruled out the last 400 meters of the southeast ridge and so we began a long traverse of the south face. At two A.M., we were beneath the col, but separated from it by the hardest climbing of the route. At 4:30 on September 17, we made it and sat down for our first rest in 22 hours. As soon as the sun warmed us, we scrambled to the west summit, only to be stopped from the real one by 25 horizontal meters of rotten rock with too much air on both sides. Our little summit was but one or two meters lower. Our long descent involved traversing toward the northwest ridge, making two spectacular rappels down the face of a hanging glacier and six rappels along the side of a gully which lies to the left of the west ridge. On the last rappel, the anchor popped and I tumbled 150 meters before miraculously coming to a stop unhurt in soft snow on a 50° slope. We descended the rest of the gully, traversed the west ridge and after another bivouac got back to Tapovan at three P.M. on the 18th.

CHRIS WARNER

Shivling. Germans Hans Raumer, leader, Dirk von Massenbach and Jimmy Rudolf reached Tapovan on October 9. They set up a camp at 5500 meters and gained the summit on October 19 via the west ridge. From Tapovan to the summit and back took them only two-and-a-half days.

KAMAL K. GUHA, *Editor, Himavanta, India*

"P 6400*" (P5969). Tapovan is a normally a beautiful Base Camp with grass and water. After we arrived on May 2, unusually heavy and continuous snowfall turned it into a torture from the start. The days went by and every morning we had to remove the snow which had fallen in the night. Our main objective, Shivling, was falling through our fingers. Our liaison officer pointed

---

*The editor, who has been in the region, finds it difficult to know what this peak can be. There is no indication on any map of a peak of this altitude where the Spaniards place it. A letter from Harish Kapadia, editor of the *Himalayan Journal* shows that he too has his doubts. Kapadia states, "From maps, their photos and other photos, it appears that they may have climbed P 6044. There is no peak of 6400 meters in that area or on that ridge." As we go to press, Sr. López informs us that they were mistaken in the altitude and that in fact they climbed P 5969, which lies just north of P 6044.

out an unclimbed 6400-meter mountain which rose above Tapovan opposite Shivling. We decided to make its ascent at night to avoid soft snow and possible avalanches. Xavi Metal González and I left Tapovan at seven P.M. on May 20. Crossing the glacier which separated us from the southwest face was arduous because the snow was still soft. As we got to the initial ramps, night had fallen and the snow had hardened. Progress was rapid on the 45° and then 50° slope in the light of a full moon. We reached a rock face a little above halfway. On leaving the rocks toward the right, the slope became steeper. For several hours, the slope was a consistent 60°. Suddenly we saw the crest 50 meters away, but the slope steepened to 65°. At 7:30 A.M. on May 21, we hugged each other on the summit. We thought of Conrado López waiting for us below, but we were happy with the ascent of a virgin peak. On May 26, we climbed Kedar Dome.

JOSEP LLUIS SASOT, *Escuela Catalana de Alta Montaña, Spain*

Bhrigupanth. An Indian team climbed this peak (6772 meters, 22,218 feet) by the northwest face and attempted the north ridge. They established Base Camp on Kedar Tal on August 18. Four experienced Sherpas with Divyesh Muni and E. Theophyllus climbed the northwest face in 15 days. The Sherpas then fixed the route ahead on the north ridge and led the leader Dr. D.T. Kulkarni and R. Jacob from Camp II on September 9 on a summit attempt. They turned back

HARISH KAPADIA, *Himalayan Club*

Thalay Sagar Attempt. Japanese Akira Kiuchi, Ken Kodachi and high-altitude porter Barubiru attempted to climb the west ridge of Thalay Sagar. They established Base Camp and Camps I and II at 4750, 4900 and 5300 meters on May 21, 25 and 29. Snowfall slowed them. It took five days to fix 13 pitches to 5750 meters. Kodachi fell sick on June 8. The other two continued. Above the schrund was a 40° to 60° ice couloir. The snow was stable but there was falling rock and ice. It snowed on June 10 and 11 and Kodachi left. On June 14 Kiuchi quit at 6150 meters after Barubiru was hit on the thigh by a falling rock while belaying.

Thalay Sagar Attempts. Difficult Thalay Sagar (6904 meters, 22,661 feet) was unsuccessfully attempted in 1989. Japanese Akira Kiuchi and a companion failed at 6200 meters on the west ridge in June. Also in June, Italian Placido Castaldi and two friends got to 5950 meters on the north face. Five Spaniards led by Venancio Soldevila did not manage to climb the east ridge in July. Italians Giambattista Gianola and four others also failed on the east ridge.

Jaonli Attempt from the South. Although Jaonli (6632 meters, 21,760 feet) has been climbed several times from the Jaonli Bamak on the north, the whole east side above the Khatling Glacier was unvisited. Our Anglo-Irish veterans party, two in our mid-sixties (one with a coronary bypass) and two in their mid-fifties, decided to attempt the east ridge from the Khatling. We were Britons Mike Banks and Alan Blackshaw and Irishmen Paddy O'Leary, Don Roberts and me. After a five-day hike from Ghuttu, we reached Base Camp at Kachhotra at 4100 meters on May 19. Deep winter snow made the route up the Khatling icefall to Advanced Base at the foot of the east ridge impracticable. We worked out a route on snow-covered moraine and over subsidiary glaciers and ridges south of the main glacier. This took time and so it was not until June 3 that we had a fully stocked Camp III below the ridge at 4550 meters. Reconnaissance showed that the rock band on the east ridge was impossible in the prevailing snow conditions. We turned to the south ridge. On June 9, Banks, Blackshaw and O'Leary reached the south ridge at 5850 meters. They endured 48 hours of heavy snowfall in very unpleasant conditions. On June 12, they attempted to move further up the ridge, which appeared fairly straightforward, but they were frustrated by the fresh snow. With supplies exhausted, they descended with some difficulty and reached Base Camp on June 14. Meanwhile, on June 8, from Camp III Liaison Officer C.P. Ravichandra and I made the first ascent of subsidiary P 5450 (17,881 feet) at the foot of the east ridge by the east face and southeast ridge.

Joss Lynam, *Federation of Mountaineering Clubs of Ireland*

Gangotri Climbs. Two members of a team from Bombay led by Uday Kolwankar climbed Gangotri I (6672 meters, 21,890 feet) in July. Jogin I (6465 meters, 21,210 feet) and Jogin III (6116 meters, 20,065 feet) were climbed on August 21 and Jogin II (6311 meters, 20,805 feet) on August 25 by an expedition led by Chinmoy Pal from Dum Dum in Bengal. There were two successful ascents of Bhagirathi II (6512 meters, 21,365 feet): British led by Amon Doran via the northeast face and Indians under the leadership of Lalthanmawia.

Kamal K. Guha, *Editor, Himavanta, India*

India—Himachal Pradesh

Himachal Pradesh Climbs by Indians, 1988. Menthosa (6444 meters, 21,140 feet) was climbed on July 30, 1988 by leader Soumitra Ganguly and Chinmoy Pal. *Kulu Pumori* was ascended on July 30, 1988 by leader Sanat Ghosh, Naresh Sabharwal, Sankar Manna, Amitava Sen, sirdar Lebat Ram Thakur and porter Thelu Ram. From the southwest ridge, they had to switch to the west face, where they fixed 600 feet of rope. *Snow Cone* (6235 meters, 20,456 feet) was climbed on July 30, 1988 by leader Kiron Mukherjee, Dhiman Haldar, Goutam Mukherjee and Subir Pal. *Kinnaur Kailas* (6473 meters, 21,237 feet) was climbed on August 14, 1988 by a six-man team from the Medical Department of the Himachal government led by G.S. Thakur.

Kamal K. Guha, *Editor, Himavanta, India*

Peaks in Himachal Pradesh. Indian climbers continued to make many ascents. *Mulkila 4 (M4)* was climbed by an expedition from Calcutta led by Goutam Dutta. On August 22, Dutta and R.S. Negi got to the summit (6517 meters, 21,380 feet). This was probably the first ascent of the peak by Indians. On the 24th, Dutta and A.N. Sapru climbed *M5* (6401 meters, 21,000 feet). Another Calcutta expedition was led by Amulya Sen. Although they had permission for M6 and M7, they climbed two other peaks. Sekhar Dutta Chowdhury, Tarak Ranjan Ghosh and Tapas Kumar Roy climbed *M10* (5852 meters, 19,200 feet) on July 16. Apurba Chakraborty, Dipak Bose, Parijat Chowdhury and Prodip Sarkar reached the summit of *M2* (5832 meters, 19,134 feet). *M1* (5730 meters, 18,800 feet) was climbed on September 3 by Ranjit Basumatari, Naren Jha, Buddhadeb Khaklari and Satyendra Singh although they had originally hoped to climb M4. *CB46* or *Akela Kila* (6005 meters, 19,700 feet) was ascended by climbers from Calcutta led by Sandip Dey. On August 21, Snehasish and Susanta Bhattarcharjee with Tek and Alam Chand reached the summit from Camp IV. In mid September, Savumoy Ghosh, Bijoy Ghale and Debashish Nath climbed CB 48 (5996 meters, 19,672 feet) from the Kulti Glacier. *Menthosa* (6443 meters, 21,140 feet) above the Miyar Nala was climbed by an expedition from Bombay led by Ajay Tasker. Base Camp was at 4400 feet and there were three high ones (Camp III at 5750 meters). Tasker, Vinay Hegde and V. Shankar climbed to the summit in ten hours on August 21. They followed the first-ascent route from the southwest. This, too, was probably a first ascent by Indians.

KAMAL K. GUHA, *Editor, Himavanta, India*

Kulu Pumori and Shigri Parbat. A 44-man expedition from the Indian Border Security Force climbed both of these peaks. Three transit camps were placed on the Bara Shigri Glacier and Advance Base at Concordia at 4900 meters. There they split into two groups. On August 14, deputy leader S.C. Negi, Constables S. Gombu, Jumma Khan, Bim Sen, Shiromani Singh, Lance Naik Diwan Singh, Havildar Naresh Singh and Assistant Commandant S.D. Thomas reached the summit of Kulu Pumori (6553 meters, 21,500 feet) from a high camp at 6065 meters on the southwest face. This mountain was first climbed by R.G. Pettigrew's British party. Negi and Thomas then joined the group on Shigri Parbat, which had established Camp III at 5320 meters. The route from Camps II to III had been difficult with crevasses and hanging glaciers. Above Camp III, they fixed 500 meters of rope to get up an ice wall which ended only 30 meters below the summit. On August 21, Negi, Thomas, Naiks T.R. Angdoo, T. Dorje and Darshan Singh, Lance Naik Jamuna Prasad, Constables Bal Bahadur, Suresh Kumar and S. Lotus climbed to the top of Shigri Parbat (6526 meters, 21,410 feet). Another team on August 22 was driven back by a blizzard. The mountain was first climbed in 1961 by Irish and British.

KAMAL K. GUHA, *Editor, Himavanta, India*

Gyagar, Spiti. We made the first ascent of remote Gyagar (6400 meters, 20,998 feet), which lies near the junction of Tibet, Ladakh and Spiti. With 10 yaks, Ramkrishna Rao, Dolphy D'Mello, Vasant Dalvi, Shridhar Vaishampayam, high-altitude porter Tikamram Thakur, cook Jagdish Thakur and I made a grueling nine-day approach. We went over Zingu Top (4150 meters), Sisbang Top (5060 meters) Lalung Dagda, Sherula, crossed the Lingti River at Phipuk, went over Kulia (5880 meters) and Chaksachhala (5260 meters) and back down to the Lingti at 4280 meters. We went upstream and established Base Camp at 4500 meters at the junction of the Lingti and Gyagar Nala. We moved north up the *nala* to place Advance Base at 5000 meters on June 29. On July 1, all seven of us climbed Gyagar by its south ridge. The return to Kaza took us until July 12.

DHIREN PANIA, *Paramount Trekkers, India*

Phabrang. A four-member Japanese group led by Shiro Sekimoto climbed Phabrang (6172 meters, 20,250 feet) twice by different routes. On August 8, all four climbed the southeast face and on the 13th they all climbed to the summit again via the east face.

HARISH KAPADIA, *Himalayan Club*

Indrasan from the North. After bicycling from Simla to Manali, our approach began on May 8. The conditions for the porters were very difficult because of abnormally deep snow at that season. We placed Base Camp at 4300 meters at the foot of the magnificent north face on May 12. Camp I was installed below the northeast col on May 14. Five climbers had to turn back at 6000 meters on May 15. On May 21, Frenchmen Yves Tedeschi, Eric Gramond, Bruno Prom, Dominique Gleizes, Philippe Renard and I, and Indians Takkur Dass and Liaison Officer S.C. Sharma reached the summit of Indrasan (6221 meters, 20,410 feet) at 12:30 P.M. I descended to Base Camp by paraglider in 15 minutes. During the descent, Gleizes slipped on ice and fell 300 meters, but did not have to be evacuated.

ALAIN ESTÈVE, *Captain, Groupe Militaire de Haute Montagne*

CB 13. A Japanese expedition with 11 climbers led by Isao Minami put two teams on the summit of CB 13 (6264 meters, 20,223 feet) via the north ridge. On August 3, Yoshichika Yamada, Yoshio Nakagawa and Hiroyuki Nakamori set out from 6000 meters and got to the summit the next day after a bivouac at 6000 meters. On August 5, leader Minami, Yosuke Minami, Etsuji Kawase, Mayumi Kobayashi and Indian liaison officer Bijai Sagar Shimedi also climbed to the summit. This was a low-budget, fast ascent with a father-son summit climb. Yosuke Minami at age 16 may be the youngest Japanese to have climbed to the top of a 6000er.

KR 3. A six-member Japanese group got to the top of KR 3 (6157 meters, 20,200 feet) in the Koa Rong valley on August 15. Katsuhei Toyama and Naoki Kondo reached the top via the south face. The leader was Atsuo Iizuka.

HARISH KAPADIA, *Himalayan Club*

India—Kashmir and Jammu

Nun and Kun, 1988. A 95-member team from the Indian Army was led by Lieutenant Colonel H.S. Mann. Nun was climbed by two different routes. Four men made the first Indian ascent of the difficult east ridge, while 21 others did the normal west route in three batches. Kun was climbed by 22 climbers in three groups.

KAMAL K. GUHA, *Editor, Himavanta, India*

Nun. Our expedition consisted of Austrians Willi Wehinger, Walter Bell, Kurt Kirchler, Götz Mayr and me as leader and German Hermann Huber. After a number of delays on the approach, we reached Tongul in the Suru valley on August 5. The porters were demanding 160 rupees per day, but after long bargaining we settled on 80 rupees. With 16 porters we reached Base Camp at 4300 meters on August 6. A day later a Japanese expedition arrived, hoping to climb the normal southwest ridge. On the 8th, we established Advance Base at 4700 meters and the next day went up the steep ice wall that leads to the plateau and continued to the site of Camp I at 5450 meters. On the way down, we fixed a rope on the steepest part. From Camp I, on August 12, we traversed the great snow plateau toward the northwest ridge on skis. After reconnaissance on the 13th, four of us climbed with heavy loads to 6200 meters on the 14th. Huber and I camped there for the night. Kirchler had to leave. On August 15, the rest climbed directly up from Camp II to 6600 meters, the last place to camp before the 400-meter slope that leads to the top. It was difficult to put up the tents in the wind. August 16 was stormy. Wehinger was having circulation problems, and Bell and Huber descended with him to Camp II to avoid frostbite. Mayr and I made a summit attempt to 6850 meters. It stormed the next day, but the 18th was clear and windless. Mayr led most of the way in tiring, firm but deep snow which averaged from 35° to 45°. We climbed through the crux, a rock barrier just below the summit ridge, in an ice-filled gully. We reached the top (7135 meters, 23,410 feet) at 12:30 P.M. "110-years-old!" said Mayr, because we were both 55. It was 29 years after our first expedition together when we had made the first ascent of Disteghil Sar in the Karakoram. We were back in Camp III by four P.M. On the 19th, we descended to Camp II where we were met by Bell, reporting that Huber had broken his leg on the descent to Camp II. Bell and Wehinger transported him to Camp I on an improvised sled. He was evacuated from there by an Indian Air Force helicopter.

WOLFGANG STEFAN, *Österreichischer Alpenverein and Alpenklub*

Nun Attempts. A number of expeditions to Nun this year failed to reach the summit. These included Netherlanders led by R.D. West, Taiwanese led by Gau Ming-Ho, British led by Patrick Littlejohn, Japanese led by Ryozo Takenami and French led by J.M. Bitdot. Italians led by Massimo Pagani failed on Nun but did climb Kun.

HARISH KAPADIA, *Himalayan Club*

Nun. Spanish Basques made the ascent of Nun by the northwest face. After establishing three high camps, leader Juan Manuel Sotillos, Juan Fernando Azcona, Josu Bereciartua and Amaya Aranzábal reached the top on July 19. A second summit attempt by this ten-member party failed because of too much new snow.

Nun and Kun, UIAA Training Camp. The training camp organized by the UIAA was a remarkable success. A team of 28 mountaineers between the ages of 18 and 56 represented nine countries, three continents and four major religions and spoke 18 different languages. They were led by Indian Hukam Singh and Greek Mike Tsoukias. They established Base Camp at 4400 meters at the eastern foot of the Nun and Kun massif. Camp I was set up at 5400 meters below the southern slope of the White Needle. On August 12, the body of Ashok Patel was found; he was the liaison officer of the Americans in 1988. From August 16 to 19, White Needle (6565 meters, 21,540 feet) was climbed by 25 climbers in five batches. Among them were 13 Indians, including Miss Santosh Yadev, the only lady member. On August 21, four Europeans and four Asians left Base Camp to climb Kun (7077 meters, 23,220 feet). German Walter Treibel, Netherlanders Frank van den Barselaar, Ray Cornips, Frank Schmidt, Iranian Ebrahim Davood and Indians Tsewang Smanla, Rajeev Sharma and Shuyeb Omer reached the summit. One of the principles of the expedition was to leave the mountain clean. From Base Camp, six bags of garbage were removed. Spaniard Jordi Pons, the oldest of the party at 56 years, made a very interesting film showing the fraternity and international friendship on the exotic mountain background. All participants except for one ascended at least one summit. For many, this was their life-time altitude record. Experienced instructors gave valuable instruction and encouragement to the young mountaineers. Dr. Walter Treibel says, "In my opinion, the most important lesson from the entire project is the very good and informative companionship of alpinists with such different cultural backgrounds and ways of thinking. Complete strangers became rope partners and mountain comrades. Even real friendships developed around the globe. This is doubtless the greatest success of the expedition." It was an excellent idea of the UIAA Expeditions Committee.

JÓZEF NYKA, *Editor, Taternik, Poland*

Kun. Three Italian expeditions attempted to climb Kun in 1989. Only the one led by Massimo Pagani succeeded. Those under the leadership of Giuseppe

Enzio and Arturo Bergamaschi (see below) did not get to the summit. French led by F. Rebuffet did get to the top, but the French expedition led by Pierre Eyssette failed. For the American attempt, see below.

Kun Attempt. A Colorado Mountain Club group attempted to climb Kun by the northeast ridge. Dick Dietz, Kent Groninger, Cathleen Richards and I left Kargil on June 11. The road was passable by truck only to near Parkachik. On June 12, we rigged a pulley system to cross the Suru River via the cable while our equipment was carried across by horses. Deep snow drifts stopped the horses beyond the river and we got to Base Camp at 14,400 feet along the Shafat Glacier only on June 16. We established Camps I, II, III and IV at 17,000, 18,500, 20,000 and 20,500 feet on June 19, 22, 25 and 26. On June 27, we went for the summit but abandoned the climb in heavy fog and waist-deep snow on a 45° slope.

KENNETH P. NOLAN

Kun Attempt. Our expedition was composed of Carla Barbanti, Claudio Ansaloni, Gian Paolo Bassi, Ermanno Boccolari, Giancarlo Calza, Loris Duzzi, Pietro Feretti, Sergio Leoni, Massimo Lugli, Antonella Mezzadri, Luciano Pasquali, Gerardo Re Depaolini, Paolo Tamagnini, Franco Vivarelli, Angelo Zatti and me as leader. Our approach was made difficult by the flooding of the Suru River. Horses could be got only to 4050 meters and the climbers had to carry everything to 4350 meters to Base Camp. We set up Camp I at 5350 meters on July 16, hoping to climb the northeast side. Camp II was established on the 17th after fixing 100 meters of rope and climbing an ice slope for 300 meters to the plateau. Camp III at 6350 meters between Kun and Pinnacle Peak was occupied on July 19. Heavy snows on July 20, 21 and 23 created great avalanche danger and we gave up the attempt on July 26.

ARTURO BERGAMASCHI, *Club Alpino Italiano*

Kun. On August 10, our group, guided by Christian Laplace and me, gathered at Base Camp at 4400 meters on the moraine of the Shafat Glacier. Camp I was placed at 5300 meters. Our plan was to divide into two parties, one of which would move up one day ahead of the other. On August 13 and 14, Camp II was established on the snow plateau to the right of the White Needle. All descended to Base Camp for a rest. Camp III was set up on August 17 on the snow plateau at 6300 meters by the first party. On the 18th, Philippe Andral, Roger Albessard, Jean-Claude Lètetu, Jean-Michel Meunier, Jean Duffort, Françoise Goudet and I reached the summit in splendid weather. On August 19, Laplace, Danièle Lavalade, Pierre Perisse, Jérome Latrubesse, Pierre Becquet and Sylvain Pigny got to the top.

FRANÇOIS REBUFFET, *Societé Allibert, France*

White Needle. Our expedition was composed of Gorka Estornés, Tomás Izco, José Luis Pérez, Mikel Repáraz, Pedro Tous and me as leader. On July 10, we crossed the Suru River and placed Base Camp at 4000 meters in the valley of the Shafat Glacier. On July 13, we occupied Advance Base at 4500 meters. Camps I and II were placed on July 14 and 18 at 5300 and 6000 meters, the latter on the snow plateau. On July 20, Estornés and I crossed the col and climbed the east ridge to the summit of White Needle (6600 meters, 21,654 feet). After three days of non-stop snowfall, another summit attempt was made along with Americans Keith Brown and Jan Harris, but equipment left on the col could not be found and the attempt failed.

FERNANDO JOSÉ FERNÁNDEZ, *Pamplona, Spain*

East Kishtwar Peaks. Our team comprised Bob Reid, Roger Webb, Dave Saddler and me. We were active to the north of the Dharlang Nala during early September. Since all high-altitude food and some equipment had been lost by the airline, the original objective, the west face of P 6400, was not attempted. Saddler and I switched our attention to the first shapely rock-and-ice peak on the east flank of the Muni Nala just above its junction with the Dharlang Nala, while Reid and Webb tackled the snow-and-ice peak on the west side. On September 7, Saddler and I finally climbed our peak (5990 meters, 19,653 feet) via the southwest face after an earlier attempt was thwarted by avalanches and bad weather. After three rock pitches, we climbed broken ground to bivouac at 400 meters height in a rock cave. Then ice chutes were climbed, mostly by moonlight, to an upper icefield and the summit ridge. We descended to the rock cave in the night, giving a total of 29 hours of continuous climbing. The face was 2200-meters-high and of Alpine D. Sup. difficulty. Reid and Webb topped out on their peak (5950 meters, 11,521 feet) on September 10 after two days of climbing. The ascent was a straightforward snow-and-ice climb (A.D.) with some objective danger.

GRAHAM E. LITTLE, *Scottish Mountaineering Club*

P 6230, South of Umasi La, Kishtwar Himalaya. On July 25, Ian Mills, Neil Brown and I climbed a new route, the north face of P 6230 (20,440 feet). It had previously been climbed by the south face. We ascended a steep 1500-foot glacial snout to 14,000 feet onto an unexplored glacier. From the head of the glacier we climbed an exposed rising line of snow and ice across the face until it ended 2000 feet below the summit. We ascended a 600-foot ice wall capped by a continuously corniced summit ridge and finally reached the loose, rocky summit. We took six days to make the climb and two to descend the same route.

CARL JOSEPH SCHASCHKE, *England*

Hagshu Attempt. A British group led by John Barry failed to climb this difficult peak, which they were attempting by the north face. Bad weather turned them back at 5790 meters.

HARISH KAPADIA, *Himalayan Club*

Hagshu, Kishtwar Himalaya. We were Tim Whitaker, Max Holliday, Phil Booth, Ken Hopper and I. Booth, Hopper and Holliday made the first legal ascent of Hagshu (6330 meters, 20,768 feet), reaching the summit on September 16 after a three-day, alpine-style climb of the east face. I returned to Base Camp with Whitaker, who had contracted pulmonary edema after we had reached 6000 meters on the north face and east ridge. Whitaker made a fast recovery but obviously was unable to make a second attempt. Both routes were approached in two days from Base Camp on the Zanskar side north of the mountain. The climbing was relatively easy, but serious.

ROBIN BEADLE, *British Mountaineering Council*

Matho Kangri I and III. Matho Kangri (or Yan Kangri) had been climbed only once before, by Japanese in 1986. A 21-member team from the Army Ordnance Corps was led by Major Harjit Singh Bawa. They reached Base Camp at 15,000 feet on the Shang River on August 29 and gained the summit (6230 meters, 20,440 feet) two days later. Further details are not known. Another expedition of ten established Camp I at 18,000 feet on September 11. On the 12th, leader Babban Prasad Singh, Sudhir Kumar, M.M. Singh, Chhering Lotto and guide Chewang Norbu set out for the summit. Although M.M. Singh very nearly had a fatal slip, all reached the summit at 12:45. That same day, others headed for Matho Kangri III but were turned back the next day by a snowstorm. They returned from Base Camp to a new Camp I at 18,500 feet on the 15th. At one P.M. on September 16, B.P. Singh, Dilip Kumar, B.K. Srivastava and Skikant Srivavasta climbed rock bands, loose boulders and snow to gain the summit of Matho III (6121 meters, 20,083 feet).

KAMAL K. GUHA, *Editor, Himavanta, India*

Kolahoi, Southeast Rib. On June 25, Jan Harris and I made what may have been the first ascent of the southeast rib of Kolahoi. There were nine pitches of difficult mixed snow and rock.

KEITH BROWN

India—Eastern Karakoram

Saser Kangri I and IV, 1988. The 144 kilometers from Leh to Panamik were covered by Army trucks via the highest road in the world; this crosses the Khardung La at 18,380 feet. Base Camp at 15,500 feet was set up on July 19,

1988 after a two-day trek from Panamik up the Pukpoche Lungpa. Camp I was established on July 26 at 17,800 feet on the Pukpoche Glacier, a kilometer short of the bifurcation of the North and South Pukpoche Glaciers. Camp II was placed at 20,300 feet above the South Pukpoche Glacier on July 28. Camp III was above a steep ice patch, followed by a sharp snow ridge and rock shoulder. The complete route from Camp II to III required 2500 feet of fixed rope. Camp III, established on August 6 at 22,600 feet, was the summit camp. For Saser Kangri IV (7420 meters, 24,330 feet) it was a three-hour climb to the top. For Saser Kangri I it would have been advisable to have a bivouac camp in the col, though we climbed it from Camp III, based on the previous year's report. It took us a little more than twelve hours to reach the summit (7672 meters, 25,170 feet), but unlike last year's expedition, we fixed 2000 feet of rope simultaneously from the col to west summit. From there to the main summit is less than an hour's descent to the col and the final ascent of 400 feet to the peak. On August 24, 1988, two summit parties left at the same time for the two different peaks. K.R. Lavaraju, Sange (senior), Pasang and I climbed Saser Kangri I. Kripa Narayan, S. Srivatsa and Sange (junior) climbed Saser Kangri IV. The other members of the team were Mahendra Sharma, S. Bhattacharjee, B.K. Gupta, J.P. Singh, Surinder Chauhan, Sandeep Goswami, Prajapati Bodhane, Tapesh Bansal, Miss Nandini Lohia and Miss Yangdu Gombu. For the first time, Indian women participated in an expedition to the Karakoram.

HEERA LOHIA, *Climbers and Explorers Club, India*

Peaks Above Chong Kumdan and Aq Tash Glaciers. Our members were Arun Samant, Muslim Contractor, Monesh Devjani, Vijay Kothari, Ashwin Popat and I as leader. We visited the last two major glaciers in the Eastern Karakoram and climbed peaks northeast of the Saser La. Our approach was fraught with difficulties. Via Sasoma, the Tulum Puti La, Changmolung, the Saser La and the Shyok River, we finally got to Base Camp at the snout of the Aq Tash Glacier on July 29. It was 28 days since we had left Bombay and 17 days from Leh (instead of the expected 6). During the ensuing days, I suffered a bout with malaria and went to Chong Tash Camp with Devjani to recover. Samant and Contractor penetrated the Aq Tash (White Stone) Glacier with porters. In six days they had Camps I and II established and stocked at 5200 and 5650 meters. In inclement weather they climbed to the col between Aq Tash (7016 meters) and P 6739. Aq Tash was too steep and sharp. They tried P 6739, east of the col, and on August 7 reached a 6400-meter black tower. They returned to Base Camp on August 9, where Devjani and I joined them after my recovery. Contractor and porter Pasang Bodh decided to continue climbing around the Aq Tash Glacier while others proceeded to the Chong Kumdan (Big Dam) Glacier. They climbed "Lokhzung" (Eagle's Nest; 6090 meters, 19,981 feet) on August 12 and "Chathung Thung" (Black-Neck Cranes; 5645 meters, 18,520 feet) on August 14. Devjani, Samant and I with three porters left for the Chong Kumdan Glacier along the Shyok River. Cutting across the Thangman Glacier, Samant and porter

Koylu Ram had a tough time crossing the ice pinnacles. We reached the four-kilometer-long plain near the Chong Kumdan Glacier. This advancing glacier has blocked the flow of the Shyok a number of times in the past, forming a huge glacial lake. Whenever the dam burst, it loosed giant floods in the Shyok (River of Death), causing destruction and death for miles downriver. The last such major flood was on August 16, 1928. We established an Advance Base on the left moraine at 5040 meters, below the peak "Skyang." In the short time we had, we could only examine the eastern and southern aspects of Chong Kumdan I (7071 meters). We placed a camp up a side glacier at 5540 meters. On August 14, we climbed to a 5900-meter pass, where I, nursing a recent fracture, had to drop out. The views of Chong Kumdan I were both enchanting and threatening. Samant, Devjani and Kolyu Ram climbed to the summit of "Chogam" (Box of Holy Scriptures; 6250 meters, 20,506 feet), up firm, steep snow to a 30-foot rock pinnacle at the summit. On August 15, Samant and Kolyu Ram climbed "Stos" (Ibex; 6005 meters, 19,700 feet) to the east of Chong Kumdan I, traversing below the slopes of Chogam. The next day Devjani and Yog Raj climbed "Skyang" (Wild Ass; 5770 meters, 18,931 feet) up the southeast slopes from Advance Base to the summit pinnacles. Our mules arrived on time and we had a quick passage to Sasoma (August 22) and to Leh the next day. The area northeast of the Saser La is absolutely barren. Weather in July was atrocious with rain and clouds. August was better but colder.

HARISH KAPADIA, *Himalayan Club*

Rimo II and IV. An Indo-International expedition, led jointly by Sonam Palzor and Doug Scott, climbed Rimo II (7373 meters, 24,190 feet) and Rimo IV (7169 meters, 23,520 feet). The Indian members were Sonam Palzor, Tsewang Smanla, Kanhaiya Lal, Mohan Singh, a radio operator, a doctor and Liaison Officer Rajiv Kakkar. The "foreigners" were Britons Doug Scott and Nick Kekus, Canadians Rob and Laurie Wood, Austrian Robert Schauer, American Stephen Sustad and Indian Sharavati Prabhu. There were interminable administrative delays and it was 19 days before they could leave Leh on June 16. Schauer was so distressed that he left the expedition at Panamik on June 18. On June 22, they arrived at Base Camp at 4200 meters on the North Terong Glacier. The original objective was to have been first to climb the unclimbed west ridge of Rimo III with fixed ropes and then for the "foreigners" to climb the also unclimbed south buttress alpine-style. Advance Base was set up at 4750 meters on June 28. Altercations had developed with some of the student porters who quit but the liaison officer and Sonam Palzor got supply going with local men. Rob Wood had severe chest pains and was obliged to leave. There was some dissension when the Indians wanted to cross Ibex Col to repeat the Fotheringham-Wilkinson route on the east of Rimo III, but the conditions for crossing the col were bad. Camp I was placed at 5300 meters. There was much new snow and it seemed preferable to the "foreigners" to switch to the west ridge

PLATE 51

Photo by Douglas Scott

**RIMO II. Indian Route on left;
"Foreigners'" Route on right.**

of Rimo II, which actually is really a shoulder of Rimo I. The Indians preferred a snow couloir between Rimo II and III. They agreed for the Indians to climb the couloir while the others would climb the technically more difficult but safer west ridge. Then, all would meet at a notch below the final steep, rocky ridge and continue on together. On June 10, Kekus and Sustad on one rope with Scott and the two women on the other climbed the ridge to bivouac at 6000 meters. The next day they ascended steep ice and rock gullies. Kekus and Sustad bivouacked on the ridge crest at 6660 meters and the others three rope-lengths lower to accommodate the expected arrival of the Indians. Having climbed the couloir, the Indians were on the col lower down, ready to move out. On July 12, Kekus and Sustad saw to their amazement that the Indians were not heading for the notch, as had been agreed on, but were climbing instead the west-southwest snow face of Rimo IV! Kekus and Sustad continued on upwards and at three P.M. completed the first ascent of Rimo II. Laurie Wood had such a bad altitude headache that she could not go on and Sharu Prabhu found the climbing too technical, and so Scott had to give up the chance to go to the summit. The Indians completed their ascent of Rimo IV, descended to the east and returned via Ibex Col. This was the second ascent of Rimo IV, which was first climbed in 1984 by Indian Army Engineers. Scott, Kekus and Sustad then hoped to make an alpine-style ascent of the south buttress of Rimo III, the original objective, but unexpectedly, without consulting co-leader Doug Scott and the other "foreigners," Sonam Palzor cancelled the expedition, much to the distress of the "foreigners." There are disquieting reports of poor relations and troubles between the two sides and foul language from the student porters brought from Leh. The Nubra valley porters worked well with the expedition.

Mamostong Kangri, Third Ascent. Indian Army Engineers led by me climbed Mamostong Kangri ("Thousand Devils Peak") by the same route as the Indo-Japanese expedition of 1984. A team of twenty climbers was supported by nine others. We made a two-day approach march from Sasoma on the traditional silk route. We established Base Camp at the snout of the Mamostong Glacier on September 15. Two camps were placed on the Mamostong Glacier at 5100 and 5600 meters on July 18 and 25. We crossed a 5885-meter pass to the Thangman Glacier and established Camp III at 6000 meters at the foot of the icefall from the east ridge. We placed Camp IV on the east ridge at 6600 meters on August 6. It took two days to secure the route to 7200 meters with soft snow all the way. On August 10, Captain Gurdyal Singh, G.K. Sharma, Mewa Singh, Nanak Chand, Thondup Dorjee and I reached the summit (7516 meters, 24,660 feet). A second summit team led by deputy leader Major Y.C. Chhibber was beaten back by bad weather on August ll. The team also climbed P 6235 (20,456 feet) and P 6190 (20,309 feet) above the Thangman Glacier on August 11 and 13.

M.P. YADAV, *Major, Indian Army*

Pakistan

K2 Attempt. Our expedition comprised 10 Basques, Balti "Little" Karim and me. The Basque members were Iñaki Carranza, Juanjo San Sebastián, Txema Camara, Ramón Portilla, Alberto Posada, Koldo Tapia, Matilde Otaduy, Antonio Trabado, Angel Selas and Martín Zabaleta. Our approach march up the Baltoro went smoothly from June 12 to the 21st. The path is taking an acute environmental beating from soldiers, trekkers and climbers. We placed Base Camp at 5000 meters in the usual place. As we were the only team on the Abruzzi Ridge this summer, logistics were simplified. Actually, we functioned as several smaller groups on the ridge, first to acclimatize and then in attempts on the mountain. We used one good spell of weather between July 7 and 12 to acclimate and to replace old fixed lines. Several members got to 7300 meters during this period. From then on, we never had more than three or four good days in a row. On July 31, all but Zabaleta, San Sebastián and I left for home. We made two more attempts. The other two spent two nights at 7350 meters in hopes the weather would clear. On August 13 we too left for home.

CARLOS BUHLER

K2 Attempt and Tragedy. An Austrian expedition was composed of leader Edi Koblmüller, Hans Bärnthaler, Robert Strouhal, Gustav Ammerer, Herbert Hutar, Dr. Herbert Habersack and Maila Pemba Sherpa. They had hoped to climb K2 by its east face but terrible weather prevented them from getting very high. Bärnthaler climbed on a subsidiary peak to take photographs on July 28. Tragically, he was carried away by a windslab avalanche and killed.

K2 Attempt. Swiss Jean Troillet and I made what hardly can be called an attempt on K2 from the west since the weather was so bad. During 42 days at Base Camp, it actually snowed for 30 with 10 to 15 centimeters of new snow each morning.

WOJCIECH KURTYKA, *Klub Wysokogórski Kraków, Poland*

Broad Peak Attempts. This was not a good year for expeditions to Broad Peak. Bernard Muller and his wife Laurence de la Ferrière led an international group of some 22 climbers but they were unsucessful. They included well known climbers such as Swiss guide Stéphane Schaffter, Yves Lambert (son of the famous Raymond Lambert) and Eric Haefelin. Italians Fabrizio Defrancesco, leader, Almo Giambisi, Mario Manica and Stefano Ventura got to Base Camp on June 22. They placed camps at 5900, 6400 and 7000 meters. After a rest at Base Camp, they left on a summit attempt but gave up on July 8 at 7500 because of steep deep snow. Japanese led by Tadakiyo Sakahara established four high camps but could get no higher than Camp IV at 7720 meters.

Other expeditions that could not reach the summit included Swiss with Romolo Nottaris and Mexicans under the leadership of Antonio Cortés.

Gasherbrum I Ascent and Tragedy. Our expedition, composed of four Japanese, Russian Igor Kurkov, Nepali Tsindi Dorje Sherpa and Austrians Gerhard Frossmann and me, was led by Dr. Makoto Hara. When we got to Base Camp in July, we discovered that the route we had hoped to climb on Gasherbrum I (Hidden Peak) was off-bounds for us because of the idiotic war between India and Pakistan. Frossmann and I started up a new route on the right side of the south face, despite its being both difficult and objectively dangerous. We ascended some 1000 meters and were at 6500 meters with about 150 meters of difficult terrain badly threatened by falling ice before it appeared that easier ground led to the summit. We would have had to traverse 70° ice that was covered with very deep powder snow. It was too risky to keep on. We bivouacked in a crevasse and descended. A 14-day period of continual snowfall followed. The whole expedition then turned to the normal route. We spent three days on a very broken glacier to get to the foot of the route. I gave up counting how many times someone fell into a crevasse. We climbed to a 6400-meter col above which 50° to 65° slopes led to a rock band at 7000 meters, where we fixed rope. At that point, we had a falling out with the Japanese when they ordered us to go back for more rope. We descended and quit the expedition. Haruyuki Endo, his wife Yuka and Tsindi Dorje Sherpa continued on and climbed to the summit. On the descent, the young Nepali got separated from the Japanese couple. He must have fallen, but they were too tired to be able to search for him.

MICHAEL LEUPRECHT, *Österreichischer Alpenverein*

Gasherbrum I. Austrian Willi Bauer was back in the Karakoram in 1989 from which he barely escaped in the disastrous 1986 tragedy on K2. He led a commercial group of 20 Austrians and Germans, including some climbers very experienced in the high mountains. Unfortunately, the extremely bad weather this season robbed the group of success.

Netherlands Gasherbrum II Ascent, 1988. On June 25, 1988, Arjan van Waardenburg, Rene de Bos, Hans van der Meulen and I reached the summit of Gasherbrum II. From Camp I at 6000 meters on the glacier plateau at the foot of the south face, we climbed alpine-style, making a partially new route on the southeast ridge. During the final climb, we had very good weather. Up to 6600 meters, where we had the first pinnacles and our first bivouac, we climbed the southeast ridge. From there we made a new variant on the glaciated southeast side east of the southeast ridge with a second bivouac. We then continued to the foot of the final pyramid and a third bivouac. After reaching the summit, we descended the normal route, where Austrian, French, Czechoslovakian and Swiss expeditions were active. We lost our leader, Ronald Naar, two weeks after leaving the Netherlands. He broke his foot and injured his back very badly in a paraglider accident and had to be evacuated by helicopter from Payu.

JEROEN JACOBSE, *Koninklijke Nederlandse Alpen Vereniging*

Gasherbrum II. Toni Fullin, Tito Planzer, Peter Stadler and I left Dassu on May 8, the first expedition of the year. For days we plowed through knee-deep snow and got to Base Camp on May 19. The glacier from Base Camp to Camp I was very dangerous, with only a little old snow covering the crevasses. We spent the night at Camp I on May 28 and bivouacked on the 29th at 6800 meters. On May 30, all four of us reached the summit at four P.M. One climber showed signs of an edema after returning to the bivouac and another was frostbitten.

CHRIS FORSTER, *Schweizer Alpen Club*

Gasherbrum II, All-Women's Ascent. The first all-women's team from Britain to an 8000er was composed of Rhona Lampard, leader, Brede Arkless, Geraldine Westrupp, Kathy Bainbridge, Becky Thorp, Dr. Sally Churcher and as a guest from Poland, Wanda Rutkiewicz. They climbed the normal route without bottled oxygen and without male support, although they cooperated with other parties. Base Camp was established on May 30. Camps were set up at 6050 and 6550 meters. A shocking experience was the sight of the dead body of Gary Silver lying in his sleeping bag at the top of the fixed lines at 7000 meters, where he collapsed on June 9, 1988. They started the summit push on July 7 and established Camp II from which on July 12 Lampard and Rutkiewicz reached the summit. Bainbridge accompanied them to 7700 meters, where she turned back. The next day a second team had to withdraw because of high-altitude problems. The weather conditions were bad; during six weeks they enjoyed only ten days without storm and snowfall. Wanda Rutkiewicz filmed the entire climbing, including summit scenes. This was her fifth 8000er, the most any woman has yet achieved.

JÓZEF NYKA, *Editor, Taternik, Poland*

Gasherbrum II Ascent and Tragedy. We were Javier Bermejo, Xabier Erro, Pili Ganuza de Goñi, Javier Garayoa, José Miguel Goñi, Anxton Ibarguren, Agustín Pagola and I. Having left Dassu on June 26, we got to Base Camp on July 5. Contrary to predictions, the weather cleared on the 7th. We carried up loads the next two days and four of us occupied Camp I on the 9th and Camp II the next day. The lead group continued up to Camps III and IV on July 11 and 12. Only a week after getting to Base Camp, on July 13, Erro, Ibarguren and Goñi reached the summit at eight A.M. During the descent, Ibarguren slipped and fell down the abrupt Chinese slope. His companions tried in vain to locate him and returned late to Camp IV with the sad news. All decided to withdraw from the mountain.

GREGORIO ARIZ, *Club Anaitasuna, Spain*

Gasherbrum II Attempts. Aside from the American attempt described below, there were two other unsuccessful tries to climb Gasherbrum II. A Spanish expedition led by Pedro Fernández and Koreans led by Kim Hong-Ki did not reach the summit.

Gasherbrum II Attempt. Ours was the first American commercial expedition to an 8000-meter peak. We were Galen Rowell, deputy leader, Bob Sloezen, guide, Dr. Peter Cummings, Lester Thurow, Scott Moore, my wife Aleja, Base Camp manager, and I, leader. We reached Base Camp on the Abruzzi Glacier at 6000 meters on June 2. Poor weather characterized the entire trip. Despite almost continuous snowfall, the whole team worked hard and established Camp I at 6000 meters on June 8. We moved to Camp I on June 13 and after a couple of severe storm days began pushing higher and occupied Camp II at 6615 meters on the 25th during a brief spell of good weather. Camp III was occupied on June 26 by Rowell and Moore. Sloezen, Cummings and Thurow joined them on the 27th. Because of the conditions, it was not feasible to bivouac at 7300 meters, as is typically done en route to the summit on the standard route. Two summit attempts were made between June 28 and July 3; Sloezen, Cummings and Moore reached our high point of 7650 meters (25,100 feet). An estimated 18 feet of snow fell during the expedition. We left Base Camp on July 6. Even on the trek out, we were in waist-deep snow and still on snow at Goro camp at 15,000 feet.

MICHAEL COVINGTON

Chogolisa Attempt, 1988. On page 245 of *AAJ, 1989,* it incorrectly stated that a French expedition led by Christian Bourgeon changed its objective from Gasherbrum I to II. It did change its objective, but it was from Sia Kangri to Chogolisa. That peak was unsuccessfully attempted in late July of 1988 but the climbers were turned back from a high point of 6400 meters by bad weather.

Masherbrum Attempt. Our team members were Mark Miller, Nigel Hillman, Bruce Hubbard, Stuart Bygrave, Adrian Bake, Mike Cross, Graham Hulme, Ewen Todd, Colin Jamieson, Keven Murphy, Alec Erskine and I as leader. We had hoped to climb Masherbrum (7821 meters, 25,660 feet) by its unclimbed east ridge. We established Base Camp on July 18 on the west side of the Masherbrum Glacier, two-days' walk from Hushe. The route surmounted three icefalls, each about 1000 feet high, before crossing a plateau at 18,000 feet and ascending windslab slopes to a snow dome at 20,000 feet, a 1-1/2-mile-wide snowfield where the separate peaks of Masherbrum East and the main peak rise. We placed Camp I at 16,800 feet on July 21 at the base of the third icefall. Camp II, reached on July 26, was just above the plateau on a ridge below the slopes leading to the snow dome. Camp III was established on July 28 on the edge of the snow dome. On August 4, we finally set Camp IV at 21,600 feet just below the southeast face of Masherbrum proper. Hillman, Miller, Jamieson, Murphy and

I attempted to climb the steep south face of Masherbrum East on August 12 but were forced down by a thunderstorm after reaching 22,000 feet. After a period of bad weather at Base Camp, there were two more attempts, but continuous snowfall prevented our getting further than Camp IV, which, on the final attempt, was completely buried and could not be found.

GINETTE HARRISON, M.D., *British Mountaineering Council*

Nameless Tower, Trango Group. A Spanish expedition made another new and very difficult route on the Nameless Tower. It rises between the 1987 Franco-Swiss route (Delale, Fauquet, Piola, Schaffter) and the 1976 British route (Anthoine, Brown, Boysen, Howells). The climbers were Miguel Angel Gallego, José Luis Clavel, Chiri Ros and José Seiquer. They got to Base Camp on June 16. The route to the base of the climb, where 1000 feet higher they established a camp and a supply dump, was very dangerous and several times they were nearly wiped out by avalanches as they were in the narrow corridor. From the high camp, they fixed a considerable amount of rope on the lower part of the tower. The weather was atrocious. In the whole month of July, they had only four good days. Other expeditions in the region quit. They spent 19 nights on the face and climbed 36 pitches in all. Although much was on extremely difficult rock, there were mixed pitches and six rope-lengths on a steep icefield. The final pitches presented an unusual problem. The summit snowcap kept releasing both powder-snow avalanches and cascades of water. In the last four pitches, they joined Piola's route. All four climbers got to the summit on August 9. (A full report with photographs appears in *Desnivel*, N° 50, November 1989.)

Trango Towers Attempts. Canadians Jim Brennan and Greg Foweraker and Americans Dan Cauthorn, Greg Collum, Matt Kerns, Pat McNerthney and Mark Wilford and I established Base Camp on the Trango Glacier in late May. Like other expeditions, we had difficulties persuading porters to carry to actual proposed campsites; they declare each year that base camps are further and further down the glaciers. An additional headache is the decision by the porters to make the crossing of the Dumordo River an additional stage, whether expeditions use the bridge or wade the river. More than a week of perfect weather in late May and early June gave opportunities for the teams to explore. Wilford and I established a camp on the Dunge Glacier, hoping to make two-man alpine ascents on the Great Trango and Nameless Towers. We humped loads to the base of the Nameless Tower and fixed 200 meters of rope up the 1988 Swiss-Polish route. On the Trango Glacier Brennan and Foweraker climbed high on the Woolums-Selters route, but being unacclimatized descended. McNerthy and Collum climbed several pitches on the huge southwest buttress of the Great Trango Tower but decided against this route because of its enormous size. Cauthorn and Kerns climbed a small peak of less than 6000 meters in the Uli Biaho chain to reconnoiter a route on the Great Trango Tower and watched a

PLATE 52

Drawings © Dee Molenaar

NAMELESS TRANGO TOWER.
Route 3, 1976 (Britons Anthoine,
Boysen, Brown, Howells); 1, 1987
(French Delale, Fouquet and Swiss
Piola, Schaffter); 5, 1987 (Yugoslavs
Cankar, Knez, Srot); 6, 1988
(Pole Kurtyka, Swiss Loretan); 2,
1989 (Spaniards Clavel, Gallego, Ros,
Senquer); 4, 1989 (Germans Albert,
Güllich)

storm approach, which lasted for three weeks, dumping much snow. On June 23, the weather cleared for four days and efforts resumed. The Canadians attempted the Yugoslav Nameless Tower route but descended after nine pitches when their stove failed. Kerns and Cauthorn tried the Rowell-Schmitz-Hennek and the Woolum-Selters routes but, like Collum and McNerthney on the latter route, found the snow too deep and dangerous. Wilford and I returned to our route, dug our gear out of the ice, pulled up our ropes behind us and committed ourselves to a new independent big-wall route right of the Swiss-Polish route on the impressive northeast face. We had difficulties of 5.10 and A4. Expanding flakes seemingly glued together by ice and much hooking characterized the route. We climbed seven pitches in five days before being trapped for seven more days in a two-man porta-ledge when a major storm moved in to coat both us and the peak with ice. Ropes, Jümars and the pulley froze and became useless necessitating desperate maneuvers to get us both united at a belay. The frozen porta-ledge collapsed twice at night in the midst of a spindrift cascade. After twelve days on the wall, we had reached 19,200 feet, but the weather remained bad. We rappelled and waded exhausted through dangerous, deep snow to Base Camp on July 4.

GREG CHILD

Nameless Trango Tower, Eternal Flame Route. Our expedition was composed of Milan Sykora, Christoph Stiegler, Wolfgang Güllich and me. Our goal was to establish a new route on the south face of the Nameless Tower in free-climbing or Rotpunkt (red point) style. Güllich and I had already done the first free ascent of the Nameless Tower in 1988 via the Yugoslavian route. At that time, we discovered a great line, a crack system to the left of the Yugoslavian route. We arrived at Base Camp on August 16. Because of bad weather, it took us more than three weeks to set up a camp on the shoulder of the Nameless Tower at 5400 meters, with equipment and ten days of food. In the following two weeks, we were able to complete the new route. It has 35 pitches of difficult climbing: 11 pitches of 5.11 and two of 5.12. The excellent cracks reminded me of Yosemite and the rock quality of Joshua Tree. We fixed several pitches before a couple of days of rest in Base Camp. After our return to the shoulder, the next day we climbed several more of the finest pitches of my life before Güllich fell and severely sprained his ankle. He was helped back to the shoulder camp, where ice packs and aspirin kept the pain somewhat in control. The following day, Stiegler and I climbed past our high point until we had ascended some 500 very difficult meters when the weather turned threatening. We rappelled back to the shoulder. The day after, September 18, Stiegler and I jümared back up but traversed some 40 meters to the right to join the Yugoslavian route, which we followed some 300 vertical meters to the summit. With the help of aspirin and plastic boots, Güllich accompanied me the next day. We pushed the route further past the crux of the whole route before being driven down by an icy wind. September 20 was for me the sixth day without a rest. We climbed back up and past our previous high point, despite a slip which took the skin off my right hand. Finally we completed this direct finish to the summit (6251 meters, 20,510 feet). We named our route "Eternal Flame." The inspiration for this was the flame-shaped rock tower and a song of a four-girl English rock group, the Bangles. The song accompanied us on the whole trip and the lyrics of the song gave us the names of every pitch. This is the hardest rock route (5.12c) yet done in the Himalaya or the Karakoram.

KURT ALBERT, *Deutscher Alpenverein*

Trango Towers Correction. On page 250 of *AAJ, 1989*, it incorrectly gives the belief that the main summit of the Trango Château or the First Tower was still unclimbed. This summit had already been reached by Japanese in 1987, as reported in *AAJ, 1988* on page 251.

P 5866 (Thunmo), Baltoro Cathedral, solo. In June, with a trekking permit and seven porters, I set up "Base Camp" on the Dunge Glacier. I made solo a VII, 5.10d, A4+ climb of 54 pitches on the Baltoro Cathedral in 13 days. I spent two days fixing three pitches, nine days climbing alpine-style to the summit and two days descending. The peak is shown on the Italian map as Thunmo and is 5866 meters (19,246 feet). I nailed a 2000-foot big wall off the Dunge Glacier, which was easy except for one "psycho" aid pitch, and climbed 3500 feet of alpine climbing (rock steps and ridges, snow gullies and two 80° ice pitches) up to the base of the 1000-foot summit pyramid of golden granite. I climbed the northwest arête of this three-sided pyramid. It went 98% free at 5.10 except for one pitch of 80° thin ice. The summit pitch was a 5.10d run-out face climb to a desperate lunge. I summited at seven P.M. and immediately started the ten rappels down the north face to reach my bivouac tent at eleven P.M. I reached my portaledge the following day at dusk and was but eight rappels off the glacier the next day when the monsoon storm broke that I had watched engulf Nanga Parbat the previous day. I ran low on food the day before my summit day. I placed three bolts, all for bivouacs. Knowing I needed good weather up high, I fixed and climbed the first four days in "bad weather" (light snow and overcast), and then got lucky. Five days up the route, I got eight days of perfect weather—the longest stretch of good weather between mid May and early August.

JAMES BEYER

Uli Biaho Tower, East Face Attempt. Our expedition was composed of Carlo Grossrubatscher, Adam Holzknecht, Dieter Demetz, Walter Pancheri and me as leader. We hoped to climb the still unascended east face of the Uli Biaho Tower (6083 meters, 19,958 feet), but bad weather prevented it. We arrived at Base Camp on the Trango Glacier at 4200 meters on May 29. The first problem was getting to the base of the wall up a rockfall-threatened couloir. The couloir is 800 meters high and has sections of 80° ice. Bad weather moved in shortly after our arrival at Base Camp and hindered us as we fixed rope in the couloir and moved up supplies. The face itself was mostly covered with new snow and the cracks were full of ice. On a second attempt on the wall from June 13 to 15, we climbed to 5200 meters, where we dug a snow cave. We were blocked there for two days by the weather. On the 17th, I had to head for home with a bad knee. More bad weather followed. From June 23 to 26, the group reoccupied the camps at the foot of the wall and on the wall and, with miserable conditions, got to 5500 meters before more bad weather moved in again. All rope and equipment was removed from the face. They started the trek out on June 29.

STEFAN STUFLESSER, *St. Ulrich, South Tirol, Italy*

Uli Biaho Spire. A New Zealand expedition was made up of leader Nicholas Craddock, Guy Cotter, Paul Rogers and Murray Judge. In July, they climbed the Uli Biaho Spire, although we do not know by which route. Details have not yet reached us.

P 6100, Choktoi Glacier. Spaniards Jon Lazcano and Javier Mugarra made the first ascent of a very difficult 6100-meters (29,013-foot) spire which rises above the Choktoi Glacier to the right of Baintha Brakk. They got to Base Camp on June 24. They then fixed rope up much of the first 600 meters of the 800-meter-high face. On July 29, they jümared up the 600 meters and climbed to the summit in a twenty-two hour day. An article on this climb with photographs appears in *Desnivel* of December, 1989, pages 33-39.

Sosbun Tower Attempt. Tilman described the peaks of the Hoh Valley as "an uncompromising rock wall crowned with jagged towers," but the attraction of these towers is deceptive; the rock everywhere is dangerous: enormous, rotten loose rocks and cracks with sandy edges. The climbing is very hard because of it. It seems useless to continue further exploration there. However, innocently J-Ph. Dolby Monet, Y. Duverney and I attempted the very beautiful east face of Sosbun Tower (c. 6000 meters, 19,685 feet). The face is 1100-meters high, very steep and in part overhanging, but its rock is nonetheless treacherous. We prepared the route on July 10 and 11 and climbed the first 700 meters from July 27 to 30. We felt we were within a rope-length of easier ground and at the end of the difficulties, but we quit there. The objective danger from rockfall was enormous even though the route we chose was relatively sheltered. The weather was also mediocre. From July 4 to August 6, we had only 11 fine days. Italians Daniele Bosisio, Adriano Carnati, Tita Gianola and Paolo Vitali climbed one of the Sosbun Needles (5400 meters, 17,717 feet), which lies southwest of Sosbun Tower. On August 19 and 20 they fixed 350 meters of rope on the southeast ridge. They then bivouacked halfway up the wall

PLATE 53

Photo by Bernard Domenech

SOSBUN TOWER, Karakoram.

and climbed to the summit on August 22. They climbed some 800 meters up compact, wet rock with rotten cracks.

BERNARD DOMENECH, *Club Alpin Français*

Baintha Brakk, North Ridge Attempt. Our expedition had as its members Andy Perkins, Chris Flewitt, Steve Hartland, Phil Butler, Dave Green, Dr. Timothy Jordan, Paul Nunn and me. After porter problems, we eventually established Base Camp on July 17 on moraine at 15,200 feet. During a week of poor weather, on skis we moved loads to Advance Base at 5060 meters on the Sim Gang (glacier). It was about a seven-hour trip with a 25-kg load. During the six weeks we had only two spells of good weather, one of four and the other of five days. We made two light-weight attempts on the left-hand spur. On the first, on August 8, Perkins, Flewitt and I were hit by severe rock-and-ice fall at 5600 meters. I was luckily unhurt, but Flewitt was severely struck on the shoulder. Perkins was a little behind and so out of the fire. Butler and Perkins on the second attempt on August 10 reached the col on the ridge at 5800 meters. They set up a tent and scanned the route above. It seemed a tottering pile of séracs and so they judged it unjustifiable and retreated. That ended our try.

ANDREW CAVE, *England*

Lawa Brakk. A British Metropolitan Police expedition was led by Gordon A. Briggs. On July 29, after a seven-day climb, Arthur Collins, Lew Hardy, Steven Sands, Philip Solt, Peter Stapely and Paul Vardon reached the summit of Lawa Brakk or Snow Lake Peak (6590 meters, 21,621 feet). They climbed the west ridge. A 6000-meter peak at the head of the glacier south of Cornice Peak was climbed on July 29 by Mark Deith, John Wakefield and Tony Walkenden.

Peaks Above the Hispar Glacier. During August and September, Mike Searle, Sean Smith, Simon Yates, Mark Crawford and I visited the Hispar Glacier to climb small peaks and study the geology of the area. Our approach was delayed by bad weather, which persisted until mid September. We established Base Camp at Bitenmal on the east side of the junction of the Kunyang and Hispar Glaciers on August 19. From August 23 to 27, Smith, Yates and I climbed a relatively simple route up the snowy north ridge of P 5700 (18,701 feet), which lies at the western end of the Bal Chhish range, reaching the summit at ten A.M. on August 26. Smith and Yates then attempted the fine ice couloir on the west face of a 6000-meter peak near the Jutmau Glacier; after a two-day approach followed by two days and 800 meters of climbing in the couloir, they were forced to retreat 400 meters from the summit in a storm. From September 14 to 17, Yates and Searle climbed P 5700 (18,701 feet) at the head of the Makrong Glacier. They reached the summit at dawn on September 16 after a steep snow-and-ice climb from a bivouac on the glacier. The peak straddles the Hispar-Chogolungma divide. We left Base Camp on September 19.

SIMON RICHARDSON, *Alpine Climbing Group*

P 6666 Attempt. A Japanese expedition led by Akira Takita was unable to get higher than 5200 meters on the northwest ridge of P 6666 (21,871 feet) because of bad weather. The unclimbed peak lies northeast of the Haramosh La.

Spantik. Our expedition was composed of Helga Kircher, Rolf-Christian Reich, Emilie-Ursula Reich, Dr. Wolgang Bunzl, Ludwig Rohrmeier, Franz Kuhnhauser, Johann Geiss, Reinhard Schönfeld, Eberhart Zindel, Netherlander Gerhard Meerten and me as leader. We approached via Doko, Arandu and the Chogolungma Glacier to reach Base Camp at 4300 meters below the southeast ridge on August 10. We occupied Camps I and II at 5150 and 6100 meters on August 14 and 17. Steep snow below and above Camp II was secured by fixed rope, where the climbers had to have good crampon technique on steep ice. There were flat stretches on the glacier between Camps I and II and on the summit climb, where the snow was deep in places. The summit (7027 meters, 23,055 feet) was reached on August 18 by all except Rohrmeier.

ARNOLD HASENKOPF, *Summit Club, Deutscher Alpenverein*

Spantik Attempt. Another group of Germans led by Herbert Streibel failed to reach the summit of Spantik.

Diran Attempts and Tragedy. Of the expeditions which went to Diran (7257 meters, 23,810 feet) in 1989, only the Japanese group led by Ken Takahashi was successful. Seven Koreans were led by Chang Su-Jeong. On June 20, Ha Sang-Woen and Lee Su-Hee died in an avalanche and the expedition was given up. Also unsuccessful were Japanese led by Katsumasa Nakamura, Germans under Norbert Nanzel and French under the leadership of Luc Berthaud.

Diran, North Ridge. The six-man expedition of the Hirosaki University Alpine Club was led by Ken Takahashi. They climbed the north ridge, which had not been climbed before, although Austrians had descended it in 1985. On July 11, Takahashi, Suzuki, Nobuo Tsutsumi, Masayuki Ando, Hiroshi Hori and Tetsuro Yoshimura reached the summit. There were three parties on the same route and some of the route fixing took place in cooperation with another Japanese party from Toyo University.

Rakaposhi Attempt. After arriving at Jaglot on July 24, José Angel Cobo, Perfecto Rodríguez, Francisco José Ruiz, Iñaki Ruiz, Pedro Sánchez and I as leader set out with 18 porters through Barit and Dobar to arrive at Base Camp at 3750 meters on July 27. We attempted the northwest ridge. This was first climbed by a Polish-Pakistani expedition in 1979 and by Netherlanders in 1986. The two routes were different in how they got onto the ridge. Our route was a slight variant of the Netherland route. We placed Camp I at 4700 meters on July

COLOR PLATE 8

Photo by Kurt Albert

NAMELESS TOWER in the Trango Towers.

29 before being stopped by bad weather. From August 3 to 8, we fixed 1100 meters of rope with UIAA difficulties of IV+ and 50° ice and established Camp II on the ridge crest at 6000 meters. From August 9 to 17, there was bad weather. On the 18th and 19th, we fixed another 100 meters of rope and set up Camp III at 6800 meters. On August 20 a team got to 7000 meters but was driven back by bad weather. We withdrew to Base Camp and gave up the attempt.

JAIME ALONSO, *Alpino Tabira Mendizale Taldea, Spain*

Shifkitin Sar, Shimshal Valley. In 1986, an Irish expedition reconnoitered the Malanguti Glacier area in the Shimshal valley and unsuccessfully attempted virgin Shifkitin Sar (c. 5800 meters, 19,029 feet). On September 9, 1989, Netherlanders established Base Camp at 3300 meters. They set up camps at 4200 and 4400 meters along the long glacier. After a snow-hole bivouac at 5200 meters, on September 16 Robert Eckhardt, Rob Lith and Tanja Merkelbach reached the summit of Shifkitin Sar, climbing snow and ice on the northwest side to get to the west ridge. It was not difficult, with a 45° snow couloir in the lower part and a 50° slope in the final section. The fourth member was Noes Lautier. Climbs up to 6000 meters require no permission in Pakistan and so are often overlooked in official records.

JÓSEF NYKA, *Editor, Taternik, Poland*

Shispare Attempt, Batura Mustagh. Our members included Kenichi Masui, Yasuyuki Uehara, Tatsuya Ohmura, Takayuki Tachibana, Yetetsu Adachi and me as leader. Our Base Camp at 4050 meters on the left moraine of the Pasu Glacier was established on June 13. On June 18, we crossed the glacier and set up Camp I on the far side at the upper end of a steep gully that led to the east ridge of Shispare (7619 meters, 24,997 feet). It took twelve days to extend the route along the long, narrow ridge to Camp II at 5600 meters. We found some decayed rope and rusted pitons from the Polish-German party 15 years earlier. At the 5800-meter junction of the east and main ridges with its massive pile of ice blocks covered by deep snow, we wondered if this was where the Polish-German expedition had met with the avalanche; the area above threatened to avalanche at any moment. The weather turned bad as we reached Camp III at 6100 meters on July 12. An ice wall on a 6300-meter peak took a week to overcome. Then came a long, snow-covered knife-edge. We continued on to a col at 6450 meters, the site of Camp IV. Three members then had to return to Japan on July 26, leaving Ohmura, Adachi and me. We established Camp IV on July 29. A further camp between Ghenta Peak and the shoulder of Shispare was not set up because of a shortage of time. We made the first summit attempt from Camp IV on August 8, taking many hours to climb the last hanging glacier. We then trudged through two feet of snow to a cirque at 7200 meters but could go no higher. The next day, despite signs of unfavorable weather, we made a second attempt into a strong head wind in waist-deep snow. We turned back 100 meters lower than the day before.

MASATO OKAMOTO, *Ryukoku University Alpine Club, Japan*

Batura Mustagh Map. Another of the excellent maps by Jerzy Wala is available, a map of the Batura group in the western Karakoram. It may be purchased for $3.00 from Jan Babicz, ul. Bajana 5B/1, 80-463 Gdańsk, Poland.

Peaks Above Barpu Glacier, West Karakoram. In mid August Ralph Atkinson, Ged Campion, Mick Curtin, John Keska, Stewart Muir and I visited the Barpu Glacier. We approached by jeep from Hunza to Hoppar, where we hired cooperative local porters for the three-day walk to Base Camp at Girgindil. The variable weather was good enough for the three small peaks we climbed. Girgindil Peak (5296 meters, 17,475 feet), an easy snow plod above Base Camp, had been climbed frequently before. We climbed the northeast, northwest ridges and two routes on the north face. Girgindil Pyramid is the symmetrical mountain to the left of Girgindil Peak, as seen from Girgindil, really the summit of a ridge running southwest from the Chukutans group. We estimate its height as 5800 meters (19,029 feet). There was no record of a previous ascent. Campion, Keska and I climbed it by the west ridge. There was awkward access to the small glacier to its north, then easy snow to the ridge. The ridge was easy at first, then awkward on loose schist and finally precarious snow crests. Yengutz I is the highest of the Yengutz group, which we estimate at 5999 meters (19,682 feet). We believe it was a first ascent. Muir and I climbed via the Yengutz Col, west ridge and southwest face, all snow and ice with a detour right to turn the rock band on the face.

DAVID WILKINSON, *Wolverhampton Mountaineering Club, England*

Hunza. Following a visit to the area by Pete Thompson and me in 1988, I returned for a second visit in 1989 with Andy Trull, Chris Lloyd-Rogers, Hilary Fouweather and Mick Wilcock. Our original intention of climbing in the Snow Lake area of the Hispar Glacier was thwarted by bad weather and so we based ourselves at Shigambarish, directly across the Hispar Glacier from the Uyum Haghuch Pass to Arandu. After climbing there, we returned to Hunza and attempted other peaks. No permits were needed as we always stayed below 6000 meters. On August 4, Trull, Wilcock and I backed off the first peak east of the Uyum Haguch Pass due to deep snow on the final north ridge. On August 9, Trull and I climbed the southern peak of the horseshoe north of the Hispar La. We climbed a wide couloir which led to the col and then traversed northward along a snow-and-rock ridge to the summit. On August 12, Lloyd-Rogers, Fouweather and Wilcock ascended the most northerly peak to the west of the Hargtum Glacier. Trull and I reached the summit block of Ibex Peak, the highest pinnacle northeast of Shigambarish on August 17. Beyond Hunza, Mick Nunwick joined Wilcock and me to attempt the highest peak south of Bubli-ma-Tim. On September 11, after reaching the col immediately north of the summit, we followed the ridge on steep, unconsolidated snow, but quit 150 meters short of the summit. The Hunza area provides a wealth of unclimbed peaks that are easily accessible for a lightweight, low-budget, liaison-officer-free expedition.

WALTER PHIPPS, *British Mountaineering Council*

Shani, Naltar Valley. Our expedition had as climbers Duncan Francis, Martin Oakes and me, as well as support members. Having arrived at Naltar by jeep, on July 29 and 30 we walked to Base Camp in the upper Shani valley by the Shani Glacier at 3700 meters. On August 4, I soloed Snow Dome (5030 meters, 16,503 feet; probably a second ascent), followed on August 7 by the other two. Our original intention was to make a northeast-west traverse of Shani. Due to unsettled weather and much snow on the northeast ridge, from August 11 to 13 we climbed the 2000-meter high, previously unclimbed southeast face. We ascended the icefall on left side and a rock spur. We then went up an icefield to a ridge on the left side of the face, climbed four pitches around a rock tower and abseiled to a second snowfield. Above this, a steep couloir led to a steeper icefield and the summit ridge. We three reached the summit of Shani (5885 meters, 19,308 feet) on August 13, a second ascent. Out of 21 days at Base Camp, we had nine days of bad weather. The longest period of continuous good weather was three days.

PETER LEEMING, *England*

Nanga Parbat Winter Attempt, 1988-9. Our expedition consisted of Maciej Berbeka, Piotr Konopka, Dr. Roman Mazik, Andrzej Osika, Andrzej Samolewicz, Włodzimierz Stoiński, Stanisław Szczerba, Zbigniew Terlikowski and me from Poland, Krzysztof Szafranski from Colombia and Kurt Walde from Italy. We arrived at Base Camp at 3600 meters on December 18, 1988. Temperatures there were between $-18°$ and $-25°$ C and higher, between $-25°$ and $-35°$. Our objective was the southeast buttress, but dangerous conditions forced a change in plans to the 1970 German route. On December 25, Camp I was established at 4750 meters. Unstable, windy weather slowed progress and we could not make Camp II at 6000 meters, the site of German Camp III, until January 17. Lack of snow cover and very hard ice required our fixing more than 2000 meters of rope. Despite attempts, we could not establish Camp III. On February 9, Berbeka, Kanopka and Osika reached a high point of 6800 meters. The weather deteriorated once again and we decided to abandon the climb.

PAWEŁ MULARZ, *Klub Wysokogórski, Zakopane*

Nanga Parbat Attempts. Few of the expeditions to Nanga Parbat this year were successful. Among those which did not get to the summit were parties made up of British and Swedes led by Michael Scott, Germans under the leadership of Fritz Schreinmoser and Koreans under Park Il-Hwan.

Nanga Parbat Attempt. We were Davorin and Luka Karničar, Sandi Marinčič and I. On June 13, we left Chilas for Base Camp, accompanied by 23 porters. We reached it four days later. In Base Camp there was a Korean expedition, which had been there for three weeks, and a German one. We had originally wanted to try the

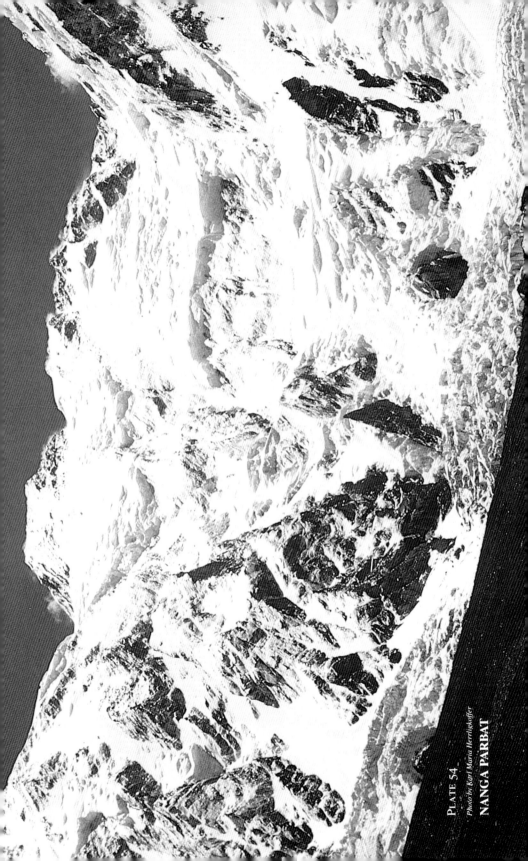

PLATE 54.

Photo by Karl Maria Herrligkoffer

NANGA PARBAT

1978 Messner route on the Diamir Face, but after we had had a look at it, we were much less enthusiastic. Séracs kept falling without any time schedule and large avalanches swept the route. We decided to join the Korean and Germans on the usual Diamir Face route. On June 18, we carried to Camp I at 5100 meters and continued on up the fixed ropes nearly to Camp II at 5600 meters before returning to Base Camp. After two days of rest, we made an acclimatization climb to 5800 meters on Ganalo Peak. Two days later, one of the Koreans, Kim Kwang-Ho, fell to his death on the face of Nanga Parbat. We climbed to Camp I, found him and brought him to the valley. The accident made us decide to return. The conditions on the face were too risky; the weather continued bad.

VLASTA KUNAVER, *Planinska zveza Slovenije*

Nanga Parbat Tragedy. A Korean expedition led by Ryoo Gil-Man attempted the Diamir face of Nanga Parbat. On June 23, Kim Kwang-Ho slipped and fell to his death. The other members of the expedition were Chae Su-San, Jung Eun-Sang, Ha Jeong-Lea and Chon Sung-Il.

Nanga Parbat, Diamir Face, German and Pakistani Success. I organized this small expedition but gave the leadership over to German Dr. Ekkert Gundelach. The other members were Swiss Diego Wellig, Philipp Zehnder and Peter Schwitter. They reached Base Camp at 4200 meters in the Diamir valley on June 18. On the first night, Schwitter fell ill with pulmonary edema and had to descend. The Mummery Rib was in wintry condition and offered no chance for an ascent. On June 21, an expedition of Pakistani army officers arrived at Base Camp; with them that made five expeditions there since another German one, plus Koreans and Yugoslavs, got there ahead of our group. On June 23, our three healthy members climbed Ganalo Peak for acclimatization and then set up a tent at 5300 meters. At that same time, a Korean fell 1000 meters down the Sigi Löw Ice Couloir to his death. Both the Koreans and the Yugoslavs abandoned the climb. On June 29, Zehnder and Wellig established Camp II and the next day advanced to Camp III before returning to Base Camp. After six days of snowfall, that pair decided to return to Switzerland. That left only Dr. Gundelach. He asked if he might join the Pakistanis. On July 9, Gundelach and six Pakistanis climbed to Camp II and the next day to Camp III at 6000 meters. On July 11, they all carried loads to 7100 meters at the top of the Kinshofer Icefield. The day after, Gundelach broke trail to the Bazhin Basin and returned to Camp IV at 7300 meters. On July 13, Gundelach, Shah Khan (son of the uncle of the Mir of Hunza) and Lieutenant Atta climbed to the summit, which they reached at five P.M. in falling snow. Gundelach and Shah Khan made it back to Camp IV which they reached at ten P.M., greeted by two Pakistanis, who had come up from Camp III in support. Atta survived a cold bivouac and got to Camp IV in the morning. All five descended to Base Camp, where they were received by the colonel with flowers. On July 18, two Pakistani generals arrived by helicopter to celebrate the first Pakistani success on Nanga Parbat.

KARL MARIA HERRLIGKOFFER, *Deutsches Institut für Auslandsforschung*

Nanga Parbat, Rupal Face Attempt and Tragedy. The members of our expedition were Hitoshi Sakurai, Nobuyoshi Sakurai, Iwao Ogasawara, Shinji Kobayashi, Tetusa Baba, Shinya Nakashima, Katsuyuki Kitamura, Masaki Akiba, Ms. Yukiko Fukuzawa, Ms. Masae Yoshino, Masanori Sato, Taro Tanigawa, Daisuke Shimizu and I as leader. On June 18, we got to Base Camp at 3650 meters on the Bazhin Glacier above Rupal. We established Camps I, II and III at 4500, 4500 and 5600 meters on June 23, July 1 and 12. On July 16, Tetsuya Baba was struck by lightning and badly injured. We called for a helicopter, but this was available only at the altitude of Base Camp. We carried him down, still alive for the next 48 hours, but he died when we reached 5250 meters. Mr. Baba's parents and sister came to attend the funeral, which lasted until July 27. On the 28th, we began a second attempt. Sato, Akiba and I placed Camp IV at 6070 meters. On August 6, we reached 6250 meters on Rakhiot Peak. At that time, we received information that one of our female members had broken her leg between Camps I and II. There was also avalanche danger. I decided not to expose the group to further dangers.

KEIJIRO HAYASAKA, *Tokyo University of Agriculture Alpine Club*

China—Southeastern China

Kang Karpo Attempt. Tom Hornbein, Robert Hornbein, Robin Houston, Brian Okonek, Robert Brown Schoene and I attempted Kang Karpo (Meili) in September. We followed the route we had previously explored in 1988 and established two camps above Base Camp. The other five members reached an altitude of 18,500 feet before being turned back by bad weather and deep snow.

NICHOLAS B. CLINCH

Kang Karpo (Meili) Attempt. Our expedition again attempted Kang Karpo, as it is known in the region, or Meili, as the Chinese call it. It was jointly organized by the Academic Alpine Club of Kyoto, the Chinese Mountaineering Associations of Beijing and Yünnan. The co-leaders were Dr. Kenji Soda and Yang Bi-Yu and I was deputy leader. There were 14 Japanese and 13 Chinese. We reached the village of Sinong on the west bank of the Langtsang Jiang (Mekong) at the beginning of October. Base Camp at 3850 meters was near the snout of the Shenchenbao Glacier. Abnormally bad weather, with heavy snow-falls, continued during most of October. It was only after 23 days that Camp I was established at 4660 meters. The following two weeks were spent in a struggle to find the way to the upper basin of the glacier. The terrible weather and a shortage of time forced us to give up and return on November 24.

TOSHIAKI SAKAI, *Academic Alpine Club of Kyoto*

Anyemaqen Attempt. When our expedition to Shisha Pangma was canceled by the authorities, Swiss Beatrice Arn, Austrians Dr. Günther Fasching and I decided to head for Anyemaqen. For a week in April we pedaled our mountain bikes from Xining through nomad country and over several 4000-meter passes. At Xiadawu we began a 60-kilometer trek with yaks. Winter conditions prevented the yaks from getting to our chosen Base Camp north of Anyemaqen. We placed a high camp at 5000 meters, hoping to make a new route over the north summit. Continuous snowstorms and cold, as well as difficult terrain in the upper part (crevasses and séracs), kept us from success. The other two got to 5700 meters just below the north summit.

BRUNO BAUMANN, *Österreichischer Alpenverein*

Cheru (Queer), Sichuan, 1988. A joint Japanese-Chinese expedition of Kobe University and the China College of Geology at Wuhan made the first ascent of Cheru (6168 meters, 20,237 feet; 31° 30' N, 99° E). There were 8 Japanese and 12 Chinese. It took them three hours on September 11 with 27 yaks to reach Base Camp at 3800 meters below the northeast face. On the 12th, they carried to Advance Base at 4150 meters. It took them two days to find the way to the glacier. Camps I and II at 4500 and 5200 meters were occupied on September 16 and 19. On September 21, Camp II was moved to 5250 meters and ropes were fixed on the snow slopes above. The first summit bid was cancelled by a heavy snowstorm. On September 23, four Japanese and four Chinese left Camp II and reached the west col. Very strong winds drove them back from the steep summit ridge. That same day other members made another camp at 5400 meters, where 14 spent the night. On September 24, Japanese Hironori Kitaguchi, Hisatake Funabara, Tetsuji Takeuchi, Ms. Naoko Sugimoto and Chinese Dong Fang, Zhang Zhijiang, Zhang Wei and Zheng Chao reached the summit. That same day, Japanese Mitsuru Kawabata and Chinese Ma Xinxiang, Meng Xinguo and Zhang Jun also got to the top. On the 25th two more Japanese, Daisuke Takechi and Hiroshi Hori, made it to the top. The route seems to have been mostly glacial with rock sections around icefalls. The honorary leaders were Yan Weiran and Kazumasa Hirai; overall leader was Chinese Hu Yansheng; climbing leaders were Japanese Hironori Kitaguchi and Chinese Zhu Sarong.

TSUNEMICHI IKEDA, *Editor, Iwa To Yuki*

Tibet

Everest Attempt. After their successful ascent of Dhaulagiri, on May 30 Oreste Forno, Graziano Bianchi, Fausto Destefani, Sergio Martini, Silvio Mondinelli and Claudio Schranz on May 30 left Kathmandu by bus for Kodari and traveled from there by jeep and truck to arrive at Rongbuk on June 2. They had originally hoped to climb the Japanese route on the north face but they changed their objective to the Great Couloir. They set up Advance Base, Camps I and II at 5400, 6100 and 7000 meters on June 7, 8 and 13. On June 14, Destefani and Martini hoped to set up Camp III at 7800 meters, but at 7500 meters the weather was so bad that they cached their loads and descended. The weather continued bad until June 21. A reconnaissance on June 22 showed the mountain out of condition. Bad weather continued and they left on June 30.

Everest Attempt. The members of our expedition were Mari Abrego, Víctor Arnal, Josema Casimiro, Antonio Ubieto, Miguel Lausín, Ignacio Cinto, Teodoro Palacín, Patxi Senosiaín, José Garcés, Iñaki Arregui, José Marciano, Jesús Gómez, Julio Benedé, Orenzo Ortas, José Rebollo and I as leader. Base Camp was placed at 5200 meters on June 15. Taking advantage of good weather, we placed Advance Base at the foot of the North Col at 6400 meters on June 23, fixed ropes, and placed Camp I on the North Col at 7060 meters on July 4. After a dump was made the next day at 7500 meters, bad weather and snowfall interrupted activity until July 20. This dump was lost under deep snow. Camp II was established at 7800 meters on July 25. A first try for the summit got back only to Camp II before being stopped by bad weather. More storms prevented establishing Camp III at 8350 meters until August 25. On August 27, four climbers and a Sherpa set out for another summit attempt but had to quit at 8530 meters because of deep snow. A final try by two members on September 3 reached the same altitude, but the conditions were equally bad.

JAVIER ESCARTÍN, *Montañeros de Aragón, Spain*

Everest Attempt. The first Greek Himalayan expedition had as members Kostas Kanidis, Kostas Passaris, Nikos Louridis and me as leader and Bulgarian Dinio Georgiev-Tomov. We got to Base Camp at 5200 meters on July 16 and acclimatized for ten days. We established Camps I, II and III on July 26, 27 and 28 at 5500, 6000 and 6400 meters. The weather turned bad. On July 3 Kanidis and I occupied Camp IV on the North Col but had to descend after two days of bad weather. The next ten days were bad. It was decided that Kanidis and Tomov should make an alpine-style try from 7100 meters with one bivouac. They set out on August 18 with good weather but deep snow. They climbed to 8100 meters but returned from that point.

STRATOS PARASKEVAIDIS, *Athenian Alpine Club, Greece*

Everest Attempt. Our Civilian-Military Expedition was composed of Captains Alfonso Juez, Francisco Gam, Franco Pelayo, César Alfaro, Pedro Expósito, Sergeants Pedro Aceredillo, Francisco Pérez, Juan Orta, Domingo Hernández, Eduardo Fernández, Avelino Mora, and civilians Dr. Joan Martínez, Leo Vogué, Miguel Vidal, Máximo Murcia and me as leader. We had hoped to climb the North Col route. We set up Base Camp, Advance Base, Camps II (on North Col), III and IV (below the Yellow Band) at 5150, 6400, 7060, 7800 and 8350 meters on June 19, July 2, 4, 25 and August 17. The highest point reached was 8550 meters on August 27. The great quantity of snow hampered our movements above the North Col at all times.

SANTIAGO ARRIBAS, *Lieutenant Colonel,*
Escuela Militar de Montaña, Jaca, Spain

Everest Attempt, Northeast Ridge. Though a large British team in 1988 succeeded in climbing through the Pinnacles, the major crux on the ridge, they did not continue on to the summit. Although the ridge between the Pinnacles and the summit has been done, ascending from the North Col, the climb of the entire northeast ridge has not been completed. Our group was made up of Americans Markus Hutnak, Tim Gage, Dr. Dick Walker, Kurt Fickeisen and me as leader and Britons Roger Mear and Paul Rose. We arrived in Kathmandu in late July and at Base Camp on August 12. Everest was whiter than I had ever seen it before. The snows had been heavy. Fickeisen, Hutnak and I, along with two of our four climbing Sherpas, established Advance Base below the northeast ridge on August 18. Two days later, we began fixing rope on "Bill's Buttress," the initial steep 3000-foot arête that leads to less steep climbing higher up. This was an exhausting slog up unconsolidated deep snow. We were able, however, to fix most rope on rock sections that occasionally showed up through the snow. When at last we three reached the top of the buttress, the site of Camp I, our presence set off enormous avalanches on either side of the buttress, emphasizing the terribly unstable conditions that monsoon snows bring to the mountain. Camp I was supplied by early September, but several attempts by almost all team members to climb higher up the otherwise easy ground on the ridge was constantly frustrated by deep snow, windslabs, avalanches and exhausting climbing. In late September, we decided that we had absolutely no chance on the northeast ridge. A guided American expedition on the North Col route agreed to share the route with us. In early October, we were well established on the North Col. The monsoon snows were replaced by a new nemesis: high winds and bitter cold. On October 12, Hutnak and Gage made a summit bid, only to watch their tent rip to shreds at 26,000 feet. We left Base Camp on October 15.

GARY SPEER

Everest Attempt. This large expedition was organized by Frenchmen Claude Jaccoux and Michel Vincent. It had two guides, Erik Decamp and Jean Clemenson, and a doctor, Corinne Beauvoir. There were 15 climbers, four of them women, and a film crew of two. I teamed up for all the trip with Véronique Perillat. The other two women were Chantal Mauduis and the Belgian Lut Vivijs. We arrived at Base Camp at 5200 meters on August 12 and placed Advance Base at 6400 meters on August 19. On September 2, Véronique and I were the first to reach Camp II at 7800 meters. There was much bad weather and snowfall. We tried for the summit in two groups on September 23. The first had to quit at 8000 meters and we in the second party at 7750 meters because of storm. On September 30, Véronique and I decided to give up because of windslab danger. One group remained on the mountain to try again. On October 3, Gallet and Asselin reached 8300 meters and Vincent got to 8200 meters.

ANNIE BEGHIN, *Club Alpin Français*

Everest Attempts from the North. There were many attempts to climb Everest from Tibet in the post-monsoon period, but none were successful. Several are noted below separately. Groups were on the North Col route. Swiss Norbert Joos and Diego Wellig, South Tyrolean Hans Kammerlander and Czech Pavel Dolecek climbed past the North Col and entered the Messner Couloir, getting to 8100 meters on September 25. American Mike Dunn led an expedition of Americans, Mexicans and Australians which got to 8600 meters on October 24. Four Italians under the leadership of Lorenzo Mazzoleni tried to climb the north face by the Japanese Couloir. On September 25, they reached their high point of 7500 meters. This same route was attempted in October by Japanese led by Yoshio Ogata. They got to 7800 meters. Chileans and Americans led by Dr. Juan Andrés Maramisio tried to climb the west ridge from Tibet. They got to 6200 meters on October 14. Americans included Keith Abell and Tim Purcell.

ELIZABETH HAWLEY

Everest Attempt. I was the leader of a 19-member expedition from Zagreb. We had hoped to climb the Australian route on Everest's north side. We established Base Camp at 5200 meters, Advance Base at the junction of the Middle and West Rongbuk Glaciers and Camp I at 5560 meters on August 15, 17 and 20. By September 8, we had fixed rope up the right side of the Great Couloir and made a snow cave for 12 people. It took us the next 37 days to gain 600 meters. Bad weather, new snow and avalanches destroyed fixed ropes and camps. In all, fourteen climbers were caught by avalanches. Marjan Kregar and Slavko Svetičič were swept down 350 meters, but luckily escaped with broken ribs and a damaged knee. Only Aco Pepevnik climbed above Camp III at 7500 meters and reached 7900 meters. We gave up on October 19.

DARKO BERLJAK, *Planinarski Savez Zagreba, Yugoslavia*

Everest Attempt and Acclimatization Experiment. An original idea I had in 1987 was able to be carried out in 1989 on the north-northeast ridge of Mount Everest thanks to a system worked out by the ARPE under the direction of Drs. Richalet and Hery. Consequently, I was able to be on the Tibetan side of Everest with Christine Janin, Fred Ancey, Michel Fauquet and Swiss Stéphane Schaffter after practicing a new kind of acclimatization. This let us omit needing a period of acclimatization and to be able to climb onto Everest without a stay at Base Camp. Before our departure, we spent a week between the summit of Mont Blanc and the Vallot Observatory with medical tests and nights on the summit and then four days in a decompression chamber at simulated altitudes between 5000 and 8000 meters. We operated under the permission of Claude Jaccoux. We left France on August 27. Our excellent physical condition and the absence of headaches let us move as follows: Base Camp, Advance Base, North Col and Camp II at 5200, 6400, 7000 and 7800 meters on September 1, 3, 5 and 9. Snow and wind kept us from showing the real results of our acclimatization in our four attemps to climb higher than 8000 meters. We hope to carry on these experiments again in 1990.

ERIC ESCOFFIER, *Groupe de Haute Montagne*

Everest Attempt. On August 20, Jan Harris and I arrived at the 5600-meter-high Rongbuk Glacier Base Camp. On the 24th, we placed Advance Base at 6400 meters at the foot of the North Col. We established Camps I and II on the North Col and north ridge at 7000 and 7500 meters on August 28 and September 8. We made three attempts to regain Camp II between September 12 and October 8 in order to cross the north face to the Great Couloir. On October 14, Harris descended to Base Camp while I established Camp III at 7600 meters. I placed Camp IV the next day at 7800 meters half way across the face between the north ridge and the couloir. This camp was partially destroyed by high winds in the predawn hours of the 16th and I abandoned further attempts.

KEITH BROWN

Changtse. Our joint expedition had nine Chinese: Jin Jun Xi, Wang Yong Feng, Luo Shen, Zhao Yue Min, Chen Jian Jun, Yang Jiu Hui, Sun Yi, Tong Lu and me as leader; and nine Hong Kong members: Zeng Luo, climbing leader, Zhong Jian Min, Zhen Yi Jia, Wu Jia Wei, Luo Wei Qiang, Huang Yan Liang, Chen Zhi An, He Zhi Ming and Ye Jin Wen. We established Base Camp, Advance Base and Camps I, II and III at 5200, 6000, 6300, 6600 and 7000 meters. We wanted to climb Changtse's north face, where the distance is short, but there were many avalanches. Therefore, we switched to the long but safe northeast ridge. We began the climb on July 1. On July 20, Chinese Wang Yong Feng, Luo Shen and I and Hong Kong climbers Zeng Luo, Zhen Yi Jia and Wu Jia Wei reached the summit.

SUN WEI QI, *Chinese Mountaineering Association*

Cho Oyu. During three days, several expeditions successfully climbed Cho Oyu via the west ridge and west face from the north. An expedition led by Alberto Bianchi put Italian Albert Brugger and Luxembourger Roland Zeyen on the summit on September 17. Italian Enrico Rosso joined with Swiss Mario Casella and Pierino Giuliani to make the climb on September 18. Two others of Casella's expedition, Michele Capelli and Conrado Margna, reached the top on September 19. Mrs. Magda Nos King, a Spaniard living in the United States, Spaniard Señorita Mónica Verge and Ang Phuri Sherpa climbed to the summit on September 19. (See below.)

ELIZABETH HAWLEY

Cho Oyu, First 8000er by Spanish Women. Society in any country is composed of men and women and I believe we have equal responsibilities. In my country, Spain, few women participate in high-altitude climbing; I felt I should do something about it. I put together a small group of women with Himalayan experience. Unfortunately, we lacked sponsorship and only Mónica Verge and I could get sufficient funds. With Ang Phuri Sherpa we left Kathmandu on August 18 by bus for Kodari. The following morning we drove to Khassa on the Tibetan border. On August 20, we arrived at Tingry and on the 21st were at the Chinese Base Camp at 4300 meters. At Tingry we contracted for yaks to take us the three-day walk to our Base Camp at 5400 meters. We wanted to get to the end of the lateral moraine on the Gyabrag Glacier, but the yak men refused to go beyond 5400 meters, where the wind funneled down from the Nangpa La. Mónica and I installed Advance Base at 5900 meters on August 30 and Camp I at 6600 meters just below the icefall on September 5. Despite unstable weather, on the 13th we placed Camp II at 7200 meters to the right of the Tichy route. I felt the weather and the snow too unstable and so we returned to Camp I to wait. On September 15, a huge avalanche caught an Italian woman and a Sherpa who were attempting the summit; both survived. The avalanche started at 8000 meters and ran past our tent at Camp II, damaging the tent somewhat. On August 18, we climbed to the rock band at 7700 meters and placed two very light tents under a prominent rock. On August 19, Mónica, Ang Phuri and I left camp at five A.M. and were on the summit at 10:45. On the way back to camp, we met the two Swiss, who reached the summit that same day after us.

MAGDA NOS KING, *Expedició Femenina, Spain*

Cho Oyu and Shisha Pangma, 1988. On page 283 of *AAJ, 1989,* it lists an ascent of Cho Oyu, by Noburu Yamada and three other Japanese on November 6, 1988. Actually there were two other Japanese: Teruo Saegusa and A. Yamamoto. Along with O. Shimuzu, they had previously, on October 24, 1988, climbed the normal route on Shisha Pangma. These ascents were the eighth and ninth 8000ers for Yamada. Tragically, Yamada died in late February on Mount McKinley.

Siguang Ri. We had as members I. Sato, S. Fukuyama, Hideo Takebe, Nobuo Yagi, Dr. H. Tanaka, Hideo Oka, Y. Nishizawa (f), H. Ogura, Takashi Okuda, M. Yagura (f), M. Komatsu, K. Shimoda, Tatsuya Ogata, Takashi Miki and me as leader. Siguang Ri lies 5.5 kilometers northeast of Cho Oyu. We left Lhasa, which was under martial law, on March 8 and approached via the Gyabrag Glacier. Our caravan was stopped by snow before we got to Base Camp and we had to use 50 yaks to go on. On March 24, we placed Base Camp at 5480 meters on the moraine of the Gyabrag Glacier and on the 27th, Advance Base at 5800 meters at the junction of the Siguang Ri and Palung Glaciers. On April 3, Camp I was established at the beginning of the route at 6100 meters. There were two steep pitches to reach the crest of the west ridge, nine more pitches to a 6600-meter dome and four more pitches with fixed rope before we could pitch

PLATE 55

Photo by Monika Nykanka

SHISHA PANGMA from the
Southwest. New Ascent Route is
marked. Other Polish ascent and 1982
British Route were to the col on the
right and along the ridge.

Camp II at 6800 meters on April 9. It took four more days to fix eight pitches to the junction peak (7010 meters) with the southwest ridge. After two unsuccessful tries on April 19 and 20, on April 21 Okuda and Miki set the first footprints on the top (7308 meters, 23,977 feet). The next day, Takabe, Yagi, Oka and Ogata also made the summit. The most difficult parts were a 200-meter-long knife-edge at 7000 meters and the rocks just below the summit. A full report in Japanese and a photograph appear in *Iwa To Yuki* N° 135, page 28.

Koichiro Hirotani, *Osaka University Alpine Club*

Shisha Pangma from the Southwest and Nyanang Ri. On a reconnaissance in 1983, Tone Škarja and I made the first ascent of the Ice Tooth, the peak just south of Nyanang Ri. Since then, I have considered Nyanang Ri to be a most convenient peak for acclimatization before the ascent of the southwest face of Shisha Pangma. Unclimbed, it is close to Base Camp and of appropriate altitude (7071 meters, 23,200 feet). We arrived at Base Camp at 5300 meters on October 7. On the 10th, Stane Belak, Filip Bence, Pavle Kozjek and I bivouacked at the foot of the face on a rocky island at 6200 meters. The next day, we climbed the southwest face to the last big notch in the northwest ridge of Nyanang Ri, where we bivouacked at 6850 meters. On October 12, we reached the summit via the west ridge. Only the first 150 meters above the notch gave us some difficulties. After a three-day rest, on October 16 Kozjek and I moved to Advance Base at 5600 meters. A three-hour walk up a broken glacier took us onto the face at 5900 meters. A steep gully led us to the large icefield of the lower face. We started up a gully above the icefield, but a stream of snow and stones forced us around the gully and to the left, where we found the first difficulties on the rock. At the bottom of the buttress, at 7200 meters, we bivouacked. A thin layer of ice and snow made it hard to dig the platform, which sufficed for only half the tent. We spent the night sitting, still roped. Just behind the tent, the face rose steeply. We climbed mostly in ice gullies, often interrupted by time-consuming rock sections and traverses. We left the edge of the buttress at the bottom of a black tower. We crossed far to the left where we placed our second bivouac on a gently-sloping snowfield at 7700 meters. On October 19, we climbed gullies. The face did not give up easily and we climbed steep rock until we were 50 meters from the top. The route ended very close to the actual summit (8027 meters, 26,336 feet). We descended to the col between Shisha Pangma and Pungpa Ri and bivouacked there at 6750 meters. Kozjek suffered severely frozen feet. We rate the route at UIAA IV to V, 50° to 65°. It is 2150 meters high. From October 18 to 20, Bence and Viki Grošelj climbed a route farther right, along the line of the 1982 British descent (with variants), to the southeast ridge. For Grošelj, this was his eighth 8000er. Meanwhile, Belak and Marko Prezelj were attempting a third line, but they had to give up at 6500 meters because of illness. The other members of the party were Tone Škarja, leader, Dr. Žare Guzej, Iztok Tomazin and Cameraman Matjaž Fištravec.

Andrej Štremfelj, *Planinska zveza Slovenije, Yugoslavia*

Shisha Pangma. Our expedition consisted of Nobuo Teranishi, M. Hongu, T. Ishikawa, Yoshiyuki Tsuji, Kiyohiko Suzuki, M. Hamatani, H. Koike, Sinji Takamura, M. Fujita, T. Suda, H. Yamaha, H. Kojiri, N. Unno, K. Sato, R. Takahashi and me as leader. We climbed the normal northwest route. We established Base Camp, Camps I, II, III, IV, V, and VI at 5100, 5500, 5700, 6000, 6500, 7000 and 7400 meters on March 11, 20, 26, 30, April 6, 11, and 14. On April 16 Tsuji, Suzuki and Takamura climbed to the summit.

MICHIO YUASA, *Aichigakuin University Alpine Club*

Shisha Pangma Tragedy. On October 4, Swiss Dr. Luca Leonardi was nearing the summit of Shisha Pangma and only a few meters away when he was swept away to his death by a windslab avalanche. Further details of this Swiss expedition from Graubünden and the Ticino are not known.

Nyanchhen Thanglha Central Peak. Dr. Erika Prokosch, Ursula Bauer, Dr. Erich Bosina, Anna Szalay, Dr. Franz Herzog, Teodor Fritsche, Herwig Schnutt, Günther and Werner Hönlinger, Fridl Widder, Karl Wuttke and I as leader crossed from Nepal into Tibet with five Sherpas. Sirdar Tashi Lama's knowledge of Tibetan allowed us to communicate well with the Tibetan nomads. We were also accompanied by an official of the Chinese Mountaineering Association and were joined by a Tibetan liaison officer. We traveled some 100 kilometers northwest from Lhasa on July 19 to Base Camp at 4800 meters at the entrance to the Pali Sui valley. From a ridge we could see the whole of the Nyanchhen Thanglha massif. The south-southwest ridge of the unclimbed central peak (7117 meters, 23,350 feet) stood out as a possible route. The higher western peak (7162 meters, 23,497 feet) had been climbed by a Japanese-Chinese group in 1986. (See *AAJ, 1987,* pages 298-9, where the name is given as Nianqintangula.) On July 27 we established Camp I at 5150 meters with the help of six yaks. The next day we reconnoitered to an idyllic spot for Camp II at 5450 meters by a small lake below the glacier. Camp III was placed at 5900 meters on a col at the foot of the ridge on July 25. Since time was limited and the weather was unstable, only the strongest members had a chance for the summit. On July 28, a strong north wind drove back the monsoon clouds and brought lovely weather and hard frozen firn snow. Fritsche, Schnutt, both Hönlingers and I climbed the 1200 vertical meters to the summit. This was a wonderful present for me on my 54th birthday. The others climbed several 6000ers that same day. We traveled back to Lhasa on August 1. The name Nyanchhen Thanglha means "Great Saint who looks over the broad plain," which is very apt.

WOLFGANG AXT, *Österreichische Himalaya Gesellschaft*

Western China

Xuelian Feng, Xinjiang. A Japanese expedition of the Tokai Section of the Japanese Alpine Club was led by Tsutomu Ogawa. They made the first ascent of the south summit (6527 meters, 21,414 feet) of Xuelian Feng but could not get to the main (north) summit. On July 14, Juniichi Shinozaki and Akihito Yamazaki got to this south summit. On July 19, these two with three other climbers repeated the ascent. From the south summit Shinozaki, Yamazaki and Morimoto tried for the main summit but were stopped 160 meters below it after climbing along the ridge for two kilometers. The final ascent of the south summit was made on July 23 by Hidehito Iwabuchi.

Aerjinshan, Kansu. Thirteen members of a joint Japanese-Chinese expedition led by Kenji Hirasawa made the first ascent of Aerjinshan (5798 meters, 19,023 feet) on August 19 including climbing leader Yoshio Maruyama. The next day, another two got to the top.

Kongur, Northwest Ridge. The expedition was composed of climbing leader Etsuro Yasuda, Tateshi Sudo, Hideo Muto, Junjiro Hori, Yukihiro Enomoto, Chiharu Yoshimura, Kazuhiro Nakato, Shogo Takahashi, Kouichi Tomoda, T. Shimuzu, Sadao Matsuda and me as general chief leader. On June 4, Base Camp was established at 3600 meters on the Kalaidark Glacier above Hozu. It took four weeks to develop the route. Camps were placed at 4850, 5300 and 6250 meters. The lower part of the route was difficult with rock walls, a snow ridge and an icefall. Ropes were fixed above Camp III on the *Kasa Iwa* (Umbrella Rock) section, the crux of the climb. On July 9, three parties of three climbers each set out from Camp III alpine-style. They bivouacked between 6650 and 6700 meters. After one more bivouac at 7450 meters, on July 11 all but Shimuzu, Matsuda and I reached the top (7719 meters, 25,325 feet). No signs were seen of the three Japanese climbers who had been lost eight years before when trying the same route. This was the second ascent of Kongur.

RYUICHI KOTANI, *Kyoto Karakoram Club, Japan*

Kongur Tiubie Attempt. An unsuccessful try on the central rib of the southwest face of Kongur Tiubie (7595 meters, 23,278 feet) was made by ten Japanese led by Suichi Torii. Bad weather stopped them at 6510 meters on the great ice wall above their Camp III at 6200 meters.

Kaxkar Attempt. A 9-member Japanese expedition tried unsuccessfully to climb Kaxkar (6347 meters, 20,824 feet), which lies 15 kilometers south of what the Chinese call Tomur and the Soviets Pik Pobedy. They got to 5200 meters on the southeast side.

Schoolboys in the Chinese Pamir. Our expedition from Aldenham School approached the Karakol Lakes in China via the Karakoram Highway from Rawalpindi in Pakistan. Although the hiring agreement was for 12 days, the camels deserted us at Atkash, about 24 kilometers east of Karakol. Our plans obviously had to change and we could not cross the Qaratash Pass. We ferried food and equipment for three days to an Advance Base at 4200 meter in the Torbelung valley. We undertook many mini-expeditions while in the area. We ascended two minor peaks, which lie south of the Qaratash Pass. We made a high camp above an extensive moraine on the tongue of a hanging glacier at 4750 meters. On August 7, P 5450 was climbed by Nick Parks, Dr. David Arathoon, Jon Rouach, Crispin Graham, David Kilborn, James Howel, John Turner, Owen Williams, Matthew Cobham, Mark Woodroffe, Donna Parks and Stephen Edwards. On August 9, Pamela MacGregor, Nick Parks, Dr. Arathoon and Cobham climbed P 5360.

DAVID MACGREGOR, *Aldenham School, Elstree, England*

Cholpanlik Mustagh, Kun Lun. Our expedition was composed of Koshi Sasaki, Eiichi Sato, Ichiro Yamagata, Hitoshi Goto, Hirofumi Oe, Toshiaki Yoshioka, Masami Hosaka, Takashi Ota and me as leader. We started from Kashgar with two jeeps and a truck on July 9 and drove to Aksaichin Lake at 4840 meters. We got to Base Camp at 5360 meters on July 19. Chopanlik was still 14 kilometers from Base Camp. We had a very long approach, first up the Valley of Wind and then up the Aksai Glacier, where we established Camps I, II and III at 5790, 6010 and 6220 meters on July 26, 31 and August 6. We fixed 350 meters of rope beyond Camp III to gain the summit of P 6510. We placed Camp IV at 6460 meters on the ridge beyond on August 13. From there we followed the ridge crest over P 6480, P 6490 and P 6449 before dropping onto the West Cholpanlik Glacier. On August 14, Yamgata, Goto and Hosaka climbed to the south ridge and reached the summit of Cholpanlik (6524 meters, 21,404 feet). They bivouacked on the descent at 6220 meters.

KAZUO SASAKI, *Sendai Ichiko Alpine Club, Japan*

Ulugh Mustagh. A joint expedition of 23 Japanese and 13 Chinese made the second ascent of Ulugh Mustagh. On August 31, six climbers got to the top, including climbing leader Fuminori Furukawa.

Gasherbrum I (Hidden Peak) Reconnaissance from the North. There were two Japanese expeditions that approached Gasherbrum I from the Chinese side. The first one conducted by Masaaki Fukushima and Jin Tamada from the Yokohama Alpine Association spent a month looking at possibilities. After arriving at Base Camp on April 30, they went from May 5 to 9 to the Urdok Glacier. On May 13 and 14, they explored the upper part of the Shaksgam River Glacier. From May 18 to 23, they investigated the Sagan Glacier where they could study both sides of the east ridge of Gasherbrum I. They were on the Gasherbrum Glacier and then the East Nakpo Glacier from May 27 to June 1.

They found the Gasherbrum Glacier very broken up and many ice towers on the Nakpo. They looked at possible routes on Gasherbrum I, Gasherbrum II and Broad Peak. A second group of 12 from Miayagi Prefecture Alpine Club was led by Hiroshi Yajima. They actually tried to get high on the mountain and reached 6100 meters on the east ridge but gave up on July 9. Yajima was nearly killed in an avalanche and they had several minor accidents.

USSR

Khan Tengri and Pik Pobedy. The 3000-meter-high snow-and-ice north face of Khan Tengri is the highest and most severe wall in the Tien Shan. There are seven routes on the face, but all had been climbed by Soviets in teams of at least six using much material and fixed ropes. Josef Nežerka and I were the first to climb this gigantic wall alpine-style. We were on the climb from July 20 to 27, reaching the summit (6995 meters, 22,950 feet) on July 26 (UIAA V, 80°). We had planned to take four days for the ascent but already on the second day the weather turned unfavorable, which slackened our pace considerably. In the lower part we followed the route of the Studentin team and in the upper part that of the Myslovski team. We descended the west ridge to the 5900-meter pass and then to the south to the International Mountaineering Camp on the South Inylcheck Glacier. Seven days after our descent to the camp, Nežerka, Miloslav Neuman and I climbed Pik Pobedy (7439 meters, 24,407 feet) over the Diki Pass and Pik Vazha Pshavel. Thus Neuman became the first Czechoslovak and the third non-Soviet climber to become a Snow Leopard. (The other two are Americans.) This title is given to mountaineers who have successfully climbed all the four peaks over 7000 meters in the Soviet Union.

ZOLTÁN DEMJÁN, *Slovenský Horolezecký Zvaz, Czechoslovakia*

Pamir Camps, 1988. The Soviet international Pamir camps continue to be popular, providing challenging high-altitude climbing at relatively moderate cost. During the 1988 season, 412 foreign mountaineers from 17 countries in Europe, Asia and America, including Messner, came together in the camps. Pik Lenina (7134 meters, 23,406 feet) was climbed by 119 foreigners, Pik Korzhenevskoy (7105 meters, 23,310 feet) by 65 and the highest in the Soviet Union, Pik Lenina (7483, 24,550 feet), by 55. Some teams used difficult routes; ski and paraglider descents were completed. Unfortunately there was quite a bit of illness, mostly high-altitude sickness. The local rescue teams intervened in 45 cases. There were also deaths. For instance, Czechoslovak Dr. Peter Čamek was killed on the descent from Pik Chetiriokh. Pik Lenina, climbed by thousands, remains the world's most popular 7000er. Pik Kommunizma has been climbed by some 2000 mountaineers on more than 20 routes. A new high-standard route with a 8500-foot rise was made in August 1988 via its south face by a Soviet team led by V. Bashkarov.

JÓZEF NYKA, *Editor, Taternik, Poland*

COLOR PLATE 9

Photo by Andrej Štremfelj

On the Southwest Face of SHISHA PANGMA.

Pik Leipzig. Near Pik Lenina, there are still rarely visited lower peaks. On August 9, East Germans Ralf Brummer, Wolfgang Hempel, Erhard Klinger and Siegfried Wittig climbed the probably virgin P 5725 (18,783 feet). They completed the ascent from the upper part of the Achik Glacier via the snow plateau at 5100 meters and then the ridge. Klinger also climbed nearby P 5347 (17,543 feet). The name of Pik Leipzig has been approved by Soviet authorities.

JÓZEF NYKA, *Editor, Taternik, Poland*

Czerski Range, 1988. A Czechoslovak expedition climbed in the Czerski Range in eastern Siberia in 1988. (The range was named for a Pole, hence the spelling.) It lies in a remote area with a harsh climate and many unclimbed peaks. The highest, Pobeda (3147 meters, 10,325 feet) was first climbed in 1966 and had been climbed only once since. Access is difficult with marshy tundra and few roads or maps. The Slovaks, led by Pavol Breier, flew to the Yukutian village of Sassyr and then traveled a day by truck to the pathless wilderness. They established Base Camp on the Leker Glacier at 2000 meters. On July 13, 1988, two pairs made the first ascent of P 3075 (10,068 feet), the second highest in the area. Breier and P. Zelina reached the summit via the southeast ridge (UIAA IV) while V. Kinčeš and J. Trst'an climbed the 700- meter-high east face (IV and 55° ice). On July 16, Kinčeš and Trst'an climbed a new route in the center of the 800-meter-high north face of Pobeda (IV, 65° ice). A trekking group accompanying them climbed Pobeda from the south and crossed the Buordakh massif. Both the climbers and trekkers then joined and made an exciting 400-kilometer paddle down the Moma River through uninhabited country to Honuu village at the junction of the Moma and Yandigirka rivers.

JÓZEF NYKA, *Editor, Taternik, Poland*

Book Reviews

EDITED BY JOHN THACKRAY

Everest: Kangshung Face. Stephen Venables. Hodder & Stoughton, London, 1989. 236 pages. Black-and-white and color photographs, maps. £14.95.

Stephen Venables, raised in a somewhat cloistered Oxford milieu (receiving a Masters degree in English literature) has been moving quietly forward in the ranks of current world-class British mountaineers. With the climb described in this book, he has leaped to their very forefront. He has also proved himself a writer of equal standing. His first book, *Painted Mountains*, attracted much attention when it won the coveted Boardman-Tasker Memorial Award for mountaineering literature in 1986. It revealed a clear, literate writing style of unaffected frankness, and the hot spark of mountaineering ambition.

This second book, with Everest as its subject, will attract a much wider audience. It is the saga of four men, Americans Robert Anderson and Ed Webster, Canadian Paul Teare and Venables, attempting the impossible—climbing Mount Everest without oxygen or Sherpas up a route that was new to 8000 meters, comprising a great variety of technical difficulties (one of which is an honest-to-God Tyrolean Traverse at 6500 meters!). The climb begins at the base of the East (Kangshung) Face of Everest at 5450 meters, weaving directly up to the South Col. From there they plan to follow the southeast (Hillary) route to the summit.

Upon reaching Base Camp, most expeditions to Everest hunker down to sort tons of gear, acclimatize and gird their loins. Not Venables et al. They go into action immediately, site Advance Base the next day and begin the push fixing ropes up their 3500-meter-high route. Here is a sample of Venables' diary entry on this push:

"Day Six on Buttress. Up very wearily at 2:30 am, determined to help Paul and Robert carry and to lead the next pitch up . . . Very slow. Pain under ribs. Cough. Sore throat. Legs like lead. Weight of 100-metre rope, gas stoves and food. Counting rope—now twelve of them in place, mostly 100 metres—like doing a major alpine route two days running, with only five or six hours' sleep in between. And at much higher altitude."

Venables later glories in the mixture of climbing terrain he gets to lead—rock, mixed and pure ice. The group makes excellent progress, with only short bouts of bad weather, well-timed to enforce rest days. Once the group surmounts the main buttress (to the left of the American buttress of 1983), the mood quickly changes to one of hard-driven exhilaration. Climbing a particularly sheer ice face, Venables exalts: "And what an ice pitch! . . . poised . . . as if on a crest of a gigantic wave about to crash down into the Kangshung basin. All my tiredness vanished and I raced on adrenalin, stabbing my way maniacally upwards as the clouds closed in, swirling grey around the Kangshung cirque."

Eventually they get to the South Col. Paul Teare is stricken with altitude sickness but within a few hours recovers enough to climb down alone. The remaining three struggle to begin their summit attempt, but they are struck by lassitude. Before midnight they leave the tent and climb through the night but the combination of wind and altitude has taken much of the heart out of them. Each spends what seems like hours sitting down to rest while precious time races by.

As Venables plods upward, Everest ghosts flutter before his eyes. When he approaches the South Summit, it is Tenzing Norgay and Raymond Lambert of the Swiss expedition of 1952 who pass into view. As he surmounts this foresummit, Evans and Bourdillon appear, who ended their attempt at this point in 1953 because of insufficient oxygen and deteriorating weather. Tenzing Norgay, this time with Hillary, rises in his mind's eye as he contemplates the Hillary Step. Hillary was able to wedge his way up while Dougal Haston floundered in deep powder snow. Venables is delighted to discover that he can climb the step which is in good condition. And finally the summit: "I wanted to savour that precious moment, storing away what memories I could in my feeble oxygen-starved brain. It would be nice to say that it was the happiest moment of my life and that I was overwhelmed with euphoria; but that would be a gross exaggeration, for at the time there was only a rather dazed feeling of—'Isn't it strange?'"

As he turns to leave, Everest's largest ghost—George Mallory—appears. Venables hurries down, not anxious to share his fate. If the ascent was carried out in a dream, the descent becomes a nightmare. A different cast of ghosts appears: Mick Burke who disappeared on the summit ridge; Peter Habeler, in terror of suffering high-altitude brain damage; Hannelore Schmatz, whose ice-encased body sat on the route for years.

Unable to continue down in the dark and nearly comatose with fatigue, Venables bivouacs in the open that still night at 8500 meters. The next morning he meets up with his companions farther down. They have a similar story to tell. They kept falling asleep. Ed Webster had reached the South Summit and realized clearly that this was the moment to turn back. Robert Anderson, an hour behind, passed Ed and attained the South Summit only to become disoriented. Ed and Robert had retreated halfway down to the South Col, reaching an abandoned Asian tent just as darkness fell.

Together all three descend to their tents on the col, melt a meager ration of water, lick their wounds and collapse. Ed Webster is the worst off. His fingers are purple with frostbite and he surmises—but cannot remember clearly—that the damage must have occurred during a dawn photography session. They cannot bring themselves to leave the comfort of their tiny tents, but finally Ed cajoles his companions to don their climbing gear and move down. For safety each climbs separately, for none could hold the other in a fall. The descent is a vivid nightmare.

In this intensely told epic of conquest and descent, the issue of how much risk climbers are justified in taking is writ large, but not deeply analyzed. Venables does not preach but describes with great realism what happened. There is not a word of psycho-babble.

While realistic and detailed, his description of the retreat below the South Col was obtained only after painstaking reconstruction after interviewing each of the climbers. Severe amnesia affected them all. Their ragged and broken states of mind raise some troubling questions. If one climbs to experience the pleasure of it, it is done to please oneself. If one cannot remember a sensational climb because it was oxygenless, does it become only a remarkable feat done to please others? In this vein the question "Why do you climb?" would be better asked "For whom do you climb?" Or is the residual sense of enormous achievement reward enough?

Stephen Venables has a wonderful knack for explaining how he surmounts a climbing problem without seeming to be writing a textbook. Serious climbers will find a trove of techniques to study which are described clearly enough for non-climbers to understand. Climbers or not, all will be interested in this mountaineering thriller of a tiny band pulling off an incredible victory, an account so stirring it will be put down only to obtain a moment's breather. It is a story that will take its place along with other outstanding sagas of Everest— Norton's *The Fight for Everest, 1924*, Lord Hunt's *The Ascent of Everest*, Hornbein's *Everest, The West Ridge* and Bonington's *Everest the Hard Way*.

The book is elegantly designed by long-time Everest publishers, Hodder & Stoughton, with 48 pages of breath-taking color photographs, all beautifully printed. Detail photos lead the reader carefully along the route. The quality of the photography is outstanding and does much to prove what an extraordinary accomplishment these four climbers achieved.

THOMAS HOLZEL

The Art of Adventure. Galen Rowell. Collins Publishers, San Francisco, 1989. 166 pages, 127 color photographs. $45.00.

There is no doubt that Galen Rowell is one of the great photographers of the world. This is clearly apparent in this new and gorgeous coffee-table book. The superb composition of each photograph, the clarity of detail, the excellent quality of the reproductions all contribute to making this an exceptionally beautiful volume. The 10 by 14-inch format makes it possible to show many of the pictures double-paged, increasing their effectiveness.

Galen Rowell combines his skills of photography with being one of the outstanding American mountaineers. For that reason, climbers will find this album of particular interest, for it is primarily in the mountains or in mountainous areas that most of the photographs were taken. The mountain scenery and the climbing shots are outstanding. Many are what might be called "mood shots" taken at sunrise, sundown or in threatening and inclement weather. However, some of the ones which are most striking are incredibly natural shots of animals in the wild. His pictures of mountain peoples show a great feeling of sympathy with them. In his many years of photography, Rowell has been in many unusual and out-of-the-way places. Represented are photographs taken in his native

California and other parts of the "Lower 48," Alaska, Canada, China, Tibet, Pakistan, Nepal, Africa, Patagonia. This is indeed an anthology of the "best of Galen Rowell."

K2—Traum und Schicksal. Kurt Diemberger. Bruckmann Verlag, Munich, 1989. 336 pages, 46 color photographs, 60 black-and-white photographs, 4 drawings, 5 maps, 4 mountain profiles, Tibetan symbols. DM 48 (about $29).

K2—Traum und Schicksal ("K2—Dreams and Fate") takes us back to 1957, when Kurt Diemberger, as a companion of Hermann Buhl, first saw the mountain from the foot of Broad Peak. His dream of actually climbing it took shape only after reading a passage in Eric Shipton's *Blank on the Map*, describing the view of the north side of K2. He did not see that view until 1982 during a small scouting expedition approved by special permit by the Chinese government. It was an inspiration and Kurt left with the firm desire of one day setting foot on the top. Visits to England followed where on the cliffs of Wales he met Julie Tullis, who later became his partner in high-altitude filming.

In 1983, Kurt returned to K2 with Julie Tullis via Sinkiang and in 1984 via Pakistan. Climbing attempts were made. The first part of the book is written in narrative style, always interesting, and one gets involved with the author's doings. The pictures are of superb quality, a joy to look at.

The second part of the book takes us to the fateful year of 1986 when nine expeditions from many lands were heading for the top of K2. That year saw the final attempt of Kurt Diemberger and Julie Tullis. It is a gripping story, full of drama, a continuous crescendo until they reach their goal. Then, on the descent, fate strikes. Kurt and Julie suffer a fall on the steep slope not far below the summit. It ends miraculously with a soft landing that leaves them without any apparent serious injuries but forces them to bivouac in the open. They manage to get back to the tents in a blinding snowstorm, where they and other climbers are trapped. The description of how death takes its toll as all the climbers lie confined to their tents in the death zone strikes with emotional and frightening force. Julie Tullis dies first, just falling asleep in the tent forever. Fate had struck again.

The reader becomes a captive in the twilight zone of life and death at 8000 meters where the altitude causes carelessness, hallucinations, and warped or totally missing memory. When, after days, the fury of the storm abates somewhat, the remaining climbers can finally dare to tackle the descent to safety, but only two of them succeed, Kurt Diemberger and Willi Bauer. All the others perish. Kurt is badly frostbitten and spends weeks recuperating in the hospital in Innsbruck.

The appendix contains a history of all K2 expeditions, a list of all climbers who attempted K2 and of those who died on the mountain. There is also a list of the main peaks in the Karakoram. There is an extensive bibliography. All this has been diligently researched and will be a valuable help to all visitors to that part of the world.

Kurt Diemberger's and Julie Tullis' film, *K2—Traum und Schicksal*, was finished by Kurt alone and received the Città di Trento Prize at the 37th International Mountain Film Festival at Trento in 1989. The Italian version of Kurt's book on K2 was picked by the jury from 60 volumes of 37 different publishers as *The Mountain Book of the Year*. The English version of the book has been translated by Audrey Salkeld and will appear in the autumn. *K2— Traum und Schicksal* is a fine book that keeps one spellbound to the very last page.

HORST VON HENNIG

Mountaineer: Thirty Years of Climbing on the World's Great Peaks. Chris Bonington. Diadem Books, London, and Sierra Club Books, San Francisco, 1989. 192 pages, numerous color illustrations. £17.95 or $29.95.

Chris Bonington's latest book, his tenth overall and his third autobiography, is certainly a pleasure to look at. With large images of ravishing mountain scenery, *Mountaineer* is a coffee-table book par excellence. The photos, well chosen and admirably reproduced, constantly remind us of the reasons we go to the mountains.

I can think of no other mountaineer except Kurt Diemberger who has climbed big Himalayan peaks over such a long time span. Since 1960, when he reached the top of Annapurna II, Bonington has made seventeen trips to Asia. And though he has climbed only one 8000-meter peak, Everest, this was in 1985, when he was 51!

Much of Bonington's early climbing life will be familiar to his followers. After surviving youthful forays to the crags of Great Britain, the author ventured to the Alps in his twenties, accomplishing some significant first ascents. In this abbreviated autobiography, these years pass quickly. Later he began his trips to the Himalaya, the subject of most of the remainder of the book.

Over the years the author climbed with dozens of legendary figures, among them John Harlin, Tom Patey, Dougal Haston, Ian Clough, Mick Burke, Nick Estcourt, Joe Tasker, and Peter Boardman. All these men are now dead, killed in action. And the last five died on Bonington's expeditions, a sobering statistic.

Those who have survived numerous Himalayan expeditions—men like Bonington, Diemberger, Scott, Messner—are the *living* legends, and an aura of respect and mystery surrounds them. Are these four survivors extra cautious? Is their karma so developed that they have become invincible? Or are they just plain lucky? Bonington, alone of the above quartet, is not known for his daring exploits. Does this make him the shrewdest—or the most timid—of the group?

There's hardly a trace of such philosophical introspection in *Mountaineer*. Bonington rarely displays emotion, though he once mentions "agonizing" about all the deaths on his trips. When Burke disappears on top of Everest and when

John Harlin dies on the Eiger Direct, the author is so casual he could be talking about total strangers.

The book is organized into ten chapters, each opening with an overview of its subject. The balance of the chapter reexamines the identical information by means of extended captions and detailed accounts of particular climbs. This format results in redundant material and confusing transitions. For instance, after a climb of Mont Blanc, with the weather still perfect, "there was only one climb to go for—the Eiger North Wall!" We turn the page, eager to hear about the dreaded Ogre . . . and instead wade through pages about the Chamonix aiguilles. Seventeen pages later we arrive at the Eigerwand.

Bonington's prose is adequate, though it is often bland and cumbersome. His thoughts can wander like a route through an icefall, causing readers to lose their way. An example: "The Mount Everest Foundation underwrote the cost of it, we were to be accompanied by a film crew, Don Whillans designed the box tents, successors to the Patagonian prefabricated hut, and also a waist harness, from which all subsequent harnesses have been developed." A sentence like this could go on forever, obviating the need for periods.

Bonington's life story is by definition exciting, unique. Yet he has trouble luring the reader into his special world. Hesitant to delve into the nuances and complexities of climbing, he instead tells us the "standard" thoughts. It's rough above 7000 meters. The mountains are soulful and yet unforgiving. Death is part of the game. Does the author spout these cliché from conviction, or because he's been advised that's the way to write about mountaineering?

I dream of perfection, I suppose. Few mountaineers write well, and we have come to accept lackluster prose as a trade-off for a well-illustrated adventure yarn. Not everyone can write like David Roberts, but why can't he at least have a few writers hot on his tail? Bonington, I regret to say, is not even in the race. But he surely takes pretty pictures!

STEVE ROPER

Ascent: The Mountaineering Experience in Word and Image. Edited by Allen Steck and Steve Roper. Sierra Club Books, San Francisco, 1989. 205 pages, illustrations. $19.95.

In the inaugural issue of *Ascent*, Royal Robbins characterized the periodical as "a delightful and tasteful mélange of mountaineering; an eclectic potpourri of adventure, polemics, cartoons, photographs, poetry, humor and information, all strung together with a few central threads: California mountaineering, significant mountaineering successes and belles-lettres of alpinism." From its inception in 1967 through 1976, *Ascent* was, in effect, an annual mountaineering magazine. A shifting band of editors, which included Dave Dornan, Chuck Pratt, David Roberts, Lito Tejada-Flores, Jim Stuart, Joe Fitschen, Edgar Boyles and Glen Denny, worked with *Ascent's* mainstays Allen Steck and Steve Roper to produce a product that focused on first hand accounts of significant mountaineering ascents. The early editions were fleshed out by mountaineering notes, book reviews, interviews, essays and a few fictional pieces. In short, it was much the same format that we now see in our bi-monthly climbing magazines, although with an undeniable flair.

After publication of the combined 1975-1976 issue, *Ascent* underwent a rather dramatic change. Steck and Roper, who by this time shouldered the editorial burden alone, came to realize that they could no longer compete with the climbing periodicals for topical climbing accounts. They began publishing every four years and shifted their focus from articles on the here-and-now to articles of "more lasting interest, favoring literature over journalism, a sometimes elusive distinction"—a distinction, that while elusive, Steck and Roper have mastered.

Ascent has become the only periodical which exists solely for the expression of mountaineering literature. Who else would have published what is probably the finest piece of climbing fiction ever written, David Roberts' 66 page novella, "Like Water and Like Wind" which appeared in the 1980 issue? The 1980 and 1984 issues of *Ascent* became full-blown anthologies of book length, combining essays, fiction and non-fictional accounts, all of which explored the mountaineering experience. In addition to leading all mountaineering publications in the pursuit of literature, *Ascent* set the standard for visual beauty with its black and white photos, illustrations and color essays.

The 1989 issue of *Ascent*, which for reasons unexplained came out a year late, would by general standards be considered visually attractive. When compared to *Ascent's* recent issues, however, it is disappointing. The contrived graphics and undistinctive photo of the cover are a marked contrast from the stunning photos which have graced the two past issues. The only photo essay is of excellent quality but of a subject—Mount Everest and environs—which we have seen time and time again. Tad Welch's illustrations are nice, but the reader yearns for the diversity and profusion of images that have accompanied past issues.

While the images in this issue of *Ascent* are disappointing, the words live up to Steck and Roper's past standards. The 1989 issue contains seventeen stories together with seven poems. As is perhaps unavoidable, there is a range in the quality of pieces, but there is plenty here to recommend. I will spare you what few criticisms I have and point out some of the best.

Among the six fictional pieces, two which stand out are "The Collector" by Anne Sauvy and "For The Record" by Steven Jervis. In "The Collector", a World War I veteran returns to find life as he has known it shattered. Turning to the mountains for consolation, he begins pursuing a game of collecting firsts so extreme that no one else would have climbed them. He is stung by the disbelief of his rivals and plots his revenge by beginning to secretly collect dozens of difficult first ascents, taking extensive photos and writing out detailed route descriptions. His prize collection of solo triumphs is officially sealed and dated by a notary. His revenge is jeopardized, however, when he dies and his voluminous record discarded as trash.

In "For The Record", two former friends vie to convince the editor of the National Alpine Club's accident reports, through their correspondence, of the veracity of their competing versions of a climb which ended in tragedy. Their bitter recriminations and conflicting accounts are certain to strike a deep chord with anyone who has experienced tragedy in the mountains.

In "Karass and Granfallons" by Alison Osius and "The Best of Times, The Worst of Times" by Joe Kelsey, the authors explore the bonds of climbing friendship. "Karass and Granfallons" centers around a far-flung, cash-short group of friends that jokingly calls itself the Fourth Avenue Alpine Club after a bar in Anchorage's seediest district.

In "The Best of Times, The Worst of Times", a group of friends, most of them admittedly long past their prime, use a May trip to Joshua Tree to push their personal limits as they prowl the crags by day and recount climbing experiences—both past and present—around the fireside by night.

A common theme in climbing literature has always been personal tragedy and loss. This issue of *Ascent* is no exception. One-half of the articles have tragedy as a theme. Perhaps the most compelling is Gary Ruggera's "The Eyes of Buddha" in which he races to save a friend dying of altitude sickness and then confronts the terrible reality of his friend's death and his own grief. You won't find route descriptions, ratings or ego-charged narratives in this story or, for that matter, any of the others. What you will find is a perceptive, heart rending tale of a mountaineering experience.

While the latest issue of *Ascent* may not be as slick or glossy as its recent predecessors, it remains the best thing going when it comes to pure mountaineering literature.

ROBERT F. ROSEBROUGH

Mountain Journeys. Edited by James P. Vermeulen. The Overlook Press, Woodstock, New York, 1989. 248 pages, $19.95.

James P. Vermeulen has compiled an anthology of mainstream first-person climbing stories. He has reasonably organized the selections into a kind of up-and-back structure: "Because It was There," about the tug of mountains on the imagination; "Up, Down and Toward," dealing with expedition planning and preparation; "Trials and Tragedies;" "Summits;" and, lastly, "Back into the World."

A sampling of the writers he has chosen includes Galen Rowell, Gaston Rebuffat, Nicholas Clinch, Tom Patey, Elizabeth Knowlton, Art Davidson, Robert Bates, Robert Craig, Dave Roberts, Julie Tullis, Rick Ridgeway, Maurice Herzog, Tenzing Norgay. The more offbeat choices are John Muir and Joe McGinniss. Before each, the editor includes a brief, competent comment on the careers and writing of each climber.

In his preface Mr. Vermeulen writes, "Not surprisingly, the question most often asked about mountaineers is: Why?" The same question can be asked about anthologies. Why? What gap in the literature is plugged by anthologizing? Mr. Vermeulen goes on to say, ". . . . The stories in this paper feast were harvested with an eye toward feeding everyone, for everyone's feast."

The trouble is that old-hand climbers who read already know these books in their entirety. To feed the experienced, the anthologist would need to have ferreted out more obscure writers or less familiar events. Terray? Tejada-Flores or John Long? Others we don't even know? In sum *Mountain Journeys* is a smorgasbord that can only be expected to whet the beginner's appetite.

In a 248-page book, including a forward, preface, and glossary, Mr. Vermeulen has included twenty-one excerpts which are too brief and tend to bleed into each other. Like ocean-voyaging literature, accounts of mountain ascents take on a general sameness. One alpine storm is pretty much like another, not in the actual experience, of course, but in the telling. Specifying, individualizing, is one of the challenges the first-person narrator faces. Most of these writers have succeeded in that their books are infused with their own personalities and a sense of immediacy. But take several great mountaineers and pull out of context their five-to-ten-page accounts of, say, tough alpine ascents, put them side by side, and something of that original character and immediacy is lost. Perhaps *Mountain Journey's* purpose would have been better served by including half as many excerpts twice as long, a feast with fewer nibbles.

DALLAS MURPHY

Gorilla Monsoon. John Long, Chockstone Press, Denver, 1989. 177 pages. $12.95.

In the eighteen largely autobiographical narratives in *Gorilla Monsoon*, John Long creates himself as a character: daring, exuberant, relentless in pursuit of experience, and only occasionally reflective. He sounds much the way he appeared in a photograph of him and his companions after the first one-day ascent of El Capitan. Cigarette dangling, bandana topping long tangled hair, shirt open over his pectorals, Long looks very tough, ready for anything. In this book we find him not merely risking but brazenly courting extreme danger. Although he never puts it this way, his survival seems miraculous—and very gripping for the reader.

Of the eighteen pieces, only two are about climbing—three, if you count a description of the world's longest rappel, performed for T.V. (It is a mild irony that Long, the free spirit, is often dependent upon the corporate whims of a major television program, which employed him to arrange and film spectacular events.) But readers of this journal will find plenty of interest in all these accounts of "adventuring," as Long twice terms it. Long is an adventurer in the good sense of the term—endlessly curious, searching out what has not been accomplished and scarcely imagined, prepared for almost any kind of risk. We find him rocketing through water pipes in Venezuela, hacking his way across Borneo, snowmobiling nearly to hypothermia in Baffin Island. At times he seems virtually suicidal, but love of life does, for some people, entail the hazard of death. To each his own terror: the story that frightened me the most has Long and his (if possible) more reckless accomplice D.B. squirming through a huge South American cave. At one point D.B. is up to his chest in slime and almost gone. "We didn't know a damn thing about caving," Long has informed us. "It's very harrowing," but D.B. is extricated to contribute two fine passages to the book.

Long's writing is usually as energetic as the experience it conveys. He is at his surest with autobiographical accounts like "The Only Blasphemy," in which he economically conveys the pressure of competitive solo climbing and the awful moment when he realizes he has taken one chance too many. But I think that with "Requiem for Ronnie," which takes the form of a twice-told tale, he strains too hard and ends up with less. Its climactic scene with a dying hero sound unreal to me. Thus I share the preferences of Alison Osius, as declared in her illuminating foreword, for the more direct and immediate of these pieces. Long is evidently an ambitious writer, who wants to go beneath and beyond adventure. But for me "Requiem" is a failed attempt to create a mythic character, only partly redeemed by its vivid description of running some amazing rapids; whereas "Blasphemy" is the real thing. It has a frightening and altogether plausible immediacy. We can feel all the fear, the triumph and the relief of the narrator. It is a small classic: brief but telling.

Although Long is himself very vivid, some of the other characters are not. A prime example is "Down and Out," which has the shape and some of the impact of a good short story. Its protagonist, the daring cliff-jumper Carl Boenish, is "the most singular individual I had ever met," but we scarcely see his singularity or "contagious enthusiasm." Long devotes considerable space to describing Carl's disjointed conversation, galvanized by "goofy mix of mysticism and personal revelations, coupled with the cryptic tenents of a religious system I could not quite discern." If only Long had let us really hear that voice! When, rarely, Carl does speak directly, he sounds rather like Long. And his young wife Jean, who should be an important figure, is little realized. This lack of vividness muffles the impact of the ending. Carl's last "crazy" jump seems merely enigmatic—extremely sad but without clear significance.

Long is attempting the difficult transition from journalism to fiction—or at least narrative that uses the devices and conventions of fiction. This movement is clearest in the last piece in the book, "A Stone from Allah," which depicts the tender, chaste relations between the narrator and a young Indonesian girl from Borneo who is resisting her inevitable descent into prostitution. The heroic action—the crossing of Borneo, described earlier in the book—is but briefly alluded to here. The burden falls on the characterization which, though fuller than in "Down and Out," relies too much on the familiar: "she smiled like the Milky Way"; "her skin was like God." Some details, however, suggest Long's gift for observation not just of action but of people—the girl's desperate attempts to distract him from the squalor of her dwelling, and the "hard corners of her mouth," sad emblems of change after his two months' absence.

In the light of Long's progression as character and writer, it is a pity that the sections of the book show no apparent order—certainly not chronological by experience. Except very sketchily in the foreword, there is no information about order of composition and place of previous publication, when appropriate. There are no photographs and no evidence of careful proofreading—spelling errors abound. But at $12.95 *Gorilla Monsoon* is a bargain which no purchaser should regret. Many sections roar at you with the energy and unstoppability of an express train, and leave you as unnerved as though you had nearly been struck by one. Long is never less than entertaining; at times he is considerably more.

STEVEN JERVIS

The Loneliest Mountain. Lincoln Hall. Photographs by Jonathan Chester. The Mountaineers, Seattle, 1989. 232 pages. $35.00

Scarcely 4000 meters high and technically not very demanding, Mount Minto is not the conventional idea of a difficult mountain. Yet because of its location in a rugged corner of Antarctica, at the beginning of 1988 it remained unclimbed despite several attempts. Its ascent was a formidable challenge to an under-financed group of Australians. As one of them writes:

> All we needed was a ship and enough fuel, food and equipment for eleven people to sail 4000 nautical miles, survive for up to eighteen months in the most inhospitable climate in the world, as well as for six of the team to travel 300 kilometers overland across unknown glaciers and through passes, in order to scale a massive unclimbed peak.

In three months they did it all and returned to Australia without serious injury or unreasonable stress.

One result of this triumph is a book (there is also a video with the same title) that is likable and informative. The mountaineering experience of the six climbers ranged from Himalayan to virtually none, and the variation adds texture to their enterprise.

Though close to Australia, Antarctica is cut off from it by a lot of cold, turbulent sea. The group got there on a 21-meter sailing vessel, with intermittently functioning motor, "endearingly named" (to quote the foreward by the Australian novelist Thomas Keneally) the *Allan and Vi Thistlethwayte.* (The Thistlethwaytes were the most important of the expedition's many patrons.) The little ship pitched constantly, relegating the most seasick climber to his bunk for the entire voyage, and was afflicted with many mechanical problems. On arrival, it had to be maneuvered carefully through the pack ice to a mooring at Cape Hallett, from which the circuitous approach to the mountain could begin. Several weeks of arduous hauling, trekking and climbing culminated in the successful ascent, all the happier because all six aspirants made the top.

The narrative is a pleasure to read. I found it interesting and at times pleasingly humorous, however, rather than compelling. One reason is that so little went wrong: the most trying moment was the loss of the skidoo, their only means of motorized hauling, along with a crucial pair of skis. Another is that despite extensive use of dialogue, the author does not effectively differentiate among his six characters. Although their speech is convincing, they sound much alike.

In the inevitable comparisons with earlier explorers like Amundsen and Scott, one can't help thinking how significantly modern technology protects our contemporaries. Hall addresses this point in his introduction: "Our aim was to climb a mountain, but the size and style of the expedition was actually more important than the goal itself. . . . The challenge is to meet the world on its own ground, because then one has no choice but to understand it." The six made the climb in good style, but they were dependent on radio communication, and the genuine risk of having to winter over—because the ship would have left to escape being trapped in the ice—was finally eliminated by a helicopter evacuation to a large, friendly ship.

The greatest virtue of the book is its production. If $35.00 sounds like a lot, then believe me, the value is excellent. The large glossy pages are studded with marvellous color photographs, thoughtfully laid out and worth the price of admission by themselves. There are also some clear, helpful maps. The Mountaineers and the printers in Hong Kong are to be applauded. Moreover, various members of the expedition contribute valuable appendices on food, photography, equipment and other matters essential for anyone contemplating a similar enterprise.

The book is animated by a strong environmental concern. A prologue describes a nighttime ascent of the Centrepoint Tower in Sydney, to display a bannner protesting nuclear warships. The note left on the summit reads in part: "We intend the ascent be used to place Mount Minto as the cornerstone in an Antarctic World Park for the physical and spiritual benefit of all humankind." Amen to that.

STEVEN JERVIS

Rocks around the World. Stefan Glowacz and Uli Wiesmeier. Sierra Club
    Books, San Francisco, 1988. 144 pages. $24.95.

There's a commercial recipe behind *Rocks Around the World*: find a reigning rock-climbing star, send him with a personal photographer on a world tour of the standard watering places (Smith Rocks, Needles, Red Rocks, Arapiles in Australia, Ogowayama in Japan, and well-known locations in France, Germany and the U.K.) crank out another coffee-table book and count the money rolling in. Since my personal coffee table's legs had buckled and collapsed long ago, I've been immune to this formula. Then I discovered, encaged in the mummified hand of this publishing convention, the photographs of Uli Wiesmeier, who accompanied the peripatetic West German ace Stephan Glowacz.

In a field where even gifted photographers can get sucked into cliché, Wiesmeier stands out as an original mind: bringing a personal vision to such standard shots as a chalked-up fist straining on a nubbin, a group of climbers at a bouldering wall. The true hero of this book is not the lantern-jawed Glowacz with his long locks and gymnast's physique in colorful tights, it is the rock — its sculpture, its fantastical textures, its place in the landscape — observed by a genius eye. At his best Wiesmeier communicates a richness of vision and fine detail akin to a canvas by a grand master. His double-page spreads on Jogasaki, Red Rocks, Mount Arapiles and Verdon are breathtaking.

In the more familiar rock-climbing sequences Wiesmeier deftly gives us shots with something urgent to say, each frame dense with information, lyrical in its evocation of scenery. With a fine sense of perspective, he balances the claims of rock climbing action and of the surroundings. The picture of the sport that emerges is full of reverence and wonderment at the properties of rock. The climber belongs here, he is integral and necessary to the properties of the land, not the gaudy alien we've seen so often. And the crags themselves are just magical.

Glowacz's short, four-part commentaries are uninformative and at times just silly. (If Rodin's Thinker could speak, would he be worth listening to? Was Nijinsky?) But the text's triviality hardly matters, such is the majesty of Wiesmeier's work.

JOHN THACKRAY

Portrait of an Explorer. Hiram Bingham, Discoverer of Machu Picchu. Alfred M. Bingham. Iowa State University Press, Ames, Iowa, 1989. 141 black and white photographs, 6 sketch maps, 382 pages. Hardbound. $29.95.

Although Hiram Bingham was not the discoverer of Machu Picchu any more than Columbus was the discoverer of the New World, it was he who put the last Inca capital on the map and who gave it back to the world. The book, written by Bingham's third son, is an efficient biography that, without omitting the necessary detail about the personal life of the person portrayed, goes to great lengths to describe the job he did. The work is divided into four parts with 27 chapters. There are also an epilogue, appendixes, bibliographies and an index.

Born in 1875, Hiram Bingham earned a doctorate at Harvard and became a lecturer at Yale. In 1906-7 he made his first South American expedition, repeating across Venezuela and Colombia the route of Bolívar's liberating army (1821). In 1907 he carried out his second South American expedition, or rather, travels. It was then that he became convinced that "the last Inca capital" remained to be discovered. This led to his 1911 expedition to Peru, his most famous one. Archaeologist A. Bandelier had written that Nevado Coropuna could very well be "the culminating point in the continent," and placed it at over 23,000 feet. Bingham, even if he actually had not been a mountaineer, had exploration in his veins and managed to set up an expedition to climb Coropuna and also to search for the last Inca capital. Unexpectedly he had to compete with another American, Annie Peck, who in 1906 had climbed Huascarán Norte. Bingham decided not to race for Coropuna and instead, to survey the land as he worked his way toward the mountain. In the end, Annie Peck climbed the easternmost peak of Coropuna (6303 meters) and Bingham's party, the highest, which his surveyor put at 6617 meters. Bingham undertook yet two more trips to Peru. In 1912 he did discover, or uncover, Machu Picchu and in 1914-15, more ruins.

This book is definitely of interest to all mountaineers fond of Peru and of South America. Of the 27 chapters that form the book, twelve deal directly with the Andes and the rest, with travels elsewhere as well as with the life of Bingham himself. A number of photos, taken some seven decades ago, will be of interest to climbers.

This book shows an involuntary mistake. The 1985 Peruvian chart (sheets Cotahuasi and Aplao) led the author, and others too of course, to believe that the north peak of Coropuna (or Coropuna Casulla), with 6377 meters, is the highest in the massif and that the dome climbed by Bingham in 1911 is 6350 meters high. This is wrong. Bingham did climb the highest peak (locally called El Toro), which later Peruvian surveys have placed at 6425 meters. This was confirmed by Mike McWherther, who in 1984 ascended Coropuna Casulla and wrote in *Summit* (no. 5, 1984, p. 21-22):

> . . . when we reached the north peak's great summit plateau . . . we looked to the dome peak. It looked about 300 ft higher.
>
> We had been misled by the topographic map and climbed Coropuna's second highest summit.

The text is complemented by quotations from Bingham's writings and from his personal letters, by adequate maps and, above all, by photos taken by the explorer himself. To summarize, then, this is a biographical book about the life and times of a well known explorer, who was besides a pioneer mountaineer.

EVELIO ECHEVARRÍA

Ecuador: Tierras Atlas.Jorge Anhalzer. Imprenta Mariscal, Quito, 1987. 154 pages, 120 color photographs, 1 sketchmap. Hardbound.

Frontera Superior de Colombia.José F. Machado et al. Banco de Occidente, Bogotá, 1987. 183 pages, 146 color photographs, 15 line drawings and sketch-maps, 5 maps. Hardbound.

The Andes: Natural Beauty of Chile. Gastón Oyarzún. Editorial Kactus, Santiago, 1988. 88 pages, 73 color photographs. Softbound.

A Chilean, an Ecuadorian and a team of Colombians directed by José F. Machado have almost simultaneously produced a color portraiture of the high mountains of their respective countries. The Chilean work is the English version of an earlier Spanish edition. All three books have a common layout. Each one alternates pictures of stark rock and ice peaks and local climbers in action, with vignettes depicting sunsets, flowers and animal life. All three also offer brief data of important mountains and of main, historical ascents. All three books, too, display here and there impressive photos of unclimbed walls, mostly rock. And all persons participating in the preparation of these books can be identified as the best climbers in their respective countries. There are also some differences among these works, differences that respond to the characteristics of the mountain scenery and of the mountain sports pertaining to each of the countries involved. The Ecuadorian volume places an emphasis on lesser peaks, particularly the very little known ones of southern and eastern Ecuador. The Chilean work, as to be expected, also describes skiing, skiers, winter mountaineering and mountain tourism. The text in Oyarzún's album is clear and to the point; it intends to supply information. And the Colombian book, the most ambitious of all three, puts a greater emphasis on the portrayal of mountain people. Anhalzer and the Colombians attempt to explain, by means of text and picture and with much feeling, the meaning of scenery for both the local highlanders and for mountaineers.

Of the seven Andean countries, only Bolivia and, partially, Argentina, have not seen their high mountain world portrayed in an album type of book like these. Ecuador has so far been the most favored, with no less than four such books published in the last few years. Every one of the three books listed above contains a challenge and an invitation for mountain adventures abroad.

EVELIO ECHEVARRÍA

The Mount Everest Maps

In the November 1988 issue of the *National Geographic* the most accurate map of Mount Everest (1:50,000) ever produced was published as a supplement. Also, in that same issue the map was described in an article "Surveying the Third Pole" by Bradford Washburn. This magnificent cartographic product culminated many years of effort by Bradford Washburn and his project team and it is one of the most dramatic cartographic accomplishments of this century.

In addition, there are ten large scale map manuscripts (1:10,000) and the resulting large-scale shaded relief map (1:15,000) which are superb and provide an outstanding and everlasting cartographic rendition of a significant part of the earth. In reaching that conclusion many considerations and realities are involved, including project area (terrain variances, terrain accessibility, climatic conditions, political boundaries); evaluation and utilization of critical earlier source materials (maps, ground control, ground photography and imagery); obtaining the most modern and space photographic imagery attainable; and using the most precise positioning, advanced photogrammetric and cartographic techniques possible. There are also twelve new sheets on a scale of 1:2,500 with five-meter contours of just Everest itself.

These maps of Mount Everest will not only serve as the base of many future scientific studies by geologists, glaciologists, geodesists, hydrologists, etc., but they will serve as factual proof and models of what can be accomplished over remote, desolate and barren areas of the world.

More importantly, the maps reflect what Washburn was able to accomplish utilizing a truly International team (United States, Switzerland, Nepal, People's Republic of China, Great Britain, West Germany, Sweden, Yugoslavia, Japan) of outstanding scientific and technical talent. Washburn stated early on "our new map would depend heavily on the diligent work of the heroes of the past, strengthened and expanded by the most sophisticated modern science." Washburn's dogged persistence, determination, and leadership have made maps of Mount Everest that will stand the test of time.

OWEN W. WILLIAMS

Winter Sports Medicine. Murray J. Casey, Carl Foster, and Edward G. Hixson. F.A. Davis, Philadelphia, 1989. 425 pages, illustrated. $65.00.

This is an excellent and needed addition to the growing library of sports medicine and will be of great value to doctors, trainers and athletes involved with competitive winter sports. To my knowledge it is the first comprehensive collection of information about virtually all winter sports.

The 47 chapters are distributed in seven sections: general topics, medical problems, and injuries which are common to all winter sports, followed by special chapters on the various types of competitive skating and skiing. Except for four brief chapters on mountaineering and winter camping, the book is directed at world-class competition. Training, nutrition, physiology, biomechanics and illness and injuries peculiar to each of the ten winter sports are considered in detail–sometimes exhaustingly so. One quarter of the book discusses preparation of the athlete and his caretakers, including nutrition, over-training, and the hazards of doping. Another quarter covers all the illnesses and general injuries to which the competitor may fall victim. Finally mountaineering, altitude problems and trekking are allotted 30 pages.

Most of the chapters are clear, complete and authoritative; a few are inadequate. Only brief mention is made of snow-blindness and "fever blisters" both common and troublesome though minor. The importance of adequate fluid and electrolyte replacement for those pushing themselves to the limit in very dry cold air appears only in the chapter on nutrition. Mountaineering is given little space, and winter camping is dealt with in a few paragraphs in an excellent chapter on trekking and camping abroad. Almost nothing is said about motivation–the spur that drives the world-class athlete to super-human effort. Despite a few shortcomings, this is an exceptionally useful and helpful book for those who feel compelled to compete in the cold.

CHARLES S. HOUSTON, M.D.

High Altitude Medicine and Physiology. Michael P. Ward, James S. Milledge
and John B. West. University of Pennsylvania Press, Philadelphia, 1989.
515 pages. $89.95.

As the golden age of Himalayan climbing climaxes, it's not surprising to
find aparallel interest in high altitude. But mountain sicknesses are not limited
to those who climb the highest mountains: in fact the greatest number of
cases occur among the millions who ski, climb, trek or simply vacation among
more moderate mountains. More than a quarter of all who visit 8000 to
10,000 feet have significant symptoms and quite a few die from altitude
illness.

So this is a timely book, aimed primarily at doctors and scientists, but a good
read for anyone going to the mountains. It's quite simply the best medical text on
high altitude.

The three authors know their stuff: all are veteran climbers and scientists
who have dealt with illness and accidents in high places and have contributed to
research as well. In this book they describe the history, geography and demog-
raphy of mountainous regions and detail the normal and abnormal reactions of
man to oxygen lack. They tell amusing stories of how we learned what we know
today and describe how and why we breathe, and how the heart, lungs, blood,
and cells function normally and when short of oxygen. Hypothermia and
frostbite are well described but oddly separated from an excellent discussion of
how thermal balance is controlled.

What we know and don't know about the various forms of altitude illnesses
is summarized, though the classification British authors use differs from ours.
Case reports lighten the text and there is some stimulating comparison of healthy
man at altitude with man hypoxic from illness at sea level—a subject still
relatively unexplored.

Though the authors draw most heavily from their own experience, and a few
disputed data are advanced as fact and others ignored, the book is quite
even-handed. There are ample references for those who want to read more.
Unfortunately the index is poor.

These are minor warts: this book, primarily a medical text, is good reading
for any one seriously interested in going high and the ideal source of information
about high altitude for the mountaineering doctor.

CHARLES S. HOUSTON, M.D.

High Altitude Medicine and Pathology. Donald Heath and David Reid Williams.
Butterworths, 1989. London, 352 pages. $95.00.

The authors are senior pathologists, well traveled in the mountains of Asia and
South America, and authorities in the pathology due to altitude. It is strictly a
scientific text, an excellent companion to the clinical book by Ward, Milledge
and West. Only minor revisions have been made since the second edition (1981),

though it falls short in describing many major advances in altitude research made during the last decade.

The authors contend that symptoms experienced by lowlanders going to altitude are "normal." Less persuasive is their case for defining altitude sickness as either "benign" or "malignant." Differences between immediate reactions and the slower changes of acclimatization, and adaptation over generations are blurred. Acclimatization is discussed throughout the book rather than summarized in one place. Short chapters on high-altitude telescopes, the Abominable Snowman, exercise at altitude and sleep aren't appropriate in a pathology text and these are weak. Some of the data are outdated.

There are many references—though too few from recent literature—and the index is excellent. This is the definitive textbook of pathology, but of interest mainly to scientists interested in altitude.

CHARLES S. HOUSTON, M.D.

International Travel Health Guide. Stuart R. Rose. Travel Medicine Inc., Northampton, Mass., 1989. 228 pages. $12.95.

Though this does not pretend to emulate the hoary "Hints to Travellers", which ran to a dozen editions beginning in 1854, it's an invaluable compendium of all you need to know — sometimes more — about how to stay well when travelling; more than a hundred countries are covered. Requirements for visas, health certificates, shots, and solid advice about medical kits, health precautions and where to find help are all covered in up-to-date detail. Which diseases are prevalent, what special precautions are needed (against resistant malaria for example) are well defined for each country. Insurance, emergency air evacuation, and internationally available expert advice are included. Its handy pocket size, good maps and index and lists of addresses and telephone numbers in many countries are the sort of practical details the traveler needs. There are a few shortcomings which the author assures me will be corrected in the next, annual edition. Strongly recommended to anyone going abroad, especially to the Third World.

CHARLES S. HOUSTON, M.D.

Climbing in the Adirondacks: A Guide to Rock and Ice Routes in the Adirondack Park. Second Edition. Don Mellor. The Adirondack Mountain Club, Inc., Lake George, N.Y., 1988. 318 pages, illustrations, charts, route diagrams, map, bibliography. $24.95.

The Adirondack Mountains in upstate New York are the centerpiece of a vast preserve, the largest in the country outside of Alaska. The preserve is a patchwork of public and private lands, small towns and large tracts of wilderness. Dispersed within this area is one of the most extensive, most attractive, and least visited climbing areas in the Northeast.

Despite a history of rugged mountain exploration dating back well into the last century, with the first "technical" climbs occurring in the first decades of this one, and despite a wealth of excellent cliffs and superb climbs, the Adirondacks have managed to be left somewhat out of the mainstream of climbing in the region. This is probably because they are just that much farther from the major population centers, the harsher weather and legendary black flies. The climbing invariably seems to be less tame and more demanding than it is in more popular areas and thus has not attracted more than a handful of devotees.

For a long time, there was strong resistance to the publication of a guidebook to the area. The locals feared that the cliffs would be overrun. Well, it didn't happen. The first guidebook appeared in 1967, followed by another in 1976. Don Mellor published his first guide in 1983, with a supplement a couple of years later. Now we have Don's newest and excellent offering, which like the previous guides have plenty to lure people from the Gunks or New Hampshire. Not only does the book provide almost up-to-date information on the better-known crags, such as Pok-O-Moonshine, Chapel Pond and Pitchoff, but it also includes first-time descriptions of many newly-developed cliffs throughout the area. Don made a decision to include only those areas on public land (with just a few exceptions), thereby excluding several of the best cliffs. The guide reveals that the locals, and a few visitors, have been very active. Numerous new routes have been done, often of very high quality and many of considerable difficulty.

All this activity, on ice as well as rock, has been chronicled with reasonable accuracy. There are undoubtedly some errors in route descriptions, and even a few concerning the best way to reach some of the rocks, but that is to be expected in a guide of such wide geographic scope and is in line with the wilderness skills required by the area. The crag photos are adequate. The grading appears to be relatively consistent, though undoubtedly anomalies exist. Quality ratings, a common feature of most modern guides, is done by means of a "✔" next to recommended routes. This is the most subjective part of any guide, and I must admit surprise that several of my personal favorites, such as Slim Pickins on the Spider's Web and Touch of Class on Moss Cliff, were not amongst those recommended.

In his introduction, and often in the text, Don makes a strong plea to maintain the wilderness ethic of Adirondack climbing. He exults in the behind-the-times feel of much of the Adirondack climbing experience and urges that the march of progress be tempered by a desire to keep this area unique. Yet he displays some ambivalence here, an ambivalence shared by many of the locals, when he acknowledges the quality and difficulty of some of the few recent routes put up by modernist methods of rappel and power bolting. In the end, his message is that what has been done is enough, but no more. This philosophy appeared to have general acceptance within the local climbing community. Unfortunately, since his book was published, some vehemently anti-modernists have chopped bolts on these routes, eliminating some put up by traditional methods in the process, and damaging the cliffs and the climbing experience far more than did the bolts themselves. It is a reflection of the changing times in our sport and deep ethical divisions among climbers that even a wonderful backwater like the "Daks" cannot be spared the negative fallout.

AL RUBIN

Front Range Bouldering. Bob Horan. Chockstone Press, Denver, 1989. 196 pages, numerous maps, diagrams and black and white photos. $11.95.

Most good climbers are good boulderers, but there are a few exceptions. Tobin Sorenson, the best climber of the Seventies, claimed he could not boulder, but he never really applied himself to it. He lacked the patience to spend weeks on a problem. Also, perhaps it just was not exciting enough to climb so close to the ground: Tobin was at his best when in mortal danger.

For me, nothing compares to the satisfaction of completing an intricate route on a boulder after working through the usual progression. At first, there is the questionable conception of the route, followed by tentative pulls on the initial holds. Then comes the training of the muscles to adapt body to the rock and the laborious assembling of individual moves into a smooth sequence. Finally, there is the supreme moment. The mental and physical practicing pays off and the body finally is able to realize what the mind had long before foreseen.

In light of the important part that bouldering plays in most climber's regimens, one would think that there would be more guides devoted to bouldering areas. Often, there is a short mention of adjacent bouldering in the back of a climbing guide, but nothing more. Pat Ament did a comprehensive bouldering guide to Flagstaff Mountain a few years back, but bouldering has never been taken seriously by writers of guides.

Perhaps this new guide by Bob Horan seriously signals a trend to better guidebook coverage of bouldering. The guide describes a number of fine areas near Denver and Boulder, Colorado, including Horsetooth, Morrison, Eldorado Canyon and Flagstaff, as well as a few lesser known areas. Horsetooth reservoir, near Fort Collins, is the best. Its Dakota sandstone is ideal–like fine-grained sandpaper for maximum adhesion, yet smooth enough so that it does not rip the fingertips on dynamic moves. And what dynamics there are! Gill established the standard here 25 years ago and the frequent flyer could not ask for a better variety of aerial moves.

Morrison, near Denver and just off Interstate 70, has similar rock and is almost as good. The prettiest setting is Flagstaff Mountain, which overlooks Boulder. Its red sandstone boulders are strewn among a pine forest with a view ranging from Boulder in the foreground, across the plains toward Kansas. On a clear day, this makes for an idyllic setting. Unfortunately, the rock does not have the quality of Horsetooth—it's too rough and holds occasionally break here.

The guide uses a birds-eye view format which makes for ease in locating the boulders, but it could use a few more photos or drawings of the rocks from a side view. Sometimes, many different routes are close together and regular topo format would be an improvement. The guide is a valuable addition to any boulderer's library and any climber's trip to climb in Colorado should reserve some time to visit these areas.

ERIC ACCOMAZZO

Boulder Climbs South. Richard Rossiter. Chockstone Press, Denver, 1989. 411 pages, numerous maps, diagrams and black and white illustrations. $25.00.

Two new guidebooks to Boulder, Colorado by Richard Rossiter have recorded the new route bonanza caused by the fall of traditional ethics under the assault of retrobolting. Boulder Climbs North covers the granite crags of Boulder Canyon and one half of the Flatirons, the tilted sandstone slabs that form the backdrop for the city of Boulder. The other half of the Flatirons and Eldorado Canyon are the subject of Boulder Climbs South.

Whatever your feelings on current climbing style (or the lack of it), it must be admitted that the new bolted routes make accessible some marvelous areas of rock and thousands of feet of great climbing that otherwise would be available only to top-roping. The holds are rough sandstone and generally very sound. Most of the new routes are well protected at a difficulty of 5.11 and harder, but the guide is conscientious in pointing out the exceptions where the bolts have been more widely spaced and the lead is "sporting" in the current argot, that is, scary. An incidental benefit of the flurry of new routes is that some of the pressure on El Dorado has been eased as climbers have flocked to the Flatirons, where there are vertical acres of crackless, but featured, sandstone faces and the setting, overlooking Boulder, is gorgeous.

Unfortunately, there is trouble in this paradise. The land managers have recently announced bans on bolts in both El Dorado (a state park) and the Flatirons (a Boulder city park). You may recall that one of the arguments against retrobolting was that it would make new routes too easy: anyone with a power drill and a vacant stretch of rock could achieve the status of route pioneer and get his or her name in print. This prediction has now come true and the sheer numbers of routes have caused the rangers to take notice. They do not like what they see. The bolting ban in the Flatirons arose after climbers bolted faces right next to a popular trail and hikers complained about the drilling and the little metal things left in the rock. Had a little discretion been shown and climbers stayed away from trails, the issue might have lain dormant for years.

The outcome of the controversy is still in doubt. The Flatirons Rangers state simply that bolting is defacement of the park resources and refuse to consider any compromise, such as zoning areas of permitted bolting, requiring a set distance between routes, or trying to camouflage the bolts to minimize the visual impact. The El Dorado Rangers have at least formed an advisory committee of climbers and are listening to suggestions, but the days of new sport climbs may be over in Boulder.

ERIC ACCOMAZZO

PLATE 56

JAMES MONROE THORINGTON
1894-1989

In Memoriam

JAMES MONROE THORINGTON
1894-1989

James Monroe Thorington, born in Philadelphia on October 7, 1894, died in nearby Germantown on November 29, 1989, at the age of 95. Roy, as his friends called him, was not only a distinguished opthalmologist, writer and collector of folk art, but one of the greatest friends of the American Alpine Club, which he joined in 1918. A member for 64 years, he had much to do with its growth. A resourceful editor of the *American Alpine Journal* from 1934 to 1946, and a long-time member of the Council (now known as the Board of Directors), he served as President during the war years of 1941-43 and was made an Honorary Member in 1949.

His ancestry can be traced to the English Bulkeley family, which stems from the Lord of the Isles and William the Conqueror. His grandfather, who joined a fur company out of St. Louis in 1837 and spent two years on the Western Plains, became United States Senator from Iowa and was American Consul on the Isthmus of Panama during the French administration. His father, James Thorington, served as surgeon of the Panama Railroad during this period before coming to Philadelphia.

Roy graduated from Princeton University in 1915, received his M.D. at the University of Pennsylvania in 1919 and after residency at the Presbyterian Hospital, began the practice of opthalmology. During 1917, he worked at the American Ambulance Hospital, Neuilly-sur-Seine, France. For six years he was Instructor in Opthalmology at the University of Pennsylvania. He edited two editions of this father's *Methods of Refraction*, and wrote papers on medical research and history.

Two summers of his youth, spent in the Bavarian Highlands, aroused his interest in mountaineering, a sport which dominated his avocational life. Fifteen seasons were spent in the Canadian Northwest, during which he explored much of the Alberta-British Columbia watershed between Mount Assiniboine and Robson, making some 50 first ascents, including Mounts Barnard, Lyell, Saskatchewan and North Twin, the latter being the highest summit entirely in Alberta. He also visited the Interior Ranges of British Columbia, with five seasons in the Purcell Range. A peak in the Purcells now bears his name. Many of the names of peaks suggested by him were accepted by the Geographic Board of Canada. He was the author of *The Glittering Mountains of Canada* (1925), *The Purcell Range of British Columbia* (1946) and the translator and editor of Conrad Kain's *Where the Clouds Can Go* (1935). He also wrote the standard guidebooks of the Canadian Rockies and the Interior Ranges of British Columbia, both of which have gone through several editions.

He climbed and traveled in the Alps as well, and he was familiar with the major groups between the Dauphiné and the Gross Glockner. He wrote *Mont*

Blanc Sideshow (1932) and *A Survey of Early American Ascents in the Alps* (1943). A list of his historical and other papers, issued in 1967, contained more than 275 titles. He also made ascents in the English Lake District, Norway, Swedish Lapland and Sicily.

In Canada and the Alps, he made a few guideless ascents, but usually he climbed with guides. These included Eduard and Ernst Feuz, Alfred Streich, Peter Kaufmann and Josef Biner. Conrad Kain climbed with him for five seasons.

Roy married Christine Rehn of Philadelphia in 1925. They were a devoted couple who over the years traveled extensively in Europe and also in Central and South America, North Africa and the Middle East.

Roy had a great interest in the running and decor of the Clubhouse of the American Alpine Club. He gave generously to the library and regularly traveled from Philadelphia to New York to attend monthly gatherings or teas, often showing his excellent slides. His exhibits in the Club Museum were often of museum calibre. After he stopped active climbing, he took to painting and would often present an oil painting of a mountain to someone who had climbed it.

Dr. Thorington was a member of the German-Austrian Alpine Club, the Swiss Alpine Club, the French Alpine Club and the Mazamas. He was made an Honorary Member of the Alpine Club of Canada in 1945 and of the Alpine Club (London) in 1946. He held other honorary memberships and was also a Fellow of the Royal Geographical Society. He edited the *Bulletin of the Geographical Society of Philadelphia* for nine years and also served as Honorary Trustee of the International Folk Art Foundation of Santa Fe, New Mexico, to whom he left his extensive collection of Alpine folk art.

Roy's guidebooks to the Canadian mountains have served thousands of climbers. On many subjects he was always interesting and informative. Few members have been involved with mountains in so many ways and few have done so much for the American Alpine Club.

ROBERT H. BATES

YUKO MAKI
1894-1989

The American Alpine Club lost a distinguished honorary member on May 2, 1989 when Yuko Maki died from a heart ailment in Tokyo. He had been an Honorary Member since 1959.

Yuko Maki was born on February 5, 1894 at Sendai, Miyagi Prefecture, Japan. In 1917, he graduated with a degree in law from Keio University in Tokyo. He studied at Columbia University in 1918 and in 1919 he continued his studies in England at the British Museum. He became interested in mountain climbing in 1914 and joined the Japanese Alpine Club that same year. From 1919 to 1921 he made many excellent ascents in Switzerland. The most notable of these was the first ascent of the difficult Mittellegi Ridge on the Eiger. In 1922 he made the first winter ascent of Yarigatake. He made many ascents in 1923 and 1924 with Prince Chichibu in the Japanese Alps.

In 1925, he was the leader of a group from the Japanese Alpine Club, sponsored by Marquis (later Count) Mori Tatsu Hosokawa. Six Japanese and three Swiss guides succeeded in making the first ascent of Mount Alberta in the Canadian Rockies. They were said to have left on the summit a silver ice axe. The peak was not climbed again until 1948, when John Oberlin and Fred Ayres retrieved the ice axe. It was not made of silver but there were the intitials MTH engraved in gold leaf in its tip. In 1926, with Prince Chichibu he enjoyed climbing around Zermatt, including the ascent of the Matterhorn.

In 1956, at the age of 62, Yuko Maki led the fourth Japanese expedition to Manaslu. After three previous unsuccessful tries, his expedition made the first ascent, placing two teams on the summit.

When he returned to Japan from Europe in 1921, he brought with him not only various kinds of improved new mountaineering equipment but also advanced climbing techniques. He was one of the most influential motive powers of mountaineering in Japan. We cannot forget his kind instruction and his fair, warm personality.

He received many awards. He was an honorary member of the Alpine Club, American Alpine Club, Swiss Alpine Club, Japanese Alpine Club and Japanese Mountaineering Association. He was president of the Japanese Alpine Club from 1944 to 1946 and from 1951 to 1955 and of the Japanese Mountaineering Association from 1967 to 1969. He was given the award of Person of Cultural Merits in 1956.

ICHIRO YOSHIZAWA

OME DAIBER
1907-1989

The "Father of Mountain Rescue," Ome Daiber, died on April 2, 1989 in his 81st year. A member of the American Alpine Club since 1937, he was made an honorary member in 1976.

The story goes that young George Daiber went to the lunch counter in grade school and said to the cashier, "Owe me 25 cents so I can buy lunch." The tale went all over school, and soon George was signing all his homework "Ome." Later he had his name officially changed.

As an outgrowth of his interest in mountain equipment, with friends he founded Ome Daiber, Inc. and began producing a long line of equipment, much of it based on his own inventions and patents. These included the two-legged "Penguin" sleeping bag, the 29-point "Birdcage" crampon, one of the first with front points, "Sno-Seal," a waterproofing compound for boots which is still on the market, special ski mits for grasping the rope tows of the 30s, windproof parkas, a strong, string-laced packboard and the "Pak Jacket," a sturdy coat with a large rear pocket and built with packstraps for converting the coat to a rucksack. His prolific inventiveness resulted in a string of several dozen patents.

In 1935 Ome was invited by Brad Washburn to join the National Geographic Society's Yukon Expedition to map North America's last blank spot on the

Alaska-Yukon border. The group also included Bob Bates, Ad Carter, Andy Taylor, Johnny Hayden and Hartness Beardsley. They spent several winter months exploring and surveying the region. They made some of the earliest flights across the St. Elias Range and the first overland journey across its glaciers to emerge on the coast at Nunatak Fiord. Upon his return to Seattle, Ome with Arnie Campbell and Jim Borrow made the first ascent of Liberty Ridge on Mount Rainier. This route, previously called "impossible," was not repeated for twenty years, though it is now today one of the most popular unguided routes on Rainier and is included in Roper and Steck's *Fifty Classic Climbs in North America*.

When Ome Daiber passed away, he was surrounded by his family. This unusual person of 81 years sadly did not have a befitting end to his great career. For five years he suffered immensely from diabetes, losing his eyesight and both legs and plagued by small strokes. As few patients in my memory, he never complained about his misfortune. All the time he looked to the future. Using artificial legs, his next aim was to climb Mount Si, and he convinced himself that this would be possible. Unfortunately, the condition of his ailments precluded his wish.

Ome was a man of strict moral standards, standards which he applied to his own life and expected in others. His standard of morality was not hypocritical. He lived by it. He saw things in black and white and had no doubts about them. He had an enormous sense of humor which helped him eliminate possible frictions. This was a quality that kept him from having enemies. Everybody respected and loved Ome Daiber. He was frank and clear in his relationships with other humans. He persuaded people to follow his way of thinking.

Ome's wry humor is illustrated by a story told by a dear friend: "When I first met Ome Daiber in 1975, our family was descending the trail from Gothic Basin as Ome and his wife Matie were hiking in. As only Ome could do, he took one look at our two-year-old daughter and gave her the ultimate Daiber compliment: 'Too bad you have such an ugly daughter.' Matie's 'Oh, Ome!' didn't slow him down a bit. Without a moment's pause, he looked at my wife and said, 'It obviously isn't your wife's fault.'"

Though not a college graduate, his influence in the Pacific Northwest was enormous. He was a practical outdoor expert. He was an advisor to the 10th Mountain Division during World War II and they made him an honorary member. He gathered many other honors. He became an Eagle Scout early in life. He was one of the founders of mountain rescue in the United States, a co-founder of the Mountain Rescue Council. He worked as a rescue man and rescue leader without hesitation all his life, beginning long before the Mountain Rescue Council was ever formed.

In the greatest rescue undertaken in Alaska, namely the successful rescue of John Day, Jim Whittaker, Lou Whittaker and Pete Schoening after they experienced a severe fall on their descent from Mount McKinley in which Day and Schoening were badly injured, Ome was the ground organizer in Talkeetna. Ome coordinated the efforts of the Navy and Army together with Mountain Rescue of Alaska, Washington and Oregon to effect the final rescue.

In Seattle, whenever a rescue was going on, Ome, together with Matie, coordinated it or was the party leader in the field. His personality was so well suited to ease the possible chances of difficulties between the different government agencies, the sheriffs, police, Park Service and others that smooth cooperation was assured. It was a great deal due to Ome's perfect contact ability that this cooperation became more and more solid. Today, Mountain Rescue organizations function all over the country in smooth, uninterrupted cooperation.

Ome's wife Matie, though keeping in the background, actually was indispensable for his timeless, unselfish efforts, as she coordinated the calling system for mountain rescue. Ome was always ready to drop everything, work or pleasure, to be available for mountain rescue activities. He was tireless. He was never able to refuse the cause.

Ome was dedicated to the education of young people in the mountains. He gave numerous talks. Very often I had the pleasure of joining with him in such educational efforts. Ome brought many others into rescue. The people who worked with him are those who will keep the organizations going, but they will never overshadow his fame and his initial efforts.

We have lost a wonderful friend. I admired Ome Daiber and with you mourn his passing.

OTTO TROTT, M.D.

DENTON FOX
1929-1988

Denton Fox was one of a small group of climbers, mostly from the Western states, who, by happenstance, found themselves attending Yale University in the late 1940s and early 1950s. Building on the skeletal remains of an organization inactive since the beginning of World War II, they rejuvenated the Yale Mountaineering Club. The Western contingent included Denny, Dick Merritt, Bill Fix, Zack Stewart, Boug Bolyard, the writer, and graduate students Larry Niesen and Dave Harrah. At its peak, about forty climbers participated.

In remembering Fox, as he preferred to be known, the collegiate years loom large. Building on his earlier experience in the Colorado Rockies and Europe, his most active mountaineering period was during the late 1940s and early 1950s. He had many fine climbs in the Rockies and Wind Rivers and was also a regular at the meccas of Eastern rock climbing, such as Shawangunks, Sleeping Giant, Quincy Quarries, ice climbing in Huntington Ravine and winter mountaineering on Mount Marcy and Katahdin.

Throughout this period, he emerged as one of the two or three figures who sustained Yale mountaineering in both spirit and substance. Fox was no stereotype student-cum-mountaineer. He was of slight physique, formal in manner and dressed, right down to the thoughtfully puffed pipe, as the professor of English and Medieval Literature he was to become. His university training through the Ph.D. was entirely at Yale and he taught there for four years before moving on to

Grinnell and then the University of Toronto, where he had an outstanding career, including a long stint as Chairman of a distinguished English Department.

Most of us from those early days remember Denny Fox for his droll humor and always sage counsel. But he also possessed that bit of madness that occasionally must surface if mountaineers are to succeed. I believe he treasured (as did his friends) those infrequent departures from his academic persona. Images leap to mind: Fox on Mount Washington's summit flats in 105 mile-per-hour winds, literally a horizontal airfoil at the end of a 35-meter rope and anchored to his partner's rock-encircling body; or Fox, the gleeful mastermind behind an insane February drive across Lake Champlain at three A.M. so that a single moment of daylight winter climbing in the Adirondacks wouldn't be missed. Not the great stuff of his serious mountaineering, but the wonderful flip side of a true intellectual and gentleman.

MELVIN MARCUS

ROBERT M. SCHWARZENBACH
1917-1988

Robert M. Schwarzenbach died on August 27, 1988 in Stamford, Connecticut. He was born in Jericho, New York and lived for some years as a youth near Zürich, Switzerland. He received a degree from the Federal Institute of Technology in Zürich.

In 1938, he was a member of the United States Ski Team in the World Championships. He climbed extensively in the Swiss Alps and also ascended the Cerro de la Encantada in Baja California in 1950. In 1951, he became a member of the American Alpine Club.

From 1952 to 1971 he was the chief executive officer of Schwarzenbach-Huber Co., a New York-based textile company, and continued as chairman of the board after the company's acquisition by Indian Head, Inc. He was a trustee and treasurer of the Maritime Center in Norwalk, Connecticut, which he had helped to found.

He is survived by his wife Brigitte, his son Peter, three daughters, Elizabeth DiLeo, Jessica and Sybyl Schwarzenbach, and three grandchildren.

W. RYLAND HILL
1912-1988

Ryland Hill, an American Alpine Club member since 1961, died on December 22, 1988. He was Dean Emeritus of the College of Engineering at the University of Washington in Seattle. He had also served in UNESCO as chief of their educational program in Africa and had supervised the allocation of U.S. State Department money to improve graduate education in both South Korea and India.

Ryland's climbing career spanned more than three decades, starting before World War II in the Sierra Nevada and continuing in the Cascades and Olympics for many years. He was also active in The Mountaineers but he climbed little in the last decade of his life.

GEORGE R. SAINSBURY

HASSLER WHITNEY
1907-1989

With the death of Hassler Whitney on May 10, 1989, the Club has lost one of the best known early climbers on the American scene and one of its most distinguished scientific members. Hassler was a friend to many of us who were active rock climbers in New England in the twenties and thirties. He has now become a byword to the present-day climbers in the region through his association with the Whitney-Gilman route on Cannon Mountain, of which he made the first ascent in 1930 with his cousin Bradley B. Gilman, who was later to become a president of the Club.

He was born in New York City on March 23, 1907. He attended Yale from which he graduated with a PhB in 1928 and a MusB in 1929, which reflect his two interests: logical thought and music. He was an accomplished performer on the violin and the viola. He went on to obtain a PhD in mathematics at Harvard in 1932 and followed that interest for the rest of his life. He continued his career at Harvard, serving as Instructor of Mathematics from 1932 to 1935 while doubling as tutor from 1933 to 1935, then becoming Assistant, Associate and finally full Professor from 1946 to 1952. That latter year he left Harvard to take the post of Professor at the Institute for Advanced Studies at Princeton, from which he retired as Professor Emeritus in 1977.

Hassler had an active family life, marrying Margaret Howell in 1930, with whom he had three children: James Newcomb, Carol and Marion. In 1955, he married Mary Garfield, and they had two children: Sarah Newcomb and Emily Baldwin. After her death, he married Barbara Osterman, by whom he is survived.

He developed early an interest in mountaineering, starting at the age of 14 with the ascents of the Breithorn, the Cime de l'Est of the Dents du Midi, and the Combin de Corbassière. The next year he returned to the Alps and started climbing without guides. He continued returning to the Alps every few years, doing guideless climbs in the Chamonix district, the Pennines and the Bernese Oberland. In 1934, he climbed the Grand Teton, but he seemed to prefer the Alps for his climbing recreation.

Hassler was not only highly regarded but very distinguished in his field of mathematics. With his perceptive mind, he developed many new lines of thought and ideas in that field. He was a Fulbright exchange professor at the Collège de France in 1957 and received several honorary degrees and special awards and honors from scientific societies. Despite the eminence of his status as a mathematician, he was a very modest and unassuming person whom we shall greatly miss.

KENNETH A. HENDERSON

RUTH DYAR MENDENHALL
1912-1989

Ruth Eleanor Dyar was born on August 16, 1912 in Kiesling, Washington, a farming hamlet near Spokane. Her father, Ralph, was a newspaper executive and playwright. Her maternal grandparents, who had emigrated from southern Germany, had founded Kiesling. Ruth's love of the outdoors developed during her early years on hikes in the hills near her family's farm. As a child, she learned that she loved climbing anything available—trees in her grandfather's orchard, the farm buildings. When her family moved to Spokane after the war, she continued to climb on a neighborhood basalt outcrop.

Ruth attended the University of Washington with a major in journalism, graduating *magna cum laude*. Although she hoped for work in her field, professional jobs were scarce. She soon moved to California because she was offered secretarial work there, but she was very lonely in her first years away from home. She frequently wrote to family and friends, beginning a lifelong tradition as a correspondent.

Ruth joined the Sierra Club in 1937 and began going on outings with the Ski Mountaineers section. She first encountered rock climbing in the spring of 1938 when most of the ski mountaineers switched to climbing for the summer. Technical climbing had recently begun in California. There were six routes on Tahquitz Rock, and Ruth did them all. She was one of a party of five that made the first ascent of the Swiss Arête on Mount Sill. There were two experienced climbers and three neophytes: two young men and Ruth. The male beginners felt extremely insecure on the exposed ridge and never climbed again, but Ruth was thrilled by the climbing and the altitude.

Ruth was one of six who established a cooperative climbers' residence, "Base Camp," in 1939. A mixed group of young people living together in a big house was a concept far ahead of its time. For the residents, Base Camp was like the home and family most of them missed. At this time, Ruth developed her lifelong interest in outdoor journalism, serving as editor of *Mugelnoos*, the spirited and irreverent newsletter of the Sierra Club's Ski Mountaineers and Rock Climbing Sections during its first four years. She later served on the Sierra Club's editorial board in 1940 and 1941.

Ruth met John Mendenhall, a structural engineer, in 1938 at the base of Tahquitz Rock. They were married in Van Nuys on September 22, 1939. They climbed extensively in California before World War II. They made first ascents of Monument Peak in the southern California desert, a route on Strawberry Peak in the San Gabriels, and Mount Whitney's southeast face. In 1940, they went to the Canadian Rockies to attempt unclimbed Mount Confederation. The approach went twenty miles through an untracked forest of deadfalls. Although they reached the mountain, bad weather prevented an ascent.

With the advent of World War II, John was transferred to defense industries in the East. In some areas, the Mendenhalls could make practice climbs on local cliffs. They managed one trip from Alabama to the Tetons in 1944. Ruth wrote, "It was good to be in that high, clean beautiful country. . . . It was so fine to be *on top* again." They made several climbs, including the first ascent of the west face of Teewinot.

When Ruth and John returned to southern California after the war, they resumed climbing. In 1948, they pioneered the route which is now the standard on the Lower Cathedral Spire in Yosemite. They also returned to Canada. In 1947, they made the first ascent of Mount Confederation. In 1952, they completed the first ascent of Aiguille Peak.

After the war, the Mendenhalls' interests also centered on their family: Vivian and Valerie. For a few years, Ruth and John alternated in attending weekend climbs. However, the children soon accompanied them on hikes and later on backpacking trips. They taught the girls to be at home in the mountains. Good judgment was learned from example and anecdote as much as from formal teaching.

In 1957, they pioneered the first route on the north face of Mount Williamson in the Sierra Nevada, whose approach is among the most arduous. There were many other pioneering ascents in the Sierra, the Palisades and Minarets. Ruth fulfilled a personal goal of climbing all the 14,000-foot peaks in California.

Ruth remained active in journalism until late in her life. After the war, she resumed the editorial leadership of *Mugelnoos* and was chairman of the editorial committee until 1978. She also contributed occasional articles to outdoor magazines. In 1966, she published her first book, *Backcountry Cookery*. Ruth believed that beginners would enjoy the mountains best if they learned simple and practical techniques and kept their sense of humor. The next year, she published *Backpack Techniques*, which was based on the same philosophy as its predecessor. In 1969, *Introduction to Rock and Mountain Climbing* was published with John as co-author. In the 1970s, in response to new technologies such as chocks and freeze-dried food, Ruth produced second editions of all three books. In 1983, a third edition of *Introduction* was published under the title of *The Challenge of Rock and Mountain Climbing*. In 1982, she co-authored *Gorp, Glop and Glue Stew*, a facetious collection of outdoor recipes. From 1978 to 1981, she was editor of the *American Alpine News*.

The Mendenhalls joined the American Alpine Club in 1966. Ruth served on the Board of Directors from 1974 to 1980. She was on the Membership Committee in 1976 and its Chairman from 1977 to 1980.

In 1978, when John retired, the couple bought a house in Seattle. Before they left California, the Sierra Club honored them with the Farquhar Award for achievement and leadership in mountaineering. They were also interviewed by the club's Oral History Project and received honorary memberships in the Rock

Climbing Section. In 1983, the American Alpine Club presented them with the Angelo Heilprin Citation for service to the Club and to mountaineering.

Ruth Dyar Mendenhall died suddenly on March 22, 1989 after a brief illness with the flu. She requested that her ashes be scattered near John's at a special spot in the mountains. Throughout her life, with all her pleasure in people, her home and her writings, she felt, as she expressed at the end of her first book, "The peaks, the snows, the ink-black skies; the waters, winds and wild flowers; the trails and campfires—all will call you back."

VIVIAN MENDENHALL

ED LINK
1914-1989

Ed (Hazel E.) Link, an AAC member since 1945, died of cancer in Seattle on April l4, 1989. He was 74. Hiking and skiing trips with his Boy Scout troop provided Ed's first mountain experiences when he was in his early teens. Later, with friends from scouting, he began to explore the summits of these mountain ranges. Ed was one of America's skiing pioneers. A member of the Sahale Ski Club in the 30s, he was an active competitor in races sponsored by it and other early ski and outdoor clubs, including the legendary Silver Skis Race from Camp Muir to Paradise on Mount Rainier.

During his military career, he made significant contributions to mountaineering and skiing. Here his path crossed or joined for a time that of many members from those communities. Drafted into the Army in 1941, he was commissioned as a second lieutenant in 1942 and served in a tank unit commanded by General George S. Patton. Because of his background, he was reassigned to the 87th Mountain Infantry Regiment. He was soon in charge of a succession of climbing and skiing schools at Mount Rainier, Mount Hale, Colorado, and Seneca Rocks, West Virginia.

In 1943, he commanded an American detachment to the Mountain School Central Mediterranean Forces in Italy. He served with the 10th Mountain Division from 1944 through to the end of the war. In 1945 he was the Winter Sports Officer for the European Theater, establishing winter sports programs for U.S. occupation troops. While in Italy, he climbed a new route on the Gran Sasso and made the first ascent of Corno Piccolo. After leaving the service as a major in 1947, he worked as a civilian sports director for the Army's Garmisch Recreation Center. In 1948, he provided skiing expertise for CBS radio coverage of the St. Moritz Olympics.

Ed was recalled to active duty in 1951 and placed in charge of rock-climbing training at Fort Carson, Colorado. As a lieutenant colonel, he saw tours of duty in Korea and in Japan, where he established the Mountain and Cold Weather Training Command. He also coordinated the preparation and publishing of the U.S. Army Skiing Manual. Ed returned to the Alps in 1958 and climbed the Matterhorn. After four years of ROTC work at the Wentworth Military

Academy, Wentworth, Missouri, he spent a year as a military advisor in South Vietnam. In 1962, Ed received what was to be his last military assignment as deputy post commander of the Yakima Firing Center. Here he was able to resume mountaineering and skiing, not only recreationally, but also as an instructor and a competitor, in the mountains of his youth.

Immediately after Ed's retirement from the military in 1966, Governor Dan Evans (AAC) selected him for the position of Washington State Civil Defense Director with the additional responsibility of supervising the establishment of a state-wide search-and-rescue program. From 1968 to 1980, he was president and general manager of the Crystal Mountain Ski Resort; he helped bring a World Cup event there in 1972. Ed continued to be active in ski racing in retirement. He served as technical director for FIS World Cups, taught FIS technical delegate symposia, was a three-time national champion in veteran racing and placed in international competition. He received numerous recognitions from ski professional organizations.

Ed is survived by his wife Eddi (Edna), two sisters and a brother, three daughters, a son from a previous marriage and two grandchildren. His son Robert climbed Kangchenjunga in 1989.

FRED C. STANLEY

EINAR NILSSON
1901-1989

Einar Nilsson, a retired electrical engineer, died of pneumonia on December 13, 1989, aged 88. He was born in Malmö, Sweden, and for forty-four years worked for the Pacific Gas and Electric Company before retiring in 1966. For the past eighteen years, he lived in Carmel, California.

During World War II, Einar worked in the Special Forces Section of the Military Planning Division of the Office of the Quartermaster General, where he was extremely resouceful and popular. A big man, with black hair, flashing eyes and an eager grin, Einar was always imaginative, practical and ready to help others. As a valuable member of the Alaskan Test Expedition of 1942, he made the third ascent of Mount McKinley while testing Army clothing and equipment. His ingenuity was continually proved on this expedition. On one occasion high on the mountain when an extra pair of snowshoes was needed, he *made* snowshoes from scraps of wood and extra shoelaces. Einar's love of wild country and the mountains was very basic to his character.

He joined the American Alpine Club in 1943. He was a life member of the American Institute of Electrical Engineers, of the Sierra Club and the Save-the-Redwoods League and a member of the photographic workshop of the Carmel Foundation.

His wife Annie survives him, as well as his daughter Cece Waldron and two grandchildren.

ROBERT H. BATES

LOUIS SAMUEL STUR
1924-1989

Do not go gently into that good night,
Old Age should burn and rave at close of day;
Rage, rage against the dying of the light.
                                        —Dylan Thomas

Everyone has a Louis Stur story. There's the one about two old climbers resting on the trail listening patiently as two younger climbers raved on about the route they'd just climbed on Mount Heyburn, the Stur-Ball route. Wild-eyed, they spoke passionately of Stur's lead up the chimney in 1958, one of the many classic routes he put up in the Sawtooths of Idaho during a climbing career of nearly four decades in the area. The old men let the boys ramble on before introducing themselves. Unknowingly, the boys were recounting their adventure for the men who had put up the route years before, Stur and Ball. The timely, delayed introduction was not an attempt to embarrass the young men. Doubtless Louis was enjoying himself, delighted by the climbers' enthusiasm for a fine line. It was the same enthusiasm, excitement and appreciation he'd come to know, enjoy and maintain for an entire lifetime, a lifetime of mountaineering.

Louis Stur's rewards from climbing were derived less from expanding the technical horizons of the day than from the fulfillment he gained simply by being in the mountains. He found pleasure in working with the stone. He enjoyed landscapes and wildlife as much as summits. He wasn't a conqueror of mountains; his love for the mountains was too deep for that. Rather than tread upon them, he chose to climb among them. Setting his eyes on Mount Heyburn in the early days, he reflected in a 1975 *Off Belay* interview that "it's such an impressive, beautiful mountain that I thought it deserved some nice routes," as if seeking to give the mountain something in return for its beauty. He went on to say, "It's the fascination of pioneering the mountains. You look at some climb and . . . it might go, it might not. Once you describe it by a decimal, part of the fascination is lost." In 1959 he wrote in the *American Alpine Journal* about his beloved Sawtooths, saying, "Though the principal peaks have been climbed, we set ourselves the modest task of discovering the best and the most enjoyable routes." He and his climbing partners became responsible for the development in the Sawtooths following a period of relative dormancy in the previous decades.

Although he had traveled widely in his sixty-five years, including visits to Africa, Patagonia, New Zealand, China, Tibet, Nepal and the Alps, he found the great mountains and the great climbs right at home. He was content to grab a local partner, or to climb solo, and explore his own adopted backyard, the Sawtooths of Idaho, which caught his eye on a visit to Sun Valley in 1951. That visit lasted the thirty-eight remaining years of his life.

As the Russians invaded his homeland of Hungary, Louis left his family, friends and the nearby Alps where he had learned to climb, ski and appreciate the mountains' offerings. Prior to leaving, he had earned a two-year law degree and was graduated summa cum laude with a degree in commerce. He continued his studies in Austria, following his exodus from Hungary, in diplomacy and international commerce and went on to study economics as well. His educational excellence earned him passage to the United States via a scholarship offered by the University of Nebraska, which became his springboard to Idaho, Sun Valley and most significantly, the Sawtooths.

While working on his doctorate in economics, he and a few friends journeyed out West in the winter of 1951. He intended to return to Nebraska the following summer but found himself working as a night clerk in a hotel and spending what came to be an endless summer in Sun Valley. He worked his way through the ranks and became director of the Sun Valley Hotels. He was considered by many as the ambassador of Sun Valley due to his endless charm, infectious generosity and genuine respect for manner and protocol.

His attraction to the Sawtooths was boundless and he went on to work out numerous new routes and winter ascents in a true pioneering spirit. His record of first ascents includes those found on Heyburn, Warbonnet, Rotten Monolith, Silicon Tower, Hyndman and Devil's Bedstead to name just a few. The mountains, indeed, were a source of inspiration to Louis, for even in the worst of times he went there for fulfillment. For example, following the tragic loss of his recently wed wife, he sought solace on Mount Heyburn where he mounted a plaque in her memory and then tossed the wedding ring into Redfish Lake never to marry again. He continued to visit the spot over the remaining twenty-six years, shedding light on the romance and passion of Louis Stur. This type of action lives in the minds of those close to him. A friend quoted in Ketchum's *Wood River Journal* said, "You've got a man who in 65 years of living had done more and touched more people than most could have done in 150 years."

In addition to mountaineering, he pursued interests in piano, accordion, French and traveling around the globe. He was fond of reading and writing poetry, but his true passion, other than mountaineering, was for flying gliders. He began to fly at the age of 14, introduced the sport to Sun Valley and enjoyed it worldwide, having once soared above the Great Rift Valley of Kenya.

Louis came to rest at the base of Mount Ebert in the heart of the Sawtooths. His camera film was developed after the fall and displayed a complete panorama; Louis had been to yet another summit that day. Louis was climbing alone so the details of his fall will remain a mystery.

Louis Stur will fade, as do all, into distant memory, but it is certain that he will never be forgotten. A movement is being initiated to name a local peak in his honor and plans for his annual birthday climb were carried out with the ascent of Mount Heyburn, just as Louis had done for years with his friends. A plaque was erected in his honor and the summit dusted with his ashes.

Louis Stur's mountaineering accomplishments were bold and monumental but difficult to trace as he chose not to exploit his endeavors other than a simple accounting offered periodically to the *American Alpine Journal*. It was his style that left the lasting impression. He loved life, which was evident in the manner he chose to play his out. We should all benefit from his example and strive to keep pace throughout our own lives with his enthusiasm and love for the mountains and for mankind.

GREG WILSON

WILLIAM E. "SMOKE" BLANCHARD
1915-1989

It was a windy spring evening in the Owens Valley when James Wilson came striding toward me with that look, the "you never want to see" look, on his face. Smoke had been fatally injured in an automobile accident. Where? The Mojave Desert. When? Just coming home, via Los Angeles, from a holiday of rambling in the Italian Alps. It seemed that Smoke would always return from his far-flung travels to his little upstairs "treehouse" apartment on Willow Street in Bishop.

Smoke would return from one string of treks and expeditions only to prepare for yet another. During his hometown layovers, he would delight his many friends in the Eastern Sierra with truly wonderful tales of things he had seen and experienced on his travels through Nepal, Bhutan, Tibet, China, India, Siberia, Kenya, Mexico, Canada, Alaska, Japan, Japan, Japan. During the past few years, Smoke had taken to living about half the time in Japan, walking and scrambling through the Japanese Alps. His visits to Bishop became less frequent and time spent with him became precious.

Many of the best times with Smoke were "Buttermilking," scrambling often moderate fifth-class routes through the crags and boulder fields of the Buttermilk Country at the foot of the eastern escarpment of the Sierra Nevada. These outings were as intriguing as any wild overseas exploration because of Smoke's unique way of sharing his deep appreciation of nature, his practice of "Picnic and Pilgrimage." The stimulating combination of his intellectual observation and physical challenge, the enjoyment and pleasure of where you were, coupled with great respect and awe for the mountains and the wilderness, was tremendous.

Though Smoke was a best friend and frequent climbing partner of the late, legendary Norman Clyde and though he was a highly respected mountain guide, he steered clear of extreme alpinism or high-standard rock climbing, preferring what he termed "mild mountaineering." His standard of climbing was mild. The technical standard of the routes he tackled was never beyond moderate fifth class, what he call "3.9" with a smile. He applied a minimalist's equipment use and environmental impact ethic. During the early 1970s, while director of the Palisades School of Mountaineering, Smoke set a strong example and often gave stern lessons in respect for the wilderness, significantly influencing the climbing style and experience of hundreds of climbing students and dozens of mountain guides. His mild style by no means diminished the physical challenges he confronted. Rather than chase the numbers in the technical climbing game,

Smoke sought the great glorious feeling of moving through the splendor of the mountains and being there.

When Smoke told his stories, they were not so much of the where and what he and his companions had just done, but what they had seen, felt, learned and experienced. Smoke was such an inspired story teller that he became a teacher without trying. He was such a good teacher that you didn't know you were learning. It seemed like magic!

Though he had more than fifty years of climbing and world travel, not all of Smoke's life was so keen. As a long-haul trucker, he drove more than three million miles, adding to time away from home. Smoke lived on the thin line of risk and adventure rather than with responsibility and family. As long as he could get to the hills, walk along, looking, seeing, listening, thinking, sharing these simple joys with friends, life was as good as it could be.

JOHN FISCHER

MARCUS MORTON
1893-1989

Marcus Morton was born on August 13, 1893 in Newton Massachusetts, the third in the family to bear that name, the first being a distinguished governor of the Commonwealth. He attended Groton School and then Yale College, from which he graduated in 1916. He then entered the Harvard Law School but left in 1917 to serve in the U.S. Army in World War I. He left the service as a captain and retured to the study of law, receiving his LLD from Harvard in 1921. He immediately entered the practice of law with the firm of Herrick, Smith, Donald and Farley. He left to become Assistant District Attorney for two years, and at the end of that service, in 1927 he founded his own firm of Hale, Sanderson, Byrne and Morton, from which he retired in 1970.

In 1924, he married Margaret M. Miner and they had three children, Marian, Lea and Margaret. He took an active part in Cambridge affairs, serving on that city's Red Feather Agency, Recreation Commission, Civic Unity Commission and Council for Aging. He also served on the City Council from 1942 to 1945 and from 1954 to 1956.

Marcus was an avid traveler as well as a climber, and he visited much of Europe as well as climbing in this country and in Canada. Although he was never a continuously active mountaineer, he ascended many peaks in the Lake Louise and Lake O'Hara areas of the Canadian Rockies. He also participated in the first ascent of Mount French in the British Military Group in 1921. He always took a keen interest in the mountaineering activities of his friends and was always ready to use his legal expertise in solving the problems of the organizations to which he belonged. He was a most interesting person and we all regret his passing.

KENNETH A. HENDERSON

DONALD MASON WOODS
1903-1989

Teacher, climber, outdoorsman, photographer, world traveler, singer, actor, dancer, Donald Mason Woods died as a result of a freak accident on September 6, 1989. While alighting from his family pick-up truck in his own driveway, he was struck by the rear of a hatchback which hurtled across the small street, totalling the truck. Although helicoptered to the Washington Medical Center, he died from complications on September 20.

Don led a very eventful life, beginning with his birth in Cottage Grove, Oregon, on May 3, 1903. Educated in the Cottage Grove and Weiser, Idaho, schools, he earned his bachelor's degree at the University of Oregon. He taught school in Oregon, but soon moved as chemistry teacher to Spokane, where he married the biology teacher, Lynda Rosalia Mueller. The young couple returned to the University of Oregon, where Don completed his master's degree in chemistry. They moved on to San Jose, California, where they lived for more than 50 years. Don taught for many years at the San Jose High School and then in the Willow Glen High School.

Don always had a strong affinity for the outdoors and was both an inveterate mountain climber and a "desert rat." In the early 1930s, he was one of the first to climb Mount Robson and also was part of an unsuccessful assault on Mount Waddington. He continued to climb mountains almost all his life. In fact, he met Lynda at a Canadian Rockies mountain camp. He climbed several thousand mountains in the US, Canada, Mexico, Peru, Japan, Africa, New Zealand, Switzerland and Norway. He joined the American Alpine Club in 1930 and was a member of the Sierra Club, Mazamas, and the Alpine Club of Canada.

He was also active in the San Jose Light Opera Association. Don and Lynda were also inveterate folk dancers. An early pioneer in 35mm photography, he shot thousands of color slides of his frequent travels to the West of the United States, the entire nation and overseas.

He leaves a son, five granddaughters and two great-grandchildren.

DAVID LYNDON WOODS

HOWARD E. STANSBURY, JR.
1913-1989

Howard E. Stansbury, an American Alpine Club member since 1965, died on May 11, 1989 while on a cruise in the Caribbean. He was born in Ronan, Montana, and lived most of his life in Seattle and on Mercer Island. Surviving him are his wife Patricia, his daughter Kathryn Brown and his sons Michael, Howard III, Richard and Charles Stansbury.

A memorial service was held at The Mountaineers clubhouse in Seattle on May 17, the day on which he would have become 76 years of age. He was a long-time and dedicated member of The Mountaineers. He was a graduate of its basic and intermediate climbing courses. For many years he was on the Climbing Committee, serving for some time as the chairman, and was an instructor in both the basic and intermediate climbing courses. He was the first business manager of The Mountaineers from 1968 until he retired in 1981. He was active in the book publishing of The Mountaineers and contributed significantly to its becoming a successful enterprise. After his retirement, he was honored in 1982 by The Mountaineers' Service Award, given each year to the member who is deemed to have given the most outstanding service to the organization.

Howard ran a successful small business, the Stansbury Chemical Company. For ten years he was a member of the Mercer Island School Board, also serving a tour as president of that board. He was an outstanding Scout Master in his home community of Mercer Island for fifteen years. In his successful Scouting program, he counted more than 50 boys who became Eagle Scouts during his tenure. He was an avid outdoor leader, taking Boy Scouts into the wilderness and into the mountains as a major part of their Boy Scout experience.

Howard served as Chairman of the Cascade Section in 1977 and was a Councilor of the American Alpine Club from 1978 to 1981. He took great interest in the affairs of the Club. His untiring work and positive contributions have made a great difference to the community, to The Mountaineers and to the American Alpine Club.

JOHN M. DAVIS

SAMUEL FINLEY THOMAS, M.D.
1913-1989

Samuel Finley Thomas was born in Paris, France on October 2, 1913. He died in Salt Lake City on May 31, 1989. He received his A.B. from Princeton University in 1935 and his M.D. from the College of Physicians and Surgeons of Columbia University in 1940. During World War II, he served as a major in the Medical Corps of the U.S. Army Air Force. Dr. Thomas practiced medicine in New York City, specializing in neurology and psychiatry. He was on the staff of St. Luke's Hospital in New York from 1946 to 1975, when he retired as Director of the Neurology Division. He was a staff member of the Neurology Institute of New York City from 1975 to 1980. He was also a Professor of Neurology at the College of Physicians and Surgeons of Columbia University.

Dr. Thomas was an avid climber. He climbed extensively in the Alps and the Dolomites, where he made first ascents of the east face of the Campanile Adele and the west face of the Campanile Bettega. He also climbed in Washington and Oregon. But it was particularly in his beloved Wasach Mountains of Utah that he roamed to find spiritual strength. He joined the American Alpine Club in 1939.

He is survived by his wife Ruth, a daughter and a stepson.

NORMAN F. ROHN
1919-1989

I first teamed up with Norm Rohn during a Sierra Club trip to the Palisades over Labor Day in 1974. We climbed the rib between the two Underhill Couloirs and proceeded to the base of the impressive summit block of Thunderbolt Peak. It was a frustrating business getting the rope over the block and I missed the target countless times. My temper flared and Norm called out, "Peace on Earth!" I laughed, relaxed and made my last throw. The rope arched perfectly over the crest of the block.

Norm was the most complete sportsman I have ever known. He climbed all of the peaks on the Hundred Peaks, Desert Peaks and Sierra Peak lists (over 600 in all) in addition to the crags of Joshua Tree and many routes at Tahquitz Rock. He climbed in the Tetons and bagged the Devils Tower (after retirement!). He joined expeditions to Huascarán and Aconcagua and climbed Mexico's volcanoes. He served as a mountaineering instructor in the Sierra Club, and everyone benefited from his experience in the outdoors and in life, whether a beginner or expert in either field. His pack was not as large as that of the legendary Norman Clyde, but Norm could be called on to repair boots, reels, zippers, carabiners or stoves from the modest collection of tools he always carried. I remember his removing a fishhook from a dog's mouth at Sallie Keyes Lakes in 1985. Norm was an enthusiastic fisherman, and he stalked the lakes of the High Sierra for rainbows and goldens before and after bagging the peak or peaks of the day. He discovered *his* secret fishing lake one month before his death. Many of his friends will long remember his expertise as a hunter. One of his favorite activities was hunting desert deer. He visited almost every hot spring in the West. He was also a blue-water sailor, delivering yachts to California after their owners had vacationed in Mexico. Norm went everywhere, knew everything, could do anything and fix anything anywhere at any time.

Norm was born in Milwaukee and graduated from Phillips Exeter Academy, Cornell University and the Massachusetts Institute of Technology, where he received two Master's degrees. He was a mechanical engineer for the U.S. Navy at the Pacific Missile Test Center at Point Mugu, rising to the post of Chief Engineer of the Fleet Weapons Engineering Program. He was never confined to his desk during his career. His duties saw him leaping out of helicopters with frogmen and breaking the sound barrier on a routine basis with naval aviators. One of his regrets was that he never made it to Mach 2, but he did reach Mach 1.97 in an F-16 from 50,000 to 10,000 feet in vertical flight shortly before his retirement in 1981.

It was during retirement, however, that the depth and breadth of Norm's interests were revealed. On the conservation front, he was a member of the National Audubon Society, Desert Bighorn Society, served as chairman of the Los Padres Chapter of the Sierra Club, and was an active volunteer for the Nature Conservancy in the Anza Borrego Desert and on Santa Cruz Island. He worked as a volunteer for Food Share, gleaning surplus crops from the fields of Ventura

County and delivering them to the needy. Norm was an excellent gardener and a member of the Ventura County Orchid Society, Theodosia Burr Fuchsia Society and Begonia Society. He was a proud member of the American Alpine Club.

Norm and I had made plans for a peak-bagging and fishing trip to Lake Basin in the High Sierra last August. Norm, out in front as usual, asked for a rest break after two hours of hiking up the Taboose Pass Trail. He became uncomfortable and collapsed shortly after noon. Fifteen minutes of frantic effort failed to revive him. Gradually I realized that my good friend was gone. He will be missed by his mother Hazel, his wife Maggie, his children Kate, Lex, Carrie and Casey, grandchildren and many friends from all walks of life. Over a hundred were present to comfort each other in Norm's house and garden a week later. Memorial donations may be made in Norm's memory to the Nature Conservancy.

Peace on Earth!

ROBERT J. SECOR

RAYMOND C. GARNER
1913-1989

Ray Garner died after a short illness on July 20 at the age of 76. His untimely death cut short yet another adventure in his life. The following month, he and his wife Jinny were planning to return to the sites of early mountaineering successes in the Tetons and Brussels Peak in the Canadian Rockies.

Ray led a life of adventure accented with enthusiasm, energy and a spirit of exploring new frontiers. Over the years he excelled as a lecturer, photographer, teacher, pilot, writer and athlete. As a world-class mountaineer, Ray made many first ascents, including the north face of the Grand Teton, Brussels Peak and Agathlan in Monument Valley. He was the first American to reach the summit of Margherita Peak in Africa's Mountains of the Moon.

Ray retained his enthusiasm for the mountains throughout his life. His climbing career started in the early 1930s when he was climbing on the Palisades of the Hudson River with a braided clothesline. Here, by chance, he met the great Fritz Wiessner, who gave him the very best climbing instruction available. Ray went on to accomplish first ascents and a career in expedition photography.

In 1935, Ray and three friends from Brooklyn visited the Tetons. One can imagine the challenge, this being his first venture away from the Palisades. It was a successful outing; they climbed all ten major summits in the Tetons! Through the years Ray trained many young climbers, using the techniques of Fritz Wiessner coupled with his own experience and spirit of sharing. In the late 1930s, he taught climbing technique to Explorer Scouts in Brooklyn and in the 1940s to the Kachina Scouts in Arizona. He stressed safety and ethical behavior in the mountains as in life.

A good friend of the Garners, Glenn Exum writes, "I consider Ray and Virginia Garner to be two of the most talented people I have ever known. They were a team all through their lives and made many contributions to all of us. Ray was a talented photographer, writer, adventurer and athlete. I had the privilege of being one of the featured climbers in his film *The Mountain*, which was made on the Exum Ridge of the Grand Teton in 1946. Paul Petzoldt and Virginia Garner were the other two. That year we had an abundance of snow and blue skies, and while we were filming, the sky was filled with cumulus clouds. We were fortunate in being able to do the entire film in just two days on the mountain. Blessed with perfect light, Ray never had to pause because of poor light. He had a special talent for photographing interesting sequences and when he had finished, he had captured the subtle character of the Grand Teton. He had a great sense of humor and loved all facets of nature. He assisted us in our guiding, and he and Virginia shepherded the great Philharmonic conductor, Dimitri Metropoulis, up the Grand Teton. Ray said that experience opened up avenues in his later life that were unbelievable. Ray truly loved people. There was a contagious excitement about him, electricity in the air. "In 1946, he, Virgina and one of our Teton guides, Jeff Lewis, were preparing to go to Canada to attempt unclimbed Brussels Peak. Having heard that some Yosemite climbers were using expansion bolts, he secured a set and wanted to test them. He drilled a hole in one of the bolders near our Jenny Lake headquarters and fixed a bolt. To test it, he tied a nylon rope to the bumper of his car and attached it to a carabiner clipped into the eye of the bolt. The bolt held, but he pulled the bumper off his car. He said, 'Fellows, we are ready for Brussels!' They went off to Canada and made the climb. The world is a much better place because Ray Garner was here. He was a gentleman and we all loved him."

Ray served in the Army Air Force during World War II and earned several medals for flying missions "over the Hump." In 1962, he received the coveted Guild Award for Directorial Achievement for *The River Nile*, one of eight television documentary specials made for NBC. He also made several other films on Africa, ancient Egypt, classical Greece and the Holy Land.

In 1965, Ray and Jinny went to Idyllwild, California to make a movie film for the Idyllwild School of Music and Art. At the end of the filming Ray said, "This is home." They sold their home on the East Coast and moved to Idyllwild. "Ray wanted to live and die here," said Jinny, his wife for 51 years. In Ray's 25-year association with the school, his greatest contribution was his work with the Elderhostel program, a nationwide educational program for senior citizens. Ray took great delight in teaching and showing his films on ancient Egypt, Greece and Israel.

Ray is survived by his wife Virgina, his daughter Gaylen MacKintosh, his son James "Chip" Garner and four grandchildren. He leaves a legacy more important than his many accomplishments: his enthusiasm for life and people and the sharing of life's experiences and accomplishments. He touched many lives, an educator in the real sense. He will be missed.

RICHARD POWNALL

Club Activities

EDITED BY FREDERICK O. JOHNSON

A.A.C., Blue Ridge Section. Closing out the decade for the Blue Ridge Section, 1989 was another year of increased activity. It is showing re-emergence as the mid Atlantic representative of the A.A.C. Meeting more often than before, the Section planned to involve itself in several activities. As the Scots bard said, though, such plans gang aft a-gley. Poor climbing weather throughout much of the spring and summer prevented some climbing activities.

The biggest event was the sponsorship of *Springstone*, a climbing competition originally planned as a local event that ultimately drew climbers from around the country. Over 100 climbers competed on a four-sided artificial wall during an all-day event that drew nearly 1000 spectators. Despite many top climbers from elsewhere, the locals managed to garner top prizes in both men's and women's categories. The Blue Ridge Section would like to thank the many manufacturers who contributed to the event's success, as well as the staff and owners of Outdoor Provisionaries and REI, without whose help the event would never have proceeded.

The Section also sponsored two young climbers who participated in the British Youth Climbing Meet, held in Plas-y-Brenin, Wales. With the invaluable help of Jim Henriot of the International Climbing Exchange Committee, two D.C. area climbers experienced British rock at its best. Both Colin Seller and Erica Walters met new climbers and exchanged ideas about the sport and laid the foundation for future climbing exchanges.

As the Section moves into the 1990s, membership growth and Section activities continue to be the biggest focus. Starting in the spring, Section member and climbing-book author John Gregory has developed plans to coordinate with the National Forest Service a work project at the new climbers' campground at Seneca Rocks. Another *Springstone* may be in the works, as well as plans to coordinate activities with other Club Sections and Committees.

As always, visiting climbers are encouraged to get in touch with the Section. Contact either Stuart Pregnall (202-543-3988 home) or Tom Hood (703-830-3919 home). And bring your gear.

STUART PREGNALL, *Chairman*

A.A.C., Cascade Section. 1988 and 1989 were very good years for climbers in the Cascade Section. As usual, members participated in expeditions all over the globe, with particularly good results on both years on Kangchenjunga. Carlos Buhler has been very active on 8000-meter peaks, doing Kangchenjunga in 1988 and Cho Oyu in 1989. Lou Whittaker led a successful trip to Kangchenjunga in 1989.

The Section hosted Soviet climbers during the summer of 1988. They climbed in the Cascades and at Squamish and Smith Rock.

Programs hosted by the Section featured Steve Boyer on Annapurna's south face at the 1988 Section Banquet. Brownie Schoene told about a trip to China to attempt Kang Karpo or Meili in Yünnan. John Hessburg talked at the 1989 Rainier Brewery Night about his trip to Bolivia the previous summer.

Membership remains high and the Section continues its support of access problems. We are still exploring ways to reopen the Peshastin Pinnacles. An agreement was reached with the U.S. Forest Service to make it easier to get permits to climb at Snow Creek Wall. We look forward to the next decade of climbing challenges.

MICK HOLT, *Chairman*

A.A.C., Rocky Mountain Section. The activity of the Rocky Mountain Section continued to increase in 1989. Quarterly meetings were held in Denver, featuring slide shows by various Section members about their international climbing expeditions. In May, the annual Section Banquet was reinstituted with great success. Almost 100 Section members attended and were treated to slide shows by Bob Horan and George Lowe. Numerous local climbing shops donated prizes for a raffle to raise funds to support Section activities.

In August, a weekend outing was held in Rocky Mountain National Park in conjunction with the National Park Service. Section members spent Saturday morning picking up litter around the popular bivouac sites below the Diamond on Longs Peak. Just as members were returning from their chores to enjoy some cold beers brought in by Park Service llamas, they were asked by the Park Service to help evacuate a hiker injured at 13,000 feet on the north face of Longs. They assisted park rangers in stablizing the victim and carrying a litter down through rugged terrain and hard rain to a helicopter pick-up. Nobody picks up the litter like the Rocky Mountain Section.

The Section was also involved in numerous access issues in 1989. Working in conjunction with the Access Committee and Access Fund, issues were addressed which had to do with limestone climbing at Shelf Rock, ice climbing in Boulder Canyon, mountaineering activities in the Boulder Watershed and several other areas. Work on these and other access issues continues to be a top priority of the Section.

MICHAEL BROWNING, *Chairman*

A.A.C., Oregon Section. The principal activity for the Section in 1989, as it has been for the past several years, was the continuing Silcox renovation project. Our group raised over $50,000 for this renovation of the second ski-lift hut in the U.S. Silcox Hut, located at Mount Hood above Timberline Lodge, is on the National Historic Register and has been used by skiers and climbers since 1935.

ROBERT MCGOWN, *Chairman*

A.A.C., New York Section. Not every year is of vintage quality, but 1989 will surely rank as one of the most memorable in New York Section history. Our illustrated lectures continue a long tradition and give members the opportunity to hear outstanding speakers followed by a social hour where new friendships and climbing partners often are generated. The season featured three colorful and absorbing programs. Rick Sylvester, the well-known climber, raconteur, extreme skier and environmentalist discussed his "Climb of the Century," or the first ascent of a dry Yosemite Falls, plus his career as a sometime stuntman in James Bond films. Jon Waterman, a former McKinley Park ranger and climbing editor, presented a visual version of his latest book, "High Alaska," on the history of Denali climbing. In May a capacity audience was on hand to hear Steve Venables, Ed Webster and other members of the 1988 Everest East Face team talk about their exciting ascent of a difficult new route on the Kangshung Face. Another tradition is our "Members' Night," which showcases New York Section members' accomplishments. This year's show presented Cathy Gibson, Ken Bailey, Fred and Jamie Golomb, and Lawrence True and Linda Brown on climbing in the Pamirs, adventure filmmaking, extreme skiing safely, and trekking in the Karakoram, respectively. Held in the late spring, this event attempts to goad otherwise deskbound New Yorkers to "go out and do it."

In June, after our annual outing at the Ausable Club in the Adirondacks, came the eagerly and long awaited first visit to New York of Reinhold Messner. During a whirlwind weekend, Reinhold was interviewed on the "Today" show, followed by a press conference, a reception for 135 members and guests at the Knickerbocker Club, a lecture on "All 8000ers" before a capacity audience of 400, and a benefactors' dinner held at the apartment of David Koch. The event was run as a fundraiser for the "Mountain Wilderness" cause, with which Reinhold has been closely associated. With the proceeds the Section has formed an Environmental Fund designed to assist in financing clean-up operations in the United States and overseas. The first designated beneficiary is the Everest Environmental Expedition organized by Bob McConnell. The support of Rolex Watch, U.S.A., was particularly helpful in achieving our financial goals.

Finally, the social season concluded with the traditional black tie Annual Dinner, held the last Saturday of October. This year's special guest was Doug Scott, who presented an absorbing retrospective of 30 years of climbing during the "Golden Age" of British mountaineering. The recipient of the John Case Award for accomplishment by a Section member was Jeremy Bernstein for his outstanding 20-year contribution to mountaineering literature. The event also featured a photographic exhibition and sale by Nathan Farb, the famed Adirondack photographer, proceeds from which were dedicated to the Library Fund. Twenty new members were introduced and presented with their membership pins to conclude the gala evening.

Club members from other Sections desirous of being placed on the New York Section's mailing list or of receiving information on clean-up grants should write to P.O. Box 5475, Rockefeller Station, New York, NY 10185.

PHILIP ERARD, *Chairman*

Alpine Club of Canada. Following are highlights of the A.C.C.'s 1989 achievements. In the facilities area, 1989 marked the completion of the Wapta Icefields project, whose centerpiece was the July construction of the new Bow Hut. This project represented an $85,000 financial commitment and the volunteer labor of more than 400 persons over five years. In October the Balfour Hut was replaced by Parks Canada with an entirely new structure.

In the activities area, the Summer Camps Committee produced yet another capacity General Mountaineering Camp and seems to have successfully reversed the financial difficulties experienced by GMCs a few years ago.

As part of many on-going services, the club launched a new Sport Climbing Committee, which initiated or sanctioned three events. These included the Second Canadian National Championships, hosted by the Edmonton Section on its new wall in December. Both the Ottawa and Winnipeg Sections also held their own sport climbing competitions.

The A.C.C. awarded the first grants from the Alpine Club Endowment Fund, with amounts totaling nearly $10,000 disbursed to seven individuals or Sections, including $5,000 to the Smoke Bluffs project. The Canadian Centre for Mountaineering has launched a major corporate fund-raising drive with the donation of $100,000 to the project by Canadian Pacific Ltd. The Education Committee hosted the 1989 Mountain Leadership Conference, which was chaired by Michael Mortimer and drew over 300 participants in November.

The budget process was more difficult than usual as the club struggles to deal with rising costs in many areas, particularly publications. After serious and significant budget cuts, the Board was able to restrict a proposed membership fee increase of 30% to just 11%. This was the first increase since 1987 and raises the individual membership fee to $45. Most of the additional revenue will go to offset increased publication costs for the *Canadian Alpine Journal*, but there will also be reductions in the appearance and form of the club's national newsletter.

DICK LATTA, *Executive Director*

Appalachian Mountain Club. In 1989 the Appalachian Mountain Club continued to maintain over 1,000 miles of hiking trails in the northeastern U.S., dozens of back-country campsites and shelters, and various public workshops in hiking leadership and group safety. The club has eight huts strategically spaced a day's hike apart along the ridges of the White Mountains. The center for its mountain activities is Pinkham Notch Camp at the foot of Mount Washington. The Appalachian Mountain Club, founded in 1876, is the oldest club of its kind in the U.S. Membership is close to 37,000. The principal administrative office is at 5 Joy St., Boston, MA, which also houses one of the oldest mountaineering libraries in the country. Twelve chapters of the club are spread from Maine to Washington, D.C.

The highlight for the A.M.C. hut system in 1989 was the addition of three new structures at Camp Dodge in New Hampshire. The bunkhouses were erected with the assistance of a local Army Reserve Unit. They will house volunteers involved in trail and conservation work in the White Mountains. Greenleaf Hut was renovated to increase capacity in order to serve the growing population of hikers along the Appalachian Trail and in the White Mountain National Forest of New Hampshire.

At the chapter level volunteers organized thousands of activities throughout the year, including rock climbing and mountaineering, day hiking and instruction in ice climbing and other technical sports. Other trips included flat and whitewater canoeing, sea kayaking, cross-country and downhill skiing, and even board sailing. Programs of instruction and conservation were also offered through the chapter committees.

The Education Department continued its program in instruction and conservation. The Mountain Leadership School, a week-long course offered each summer to train leaders in outdoor survival skills, is 31 years old this year. The Boston-based A.M.C. Youth Opportunities Program, offering wilderness and outdoor survival and camping skills to leaders of youth from urban areas, is continuing to reach out to surrounding communities.

The Excursions Committee conducted a variety of local outings and extended excursions, both domestic and foreign. Members participated in over 40 excursions throughout the year from birding in Trinidad and hiking in Patagonia to hut-to-hut skiing in Norway.

Each year the Trails Program participates in maintaining and establishing trail systems to accommodate the increasing number of people who want to enjoy natural areas, and simultaneously to regulate the impact on fragile environments. In 1989 A.M.C. Trails Service trips went to many areas, among them Alaska's Kenai National Park and Virgin Islands National Park. Over the summer a group of Soviet citizens joined A.M.C. volunteers in a conservation and trail management exchange. The International Committee is arranging more service project exchange trips with foreign groups with similar interests for next year.

BARBARA STEFFINS

Arizona Mountaineering Club. In 1989 the club fielded 72 outings including 53 climbing trips with climbs averaging a 5.7 rating. Seven of the outings were to adjacent states. Successful ascents were made of Pik Lenin in the Soviet Pamirs, Prusik Peak in Washington, the East Face of Mount Whitney, and the Red Rocks in Nevada by various routes.

Training and safety courses taught by our members are open to the public. We teach basic rock climbing, advanced leading, advanced rope and rescue techniques, orienteering, and a rescue team which helps the Phoenix Fire Department with rescues.

For further information about our activities, contact the Arizona Mountaineering Club, Box 1695, Phoenix, AZ 85001.

KIM A. HUENECKE

Idaho Alpine Club. The year began with the best ice climbing in the Tetons and Snake River Gorge since 1986, inspiring several beginners to take the club's ice-climbing class. In February we held our first avalanche school, which we hope to make an annual event. Several dozen members attended the spring rock-and-snow schools to learn or to brush up on techniques for snow-and-glacier travel as well as rock-and-ice climbing. Soon after, the club became involved in the bolting controversy at City of Rocks National Reserve. We would like to thank John Steiger and Armando Menocal of the A.A.C. Access Committee for helping to organize meetings between climbers and the National Park Service in which a diplomatic resolution was made.

Local climbers had an active year in foreign expeditions. Honorary member Kellie Rhoads and her husband Jeff were members of the successful American Mount Everest Expedition. Dirk Burgard and two others attempted Mount McKinley, retreating in high winds near 18,000 feet. Steve and Katie Reiser joined the Iowa Mountaineers in Peru, where Steve summitted Huascarán Sur. Ron Mizia and Bob Hammer were in Tanzania to climb Kilimanjaro.

In the fall the club assisted in providing judges for the annual Pocatello Pump climbing competition and started two projects: building an indoor climbing wall and writing a guidebook to over 20 bouldering areas in southeast Idaho.

We invite visiting climbers to help us celebrate the I.A.C.'s 30th anniversary in 1990. Drop us a letter to P.O. Box 2885, Idaho Falls, ID 83403.

STEVEN REISER

Dartmouth Mountaineering Club. 1989 saw the direction and function of the Dartmouth Mountaineering Club change noticeably. In the spring the D.M.C. continued to offer comprehensive rock-climbing instruction to Dartmouth students and community members. In the fall the club changed its focus to more intense climbing for personal gratification, although several members continued to instruct in a separate climbing course.

Throughout the year members climbed at the Gunks, Cannon Mountain, Cathedral and Whitehorse Ledges, and many less well known but high quality crags in New Hampshire and Vermont. Several difficult new routes were put up in New Hampshire. The D.M.C. also sponsored several climbing workshops led by professional guides.

The Dartmouth tradition of Freshman Trips was given new life in 1989 with the addition of the first Rock Climbing Freshmen Trip. It included three days of hiking and climbing in the Franconia Notch area and stimulated widespread interest among its participants. As a result, the D.M.C. experienced a significant growth in membership. Owing to this success, the new trip will remain an integral part of the Freshmen Trips Program in the future.

Andy Harvard, a Dartmouth graduate, returned to his alma mater to give a presentation on his ascent of Mount Everest. Brian Kunz also gave a program on climbing in the Soviet Union.

The D.M.C. is currently involved in efforts to obtain an indoor climbing wall on college grounds. This facility will be available to recreational climbers and may be used for climbing competitions as well.

KAREN L. CRAMER, *President*

Iowa Mountaineers. Club membership has grown to 1,400 after another very active year. Over 2,500 people participated in one of the many instructional courses, mountaineering camps, or foreign expeditions.

Under Jim Ebert's instruction over 492 members learned cross-country skiing at Devils Lake State Park, Wisconsin, during January and February. Winter survival skills, proper dress, hypothermia, frostbite and avalanche precautions were discussed. Devils Lake was also the site of eight weeklong basic rock-climbing courses in May, June and August. Over 100 members from nine states participated. Throughout the year the club taught over 1,720 University of Iowa students the basic skills of rock climbing for credit in weekend courses at Devils Lake. Over the Memorial Day weekend 30 members took an intermediate rock-climbing course, with over 60 manned ascents made on six different routes.

In March 75 members spent five days hiking in the Grand Canyon in Arizona. In August Jeff Statler led an outing to the Tetons. Eight members climbed the Exum Ridge of the Grand Teton, while four ascended the Middle Teton.

The club sponsored a mountaineering camp in Idaho's Sawtooth Mountains August 1-11. With over 59 members participating, climbs were made of Warbonnet Peak, Finger of Fate and Mount Heyburn.

The Iowa Mountaineers celebrate their 50th anniversary in 1990.

The 50th Annual Banquet will be held May 19-20 in Iowa City at the University of Iowa Memorial Union Ballroom. Members are registering to attend from 14 states. Trips for 1990 include: a four-week hiking and climbing trip to New Zealand in January-February; a Devils Tower, Wyoming, trip in June; a trip to five European countries in June-July to climb eight major peaks in the Alps; and finally, a 10-day Canadian Mountaineering Camp in August in Banff National Park.

JOHN EBERT, *President*

The Mazamas. Climbing activities, the prime activity of The Mazamas, are planned and supervised under the Climbing Committee, this year chaired by Bruce Coorpender. The summer schedule, May through September, included 191 weekend activities and 25 on week days. Training programs continued as a major function of the Climbing Committee. Basic School began at the end of March, with 14 groups of 15 students each attending five Monday evening lectures, a session on knots and belay, a rock trip, a snow trip, and several difficult conditioning hikes on minor peaks of the Columbia River Gorge.

The Intermediate Climbing School admitted 40 students. It featured a day of high-angle snow, a snow bivouac, and trips to Horsethief Butte and Smith Rocks. Routes rated from 5.6 to 5.9 were used for training. The Advanced Rock Program took 22 of the 34 applicants, with 27 volunteer instructors supporting the course. The club embarked on a new Ice Climbing Program focusing on leads on high-angle ice and snow. Of 15 students, eight dropped out after the first session.

The Climbing Committee selected 16 candidates for new leaders, and seven became fully qualified. The Mazamas now have 108 active, qualified leaders. The early spring Leadership Update Weekend continued its effective maintenance program for all climb leaders. Stacy Allison, the first American woman to climb Mount Everest, was our guest speaker.

The Expeditions Committee, under chairman David Schermer, involves only a few active Mazama participants, but the results are impressive. Jim Lathrop led a party to Peru, placing four members on the summit of Huascarán. The club will sponsor a 1990 Manaslu Expedition, which has enlisted a strong climbing team from the Pacific Northwest, including Stacy Allison. The Mazamas will also sponsor a 1990 Arrigetch Expedition with attempts on several unclimbed faces of Alaska's Brooks Range. The Committee has generated funds with an annual biathlon each April, and in January 1989 they featured Dick Bass as speaker for an evening program.

The Trail Trips Committee, chaired by Phyllis Towne, planned and appointed leaders for 325 hikes ranging in difficulty from "A" to "C," and totalling 3,760 hiker-trips. Trail Trips create a friendly "melting pot" that helps to bond the club's 2,700 members and their many friends of all skill and age levels into a more cohesive group. Activities range from evening hikes in the city, walks on nearby trails, snowshoe bivouacs, backpacks, and severe "man-killers" in the Northwest mountain areas.

The Outing Committee was created in the 1980s to manage The Annual Outing, a huge event involving most of the membership. It has evolved into managing many small outings, many traveling to other continents. Chairman Homer Brock's committee planned and supervised 11 outings in 1989 with 193 participants, who ranged from Yellowstone, Mount Rainier, the Sierra Nevada, and Hawaii in the United States, the Yucatán in Mexico, and the mountains of France, Austria, and Italy.

No hiking and climbing club spends all of its time in the outdoors. The club's Conservation Committee, chaired by Clarence Mershon, has shared the battlefront with the other outdoor clubs for generations, keeping firm pressure on government decision makers to preserve our environment. Recent focus has been on preservation of old-growth timber, but a real threat has emerged at Mount Hood, deserving the attention of all Americans who prize their wilderness. Mount Hood Meadows, having gained a toe-hold on the east slopes of Mount Hood two decades ago, now is planning disastrous expansion. The impetus now is for a "destination ski resort," a euphemism for a new city sprawling across mountain meadows. This sort of development brings in megabucks for the resort operator, but it squeezes out ordinary, moderate-budget skiers.

The Research Committee, under Paul Staub, pursued its purpose of making grants to students of mountain-related studies. The process includes mailings to universities, organizations, and individuals, then evaluating the applicants for the final awards. In 1990 seven awardees shared $5,850 in assistance.

The Library Committee, chaired by Linda McNeil, entered its second year of active restructuring of the Mazama Library, one of the outstanding mountaineering collections of America. Some nature guide, geology, and weather books have been retired from the library because of advancing knowledge in these fields. Duplicate books have been sold or traded for volumes needed for a more complete mountaineering collection. Video tapes are to be added. The Mazama museum, under the direction of Vera Dafoe, is a library activity which has added greatly to the preservation of historically significant mountain equipment.

The Publications Committee, chaired by Vera Dafoe, publishes the monthly Bulletin to notify members of club events and activities, as well as an annual membership list. However, the noteworthy effort of this committee is the annual journal, *Mazama,* published sporadically since 1894 and continuously since 1913. Sentiment is strong to preserve this valued record of the club's accomplishments, although some other large clubs have discontinued their annual publication. From an extended viewpoint, The Mazamas have found, just as has the American Alpine Club, that an annual journal is sometimes the only thread of continuity for the organization over long periods of time.

JACK GRAUER

Memphis Mountaineers, Inc. 1989 proved to be a very productive year for the Memphis Mountaineers. The total membership of 66 included 42 regular members in the Memphis, Tennessee, area, eight honorary members, and 16 associate members scattered throughout the United States.

The club's 11th year began with an expedition to Ecuador, where successful ascents of Chimborazo and Cotopaxi, both 5000-meter peaks, were made. In addition, the club sponsored numerous shorter outings to Mid-South bluffs, as well as longer trips to Devils Tower, Yosemite, and the Shawangunks, among others.

Two members participated in sport-climbing competitions in Washington, D.C., and Carbondale, Illinois, where they placed first and second, respectively, in their divisions.

Individual members were active afield, and successes included a variety of activities ranging from mountaineering in England to ice climbing in Canada. Recreational Equipment, Inc. recognized the Memphis Mountaineers by awarding the club a grant which made it possible to continue to teach climbing courses. Finally, the year ended with yet another expedition to South America, this time to attempt Aconcagua (6960 meters) in northern Argentina.

The Memphis Mountaineers met monthly on second Mondays at 7:00 p.m. in the Highland Branch of the Memphis Public Libarary. Programs presented at 1989 meetings covered various topics such as ice climbing in the Cascades, Wyoming's 1988 Everest Expedition, and outdoor photography. Other club functions involved four basic rock climbing courses, informative mountaineering tips, and occasional social events. Members were notified of club activities through the monthly newsletter, the *Memphis Mountain News.*

Club officers included Scott Hall, president; Suzy Ferrenbach, vice president; Robin Daniels, treasurer; Bill Henson, secretary; and Jim Detterline, Argentina Expedition Leader. Anyone with an interest in promoting climbing in the Mid-South is encouraged to join Memphis Mountaineers. For more information, write Memphis Mountaineers, Inc., P.O. Box 11124, Memphis, TN 38111.

SCOTT HALL, *President*

Mountaineering Club of Alaska, Inc. The Mountaineering Club of Alaska, Inc. was formed in 1958 and currently has approximately 250 members. Membership is open to the general public. There are no prerequisites for membership.

The M.C.A. holds annual classes in rock climbing, mountaineering, ice climbing and glacier travel. The M.C.A. also conducts classes from time to time on subjects such as backcountry skiing, telemarking, winter camping, avalanche beacon searches, snow-shelter construction, stream crossings and orienteering. The club has also organized an avalanche safety course for club members in conjunction with the Alaska Mountain Safety Center and has organized public service projects such as trail clearings.

The club publishes a monthly newsletter, the *Scree*, which serves as an information source for climbers and hikers in Alaska. The *Scree* lists upcoming club trips, reports on completed trips, describes new routes and climbs, and reports on environmental and conservation issues of interest to club members. The club also maintains an extensive library of climbing related publications which is open to the public.

The club conducts monthly meetings, which are open to the public, at the Pioneer School House in Anchorage. In addition to the business portion of the meeting, the club hosts a slide presentation each month on a notable climb, trip or other topic of interest to the club. M.C.A. climbs and trips are often the subject of the monthly presentation. The topics can cover a broad range of subjects, however, and have included members' climbs in South America and the Himalayas, a recent geographic survey expedition in the Alaska Range and the prevention and treatment of frostbite. The club has also sponsored public talks, an example of which is the November 30, 1989, presentation by club member David Staeheli on his first solo winter ascent of Denali's West Rib.

The club organizes a broad range of club trips for all different skill levels. The trips are open to the general public. One need not be a M.C.A. member to participate in a club trip (although one must sign a club waiver form). The club does not charge for participation in club trips.

Over the past year, for example, the club has organized climbs of numerous peaks in the Anchorage area, numerous day and weekend hikes requiring no mountaineering skill, numerous day and weekend backcountry ski trips, a traverse of the Harding Icefield, a two-week traverse of the Aleutian Range from Shelikof Straits over Mount Katmai to the Valley of the 10,000 Smokes, a mountain-bike trip to the Kennecott Mine, a two-week hike in the Arrigetch Peaks area of the Brooks Range, and fly-in expeditions to the Tazlina and Matanuska Glaciers.

Noteworthy accomplishments of our members include a winter solo ascent of Denali's West Rib by Dave Staeheli in March, an attempt on Mount Everest in April by George Rooney, and the first ascent of Nagishlamina Peak (11,068 feet) in the Tordrillos, one of the highest unclimbed peaks in North America, by Tom Meacham et al. Members also made first ascents of Hearth Mountain in the Kenai Range and of Greenland Peak, Devil's Club Peak and Mountaineer's Peak in the Chugach Range, and completed a glacier traverse of the Isthmus Icefield from Kenai Lake to Whittier. Three of our members also ascended Mount Foraker via the Sultana Ridge.

The M.C.A. membership fee is $10 annually. The club's address is Mountaineering Club of Alaska, Inc., P.O. Box 102037, Anchorage, AK 99510.

NEIL T. O'DONNELL, *President* and WILLY HERSMAN, *Newsletter Editor*

Potomac Appalachian Trail Club. Our Mountaineering Section topped off another good year in 1989. Membership growth continued as the sport becomes more popular, activities keep expanding and members have even found time to go climbing!

The Second Annual Washington Mountain Film Festival drew over 500 viewers. Attendance at the PATC-MS instruction courses was at an all-time high. Many club members participated in the local climbing competition, *Springstone.* Perhaps the best indication that climbing is alive and well in Washington comes from the list of places the Mountaineering Section members went. They were active in the Alps and on French limestone, in the Tetons and on California granite. The icy summits of the Canadian Rockies were visited as well as desert sandstone. Many members experienced new forms of climbing. Some began their first mountaineering trips and others started leading on rock. Ice proved elusive in January, but the record cold of December made up for that.

As the Mountaineering Section moves into 1990, plans are continuing for trips to New England, the Tetons and some are making noises about Denali, the Pamirs and Pakistan. Hard rock as always is a constant pursuit. The Film Festival promises to be bigger and better than before. An indoor climbing wall group has been formed. As the 1990s take shape, the PATC-MS plans to be on top.

STUART PREGNALL, *Chairman*

AAC BOOKS

THE AMERICAN ALPINE JOURNAL, edited by H. Adams Carter.

THE AMERICAN ALPINE JOURNAL INDEX
1929-1976, Edited by Earlyn Church.
1977-1986, Edited by Patricia A. Fletcher.

ACCIDENTS IN NORTH AMERICAN MOUNTAINEERING, edited by John E. Williamson and Jim Whitteker.

ACONCAGUA, Topographic map by Jerzy Wala. Text by Carles Capellas and Josep Paytubi.

CITLALTÉPETL: A History of Pico de Orizaba, by Winston Crausaz.

CLIMBING ICE, by Yvon Chouinard.

CLIMBING IN NORTH AMERICA, by Chris Jones.

THE COLUMBIA MOUNTAINS OF CANADA—CENTRAL (The Interior Ranges of B.C.), by Earle R. Whipple, John Kevin Fox, Roger Laurilla and William L. Putnam.

THE COLUMBIA MOUNTAINS OF CANADA—WEST & SOUTH (The Interior Ranges of B.C.), Earle R. Whipple and William L. Putnam.

THE GREAT GLACIER AND ITS HOUSE, by William L. Putnam.

HIGH ALASKA, by Jonathan Waterman.

THE INTERIOR RANGES OF BRITISH COLUMBIA—SOUTH, by Robert Kruszyna and William L. Putnam.

MOUNTAIN SICKNESS, by Peter Hackett, M.D.

THE MOUNTAINS OF NORTH AMERICA, by Fred Beckey.

MOUNTAINS OF THE MIDDLE KINGDOM, by Galen Rowell.

THE RED ROCKS OF SOUTHERN NEVADA, by Joanne Urioste.

THE ROCKY MOUNTAINS OF CANADA—NORTH, by Robert Kruszyna and William L. Putnam.

THE ROCKY MOUNTAINS OF CANADA—SOUTH, by Glen W. Boles, with Robert Kruszyna and William L. Putnam.

SHAWNGUNK ROCK CLIMBS: The Third Edition, by Dick Williams.

SURVIVING DENALI, by Jonathan Waterman.

TAHQUITZ AND SUICIDE ROCKS, by Chuck Wilts.

TOUCH THE SKY: The Black Hills in the Needles of South Dakota, by Paul Piana.

TRAPROCK: Rock Climbing in Central Connecticut, by Ken Nichols.

A WALK IN THE SKY, by Nicholas Clinch.

WASATCH ROCK CLIMBS, by Les Ellison and Brian Smoot.

WHERE THE CLOUDS CAN GO, by Conrad Kain.

THE WORST WEATHER ON EARTH: A History of the Mount Washington Observatory, by William Lowell Putnam.

YURAQ JANKA: The Cordilleras Blanca and Rosko, by John Ricker.

Prices and order information on request from The American Alpine Club, 113 East 90th Street, New York, NY 10128-1589.

INDEX

Volume 32 ● Issue 64 ● 1990

Compiled by Patricia A. Fletcher

This issue comprises all of Volume 32

Mountains are listed by their official names and ranges; quotation marks indicate unofficial names. Ranges and geographic locations are also indexed. Unnamed peaks (e.g., P 2037) are listed following the range or country in which they are located.

All expedition members cited in major articles are included, whereas only the leaders and persons supplying information in the **Climbs and Expeditions** section are listed.

Titles of books reviewed in this issue are grouped as a single entry under **Book Reviews**. Abbreviations used: Article: *art.*; Bibliography: *bibl.*; Obituary: *obit.*

A

Aasheim, Stein P., 63
Abi Gamin (Garhwal Himalaya), 258
Academy Glacier (Greenland), 61, 64
Accidents: Annapurna, 249; Annapurna II, 251; Chetiriokh, 311; Cho Oyu, 239; Denali, 153-55, 155-56, 157; Denali National Park and Preserve, 153-56; Dhaulagiri, 253-54, 255; Diran, 292; Egger, 205; Everest, 224, 228-29, 231, 234; Gasherbrum II, 283; Hidden Peak, 282; Himalchuli, 246; Johnson, 155; K2, 281; Langtang Lirung, 240; Lhotse, 227; Manaslu, 244; Nanga Parbat, 298, 299; Poincenot, 205; Pumori, 236; Shishapangma, 308; Yalung Kang, 216
Accidents in North American Mountaineering, *art.*, 66-70; *bibl.*, 70
Accomazzo, Eric, 334-35
Aconcagua (Argentina), 202-4; *altitude of*, 202-3; *statistics*, 203
Acontango (Chile), 200
Adamson, Stephen, 247
Addison, Tom, 61
Aerjinshan (Kansu, China), 309
Africa, 211
Ahab, Mount (Selkirk Mountains, British Columbia), 180

Ahmed, Manzoor, 258
Aisthorpe, Steven, 192
Aitwal, Chandra Prabha, 257
Ajako (Greenlander), 58
Akela Kila. *See* CB 46.
Alaska, *arts.*, 21-27, 28-35, 37-42, 43-49, 50-53, 79-149; 152-64
Alaska Range, *arts.*, 21-27, 28-35, 37-42, 43-49, 50-53; 152-59; *glaciers in*, 132-35
Alaska Range: Peak 7400, 159
Albert, Kurt, 287-88
Albino, Björn, 61
Aleutian Islands (Alaska), *glaciers on*, 138-39
Aleutian Range (Alaska), *glaciers in*, 136-38
Alexander Archipelago (Alaska), *glaciers on*, 135-36
Alonso, Jaime, 292-94
Alpamayo (Cordillera Blanca, Peru), 187
Alpine Club of Canada, 360
Ama Dablam (Nepal Himalaya), 222-23
American Alpine Club, The: Blue Ridge Section, 357; Cascade Section, 357-58; New York Section, 359; Oregon Section, 358; Rocky Mountain Section, 358
"Anco Collo." *See* Cordillera Quimsa Cruz, Peak 5460.
Andersen, John, 60

Andersen, Kjell Einar, 62
Andes (South America), *indian remains in*, 201
Andrés Maramisio, Juan, 303
Angel Wings (Sierra Nevada, California), 168
Angmagssalik (Greenland), 55, 58, 59, 60, 61, 62, 63, 64
Anker, Conrad D., *art.*, 37-38
Anker, Daniel, 206-8
Annapurna (Nepal Himalaya), 247-49; *paraglider descent from*, 248
Annapurna II (Nepal Himalaya), 251
Annapurna IV (Nepal Himalaya), 251
Annapurna Dakshin (Nepal Himalaya), 251
Antarctica, 212-13
Antu Pirén (Arhuelles, Nevados de, Chile), 201
Anyemaqen (Kunlun Mountains, China), 299-300
Appalachian Mountain Club, 360-61
Aprin, Hooman, 216-17, 221
Aq Tash (Karakoram Range, India), 277
Arctic, 180-81
Ardencaple Fjord (Greenland), 62, 64
Argentina, 201-4
Argentina: Peak 4596, 204; Peak 4650, 201; Peak 4764, 204; Peak 5036, 202; Peak 6050, 201; Peak 6175, 201; Peak 6660, 201
Arhuelles, Nevados de (Chile), 201
Ariz Martínez, Gregorio, 283
Arizona Mountaineering Club, 361
Arko, Vojslav, 205, 206
Aronsson, Dag, 63
Arribas, Santiago, 301
Arrigetch Peaks (Brooks Range, Alaska), 163
Asia, 213-311
Astier, Yves, 195-200
Astrup, Eyvind, 54
Atacama, Puna de (Chile), 202-3
Athens, Peter, 231
Auble, David, 21-27
Ausangate (Cordillera Vilcanota, Peru), 192
Austmannadalen (Greenland), 54, 63, 64
Auyuittuq National Park (Baffin Island), 180-81
Axt, Wolfgang, 308

B

Baba, Shigeyuki, 251
Bae, Seung-Youl, 265
Baffin Island (Canada), 180-81
Baillet, Christian, 246-47

Baintha Brakk (Karakoram Range, Pakistan), 291
Ball, Gary, 230
Balto, Samuel Johannesen, 54
Baltoro Cathedral (Karakoram Range, Pakistan), 288
Banks, Michael, 59
Barpu Glacier Region (Karakoram Range, Pakistan), 295
Barrille, Mount (Alaska Range), *ascents of*, 154
Barry, John, 276
Baruntse (Nepal Himalaya), 219-20
Batard, Marc, 227, 248
Bates, Robert H., 337-38, 347
Batura Glacier Region (Karakoram Range, Pakistan), 294; *map of*, 295
"Bauchac, Nevado de" (Argentina), 201
Bauer, Willi, 282
Baumann, Bruno, 299-300
Bawa, Harjit Singh, 276
Beacon Rock (Cascade Mountains, Washington), 166-67
Beadle, Robin, 276
Beatty, John, 62
Bebie, Mark, *art.*, 28-35; 165-66
Becher, Gianni Pais, 184-85
Beckey, Fred, 163, 177, 179, 180, 259-60
Beggio, Giulio, 63
Beghin, Annie, 302
Beghin, Pierre, *art.*, 1-6; 218
Bell, Stephen, 245-46
Bella Coola Icecap (Coast Mountains, British Columbia), 179
Bellido Trullenque, José, 62
Berg, Agnar Thoralf, 62
Bergamaschi, Arturo, 274
Berger, Hans, 240
Berggren, Anders, 63
Berle, Morten, 61
Berljak, Darko, 303
Berthaud, Luc, 292
Bertulis, Alex, 167,179
Beyer, James, 176,288
Bhagirathi (Garhwal Himalaya), 265
Bhagirathi II (Garhwal Himalaya), 266, 269
Bhagirathi III (Garhwal Himalaya), 265
Bhrigupanth (Garhwal Himalaya), 268
Bianca, Anna, 63
Bibler, Todd, 159
Bífida (Patagonia), 206

Bigey, Alain, 253
Bilbao Barruetabena, Dina, 63
Birnbacher, Eduard, 161
Biswas, Shankar, 259
Bitdot, J.M., 273
Black-Neck Cranes. *See* "Chathung Thung."
Blaersterdalen, Ståle, 61
Blanchard, William E. (Smoke), *obit.,* 350-51
Bock, Günther, 60
Bodycote, Steve, 61
Boick, Martin, 63
Bolivia, 192-200, 201

BOOK REVIEWS
    The Andes: Natural Beauty of Chile, Gastón
        Oyarzún, 328-29
    The Art of Adventure, Galen Rowell, 317-18
    Ascent: The Mountaineering Experience in Word
        and Image, Allen Steck and Steve Roper,
        editors, 320-22
    Boulder Climbs South, Richard Rossiter, 335
    Climbing in the Adirondacks: A Guide to Rock
        and Ice Routes in the Adirondacks, 2nd
        edition, Don Mellor, 332-34
    Ecuador: Tierras Atlas, Jorge Anhalzer, 328-29
    Everest: Kangshung Face, Stephen Venables,
        315-17
    Front Range Bouldering, Bob Horan, 334-35
    Frontera Superior de Colombia, José F. Machado
        et al, 328-29
    Gorilla Monsoon, John Long, 323-25
    High Altitude Medicine and Pathology, Donald
        Heath and David Reid Williams, 331-32
    High Altitude Medicine and Physiology, Michael
        P. Ward, James S. Milledge and John B. West,
        331
    International Travel Health Guide, Stuart R.
        Rose, 332
    K2: Traum und Schicksal, Kurt Diemberger,
        318-19
    The Loneliest Mountain, Lincoln Hall, 325-26
    Mountain Journeys, James P. Vermeulen, editor,
        322-23
    Mountaineer: Thirty Years of Climbing on the
        World's Great Peaks, Chris Bonington, 319-20
    Portrait of an Explorer—Hiram Bingham:
        Discoverer of Machu Picchu, 327-28
    Rocks Around the World, Stefan Glowacz and
        Uli Wiesmeier, 326-27

Winter Sports Medicine, Murray J. Casey, Carl
    Foster and Edward G. Hixson, 330
Boucht, Christer, 60
Boucht, Peter, 60
"Bounty Peak" (Chugach Mountains, Alaska), 160
Bowdoin Fjord (Greenland), 55, 64
Box of Holy Scriptures. *See* "Chogam."
Boyarski, Viktor, 63
Bravo, Claudio, 201-2
Bravo, Orlando, 201
Breier, Pavol, 314
Brennodden, Kjell, 61
Briggs, David G., 166
Briggs, Gordon A., 291
Brill, Timothy, 255
British Columbia, *art.,* 79-149; 179-80
Broad Peak (Karakoram Range, Pakistan), 281-82
Bronken, Arild, 61
Bronken, Kjell, 61
Brooks, Mount (Alaska Range), 158; *ascents of,*
    154
Brooks Range (Alaska), 163; *glaciers in,* 139-40
Brown, Keith, 244, 276, 304
Browning, Michael F., 358
Buck Rock (Sierra Nevada, California), 169
Buhler, Carlos, 237-38, 281
Bull, C.B.B., 59
Bunnell Point (Yosemite, California), 168
Burgess, Adrian, 231, 244-45
Burns, Cameron M., 169-72, 175, 176-77
Burrill, Mount (Ellesmere Island), 181
Buscaini, Silvia Metzeltin, 204

C

Cadot, Michel, 1-6
Caliban (Brooks Range, Alaska), 163
California, 168-76
Campbell, Iain, 62
Campodónico, Renato, 201
Canada, 177-80
Cap Georg Cohn (Greenland), 59, 64
Capurata (Chile), 200
Carsolio, Carlos, 232
Casas, Toni, 187-90
Cascade Mountains (Washington), 164-67
Cattaneo, Luigi, 265
Cave, Andrew, 291
Cayambe (Ecuador), 186

Cayesh (Cordillera Blanca, Peru), 187, 190
Cazadero. *See* Argentina, Peak 6660.
Cazzaniga, Giuseppe, 63
CB 13 (Himachal Pradesh), 271
CB 46 (Himachal Pradesh), 270
CB 48 (Himachal Pradesh), 270
Centrum Sø (Greenland), 59, 64
Česen, Tomo, *art.*, 7-13; 216
Chablis Spire (Cascade Mountains, Washington), 164
Chabot, Douglas, 158
Chachacomani (Cordillera Real, Bolivia), 194-95
Chambers, Ron, 177-78
Chamoli, S.P., 257
Chamoux, Benoît, 242
Chang, Su-Jeong, 292
"Chango." *See* Argentina, Peak 4650.
Changtse (Tibet), 304
Charlet, Jean-Franck, 232
"Chathung Thung" (Karakoram Range, India), 277
Chaudhara (Garhwal Himalaya), 256
Chearoco (Cordillera Real, Bolivia), 194
Cheru (Sichuan, China), 300
Child, Gregory, 285-87
Chile, 200-201, 202-3, 204
Chimney Rock (Cascade Mountains, Washington), 165
China, 299-300, 308-11
China. *See also* Tibet.
Cho Oyu (Nepal Himalaya), 237-39
Cho Oyu (Tibet), 304-5
"Chogam" (Karakoram Range, India), 278
Chogolisa (Karakoram Range, Pakistan), 284
Cholpanlik (Kunlun Mountains, China), 310
Chong Kumdan (Karakoram Range, India), 278
Christensen, Guttom, 62
Christianshåb (Greenland), 61, 64
Chrobak, Eugeniusz, 228-29
Chuchillo (Cordillera Vilcanota, Peru), 190
Chugach Mountains (Alaska), 160-61; *glaciers in,* 116-25
Chugach Mountains: Peak 5651, 161; Peak 6283, 161; Peak 6600, 160; Peak 6842, 161; Peak 7138, 161; Peak 7240, 160; Peak 7254, 161; Peak 7265, 160; Peak 7401, 161; Peak 7420, 160-61; Peak 7455, 160; Peak 7724, 161
Chulu East (Nepal Himalaya), 246
Chung, Chai-Hong, 246
Churen Himal (Nepal Himalaya), 255

Cicilia Nunatak (Greenland), 59, 64
Clarke, Charles, 212
Clarke, Michael D., 266
Clements Markham Glacier (Greenland), 55, 64
Climbing exchanges: Lithuanian, 167
Clinch, Nicholas B., 299
Coast Mountains (Alaska), *glaciers in,* 91-96
Coast Mountains (British Columbia), 179; *glaciers in,* 91-96
Coco Rico (Cordillera Real, Bolivia), 194
Cololo (Cordillera Apolobamba, Bolivia), 193
Colque Cruz (Cordillera Vilcanota, Peru), 192
Colque Cruz II (Cordillera Vilcanota, Peru), 192
Colque Cruz IV (Cordillera Vilcanota, Peru), 190
Colque Cruz V (Cordillera Vilcanota, Peru), 190-92
Colque Cruz VI (Cordillera Vilcanota, Peru), 190
Columbia Glacier (Chugach Mountains, Alaska), 120-21
Condoriri (Chile), 201
Condoriri (Cordillera Real, Bolivia), 195-200
Cook, Frederick A., 54
Cooke, Simon, 190-92
Cordillera Apolobamba (Bolivia), 192-94
Cordillera Apolobamba: Peak 5375, 193
Cordillera Blanca (Peru), 187-90
Cordillera Darwin (Tierra del Fuego), 211
Cordillera Quimsa Cruz (Bolivia), 200
Cordillera Quimsa Cruz: Peak 5460, 200
Cordillera Real (Bolivia), 194-200, 201
Cordillera Vilcanota (Peru), 190-92
Cordillera Vilcanota: Peak 5300, 192; Peak 5370, 192; Peak 5400, 192
Coricampana (Cordillera Quimsa Cruz, Bolivia), 200
Cortés, Antonio, 282
Cotopaxi (Ecuador), 186-87
Cottontail Tower (Utah), 176
Courtnay, Ted, 62
Covington, Michael M., 284
Craddock, Nicholas, 289
Cramer, Karen L., 362-63
Cran, Mike, 61
Creigh, Andrew, 240
Croft, Andrew, 58
Crown Jewel (Alaska Range), 159
Cunuareya (Cordillera Apolobamba, Bolivia), 193
Cutthroat Peak (Cascade Mountains, Washington), 167

Czerski Range (Siberia), 314
Czerski Range: Peak 3075, 314

D

Dacher, Michael, 60
Daiber, Ome, *obit.*, 339-41
Dan Beard, Mount (Alaska Range), *ascents of,* 154
Daniel Bruun Glacier (Greenland), 58, 64
Danmark Fjord (Greenland), 55, 64
Danmarks Havn (Greenland), 55, 64
Dannebrog Ø (Greenland), 63, 64
Dartmouth Mountaineering Club, 362-63
Davidson, Sam, *art.*, 76-78
Davis, John M., 352-53
Daynes, Roger, 62
Defrancesco, Fabrizio, 281
Della Libera, Maurizio, 63
Demján, Zoltán, 311
Denali (Alaska Range), *art.,* 50-53; 152-57;
    altitude of, 153; *ascents of,* 154
Denali National Park and Preserve (Alaska Range),
    152-57; *accidents in,* 153-56; *ascents in,* 154;
    foreign climbers in, 153, 156; *rescues in,* 155-56;
    statistics, 152-57
Deoskar, Avinash, 257-58
"Devil's Club Peak." *See* Chugach Mountains,
    Peak 7240.
Dewint, Jos, 218, 253
Dey, Sandip, 270
Dhampus. *See* Dhapa.
Dhapa (Nepal Himalaya), 251
Dhar, S.N., 256
Dhaulagiri (Nepal Himalaya), 251-55
Dickey, Mount (Alaska Range), 159; *ascents of,*
    154
Dietrichson, Oluf Christian, 54
Diran (Karakoram Range, Pakistan), 292
Dixon, Mark, 245
Dølven, Ola, 61
"Dome 2" (Cordillera Real, Bolivia), 195
Domenech, Bernard, 185, 289-91
Doran, Amon, 269
Dorje, Sangya, 217
Dorje Lhakpa (Nepal Himalaya), 239
Down, Michael, 163-64
Dragontail Peak (Cascade Mountains, Washington),
    166
Drew, Dan, 61

Drouet, Didier, 62
Dujmovits, Ralf, 228
Dumbbell Mountain (Cascade Mountains,
    Washington), 166
Dundas (Greenland), 55, 58, 65
Dunn, Mike, 303
Duthil, François, 236
Dutta, Goutam, 270

E

Eagle's Nest. *See* "Lokhzung."
Early Mountain Spire, North (Cascade Mountains,
    Washington), 167
Early Winter Spire, North (Cascade Mountains,
    Washington), 165
Ebert, John, 363
Echevarría, Evelio, 200-201, 204, 327-29
Ecuador, 185-87
Egger (Patagonia), 205
Eismitte (Greenland), 64
El Capitan (Yosemite, California), 168
Eliasen, Odd, 63
Ella Ø (Greenland), 59, 64
Ellesmere Island (Canada), 181
Ellesmere Island: Peak 3500+, 181; Peak 3860+,
    181; Peak 5000+, 181; Peak 5300+, 181
Enget, Jan, 61
Enzio, Giuseppe, 273-74
Eqip (Greenland), 55, 58, 59, 64
Erard, Philip, 359
Erickson, Paul, 61
Ertsaas, Jan Morten, 62
Escartín, Javier, 301
Escoffier, Eric, 303-4
Estève, Alain, 253-54, 271
Etherington, David, 237
Ethics, *art.,* 76-78
Etienne, Jean-Louis, 63
Etukussuak (Greenlander), 58
Europe, 212
Evans, Chuck, 255
Everest, Sir George, *art.,* 71-73
Everest (Nepal Himalaya), 214, 224, 228-34, 248;
    maps of, reviewed, 329-30; *relief map of,* 75
Everest (Tibet), 300-304; *acclimatization*
    experiment, 303; *maps of, reviewed,* 329-30;
    relief map of, 75
Eyssette, Pierre, 274

F

Fairweather, Mount (Fairweather Range, Alaska), 163-64
Fairweather Range (Alaska), 163-64
Fasciolo, Gianfranco, 63
Fellerhoff, Karen, 231
Femstjernen (Greenland), 64
Fernández, Pedro, 284
Ferrière, Laurence de la, 281
Ferris, Benjamin G., Jr., *art.*, 66-70
Fick, Roderick, 55
Field, William Osgood, *art.*, 79-149
Films: Kun, 273
Fischer, John, 350-51
Fisher Towers (Utah), 176
Fitz Roy (Patagonia), 205, 206; *paraglider descent from*, 206
Fletcher, David, 259
Foraker, Mount (Alaska Range), *art.*, 28-35; 153, 158; *ascents of*, 154
Forbidden Peak (Cascade Mountains, Washington), 167
Fordham, Derek, 60
Forel, Mount (Greenland), 182-83
Forno, Oreste, 252
Forster, Chris, 283
Fox, Denton, *obit.*, 341-42
Frachon, Jean-Pierre, 223
Francis, Mount (Alaska Range), *ascents of*, 154
Frank, Joe, 219
Frankhauser, Horst, 245
Frederika Mountain (Wrangell Mountains, Alaska), 163
Freese, Lloyd, 178
Freuchen, Peter, 55
Fuchs, Arved, 62
Fukushima, Masaaki, 245, 310
Funatzu, Keizo, 63
Furukawa, Fuminori, 310

G

Gálvez, Claudio, 201
Ganesh II (Nepal Himalaya), *altitude of*, 213
Ganesh IV. *See* Pabil.
Gangapurna (Nepal Himalaya), 249
Gangotri (Garhwal Himalaya), 269

Ganguly, Soumitra, 269
García, Adolfo, 236
García, Faustino, 240-42
Gardenas Sarralde, Gabriel, 62
Gardenas Sarralde, Gonzalo, 62
Garhwal (India), 256-69
Garhwal: Peak 6352, 266; Peak 6400, 267-68; Peak 6702, 266
Garner, Raymond C., *obit.*, 355-56
Garrard, Johan, 60
Garratt, Jonathan, 251
Gasherbrum. *See* Hidden Peak.
Gasherbrum II (Karakoram Range, Pakistan), 282-84
Gatt, Erich, 195
Gau, Ming-Ho, 273
Gaule, K., 55
"Gendarme Argentino." *See* Argentina, Peak 6050.
Gendey, Patrick, 256
Gessain, Robert, 58
Ghersen, Alain, 1-6
Ghosh, Bilwanath, 258
Ghosh, Sanat, 269
Giacometti, Marino, 236
Gibson, Langdon, 54
Gimli Peak (Selkirk Mountains, British Columbia), 180
Girgindil Peak (Karakoram Range, Pakistan), 295
Girgindil Pyramid (Karakoram Range, Pakistan), 295
Giro, Pere, 219
Glacier Bay (Alaska), 97-103
Glacier de France (Greenland), 60, 64
Glacier Dome. *See* Tarke Kang.
Glaciers: Alaska, *art.*, 79-149; *bibl.*, 145-49; British Columbia, *art.*, 79-149; *bibl.*, 145-49; *lengths of*, 141-43; Yukon Territory, *art.*, 79-149; *bibl.*, 145-49
Gleed, Daniel, 61
Godfrey, Daniel, 58
Godthåb (Greenland), 64
Goggi, Ezio, 239
Gooding, Dunham, 194
Grandjean, Jacques, 220
Grauer, Jack, 363-65
Greenland, *art.*, 54-65; 181-85; *coordinates in*, 64-65; *history of crossings in*, *art.*, 54-65
Grigorov, Todor, 248
Gronau Nunatakker (Greenland), 58, 64

Groom, Michael, 223
Guallatiri (Chile), 200
Guaneguane (Chile), 201
Guevara Martínez, Pedro, 62
Guha, Kamal K., 245, 256, 258, 259, 267, 269-70, 272, 276
Guillaumet (Patagonia), 205, 208
Gundelach, Ekkert, 298
Gundersen, Øyvind Bay, 60
Gunnbjørns Cone (Watkins Mountains, Greenland), 182, 183; altitude of, 182
Gunnbjørns Dome (Watkins Mountains, Greenland), 182, 183; altitude of, 182
Gunnbjørns Fjeld (Watkins Mountains, Greenland), 181-83; altitude of, 182; climbing history of, 182
Gurja Himal (Nepal Himalaya), 256
Gyagar (Himachal Pradesh), 271

H

Haaland, Chris, 158, 246
Haapala, Viljo, 60
Hagen, Nils U., 63
Hagshu (Kishtwar Himalaya), 276
Hall, Henry S., Jr., 75
Hall, Scott, 365-66
Hampton, W.E., 58
Han, Gwang-Geol, 223
Han, Seung-Kwon, 246
Hann Glacier (Greenland), 60, 61, 63, 64
Harding Icefield (Kenai Mountains, Alaska), 129-30
Harefjord (Greenland), 62, 64
Harrington, Randal R., 236
Harrison, Ginette, 284-85
Härter, Günther, 223
Hasenkopf, Arnold, 292
Haslund-Christensen, Michael, 63
Hawley, Elizabeth, 216, 218, 219-20, 223, 227-28, 232-37, 238, 239-40, 242, 245, 246, 247, 248, 249, 251, 253, 254, 255, 256, 303, 304
Hayasaka, Keijiro, 299
Heartstone, Mount (Coast Mountains, British Columbia), 179
Henderson, Kenneth A., 343-44, 351
Hendrik Ø (Greenland), 64
Henson, Matthew A., 55
Heo, Young-Ho, 227
Hernando de Larramendi, Ramón, 62
Herrligkoffer, Karl Maria, 298

Hersman, William G. (Willy), 157-58, 160, 366-67
Hessburg, John, 194-95
Hidden Peak (Karakoram Range, China), 310-11
Hidden Peak (Karakoram Range, Pakistan), 282, 284
Hill, Mike, 61
Hill, W. Ryland, obit., 342-43
Hillebrandt, David, 211
Hillen, Stephen, 192-93, 210
Himachal Pradesh (India), 269-72
Himalchuli (Nepal Himalaya), 246
Himalchuli West (Nepal Himalaya), 245-46
Hirasawa, Kenji, 309
Hirotani, Koichiro, 305-7
Hispar Glacier Region (Karakoram Range, Pakistan), 291
Hjemlar, Erik, 60
Hoessly, H., 55
Hoff, Ole, 63
Holdsworth, Gerald, 178
Holsteinsborg (Greenland), 58, 64
Holt, Michael (Mick), 357-58
Holzel, Thomas, 315-17
Holzer, Josef, 236
Houston, Charles S., 330-32
Høybakk, Ralph, 60
Høygaard, Arne, 58
Hu, Yan-Sheng, 300
Huanacuni (Cordillera Apolobamba, Bolivia), 193
Huandoy Norte (Cordillera Blanca, Peru), 187, 190
Huandoy Sur (Cordillera Blanca, Peru), 187
Huantsán Oeste (Cordillera Blanca, Peru), 187
Huayna Potosí (Cordillera Real, Bolivia), 195, 200
Hubbard Glacier (Saint Elias Mountains, Alaska), 109-10
Hubert, Alain, 238-39
Huenecke, Kim A., 361
Huerancalloc (Cordillera Apolobamba, Bolivia), 193
Hulton, Nicholas, 62
Humboldt Glacier (Greenland), 63, 64
Hunstad, Tor-Jostein, 63
Hunter, Mount (Alaska Range), art., 37-42; 153, 158; ascents of, 154
Huntington, Mount (Alaska Range), art., 46-49; ascents of, 154
Hunza (Pakistan), 295
Huyberechts, Karl, 232

I

Ibex. *See* "Stos."
Ibex Peak (Karakoram Range, Pakistan), 295
Icefield Ranges (Alaska), 106, 116
Icefield Ranges (Yukon Territory), 105-6, 116, 177-78
Idaho, 177
Idaho Alpine Club, 362
Ignasiussen, Henning, 60
Iizuka, Atsuo, 272
Ikeda, Kaneshige, 60
Ikeda, Tsunemichi, 300
Imjatse (Nepal Himalaya), 222
Independence Fjord (Greenland), 58, 64
Index, Mount (Cascade Mountains, Washington), 165-66
India, 256-80
Indian remains. *See* Andes (South America).
Indrasan (Himachal Pradesh), 271
Ingalls Peak (Cascade Mountains, Washington), 167
"Ingemars Fjeld." *See* Gunnbjørns Dome.
Inhöger, Sepp, 252-53
Innominata (Patagonia), 206, 208
Inuiterk (Greenlander), 58
Inukitsoq (Greenlander), 55, 58
Iowa Mountaineers, 363
Iscacuchu (Cordillera Apolobamba, Bolivia), 192-93
Isertoq (Greenland), 60, 62, 64
Iversen, Iver P., 55
Ivigtut (Greenland), 58, 64
Iztueta Azkue, Josu, 63

J

Jaccoux, Claude, 302
Jacobse, Jeroen, 282-83
Jakes, Miroslav, 62
Jakobshavn (Greenland), 60, 62, 64
Jammu (India), 272-76
Jang, Bong-Wan, 248
Jannu. *See* Kumbhakarna.
Jaonli (Garhwal Himalaya), 268-69
Jarosz, Mieczysław, 264
Jemez Mountains (New Mexico), 176-77
Jensen, Gunnar, *art.,* 54-65
Jervis, Steven, 323-26
Joe, Edwin C., 168
Jogin (Garhwal Himalaya), 269
Jogin II (Garhwal Himalaya), 269

Jogin III (Garhwal Himalaya), 269
Johan Petersen Fjord, 59-60, 61, 63, 64
Johansen, Asle T., 62
Johansson, Jan O., 63
Johnson, Mount (Alaska Range), 155
Jones, Lewis, 183-84
José Fernández, Fernando, 275
Jost, W., 55
Juriques (Chile), 200

K

K2 (Karakoram Range, Pakistan), 281
Kahiltna Dome (Alaska Range), *ascents of,* 154
Kahiltna Peak, East (Alaska Range), *ascents of,* 154
Kamet (Garhwal Himalaya), 257-58
Kanazawa, Ken, 232
Kande Hiunchuli (Nepal Himalaya), 256
Kang Karpo (Yünnan Province, China), 299
Kangchenjunga (Sikkim Himalaya), 213-15, 230
Kangchungtse (Nepal Himalaya), 219
Kanjeralwa (Nepal Himalaya), 256
Kap Farvel (Greenland), 185
Kap Farvel: Peak 2100, 185
Kapadia, Harish, 267, 268, 271, 272, 273, 276, 277-78
Kapisigdlit (Greenland), 63, 64
Karakoram Range (China), 310-11
Karakoram Range (India), 276-80, 284
Karakoram Range (India): Peak 6739, 277
Karakoram Range (Pakistan), 229, 281-96
Karakoram Range (Pakistan): Peak 5866. *See* Baltoro Cathedral. Peak 5700, 291; Peak 6100, 289; Peak 6666, 292
Karchakund (Garhwal Himalaya), 265
Kashmir (India), 272-76
Kaxkar (Tien Shan, China), 309
Kearney, Alan J., *art.,* 14-20; 164, 222
Kearney, Shari, 234
Kedar Dome (Garhwal Himalaya), 268
Kedarnath (Garhwal Himalaya), 259-60
Kedarnath Dome (Garhwal Himalaya), 259, 260
Kelkar, V.G., 258
Kenai Mountains (Alaska), *glaciers in,* 125-30
Kennard, Garry, 256
Kennedy, Mount (Saint Elias Mountains, Yukon Territory), 177-78
Kerber, Günther, 63

Khan Tengri (Tien Shan, USSR), 311
Kilimanjaro, Mount (Tanzania), 211
Kim, Ha Kyung, 234
Kim, Hong-Ki, 284
Kim, In-Tae, 232
Kim, Teuk-Hee, 216
King, Magda Nos, 304-5
King's Canyon (Sierra Nevada, California), 169
Kinnaur Kailas (Himachal Pradesh), 269
Kiru (Cordillera Vilcanota, Peru), 190
Kishtwar Himalaya (Kashmir), 275-76
Kishtwar Himalaya: Peak 6230, 275
Kitaguchi, Hironori, 300
Kito, Gordon, 14-20
Knudsen, Kai, 62
Knuth, Eigil, 58
Koa Rang III (Himachal Pradesh), 272
Kobler, Karl, 238
Koblmüller, Edi, 281
Koch, Jens Peter, 55
Koch, Lauge, 55, 58
Kodiak Island (Alaska), *glaciers on,* 136
Kolahoi (Kashmir), 276
Kolev, Svetoslav, 214-15
Kolwankar, Uday, 269
Komatsu, Kozo, 152
Kongur (Pamirs, China), 309
Kongur Tiubie (Pamirs, China), 309
Korzhenevskoi (Pamirs, USSR), 311
Kost, Danny W., 160-61, 163
Kotani, Ryuichi, 309
Kraulshavn (Greenland), 62, 64
Krieger, Udo, 63
Kronqvist, Pentti, 61
Krug, Michael, 63
Kukuczka, Jerzy, 227; *death of,* 227
Kulkarni, D. T., 268
Kullerud, Kåre, 62
Kulu Pumori (Himachal Pradesh), 269, 270
Kumaon Himalaya. *See* Garhwal.
Kumbhakarna (Nepal Himalaya), *art.,* 7-13;
    216-17
Kun (Kashmir), 272, 273-74; *garbage removal
    from,* 273
Kunaver, Vlasta, 296-98
Kunlun Mountains (China), 299-300, 310
Kunyang Chhish (Karakoram Range, Pakistan),
    229
Kurtyka, Wojciech, 281

Kusum Kanguru (Nepal Himalaya), 220-21
Kwaiton, Jan, 257
Kwangde Central (Nepal Himalaya), *art.,* 14-20;
    222
Kwangde Nup (Nepal Himalaya), 221-22

L

Ladakh (India), 276
Lagos, Edmundo, 201
Lalthanmawia (Indian climber), 269
Lamjung (Nepal Himalaya), 247
Lampard, Rhona, 283
Landázuri, Freddy, 186-87
Lang, Patrick M., 177
Langshisha Ri (Nepal Himalaya), 239-40
Langtang Lirung (Nepal Himalaya), 240; *altitude
    of,* 213
Langtang Ri (Nepal Himalaya), 240
Larancagua (Chile), 201
"Lars Fjeld." *See* Gunnbjørns Cone.
Larsen, Lars, 55
Latta, Dick, 360
Laub, Wilhelm, 55
Lawa Brakk (Karakoram Range, Pakistan), 291
Lazo, Walter, 190
Le Bon, Leo, 182
"Leaning Tower" (Jemez Mountains, New Mexico),
    176-77
Lechhart, Peter, 60
Lee, Dong-Myung, 251
Lee, Ho-Sang, 239
Lee, Hugh J., 55
Lee, Suk-Woo, 232
Leeming, Peter, 296
Leipzig (Pamirs, USSR), 314
Leith, Mount (Ellesmere Island), 181
Lemhi Mountains (Idaho), 177
Lemhi Mountains: Peak 10240, 177
Lenin (Pamirs, USSR), 311
Leuprecht, Michael, 282
Leversee, Richard (Dick), 169
Lexington Tower (Cascade Mountains,
    Washington), 164-65, 167
Lhotse (Nepal Himalaya), 224-28
Lhotse Shar (Nepal Himalaya), 223
Lindsay, Martin, 58
Link, Ed, *obit.,* 346-47
Litch, James, 158-59

Little, Graham E., 275
Little Switzerland (Alaska Range), 158-59; *ascents in*, 154
Littlejohn, Patrick, 273
Lluis Sasot, Josep, 267-68
Lobuje East (Nepal Himalaya), 237
Logan, Mount (Saint Elias Mountains, Yukon Territory), 177, 178
Lohia, Heera, 276-77
"Lokhzung" (Karakoram Range, India), 277
Lowther, James N., 62, 182-83
Lucas, Enric, 227-28
Luis Zuloaga, José, 218
Lukie, Laurent, 254
Lüthi, Peter, 206
Lynam, Joss P.O.F., 268-69

M

MacGregor, David, 309-10
Magriñá i Güell, Jordi, 254
Maiden, East (Brooks Range, Alaska), 163
Maiden, West (Brooks Range, Alaska), 163
Makalu (Nepal Himalaya), *art.*, 1-6; 218-19
Maki, Yuko, *obit.*, 338-39
Malaspina Glacier (Saint Elias Mountains, Alaska), 110
Mamostong (Karakoram Range, India), 280
Manaslu (Nepal Himalaya), 242-45
Mandir Parbat (Garhwal Himalaya), 259
Mann, H.S., 272
Manuel Sotillos, Juan, 273
Maparaju (Cordillera Blanca, Peru), 187
Marciniak, Andrzej, 228-30
Marcus, Melvin, 341-42
Marmorilik (Greenland), 62, 64
Marshall, David, 200
Marshall, Shaun, 61
Martin, Franz, 60
Masherbrum (Karakoram Range, Pakistan), 284-85
Mason, Nicholas, 220-21
Masuda, Massa, 61
Masuda, Monica, 61
Matho Kangri (Ladakh), 276
Matho Kangri III (Ladakh), 276
Matthews, David, 62
Mazamas, The, 363-65
Mazzoleni, Lorenzo, 303
McAllister, Dennis C., 61

McArthur Peak (Saint Elias Mountains, Yukon Territory), 178
McConnell, Walter, 230-31
McCormick Fjord (Greenland), 54, 64
McGown, Robert, 166-67, 358
Meacham, Thomas, 159-60
Medicine, *information on*, 212
"Medusa." *See* Argentina, Peak 6175.
Mehren, Herman, 60
Mehren, Martin, 58
Meili. *See* Kang Karpo.
Memphis Mountaineers, Inc., 365-66
Mendenhall, Ruth Dyar, *obit.*, 344-46
Mendenhall, Vivian, 344-46
Menthosa (Himachal Pradesh), 269, 270
Mercanton, Paul-Louis, 55
Mermoz (Patagonia), 208-10
Meru (Garhwal Himalaya), 266
Messner, Reinhold, 224
Meza, Julia, 200
Middle Palisade (Sierra Nevada, California), 175
Miguel Montero, Luis, 220
Mikkelsen, Ejnar, 55
Milne Land (Greenland), 184
Milne Land: Peak 1867, 184
Minami, Isao, 271
Miosga, Gerhard, 63
Mirador del Olivares (Argentina), 202
Misner, Allain, 62
Mita (Cordillera Apolobamba, Bolivia), 193
Miyoshi, Katuhiko, 60
Moby Dick Mountain (Selkirk Mountains, British Columbia), 180
Mocho (Patagonia), 208
Monier, Eric, 215
Moose's Tooth (Alaska Range), *art.*, 43-46; *ascents of*, 154
Mørdre, Simen, 62
Mørdre, Sjur, 62
Moro Rock (Sierra Nevada, California), 168
Morton, Marcus, *obit.*, 351
Mountain Medicine Centre (London), 212
Mountaineering, Solo: Annapurna, 248; Baltoro Cathedral, 288; Denali, *art.*, 50-53; Everest, 248; Kangchenjunga, 215; Kumbhakarna, *art.*, 7-13; Lhotse, 227-28; Pokalde, 237; Pumori, 236; Shinn, 213; Tyree, 213
Mountaineering, Winter: Annapurna, 247, 249; Cho Oyu, 238-39; Denali, *art.*, 50-53, 157;

Everest, 234; Fitz Roy, 205; Langshisha Ri, 240; Langtang Ri, 240; Lhotse, 227-28; Lobuje East, 237; Nanga Parbat, 296; Paine Central, 211; Pokalde, 237; Pumori, 236; San Valentin, 204; Tawoche, 237; Thamserku, 221; Tilitso, 247; Yalung Kang, 215-16

Mountaineering Club of Alaska, 366-67

Mountaineers, Handicapped, 168

"Mountaineer's Peak." *See* Chugach Mountains, Peak 7265.

Mukherjee, Kiron, 269

Mukut Parbat (Garhwal Himalaya), 258-59

Mularz, Paweł, 296

Mulkila (Himachal Pradesh), 270

Mulkila II (Himachal Pradesh), 270

Mulkila IV (Himachal Pradesh), 270

Mulkila V (Himachal Pradesh), 270

Mulkila X (Himachal Pradesh), 270

Muller, Bernard, 281

Murphy, Dallas, 322-23

Myslovsky, Eduard, 214

N

Naar, Ronald, 282-83

Nacimiento II (Argentina), 202

Nacimiento V (Argentina), 202

"Naglishlamina Peak" (Tordrillo Mountains, Alaska), 159-60

Nakamura, Katsumasa, 292

Namba, Teijiro, 222

Nameless Tower (Karakoram Range, Pakistan), 285, 287-88

Nanda Devi East (Garhwal Himalaya), 257

Nanda Ghunti (Garhwal Himalaya), 257

Nanda Kot (Garhwal Himalaya), 257

Nanga Parbat (Himalaya, Pakistan), 230, 296-99

Nansen, Fridtjof, 54, 62, 63

Nansens Teltplads (Greenland), 59, 60, 63, 64

Nanzel, Norbert, 292

Narssaarssuaq (Greenland), 63, 64

Nasaitordluarsuk (Greenlander), 58

Navy Cliff (Greenland), 54, 55, 64

Negi, S.C., 270

Negra (Patagonia), 210

Negro (Argentina), 204

Negro Aspero (Argentina), 202

"Negro del Inca." *See* Negro (Argentina).

Neil Peninsula (Ellesmere Island), 181

Nelson, James, 28-35

Nepal, *arts.*, 1-6, 7-13, 14-20; 213, 214, 216-56

Nepal Peak (Sikkim Himalaya), *altitude of*, 213

Neqe (Greenland), 55, 64

Nettle, David, 43-49

Neuber, Rainier, 62

Neuenschwander, Dominique, 260-64

Neuspiel, Jan, 236

Nevada (Cordillera Blanca, Peru), 187

New Mexico, 176-77

Newsom, Robert, 14-20

Nilsson, Einar, *obit.*, 347

Nolan, Kenneth P., 274

Nordenskjöld Glacier (Greenland), 58, 65

Nordfjord (Greenland), 65

Nordseth, Håkon, 62

Norte, Pico del (Cordillera Real, Bolivia), 194

North Palisade (Sierra Nevada, California), 172-75

Northice (Greenland), 59, 65

Nottaris, Romolo, 282

Nubi (Cordillera Apolobamba, Bolivia), 193

Nugapiinquak (Greenlander), 58

Nun (Kashmir), 272-73

Nuñu Collo (Cordillera Quimsa Cruz, Bolivia), 200

Nuptse (Nepal Himalaya), 228

Nuuk (Greenland), 54, 62, 63, 65

Nyanang Ri (Tibet), 307

Nyanchhen Thanglha (Tibet), 308; *nomenclature of*, 308

Nyeboe Land (Greenland), 59, 65

Nyka, Józef, 210, 230, 247, 248-49, 273, 283, 294, 311, 314

O

Oakley, J.W., 59

O'Brien, Bart, 168

Obster, Walter, 63

O'Connor, William, 222

Ocshapalca (Cordillera Blanca, Peru), 187, 190

O'Donnell, Neil T., 366-67

Ogata, Yoshio, 303

Ogawa, Tsutomu, 308

Ohmi Kangri (Nepal Himalaya), 217-18

Ojos del Salado (Atacama, Puna de, Chile), *altitude of*, 202-3

Okamoto, Masato, 294

Olaizola, Ignacio, 253

Olsen, Hans P., 55
Olsen, Hendrik, 55
Olsson, Ingemar, 181-82
Orłowski, Jan, 217
Ortiz Zabala, Angel, 63
Ostgaard, Wendy L., 223
Ousland, Børge, 62
Ozsváth, Attila, 260

P

Pabil (Nepal Himalaya), 240-42
Pagani, Massimo, 273
Paine Central (Patagonia), 211
Paine Norte (Patagonia), 210
País de Galles (Cordillera Darwin, Tierra del Fuego), 211
Pakistan, 229-30, 281-99
Pal, Bachendri, 257
Pal, Chinmoy, 269
Palomani Grande (Cordillera Apolobamba, Bolivia), 193-94
Palta Thumba (Nepal Himalaya), *altitude of,* 213
Palzor, Sonam, 278-80
Pamir, Alto de (Arhuelles, Nevados de, Chile), 201
Pamir, Centinela del (Arhuelles, Nevados de, Chile), 201
Pamirs (China), 309-10
Pamirs (China): Peak 5360, 310; Peak 5450, 310
Pamirs (USSR), 311, 314; *statistics,* 311
Pamirs (USSR): Peak 5347. *See* Leipzig. Peak 5725, 314
Pania, Dhiren, 271
Paraskevaidis, Stratos, 301
Park, Il-Hwan, 296
Park, Sang-Yeol, 238
Park, Soo-Jo, 216
Park, Young-Seok, 240
Parra, Luis A., 203, 204
Patagonia (Argentina/Chile), 204-11
Paterson, S., 59
Patricia Bowl (Sierra Nevada, California), 169
Patscheider, Reinhard, 248
Paul, J.K., 256
Pavlicek, Jaroslav, 62
Peary, Robert Edwin, 54, 55
Peary Land (Greenland), 59, 65
"Peñas Colorados" (Argentina), 204
Perez, Michel, 58

Peroni, Robert, 62
Peru, 187-92
Petersen, Carl Emil, 62
Phabrang (Himachal Pradesh), 271
Phipps, Walter, 295
Pier Giorgio (Patagonia), 208
Pihkala, Erik, 60
Pirámide Blanca (Cordillera Real, Bolivia), 200
Pisco (Cordillera Blanca, Peru), 190
"Pismanta" (Argentina), 202
Plata, Cerro (Argentina), 204
Plata, Pico de la (Argentina), 204
Plaza Tadeo, Miguel Angel, 63
"Plunger" (Alaska Range), 159
Pobeda (Czerski Range, Siberia), 314
Pobedy, (Tien Shan, USSR), 311
Pobedy. *See also* Tomur.
Poincenot (Patagonia), 205, 208
Pokalde (Nepal Himalaya), 237
Pollard, John, 61
Pollone (Patagonia), 208
Poposki, Jovan, 224
Porcella, Steve, 172-75, 176
Posnansky (Cordillera Apolobamba, Bolivia), 193
Potomac Appalachian Trail Club, 367
Poulsen, Georg, 55
Poulsson, Sven, 60
Pownall, Richard, 355-56
Pregnall, Stuart, 357, 367
Preston, Jonathan, 37-42
Prince William Sound (Alaska), *glaciers in,* 136
Prøven (Greenland), 55, 65
Prud'homme, Bernard, 63
Pumori (Nepal Himalaya), 234-36
Purto, Mauricio, 251-52
Pušnik, Franc, 249
Putlersbak (Greenland), 58, 65

Q

Qaumarajuk Glacier (Greenland), 58, 65
Queen Mary, Mount (Saint Elias Mountains, Yukon Territory), 178
Queer. See Cheru.
Quervain, Alfred de, 55
Quirk, James, *art.,* 43-49
Quitaraju (Cordillera Blanca, Peru), 187

R

Rainier, Mount (Cascade Mountains, Washington), 167
Rakaposhi (Karakoram Range, Pakistan), 292-94
Rasmussen, Knud, 55
Raumer, Hans, 267
Ravna, Ole Nielsen, 54
Rebuffet, François, 274
Red Crags. *See* "Peñas Colorados."
Reese, Bjørn, 59
Reiser, Steven, 362
Research, Scientific: Denali, 152; Glaciers, *art.*, 79-149; Logan, 178
Richard, Michel, 236
Richards, Rick, 217
Richardson, Simon, 291
Righetti, Stefano, 259
Rimo II (Karakoram Range, India), 278-80
Rimo III (Karakoram Range, India), 278-80
Rimo IV (Karakoram Range, India), 280
Risse, Steven C., 164-65
Rohn, Norman F., *obit.*, 354-55
Roncagli (Cordillera Darwin, Tierra del Fuego), 211
Rooster Comb (Alaska Range), *ascents of*, 154
Roper, Steve, 319-20
Rosebrough, Robert F., 320-22
Rosso, Enrico, 228
Roy, Bidyut, 266
Rubin, Alan, 332-34
Ruby Lake Wall (Sierra Nevada, California), 169
Ruddle, Roy, *art.*, 39-42
Ruevski, Alexandr, 210
Ruggera, Gary, 223
Russell, Mount (Alaska Range), *art.*, 21-27; *ascents of*, 154; *paraglider descent from*, 27
Russell, Mount (Sierra Nevada, California), 169-72
Ruth Glacier Gorge (Alaska Range), 159; *ascents in*, 154
Rutkiewicz, Wanda, 215-16
Rymill, John, 58
Ryoo, Gil-Man, 298

S

S, Ajuga del (Patagonia), 210
"Sabine" (Fairweather Range, Alaska), 164
Saegusa, Teruo, 152
Safety, *art.*, 66-70
Sagano, Hiroshi, 60
Sainsbury, George R., 342-43
Saint Elias Mountains (Alaska), *glaciers in*, 96-116
Saint Elias Mountains (Yukon Territory), 177-78; *glaciers in*, 96-116
Sajama (Cordillera Real, Bolivia), 201
Sakahara, Tadakiyo, 281
Sakai, Toshiaki, 299
Sales, Malcom, 184
Salkeld, Audrey, *art.*, 71-73
Salomaki, Seppo, 61
San Valentin (Patagonia), 204
Sandhu, Balwant, 258-59
Sangay (Ecuador), 185-86
Sangmiliq Glacier (Greenland), 62, 65
Santa Cruz (Cordillera Blanca, Peru), 187
Saotome, Tsuguo, 60
Sarqaq (Greenland), 60, 65
Sasaki, Kazuo, 310
Sasaki, Takeomi, 265
Saser Kangri (Karakoram Range, India), 276-77
Saser Kangri IV (Karakoram Range, India), 276-77
Satopanth (Garhwal Himalaya), 260-64
Saunders, Victor, 218-19
Savenc, Franci, 224
Savov, Metodi, 247
Scanu, Marcelo, 202
Schaschke, Carl Joseph, 275
Schier, Peter, 264
Schiller, Werner, 63
Schmidt, Udo, 220
Schreinmoser, Fritz, 296
Schrott, Josef, 62
Schuchert, Mount (Ellesmere Island), 181
Schwarzenbach, Robert M., *obit.*, 342
Schweizerland (Greenland), 183-85
Schweizerland: Peak 1910, 184; Peak 1950, 184; Peak 2010, 185; Peak 2050, 184; Peak 2080, 184; Peak 2100, 184; Peak 2180, 184; Peak 2250, 184
Scott, Charles, 178
Scott, Douglas K., 278-80
Scott, James Maurice, 58
Scott, Michael, 296
Secor, Robert J., 354-55
Seibert, Robert R., 152-57
Sekimoto, Shiro, 271
Selkirk Mountains (British Columbia), 180
Sen, Amulya, 170

Sentinel Range (Antarctica), 213
Sequoia National Park (California), 168
Sese, Ana, 219
Seward Peninsula (Alaska), *glaciers on,* 140-41
Seward-Malaspina Glacier (Saint Elias Mountains, Alaska), 110-11
Shani (Karakoram Range, Pakistan), 296
Shannon Ø (Greenland), 55, 65
Shellabear, Michael, 192-93
Sherpa, N., 258
Shifkitin Sar (Karakoram Range, Pakistan), 294
Shigeno, Tatsuji, 234
Shigri Parbat (Himachal Pradesh), 270
Shinn, Mount (Sentinel Range, Antarctica), 213
Shishapangma (Tibet), 305, 307-8
Shispare (Karakoram Range, Pakistan), 294
Shivling (Garhwal Himalaya), 266-67
Shot Tower (Brooks Range, Alaska), 163
Shuksan, Mount (Cascade Mountains, Washington), 167
Sia Kangri (Karakoram Range, India/Pakistan), 284
Sie, Vidar, 62
Sierra Nevada (California), 168-76
Sif, Mount (Baffin Island), 180, 181
Siguang Ri (Tibet), 305-7
Sigurdsson, Vigfus, 55
Sikkim Himalaya, 213-16, 230
Silla (Patagonia), 206
Silverio, Walter, 187
Silverthrone, Mount (Alaska Range), *ascents of,* 154
Simpson, Hugh, 59
Simpson, Myrtle, 59
Singh, Babban Prasad, 276
Singh, Hukam, 273
Škarja, Tone, 307
Ski mountaineering: Antarctica, 212-13; Baffin Island, 180
"Skyang" (Karakoram Range, India), 278
Snow Cone (Himachal Pradesh), 269
Snow Lake Peak. *See* Lawa Brakk.
Søborg, Morten, 63
Soda, Kenji, 299
Søftestad, Svein R., 60
Solberg, Eilif, 60
Soldevila, Venancio, 268
Somers, Geoff, 63
Søndre Strømfjord (Greenland), 58, 60, 61, 62, 63, 65
Sosbun Spires (Karakoram Range, Pakistan), 289-91

South America, 185-211
South Pole, 212
Spantik (Karakoram Range, Pakistan), 292
Speer, Gary, 302
Spinelli, Giovanni, 63
Spiti (India), 271
Split Mountain (Sierra Nevada, California), 176
Staeheli, David, *art.,* 50-53
Staib, Bjørn, 59
Stanhardt (Patagonia), 210
Stanley, Fred C., 346-47
Stansbury, Howard E., Jr., *obit.,* 352-53
"Station Centrale" (Greenland), 59, 62, 65
Steele Glacier (Saint Elias Mountains, Alaska), 112
Stefan, Wolfgang, 272
Steffins, Barbara, 360-61
Steger, Will, 63
Stephenson, A., 58
Stepień, Józef, 215
Stocker, Anton, 236
Stolberg, A., 55
Storstrømmen (Greenland), 55, 65
"Stos" (Karakoram Range, India), 278
Streibel, Herbert, 292
Štremfelj, Andrej, 307
Stuart, Mount (Cascade Mountains, Washington), 167
Stuflesser, Stefan, 288-89
Stur, Louis Samuel, *obit.,* 348-50
Styx Mountain (Coast Mountains, British Columbia), 179
Sugiyama, Yoshiaki, 247
Sun, Wei-Qi, 304
Sunchuli (Cordillera Apolobamba, Bolivia), 193
Sverdrup, Otto Neumann, 54
Swenson, Steven J., 221-22

T

Tabin, Geoffrey C., 213
Tacusiri (Cordillera Vilcanota, Peru), 192
Takahashi, Ken, 292
Takenami, Ryozo, 273
Takita, Akira, 292
Talkeetna Mountains (Alaska), *glaciers in,* 136
Tamada, Jin, 310
Tanzania, 211
Tarditti, Alberto, 203-4, 205
Tarke Kang (Nepal Himalaya), 249

Tasker, Ajay, 270
Taulliraju (Cordillera Blanca, Peru), 187
Tawoche (Nepal Himalaya), 237
Teasdale, Ian, 257
Thackray, John, 326-27
Thakur, G.S., 269
Thalay Sagar (Garhwal Himalaya), 268
Thamserku (Nepal Himalaya), 221
Thelu (Garhwal Himalaya), 266
Thodoroff, Michel, 256
Thomas, Samuel Finley, *obit.*, 353
Thomaseth, Wolfgang, 62
Thompson Ridge (Chugach Mountains, Alaska),
    160, 161
Thorington, James Monroe, *obit.*, 337-38
"Thousand Devils Peak." *See* Mamostong.
Throne (Alaska Range), 159
Thule (Greenland), 55, 58, 65
Thule Air Base (Greenland), 59, 65
Thunmo. *See* Baltoro Cathedral.
Tibet, 300-308
Tien Shan (China), 309
Tien Shan (USSR), 311
Tierra del Fuego, 211
Tikchik Mountains. *See* Wood River Mountains.
Tilicho. *See* Tilitso.
Tilitso (Nepal Himalaya), 246-47
Tiniteqilaq (Greenland), 62, 65
Tocllaraju (Cordillera Blanca, Peru), 190
Toftdahl, Jo, 63
Tomur. *See also* Pobedy.
Tordrillo Mountains (Alaska), 159-60
Torii, Suichi, 309
Torre, Cerro (Patagonia), 205, 206; *paraglider
    descent from,* 206
Torreblanca, Alfredo, 264
Towada, Tadashi, 60
Townsend, Charles, *art.*, 21-27
Trana, Kristian Kristiansen, 54
Trango Towers (Karakoram Range, Pakistan),
    285-88
Traverses: Antarctica, 212-13; Kangchenjunga,
    213-14; Makalu, 218; Patagonian Icecap, 210
Tridente (Patagonia), 210
Trott, Otto, 339-41
Tsoukias, Mike, 273
Tsurup (Cordillera Blanca, Peru), 187
Tuft, Roger, 59
Tungurahua (Ecuador), 187

Tyndall, Mount (Sierra Nevada, California), 172
Tyree, Mount (Sentinel Range, Antarctica), 213

U

Uemura, Naomi, 61
UIAA Mountain Medicine Centre. *See* Mountain
    Medicine Centre (London).
Uli Biaho Tower (Karakoram Range, Pakistan),
    288-89
Ulugh Muztagh (Xinjiang, China), 310
Umanaq (Greenland), 62, 65
Umivik (Greenland), 54, 59, 62, 63, 65
Umrata (Chile), 201
United States, 152-77
Untch, Steven Donald, 185-86
Uranga, Raúl, 253
Urkia Arana, Nekane, 63
USSR, 311-14
Utah, 176
Uvdloriaq (Greenlander), 55

V

Valentini, Paul, 62
Valet, Frédéric, 242
Valhalla Group (Selkirk Mountains, British
    Columbia), 180
Vallunaraju Sur (Cordillera Blanca, Peru), 187
Variegated Glacier (Saint Elias Mountains, Alaska),
    111-12
Varma, B. S., 258
Varonen, Eero, 60
Vasuki Parbat South. *See* Garhwal, Peak 6702.
Vermeulen, James, 180-81
Victor, Paul-Emile, 58, 59
Viento, Volcán del (Argentina), 201-2
Vincent, Michel, 302
Vinson Massif (Sentinel Range, Antarctica), 213
Vittorangeli, Roberta, 259
Vogeley, Michael, 63
von Hennig, Horst, 318-19
Vylchev, Ivan, 248-49

W

Wagner, Frank, 63
Walker, David, 181

Wallace, William, 59
Wallgren, Lars, 63
Wampa (Cordillera Real, Bolivia), 194
Warecki, Ryszard, 227
Warner, Chris, 266-67
Washburn, Bradford, *art.*, 75
Washington, 164-67
Washington Pass Overlook (Cascade Mountains, Washington), 165
Watkins Mountains (Greenland), 181-83
Watkins Mountains: Peak 3190, 183; Peak 3330, 183; Peak 3400, 183; Peak 3500, 183; Peak 3550, 183; Peak 3600, 183
Wegener, Alfred, 55
Weigner, Vladimir, 62
Wellencamp (Cordillera Apolobamba, Bolivia), 193
Wellman, Mark, 168
Welsch, Adi, 249
West, R. D., 273
White Needle (Kashmir), 273, 275
Whitney, Hassler, *obit.*, 343-44
Whittaker, Lou, 215
Wiedman, Michael, 211
Wielicki, Krzysztof, 224
Wigley, Andrew, 219
Wild Ass. *See* "Skyang."
Wilkinson, David, 295
Williams, James, 212-13
Williams, Martyn, 213
Williams, Owen W., 329-30
Williamson, Mount (Sierra Nevada, California), 172
Wilson, Greg, 215, 348-50
Wind River Range (Wyoming), 177
Wirski, Ziemowit J., 230
Wolverine Peak (Wind River Range, Wyoming), 177
Wood, Mount (Saint Elias Mountains, Yukon Territory), 178

Wood River Mountains (Alaska), *glaciers in,* 140
Woodcock, David, 193-94
Woods, David Lyndon, 352
Woods, Donald Mason, *obit.,* 352
Wooley, W. S. L., 62
Woolridge, Mike, 218, 219
Wörgötter, Peter, 248
Wrangell Mountains (Alaska), 163; *glaciers in,* 130-32
Wulff, Thorild, 58
Wyoming, 177

X

Xanadu (Brooks Range, Alaska), 163
Xuelian Feng (Xinjiang, China), 308-9

Y

Yadav, M. P., 280
Yajima, Hiroshi, 311
Yakutat Bay (Alaska), 106-8
Yalung Kang (Sikkim Himalaya), 214, 215-16
Yamada, Noburo, 152
Yan Kangri. *See* Matho Kangri.
Yang, Bi-Yu, 299
Yengutz (Karakoram Range, Pakistan), 295
Yosemite (California), 168
Yoshizawa, Ichiro, 338-39
Yuasa, Michio, 308
Yukon Territory, *art.,* 79-149; 177-78

Z

Zachenberg (Greenland), 59, 65
Zafren, Ken, 217-218
Zaugg, Bruno, 219
Zhu, Sa-Rong, 300